RAGNARÖK

Volume 7:
Seeds of Betrayal

By
Myung-Jin Lee

English Version
by
Richard A. Knaak

TOKYOPOP®

Los Angeles • Tokyo • London • Hamburg

Translator - Lauren Na
Copy Editor - Carol Fox
Retouch & Lettering - Monalisa de Asis
Cover Layout - Anna Kernbaum

Editor - Jake Forbes
Digital Imaging Manager - Chris Buford
Pre-Press Manager - Antonio DePietro
Production Managers - Jennifer Miller, Mutsumi Miyazaki
Art Director - Matt Alford
Managing Editor - Jill Freshney
VP of Production - Ron Klamert
President & C.O.O. - John Parker
Publisher & C.E.O. - Stuart Levy

E-mail: info@TOKYOPOP.com
Come visit us online at www.TOKYOPOP.com

A 🐾TOKYOPOP® Manga

TOKYOPOP Inc.
5900 Wilshire Blvd. Suite 2000
Los Angeles, CA 90036

Ragnarok Vol. 7: Seeds of Betrayal

ISBN: 1-59182-206-8

First TOKYOPOP® printing: July 2003

10 9 8 7 6 5 4
Printed in the USA

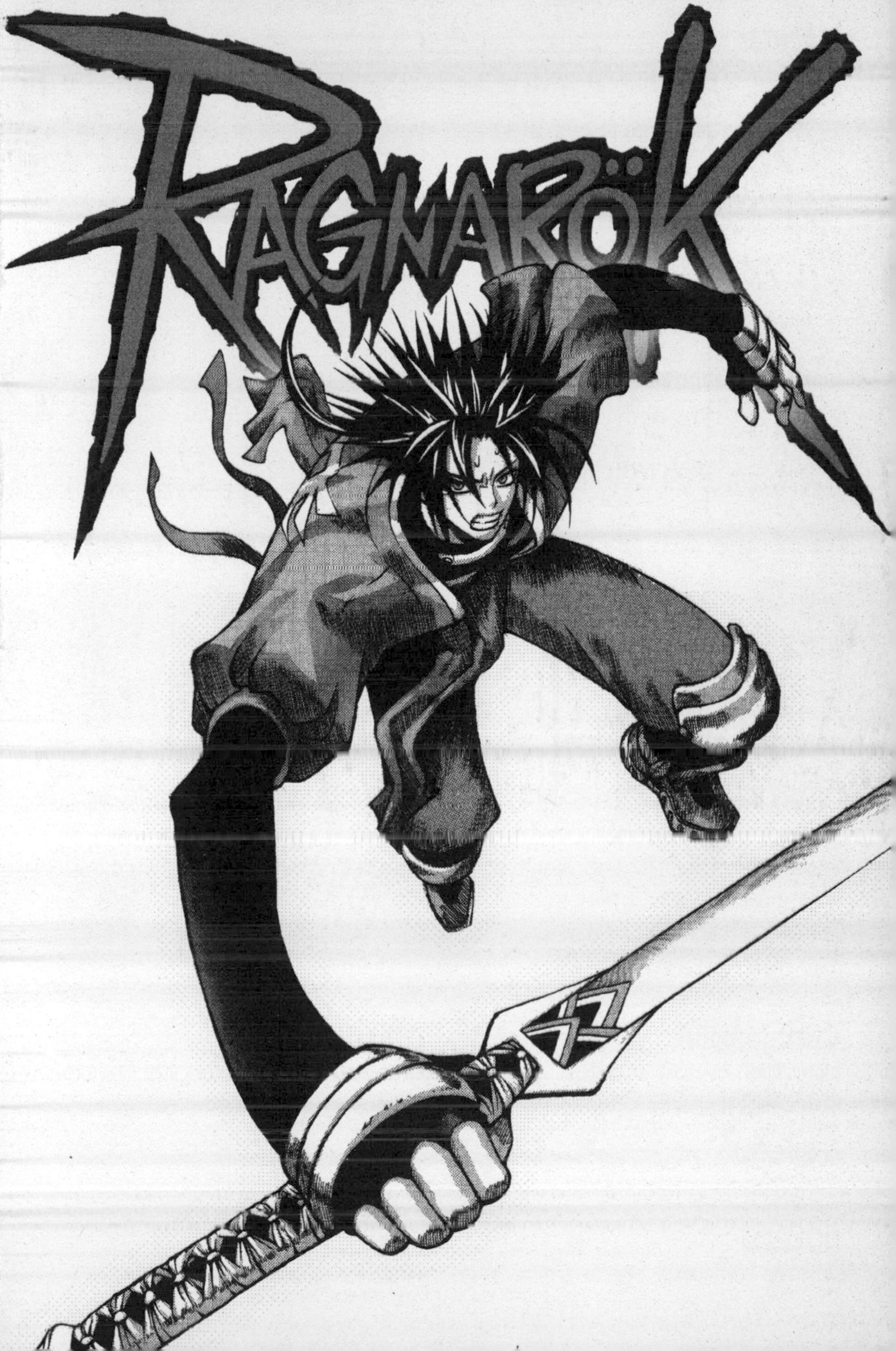
RAGNARÖK

ALSO AVAILABLE FROM

MANGA

.HACK//LEGEND OF THE TWILIGHT BRACELET (September 2003)
@LARGE (COMING SOON)
ANGELIC LAYER*
BABY BIRTH* (September 2003)
BATTLE ROYALE*
BRAIN POWERED*
BRIGADOON* (August 2003)
CARDCAPTOR SAKURA
CARDCAPTOR SAKURA: MASTER OF THE CLOW*
CHOBITS*
CHRONICLES OF THE CURSED SWORD
CLAMP SCHOOL DETECTIVES*
CLOVER
CONFIDENTIAL CONFESSIONS*
CORRECTOR YUI
COWBOY BEBOP*
COWBOY BEBOP: SHOOTING STAR*
DEMON DIARY
DIGIMON*
DRAGON HUNTER
DRAGON KNIGHTS*
DUKLYON: CLAMP SCHOOL DEFENDERS*
ERICA SAKURAZAWA*
FAKE*
FLCL* (September 2003)
FORBIDDEN DANCE* (August 2003)
GATE KEEPERS*
G GUNDAM*
GRAVITATION*
GTO*
GUNDAM WING
GUNDAM WING: BATTLEFIELD OF PACIFISTS
GUNDAM WING: ENDLESS WALTZ*
GUNDAM WING: THE LAST OUTPOST*
HAPPY MANIA*
HARLEM BEAT
I.N.V.U.
INITIAL D*
ISLAND
JING: KING OF BANDITS*
JULINE
KARE KANO*
KINDAICHI CASE FILES, THE*
KING OF HELL
KODOCHA: SANA'S STAGE*
LOVE HINA*
LUPIN III*
MAGIC KNIGHT RAYEARTH* (August 2003)
MAGIC KNIGHT RAYEARTH II* (COMING SOON)

MAN OF MANY FACES*
MARMALADE BOY*
MARS*
MIRACLE GIRLS
MIYUKI-CHAN IN WONDERLAND* (October 2003)
MONSTERS, INC.
PARADISE KISS*
PARASYTE
PEACH GIRL
PEACH GIRL: CHANGE OF HEART*
PET SHOP OF HORRORS*
PLANET LADDER*
PLANETES* (October 2003)
PRIEST
RAGNAROK
RAVE MASTER*
REALITY CHECK
REBIRTH
REBOUND*
RISING STARS OF MANGA
SABER MARIONETTE J*
SAILOR MOON
SAINT TAIL
SAMURAI DEEPER KYO*
SAMURAI GIRL: REAL BOUT HIGH SCHOOL*
SCRYED*
SHAOLIN SISTERS*
SHIRAHIME-SYO: SNOW GODDESS TALES* (Dec. 2003)
SHUTTERBOX (November 2003)
SORCERER HUNTERS
THE SKULL MAN*
THE VISION OF ESCAFLOWNE
TOKYO MEW MEW*
UNDER THE GLASS MOON
VAMPIRE GAME*
WILD ACT*
WISH*
WORLD OF HARTZ (COMING SOON)
X-DAY* (August 2003)
ZODIAC P.I. *

For more information visit www.TOKYOPOP.com

*INDICATES 100% AUTHENTIC MANGA (RIGHT-TO-LEFT FORMAT)

CINE-MANGA™

CARDCAPTORS
JACKIE CHAN ADVENTURES (COMING SOON)
JIMMY NEUTRON (September 2003)
KIM POSSIBLE
LIZZIE MCGUIRE
POWER RANGERS: NINJA STORM (August 2003)
SPONGEBOB SQUAREPANTS (September 2003)
SPY KIDS 2

NOVELS

KARMA CLUB (COMING SOON)
SAILOR MOON

TOKYOPOP KIDS

STRAY SHEEP (September 2003)

ART BOOKS

CARDCAPTOR SAKURA*
MAGIC KNIGHT RAYEARTH*

ANIME GUIDES

COWBOY BEBOP ANIME GUIDES
GUNDAM TECHNICAL MANUALS
SAILOR MOON SCOUT GUIDES

5-12-03

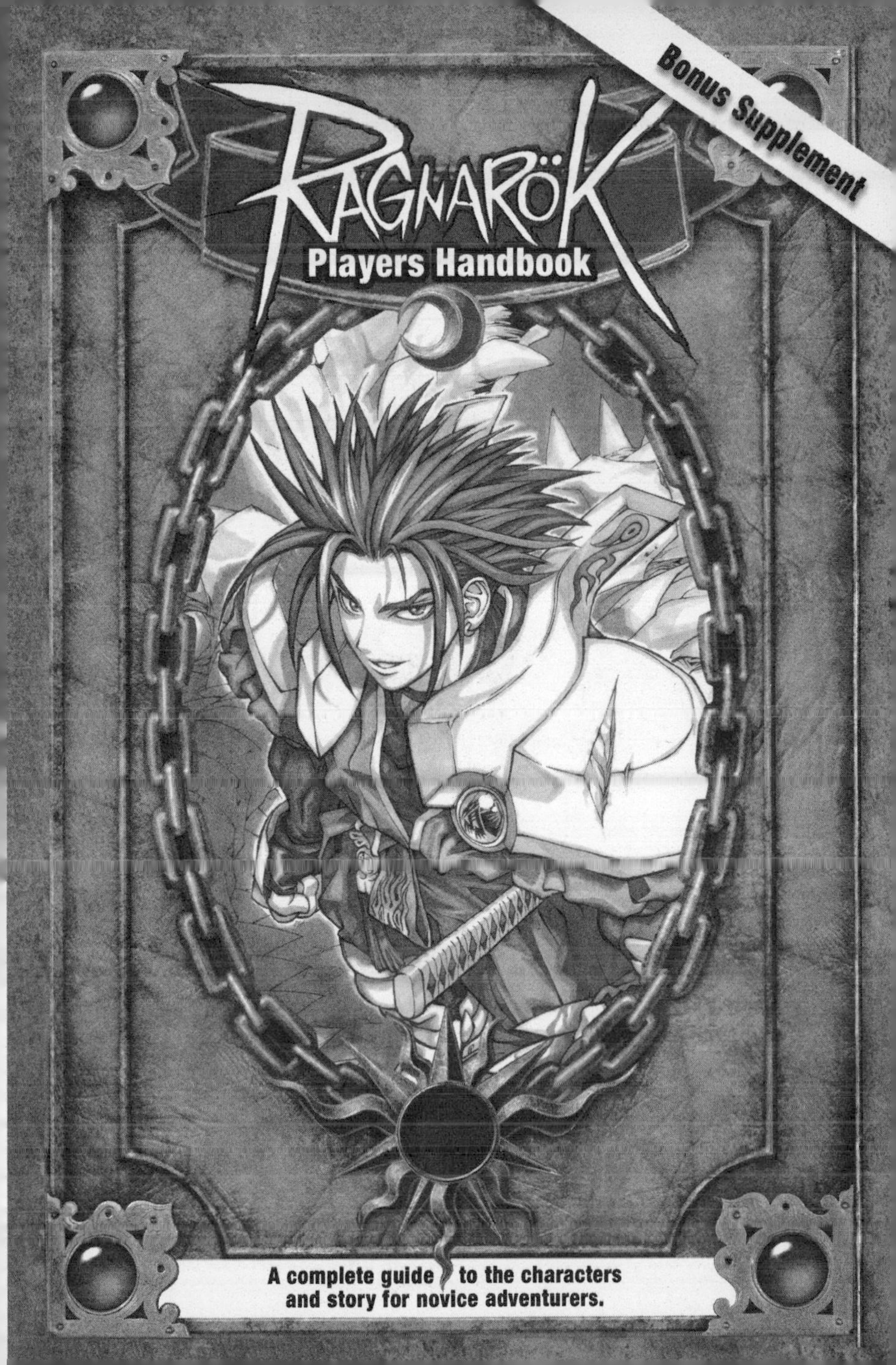
Bonus Supplement
RAGNARÖK
Players Handbook
A complete guide to the characters
and story for novice adventurers.

HEROES

NOTE: THE FOLLOWING STATISTICS ARE INSPIRED BY THE MANGA, BUT DO NOT REFLECT ANY OFFICIAL RAGNAROK RPG. – EDITOR

NAME: Chaos
Class: Rune Knight
Level: 9
Alignment: Chaotic Good
STR: 17
DEX: 10
CON: 15
INT: 12
WIS: 14
CHR: 16

Equipment:
Vision- Enchanted sword- STR +2

Rune Armor- AC -4, 20% bonus saving throw vs. magical attacks.

Notes:
The reincarnation of the fallen god Balder, Chaos has been told by his divine mother, Frigg, that the fate of the world rests in his hands. He may also be tied to the legendary "Dragon Knights."

NAME: Iris Irine
Class: Cleric
Level: 5
Alignment: Lawful Good
STR: 7
DEX: 12
CON: 9
INT: 13
WIS: 16
CHR: 16

Equipment:
Chernryongdo- Enchanted dagger- STR +1, DEX +1, 1D4 damage if anyone but she touches it.

Irine Family Armor- AC -5, WIS +1

Notes:
Iris would have become the new leader of the city of Fayon... that is, if it weren't destroyed by her sister, the Valkyrie Sara Irine. She now follows her close friend Chaos.

HEROES

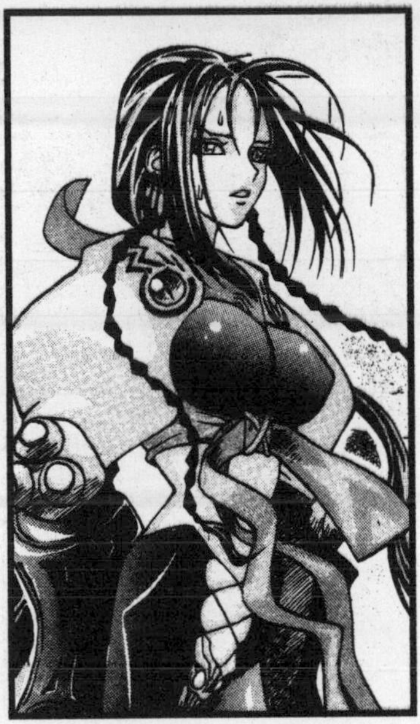

NAME: Fenris Fenrir
Class: Warlock
Level: 9
Alignment: Neutral Good
STR: 14
DEX: 15
CON: 13
INT: 16
WIS: 12
CHR: 14

Equipment:
Psychic Medallion: Magic compass which leads its bearer to whatever his or her heart most desires.

Laevatein, Rod of Destruction- STR+1, extends to staff on command.

Notes:
The reincarnation of the Wolf God, Fenris helped Chaos to realize his identity. She now follows him on his quest.

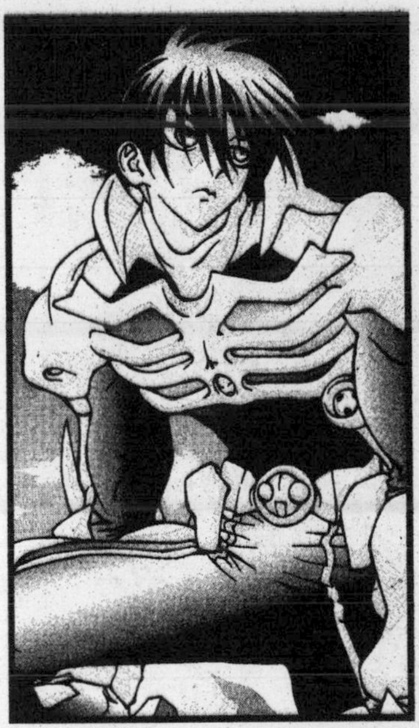

NAME: Loki
Class: Assassin
Level: 9
Alignment: Lawful Neutral
STR:14
DEX: 18
CON: 12
INT: 12
WIS: 14
CHR: 10

Equipment:
Sword of Shadows: + 4 to hit, damage +2

Bone Armor: AC -5, STR +2

Notes:
Greatest of the Assassins, Loki's anonymity is a testament to his skill at going unseen. An enigma himself, his curiosity and respect for the even more mysterious Chaos caused him to join the Rune Knight for as long as they follow the same road.

HEROES

ENEMIES

NAME: Lidia
Class: Thief
Level: 4
Alignment: Neutral Good
STR: 8
DEX: 15
INT: 13
WIS: 10
CHR: 15

Equipment:
Treasure Hunter's Bible: 50% chance of
identifying magical items

Follower: Sessy, Cat o' Two Tails: +50%
saving throw to pick pockets

Notes:
An "expert treasure hunter" by trade,
Lidia "borrows" whatever she can get her
hands on while she looks for bigger
hauls. She was last seen leaving the city
of Prontera. Her current whereabouts
are unknown.

NAME: Sara Irine
Class: Valkyrie
Level: 7
Alignment: Chaotic Neutral
STR: 14
DEX: 12
CON: 13
INT: 14
WIS: 15
CHR: 17

Equipment:
Haeryongdo, Sword of Retribution-
STR+2

Enchanted Parchments x24

Notes:
One of the 12 Valkyries of Valhalla,
Sara was once the heir to Fayon until
the villiage elders cast her out in favor
of her sister, Iris. Sara returned to
Fayon and destroyed everything,
including her parents. She now joins
Himmelmez in her quest.

ENEMIES

NAME: Himmelmez
Dual Class: Necromancer/Valkyrie
Level: 10
Alignment: Lawful Evil
STR: 9
DEX: 16
INT: 18
WIS: 12
CHR: 14

Equipment:
Wand of Hela: damage +6; 70% chance
that those killed by it will become undead

Fortress- "Dark Whisper"

Notes:
One of Freya's strongest generals,
Himmelmez's arrogance is justified by her
effectiveness. All who stand against her
army have fallen, only to join her undead
legion. Perhaps her only weakness is her
overconfidence.

NAME: Bijou
Class: Witch
Level: 5
Alignment: Chaotic Evil
STR: 15
DEX: 10
INT: 13
WIS: 16
CHR: 7

Equipment:
Claw of the mantis: STR +4; CHR -3

Follower: Geirrod, the Troll:
HP: 120; damage- 2d6 +4; regeneration;
+60% saving throws against magic attacks

Notes:
A witch who began sacrificing her body
at a young age in order to increase her
occult powers. An abomination of her
former self, Bijou now serves Himmelmez,
lending her cruel and unorthadox tech-
niques to Freya's cause.

The Story so Far...

Legend has it that the world was created from the giant Ymir. Odin, wisest of the gods, slayed Ymir and from his body created Midgard, the human realm. Ymir's blood became the seas, his flesh the land, his bones the mountains. But the source of all power, the thing that gave life to this new realm, was Ymir's heart.

After the first coming of Ragnarok, 1,000 years ago, the location of the heart was forgotten by all but a few. What brought the heart back from obscurity was the growing war among gods, demons and men. The goddess Freya, leader of the Valkyries, seeks the heart in order to use its power to control Midgard for the next 1,000 years. Learning of its location beneath the capital city of Prontera, Freya sent the necromancer Himmelmez and the witch Bijou in order to secure it.

As the fates would have it, the only ones with the power and heart to oppose Freya's forces just happened to be in Prontera in time for the attack. Chaos, the reincarnation of the God Balder, and Loki, master assassin, entered Himmelmez's flying fortress, the Dark Whisper, and after much hardship they have reached the necromancer's inner sanctum. Meanwhile, Fenris the warlock and Iris the cleric journeyed to the caverns beneath Prontera where Ymir's heart lies. Now they are locked in fierce magical combat with the witch Bijou. The matter further complicates when Sara Irine, Iris' sister and a powerful Valkyrie, comes to put her mark on the proceedings. The seeds of Betrayal have been sown.

Let us return now to the battles...

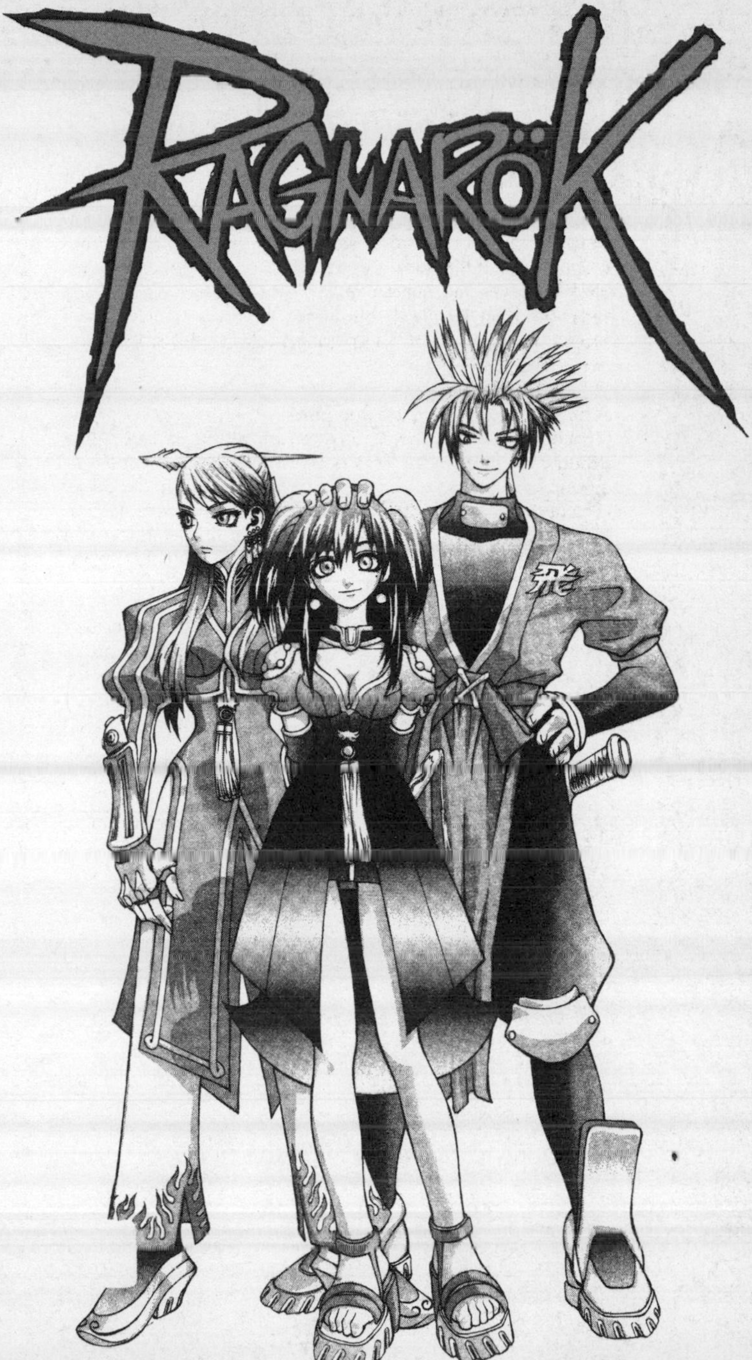
RAGNARÖK

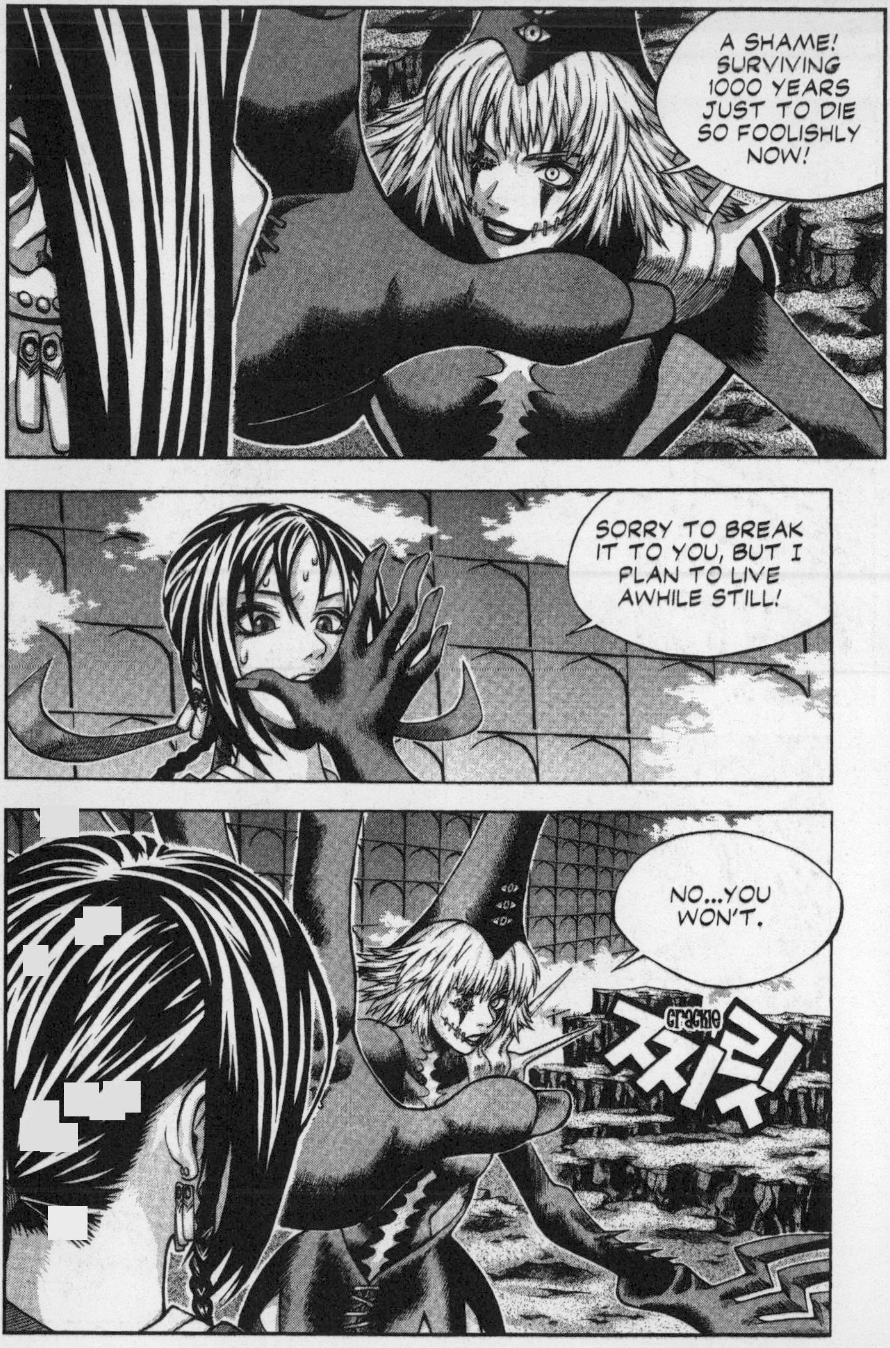
A SHAME! SURVIVING 1000 YEARS JUST TO DIE SO FOOLISHLY NOW!
SORRY TO BREAK IT TO YOU, BUT I PLAN TO LIVE AWHILE STILL!
NO...YOU WON'T.
crackle

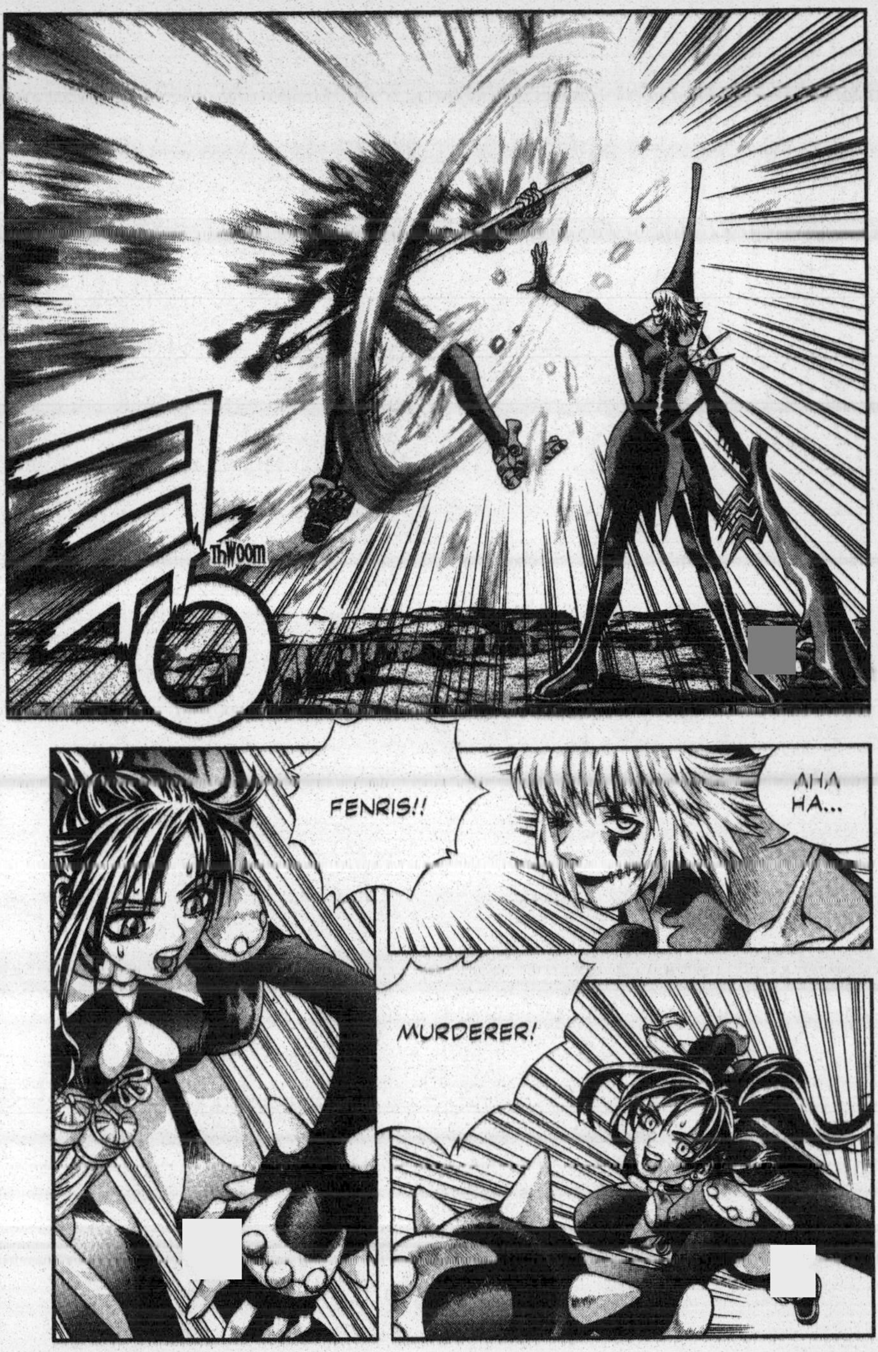
ThWoom
FENRIS!!
AHA HA...
MURDERER!

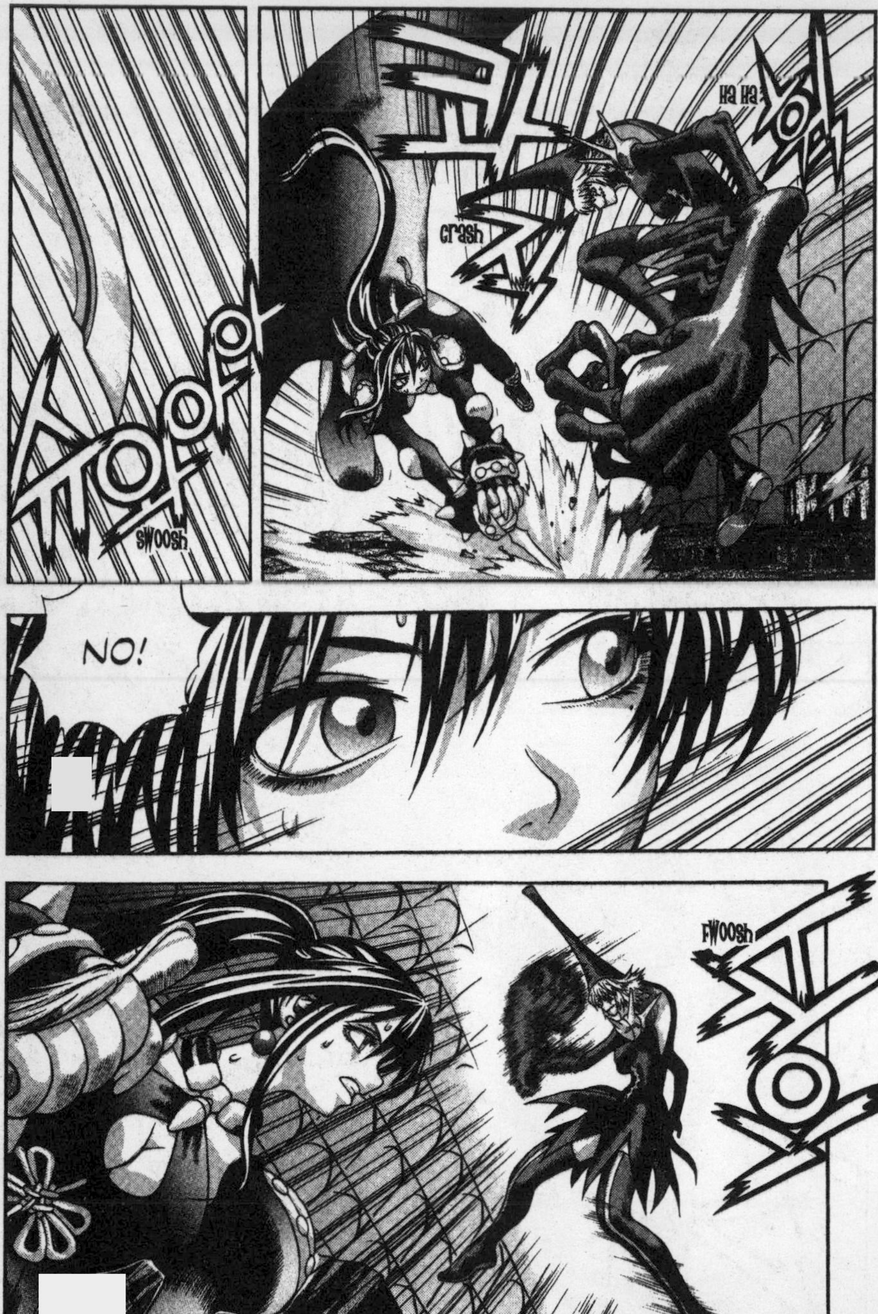
swoosh
crash
HA HA
NO!
fwoosh

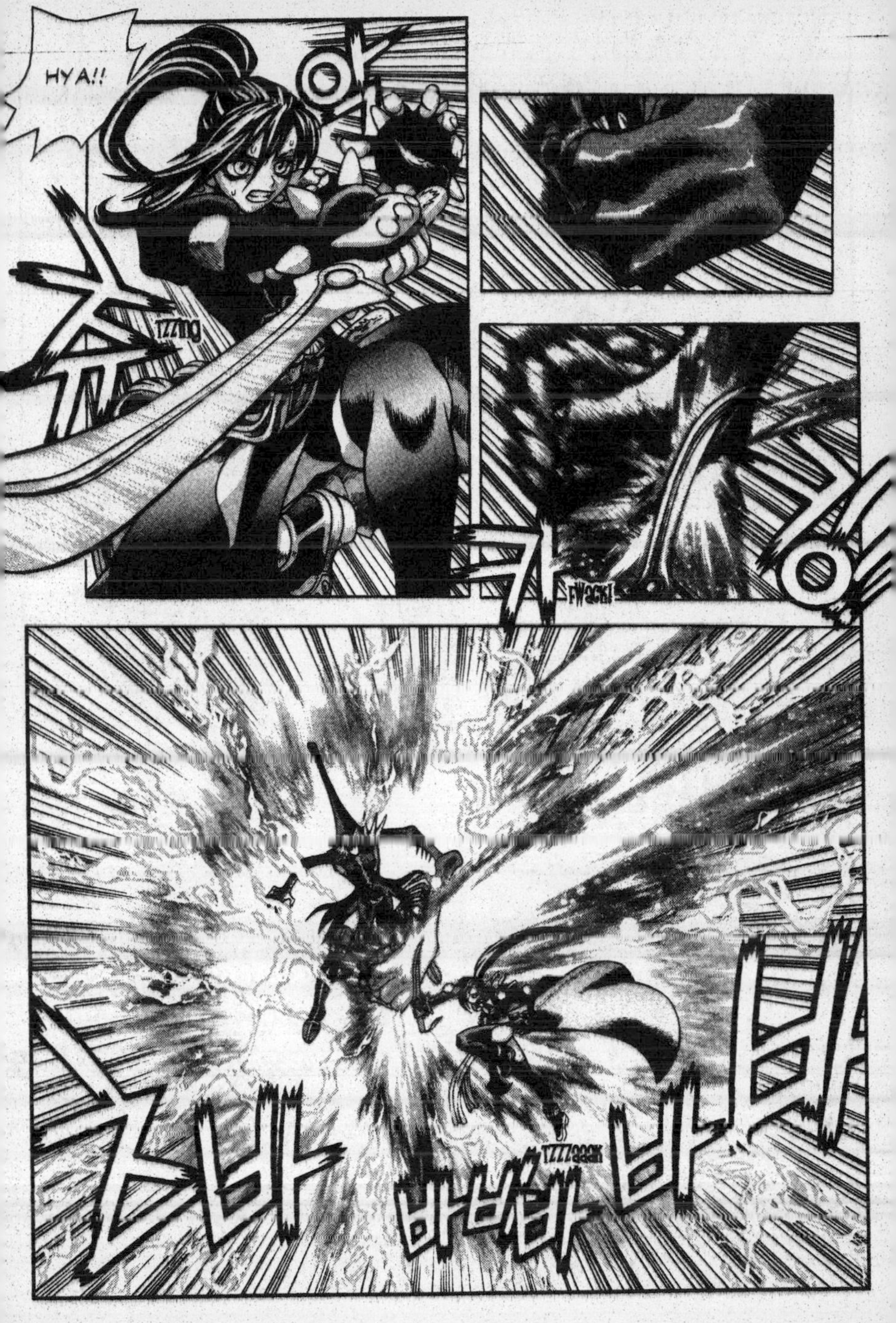
HYA!!
TZZING
FWACK!
TZZZAAAK

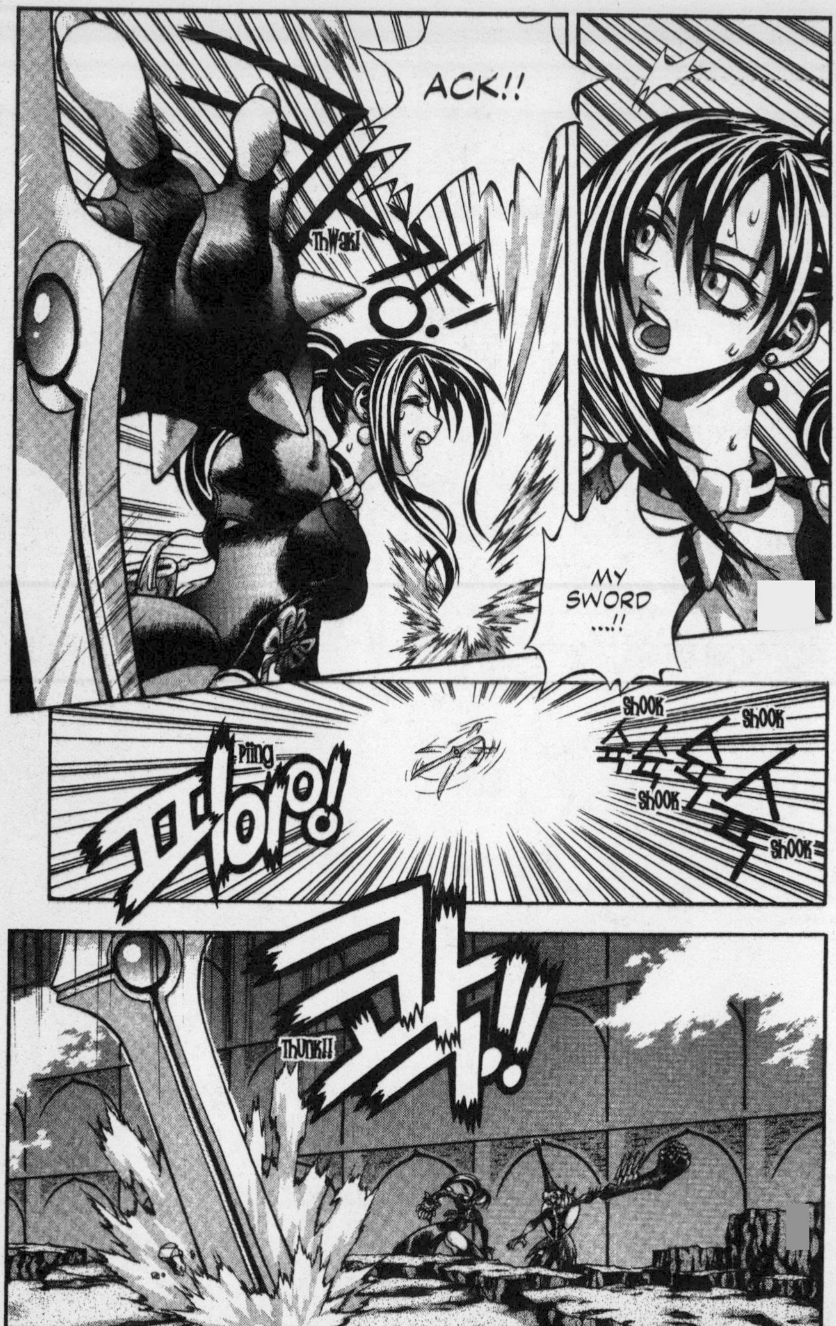
ThWAK!
ACK!!
MY SWORD ...!!
Piing
Shook
Shook
Shook
Shook
ThUNK!!

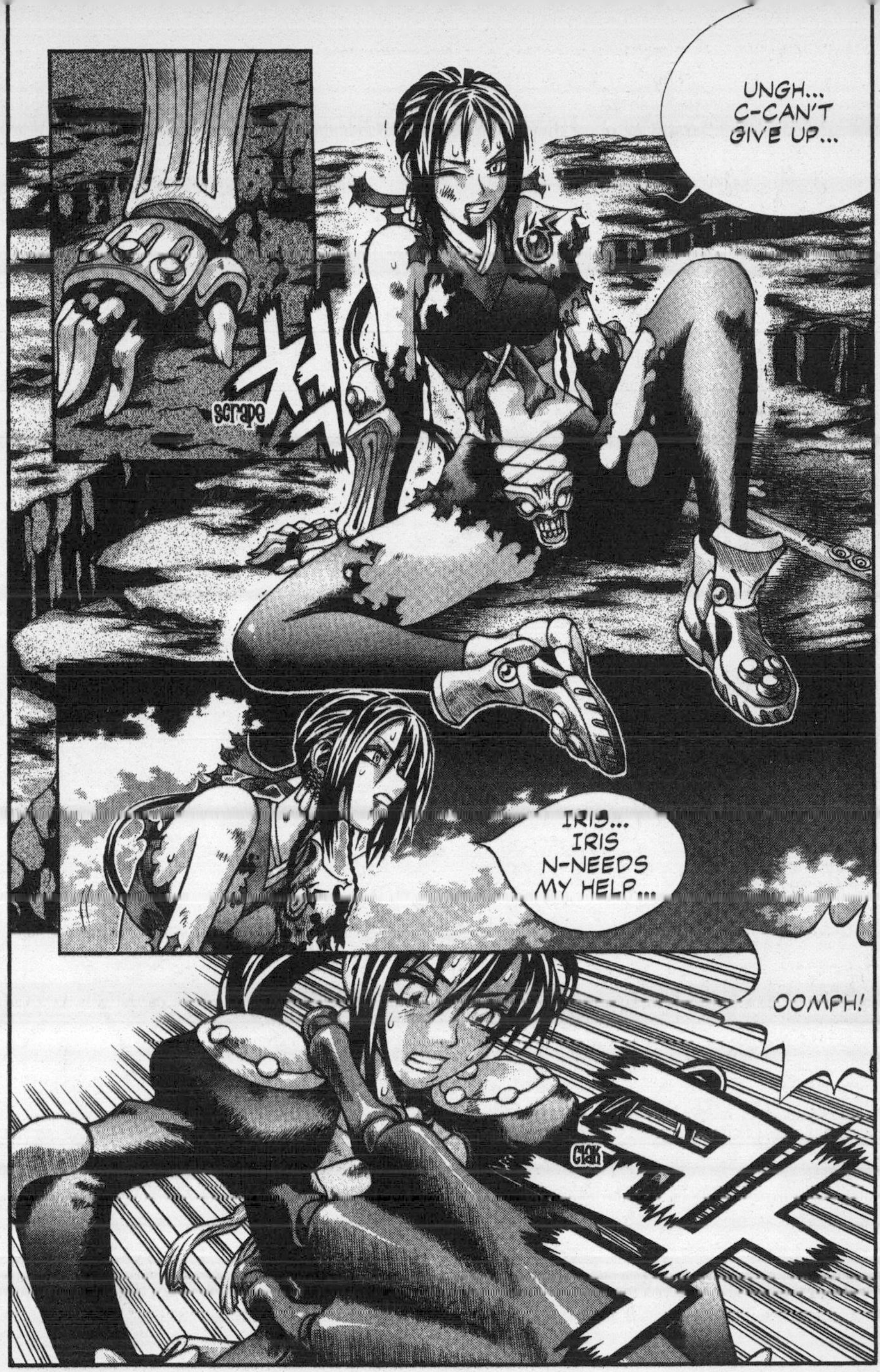
UNGH... C-CAN'T GIVE UP...
SCRAPE
IRIS... IRIS N-NEEDS MY HELP...
OOMPH!
CLAK

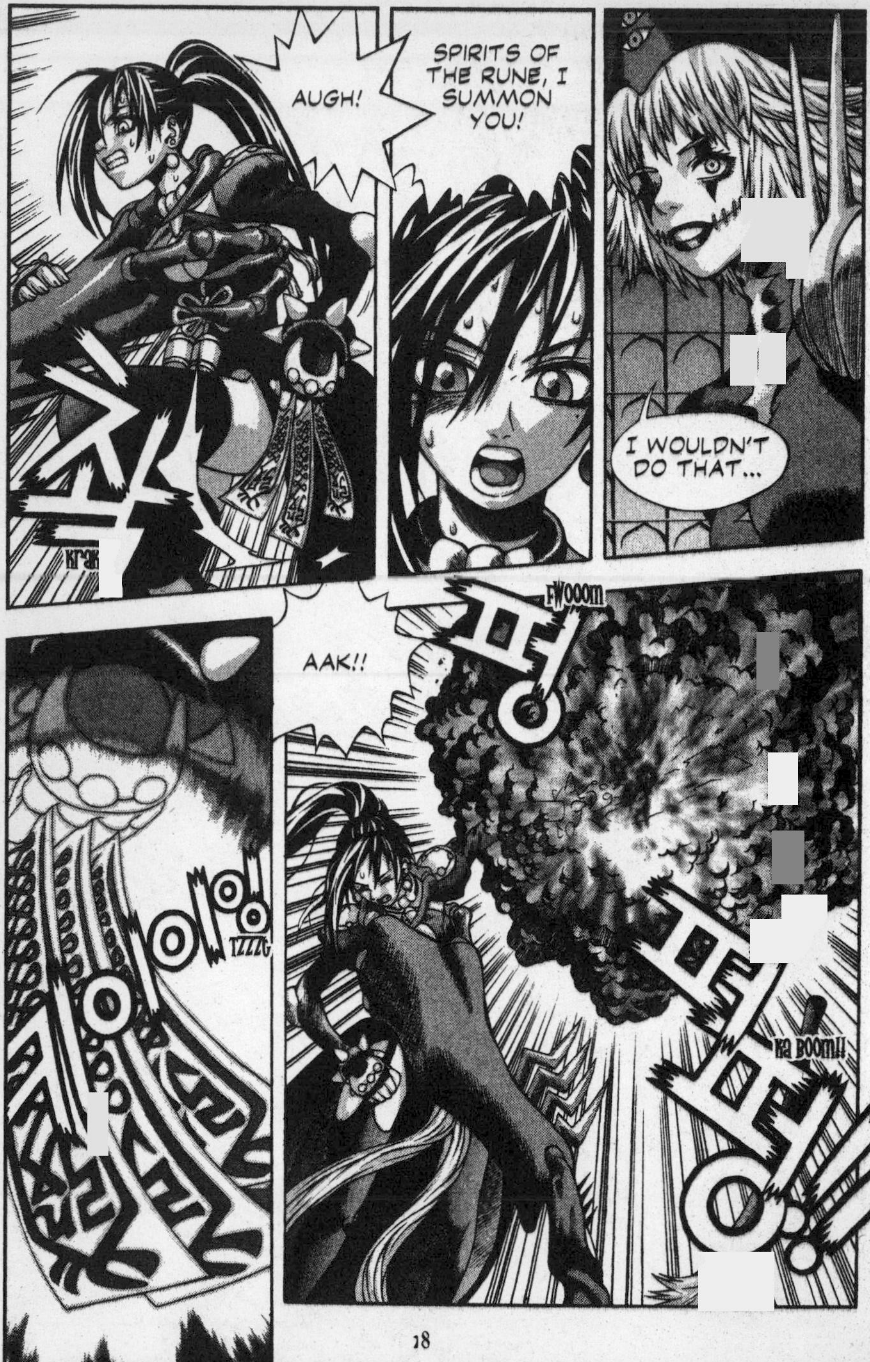
AUGH!
KRAK
SPIRITS OF THE RUNE, I SUMMON YOU!
I WOULDN'T DO THAT...
TZZZG
AAK!!
FWOOOM
KA BOOM!!

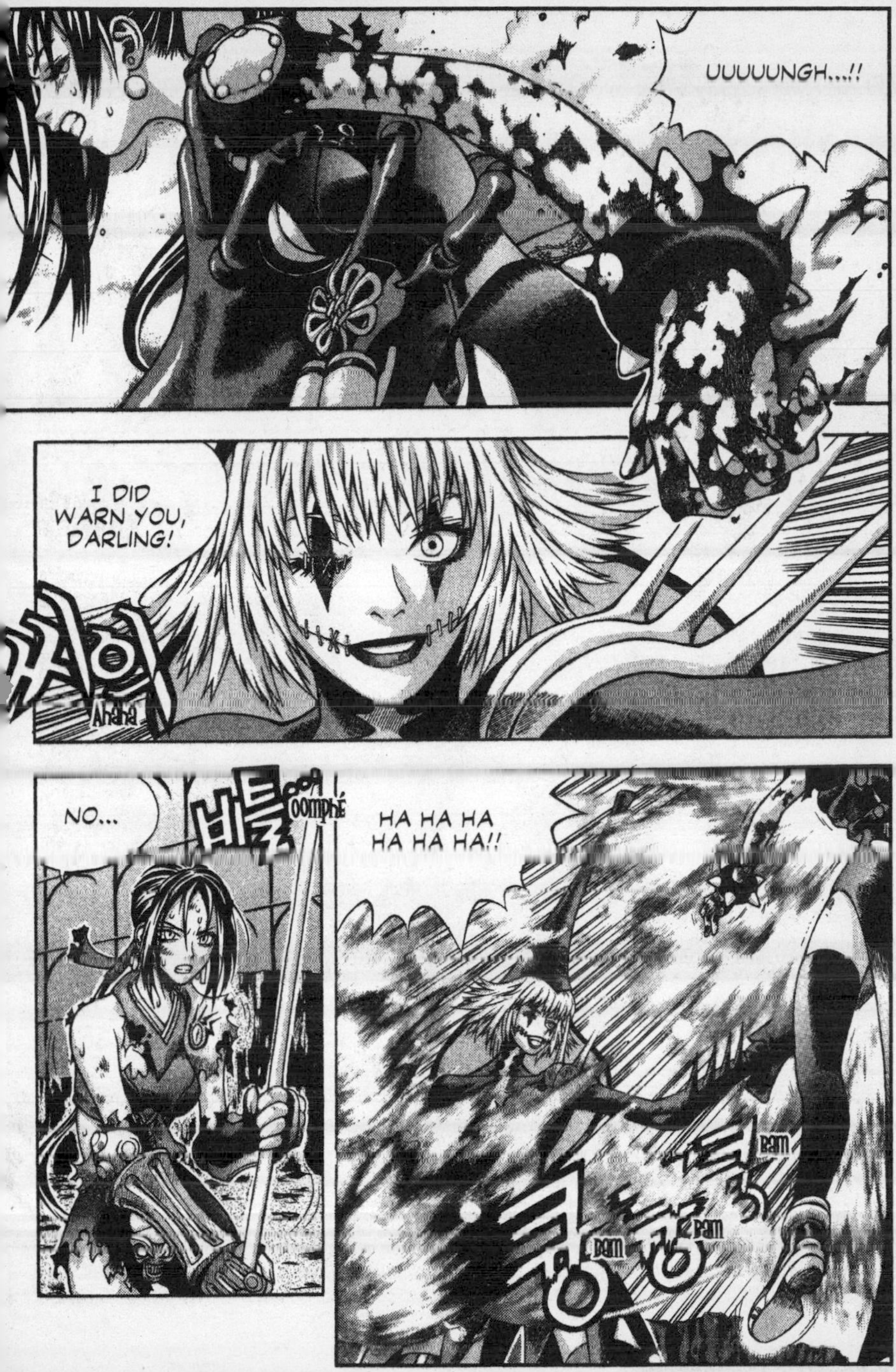

UUUUUNGH...!!
I DID WARN YOU, DARLING!
Ahaha
NO...
oomph
HA HA HA HA HA HA!!
Bam
Bam
Bam

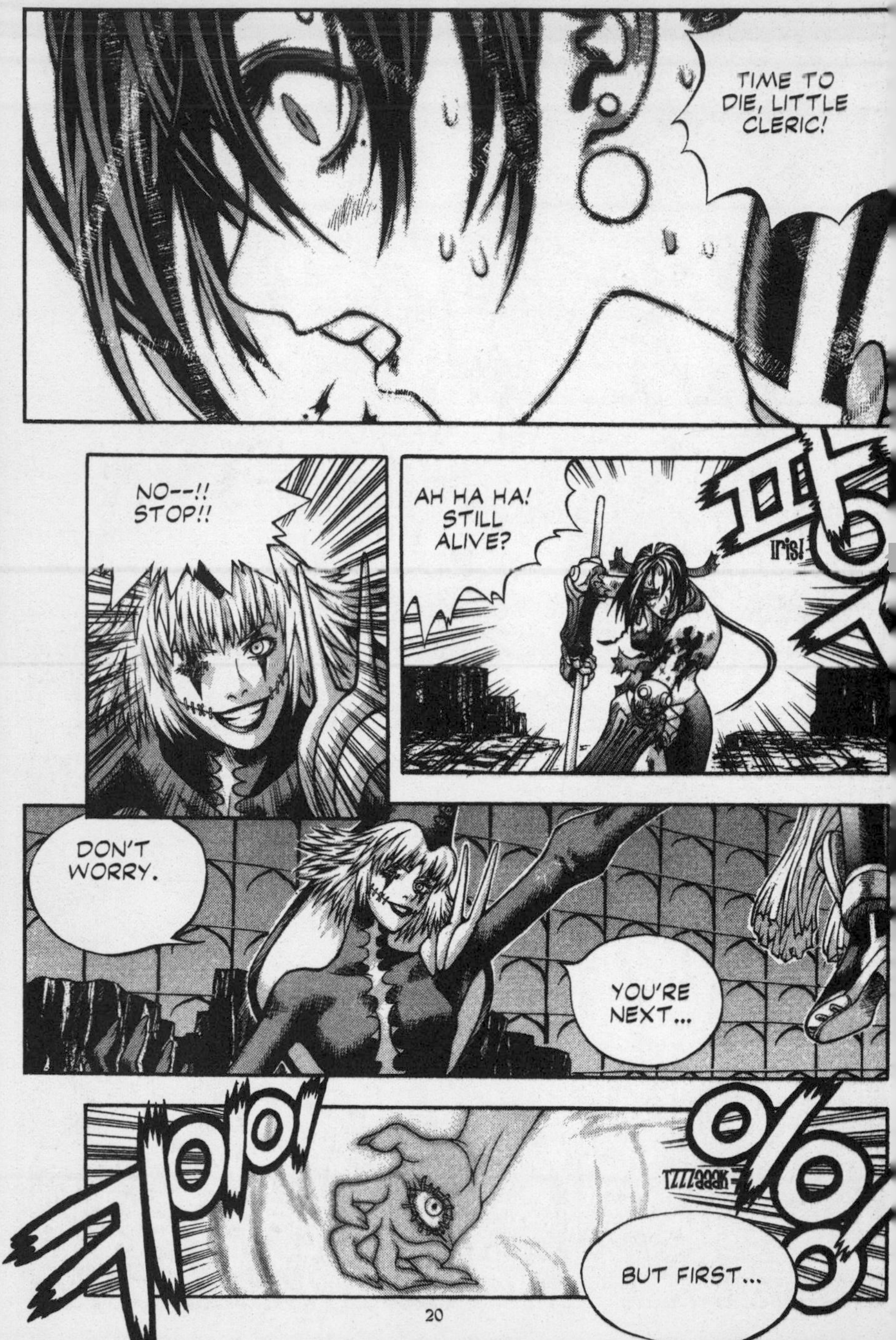
TIME TO DIE, LITTLE CLERIC!
NO--!! STOP!!
AH HA HA! STILL ALIVE?
Iris!
DON'T WORRY.
YOU'RE NEXT...
BUT FIRST...

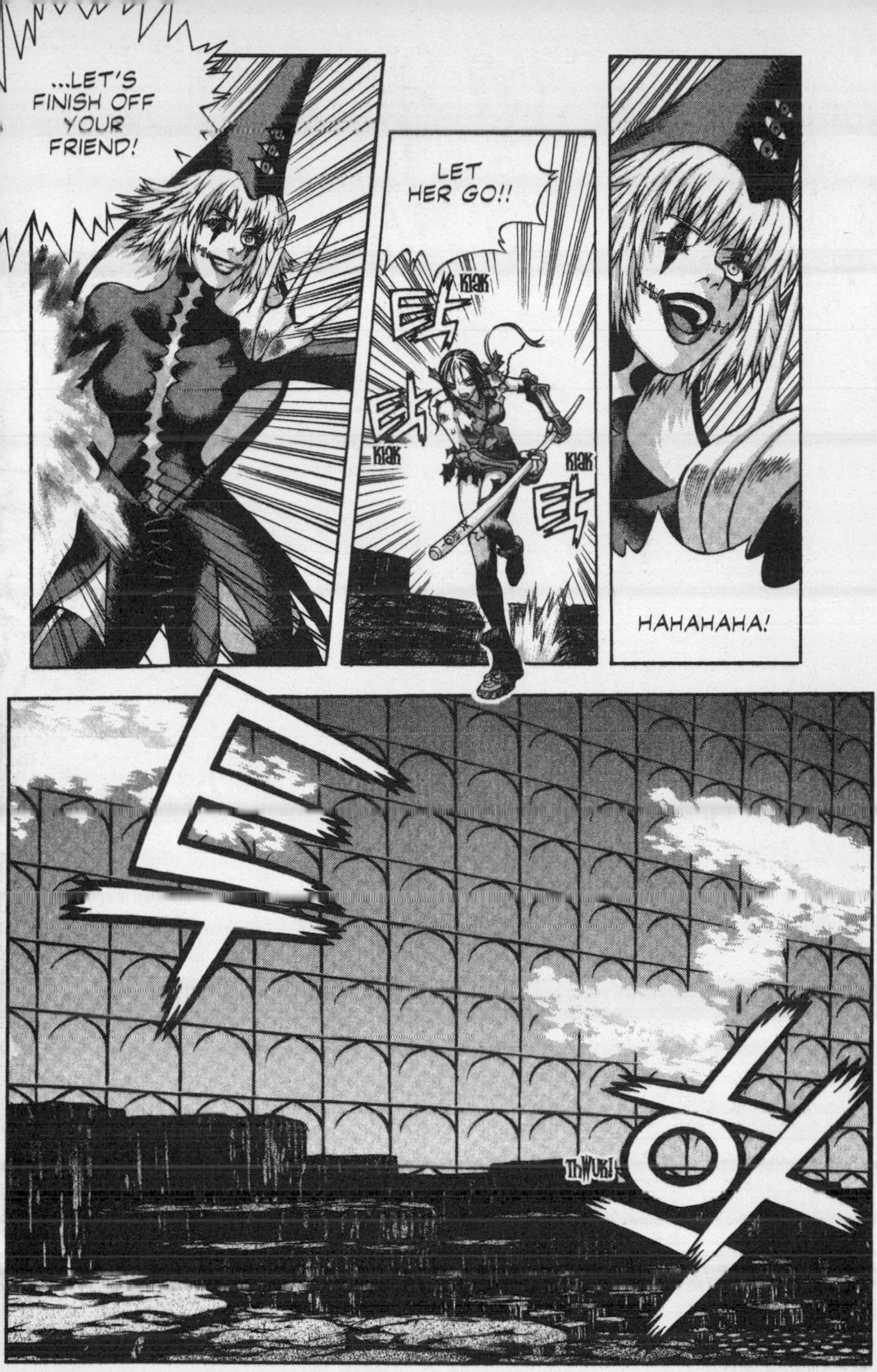
...LET'S FINISH OFF YOUR FRIEND!
LET HER GO!!
KIAK
KIAK
KIAK
HAHAHAHA!
THWUK!

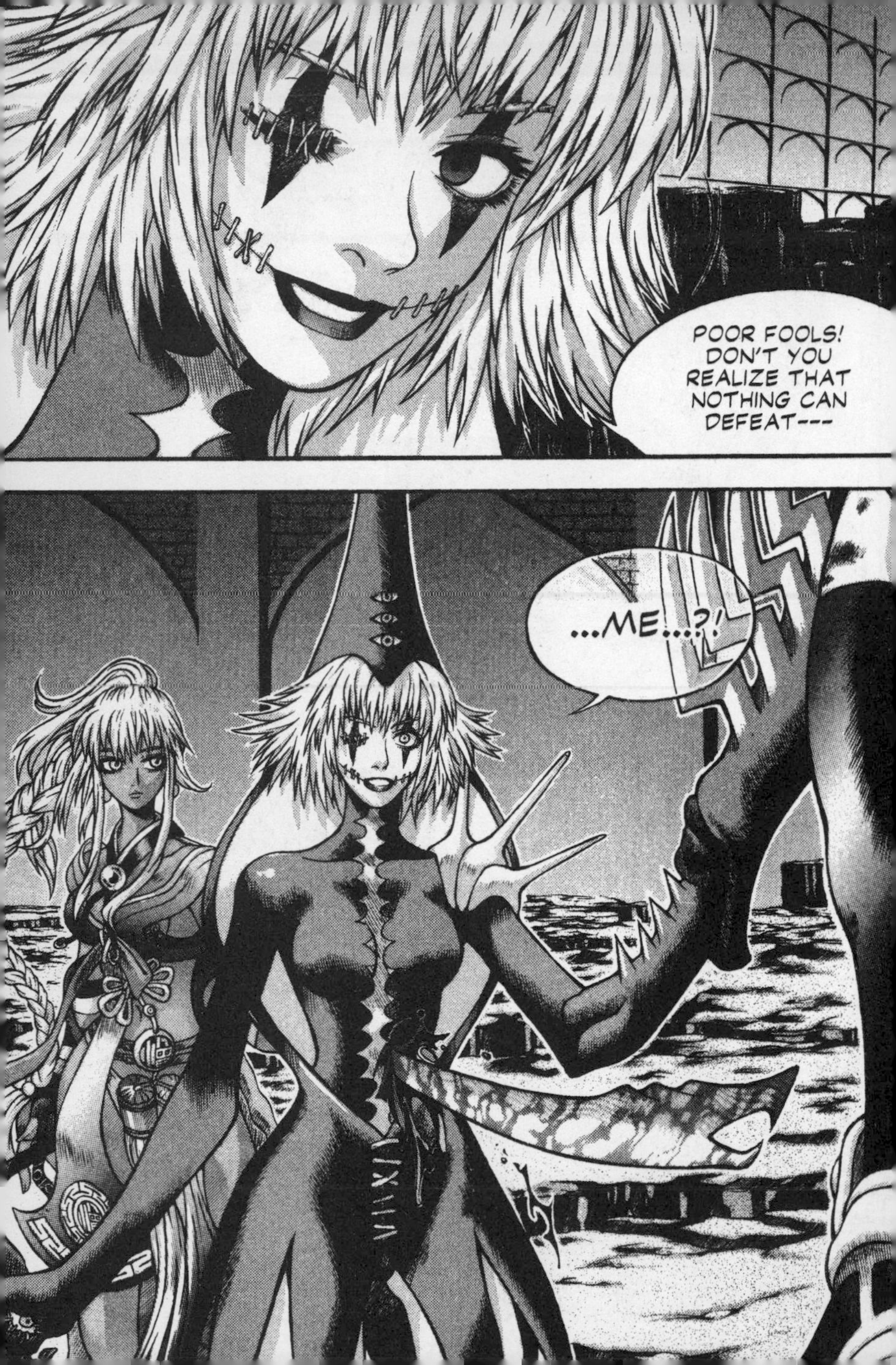
POOR FOOLS! DON'T YOU REALIZE THAT NOTHING CAN DEFEAT---
...ME...?!

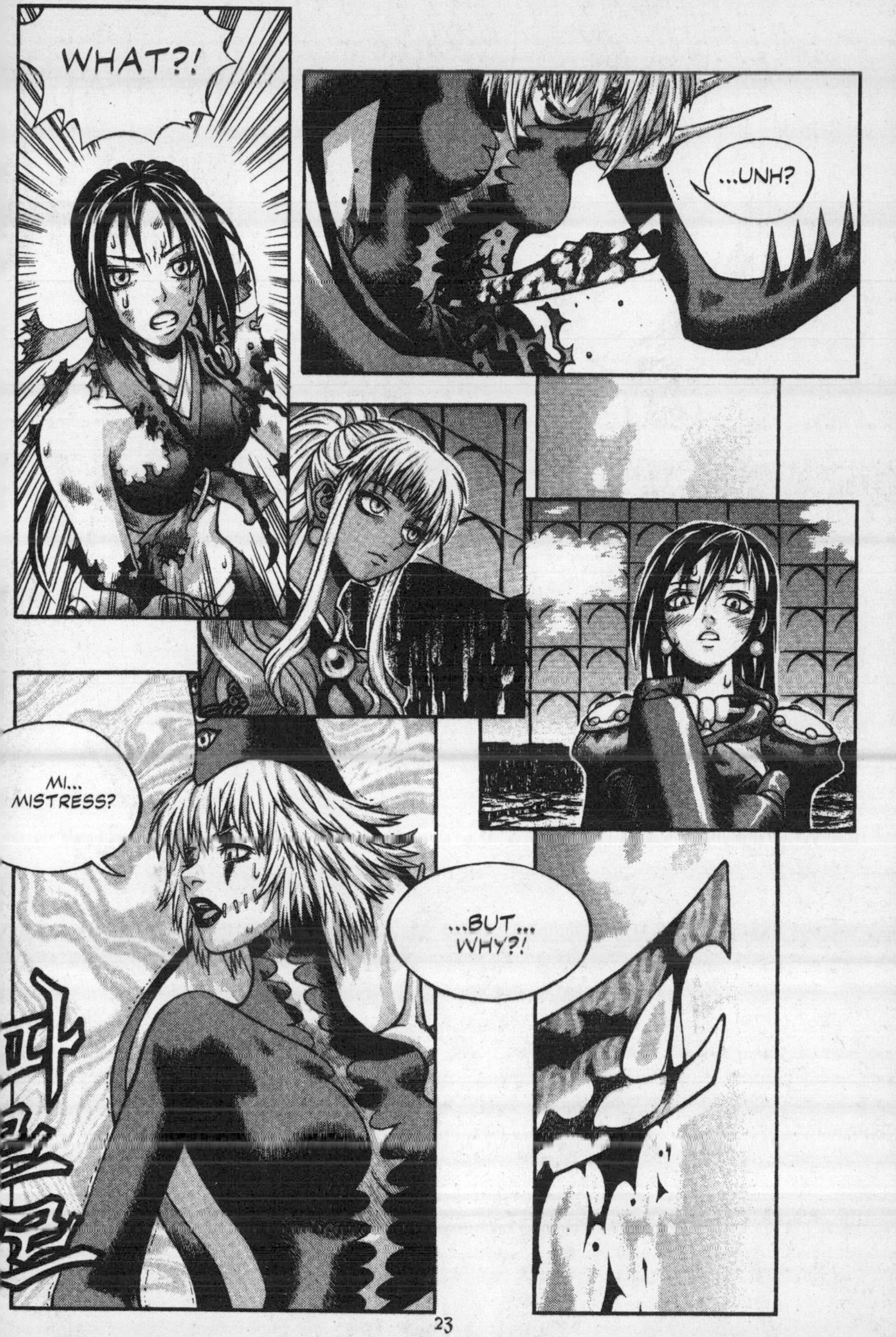
WHAT?!
...UNH?
MI... MISTRESS?
...BUT... WHY?!

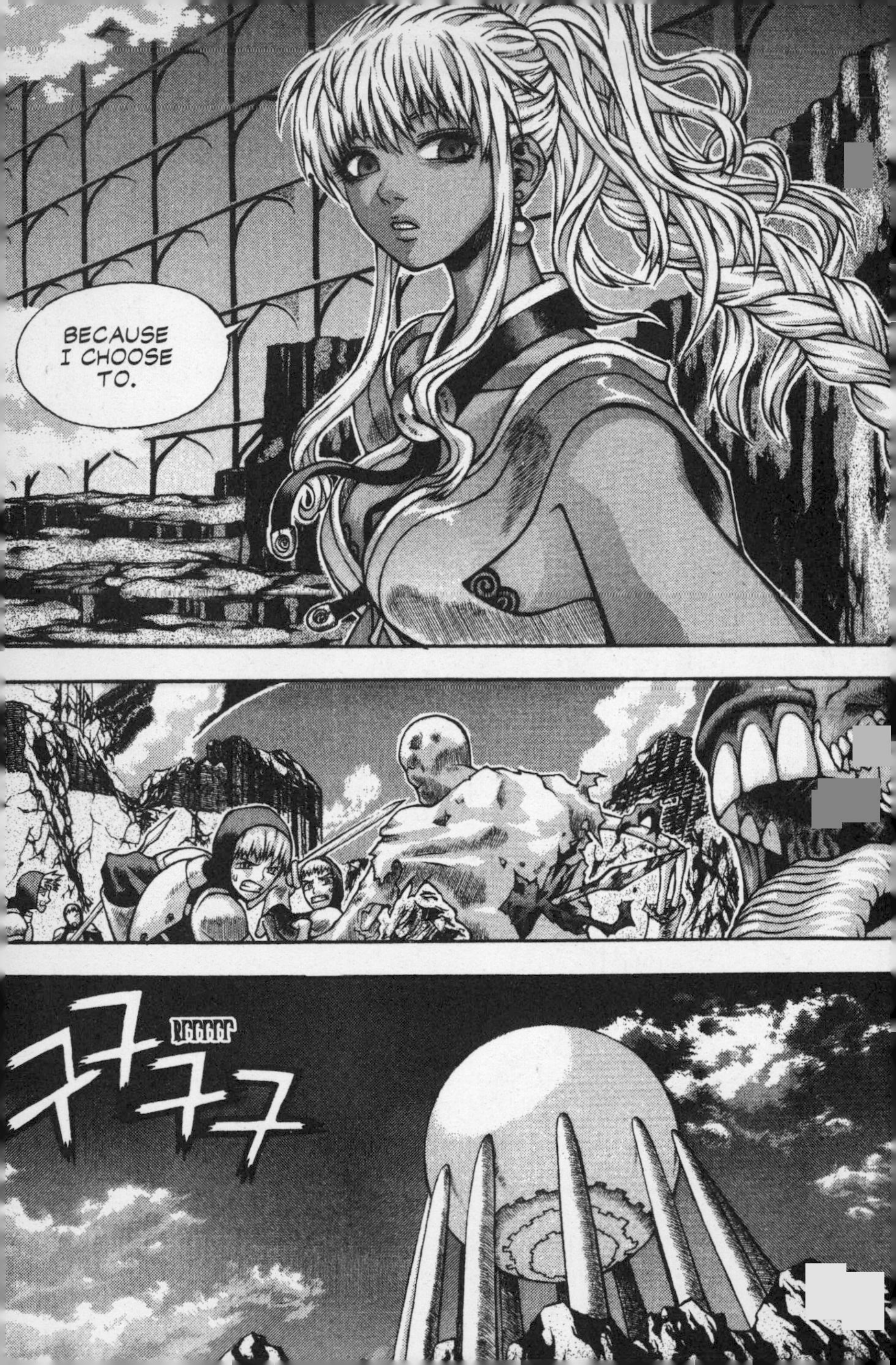
BECAUSE I CHOOSE TO.
RGGGGR

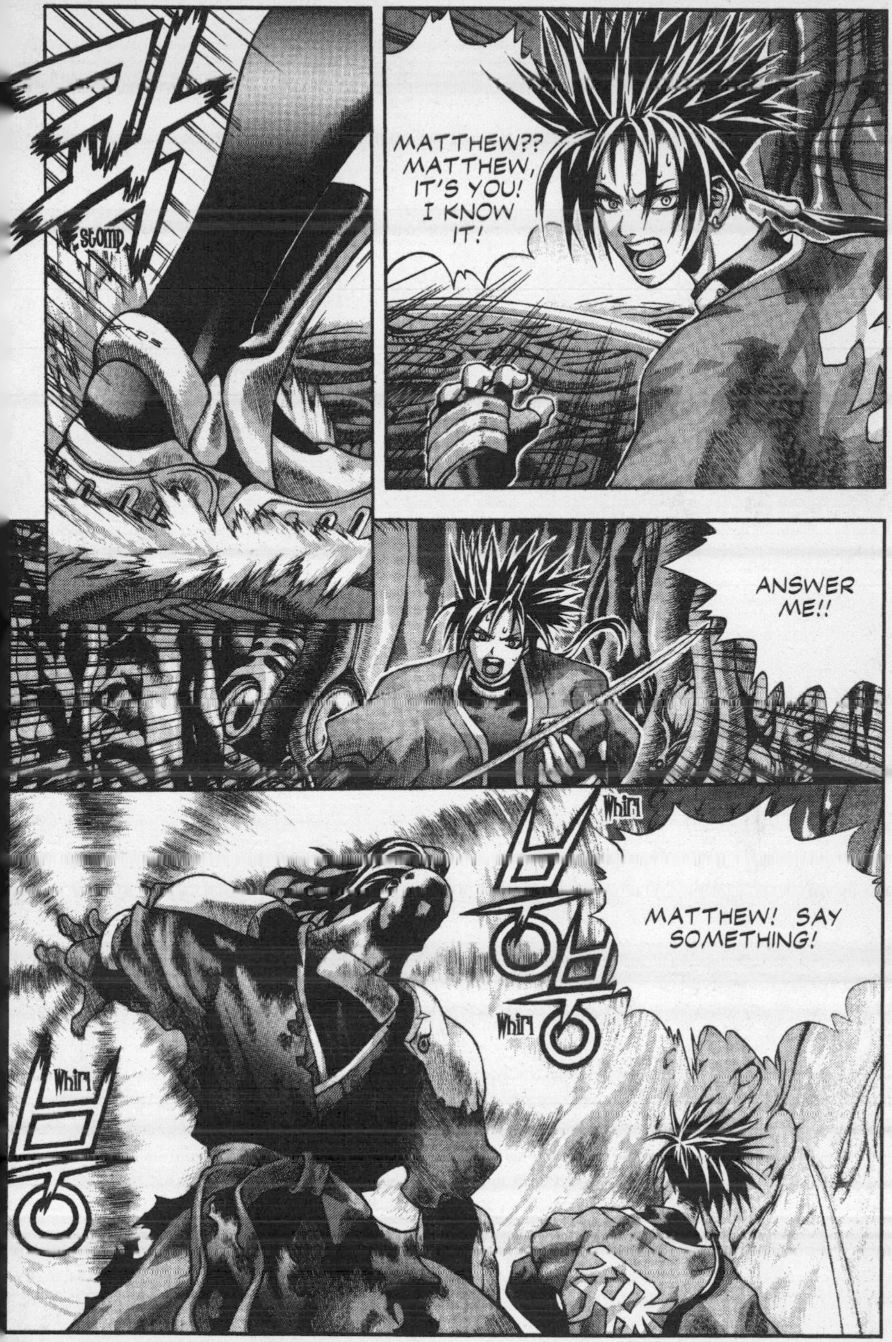
stomp
MATTHEW?? MATTHEW, IT'S YOU! I KNOW IT!
ANSWER ME!!
Whirl
MATTHEW! SAY SOMETHING!
Whirl
Whirl

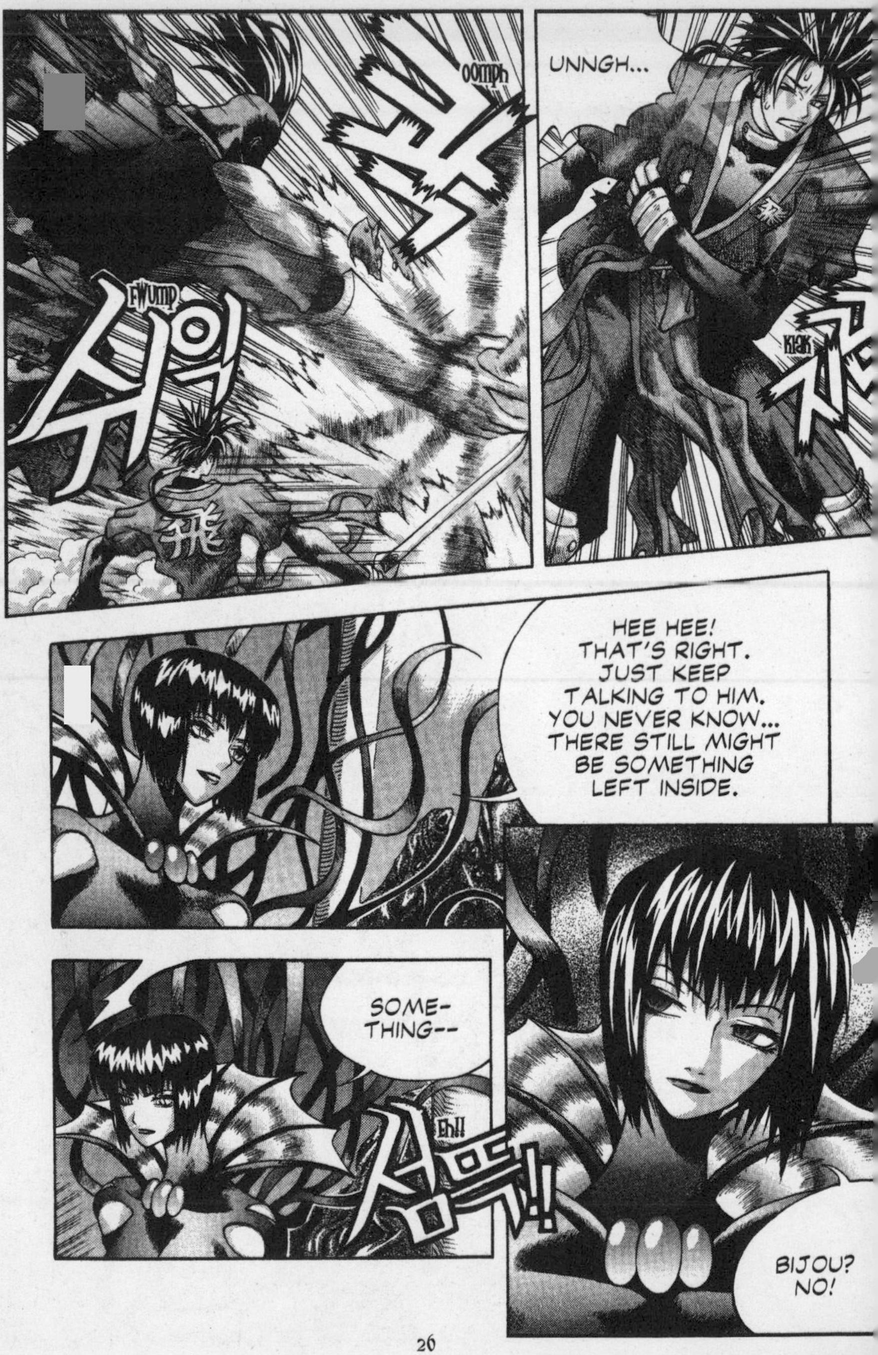
oomph
FWUMP
UNNGH...
KLAK
HEE HEE! THAT'S RIGHT. JUST KEEP TALKING TO HIM. YOU NEVER KNOW... THERE STILL MIGHT BE SOMETHING LEFT INSIDE.
SOME-THING--
Eh!!
BIJOU? NO!

RAGNAROK
라그나로크
IN TO THE ABYSS

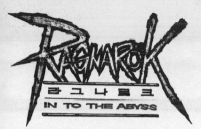

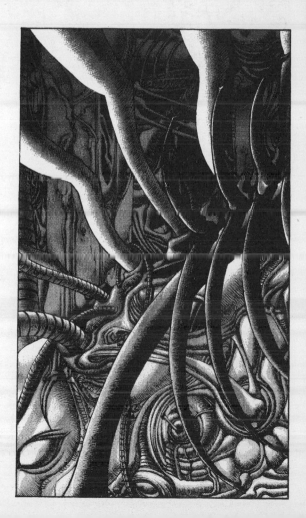

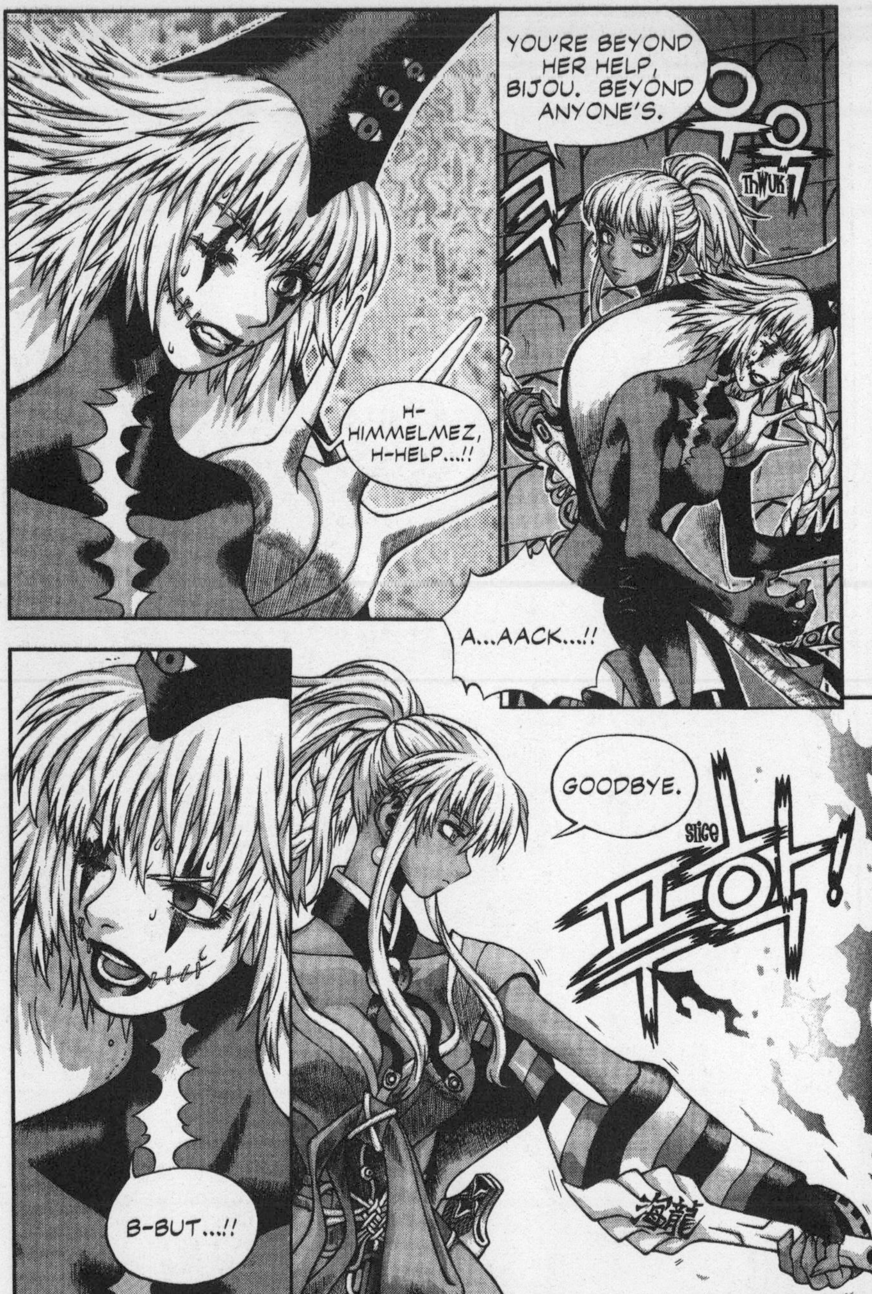
H-HIMMELMEZ, H-HELP...!!
YOU'RE BEYOND HER HELP, BIJOU. BEYOND ANYONE'S.
ThWUK
A...AACK...!!
B-BUT...!!
GOODBYE.
slice

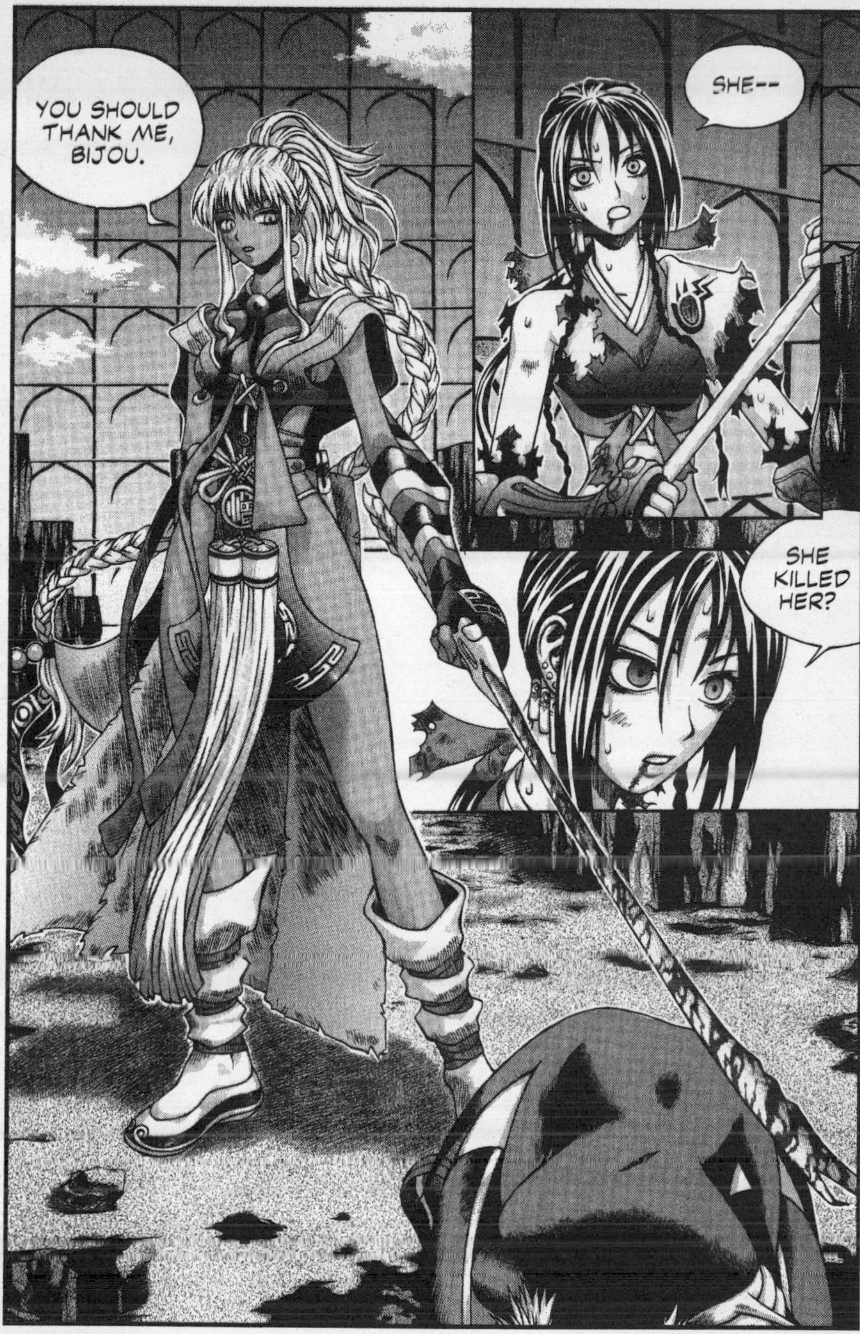
YOU SHOULD THANK ME, BIJOU.
SHE--
SHE KILLED HER?

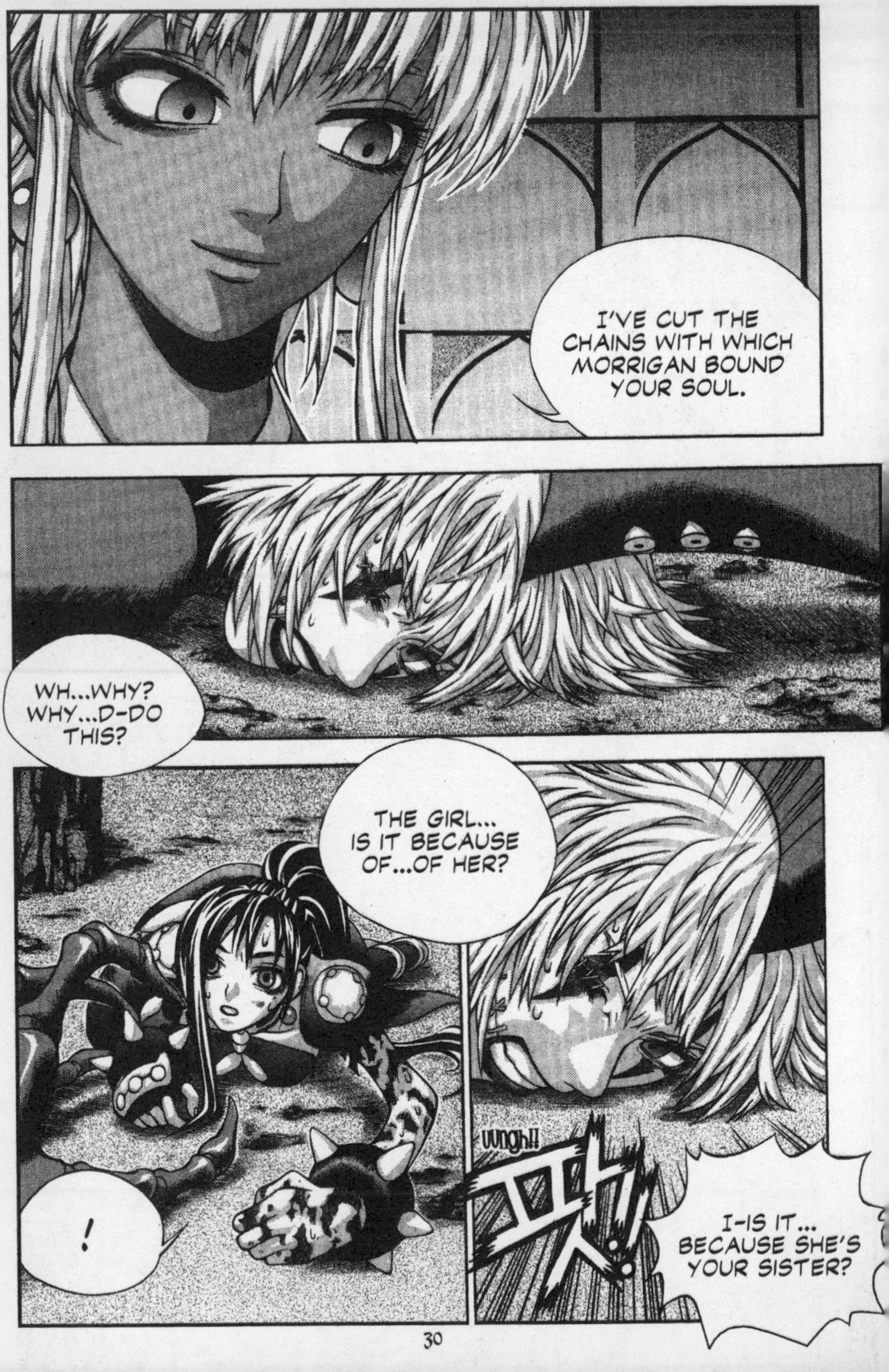
I'VE CUT THE CHAINS WITH WHICH MORRIGAN BOUND YOUR SOUL.
WH...WHY? WHY...D-DO THIS?
THE GIRL... IS IT BECAUSE OF...OF HER?
!
uungh!!
I-IS IT... BECAUSE SHE'S YOUR SISTER?

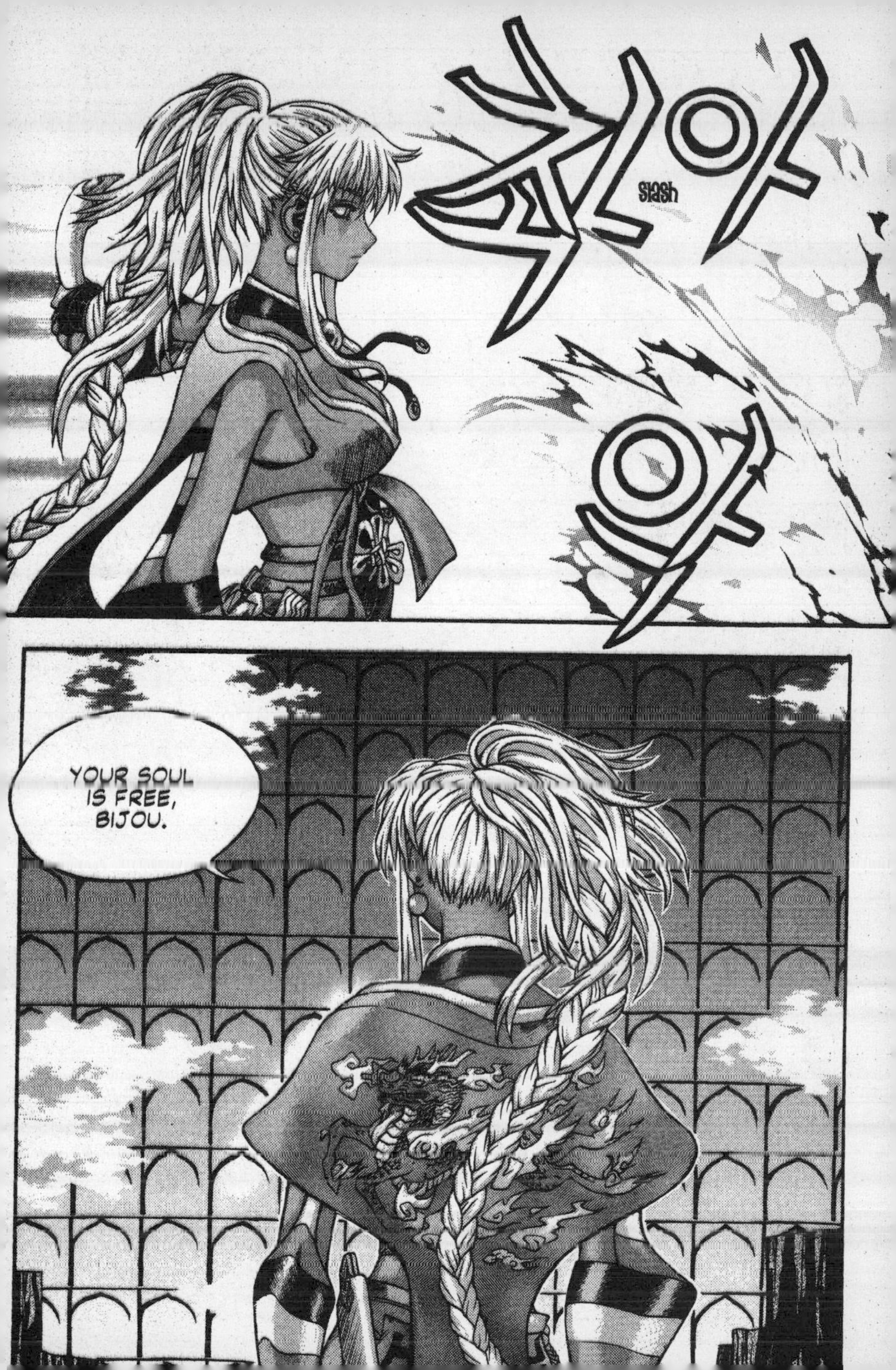

SLASH
YOUR SOUL IS FREE, BIJOU.

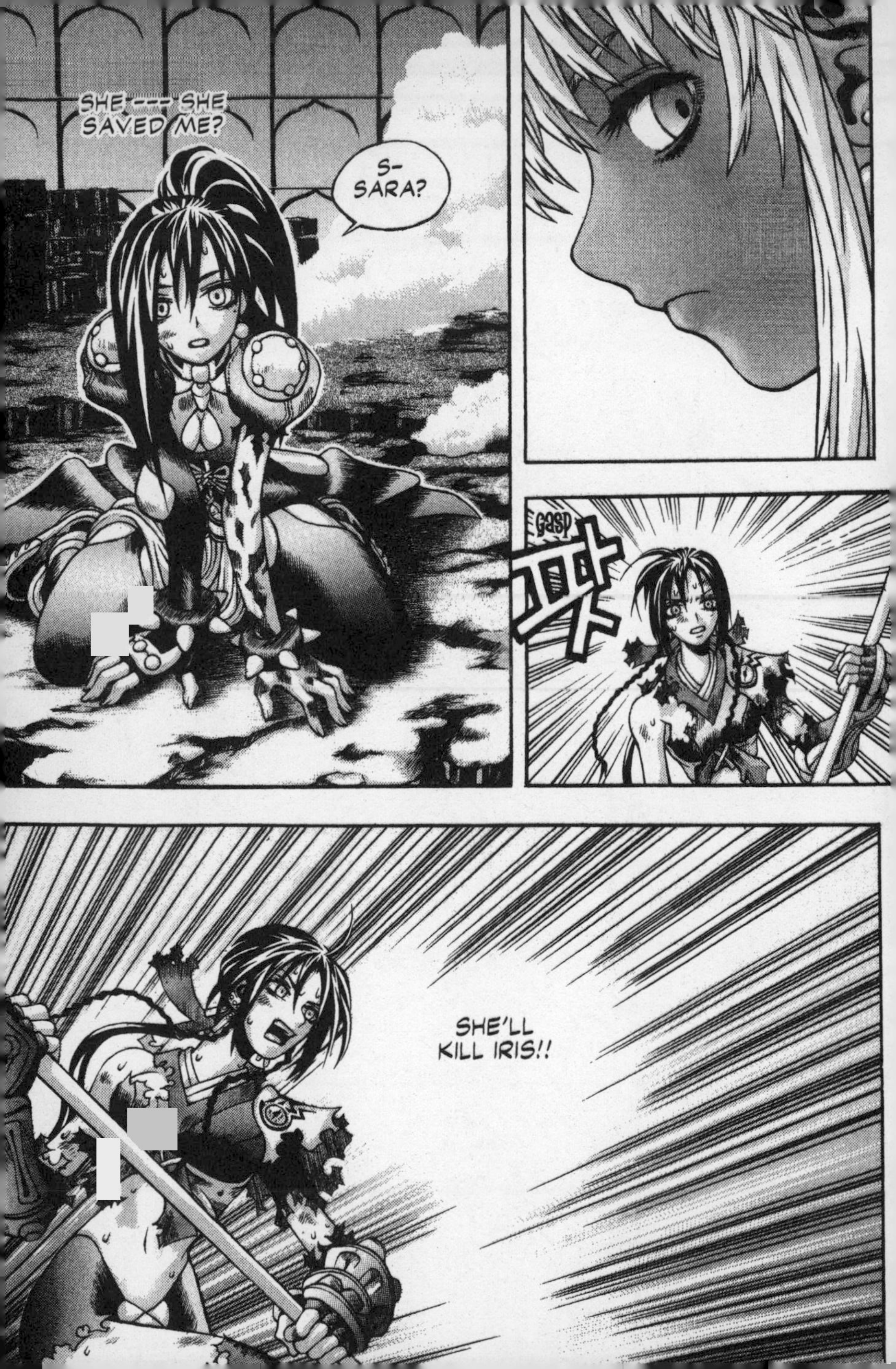
SHE --- SHE SAVED ME?
S- SARA?
GASP
SHE'LL KILL IRIS!!

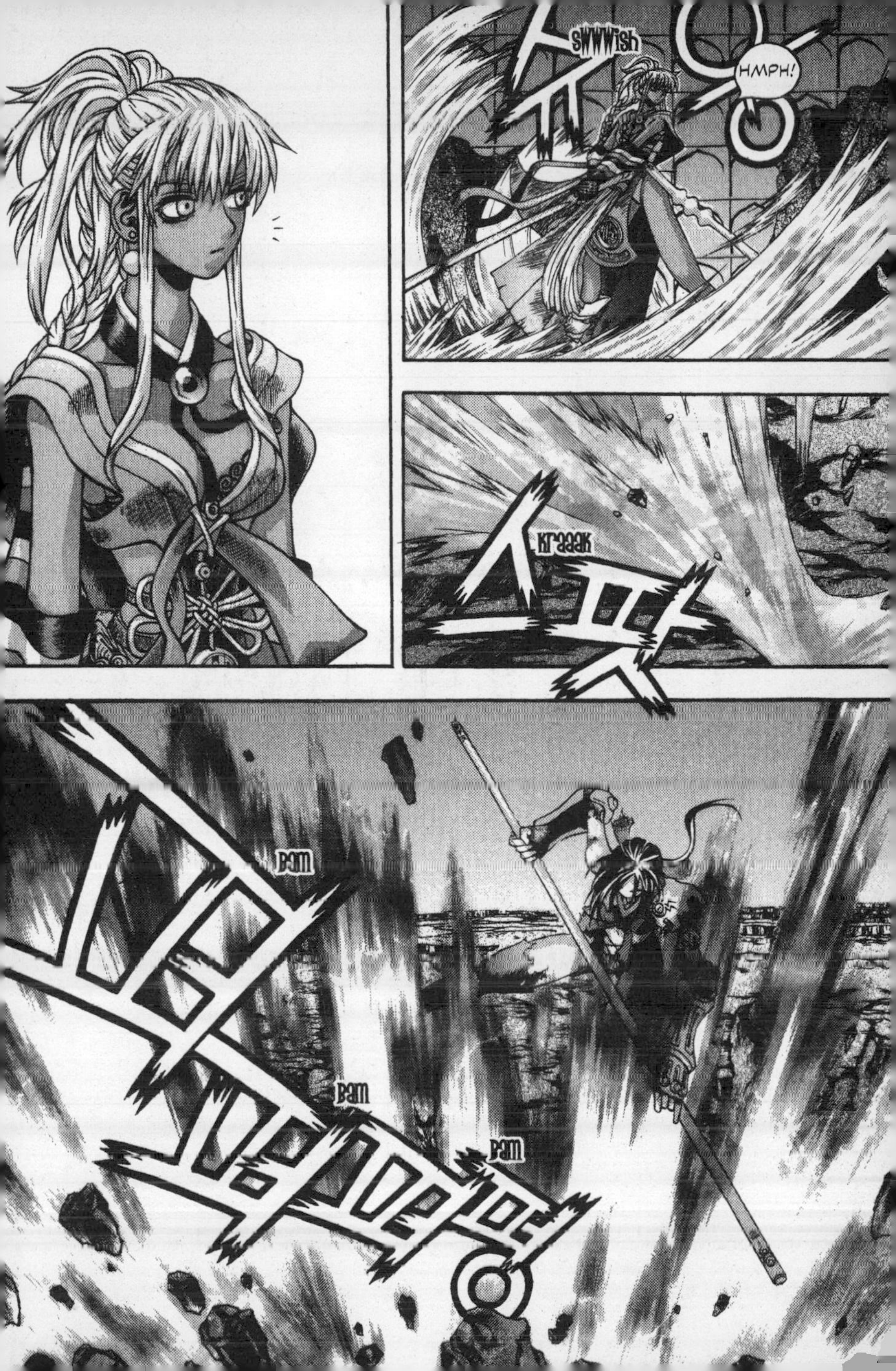
SWWWISH
HMPH!
KRAAAK
BAM
BAM
BAM

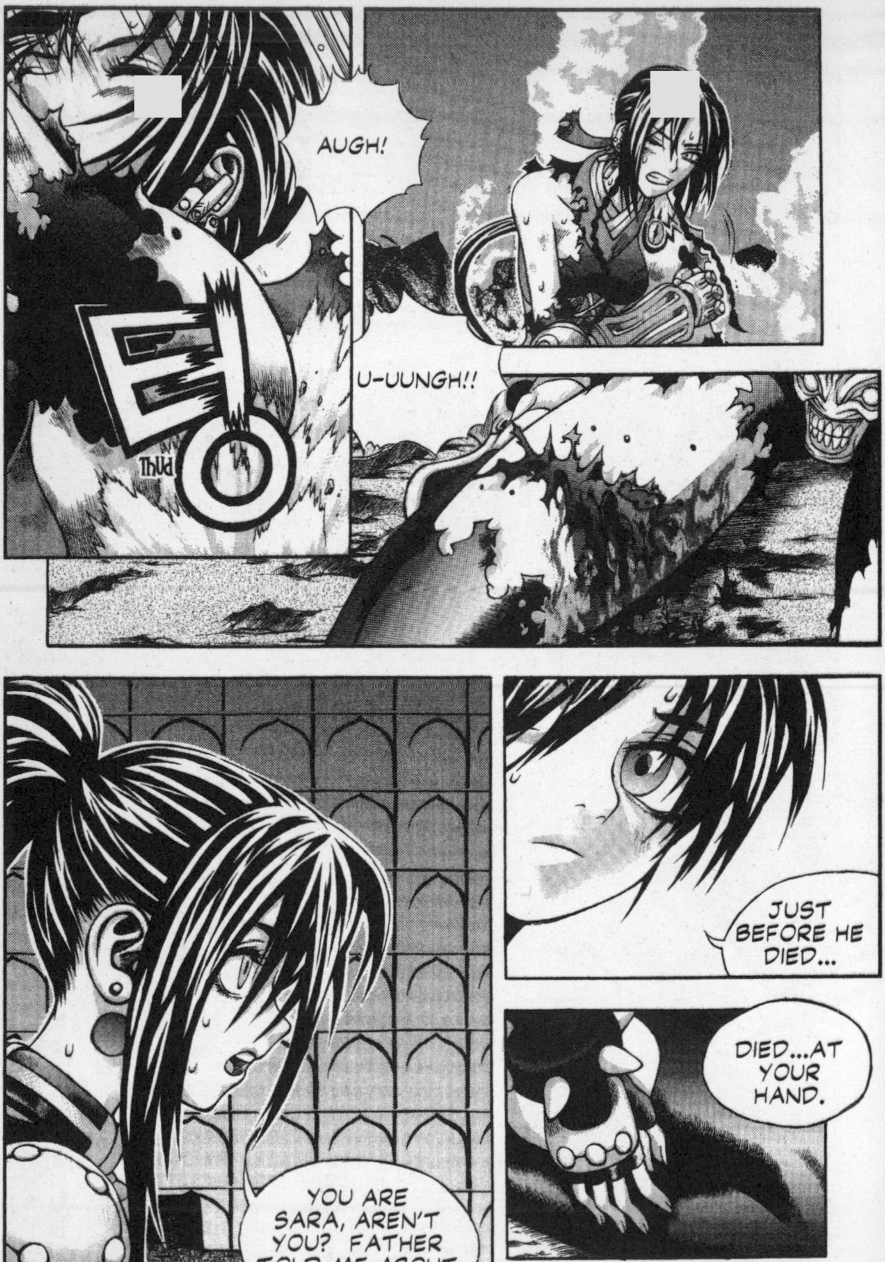
AUGH!
ThUd
U-UUNGH!!
YOU ARE SARA, AREN'T YOU? FATHER TOLD ME ABOUT YOU!
JUST BEFORE HE DIED...
DIED...AT YOUR HAND.

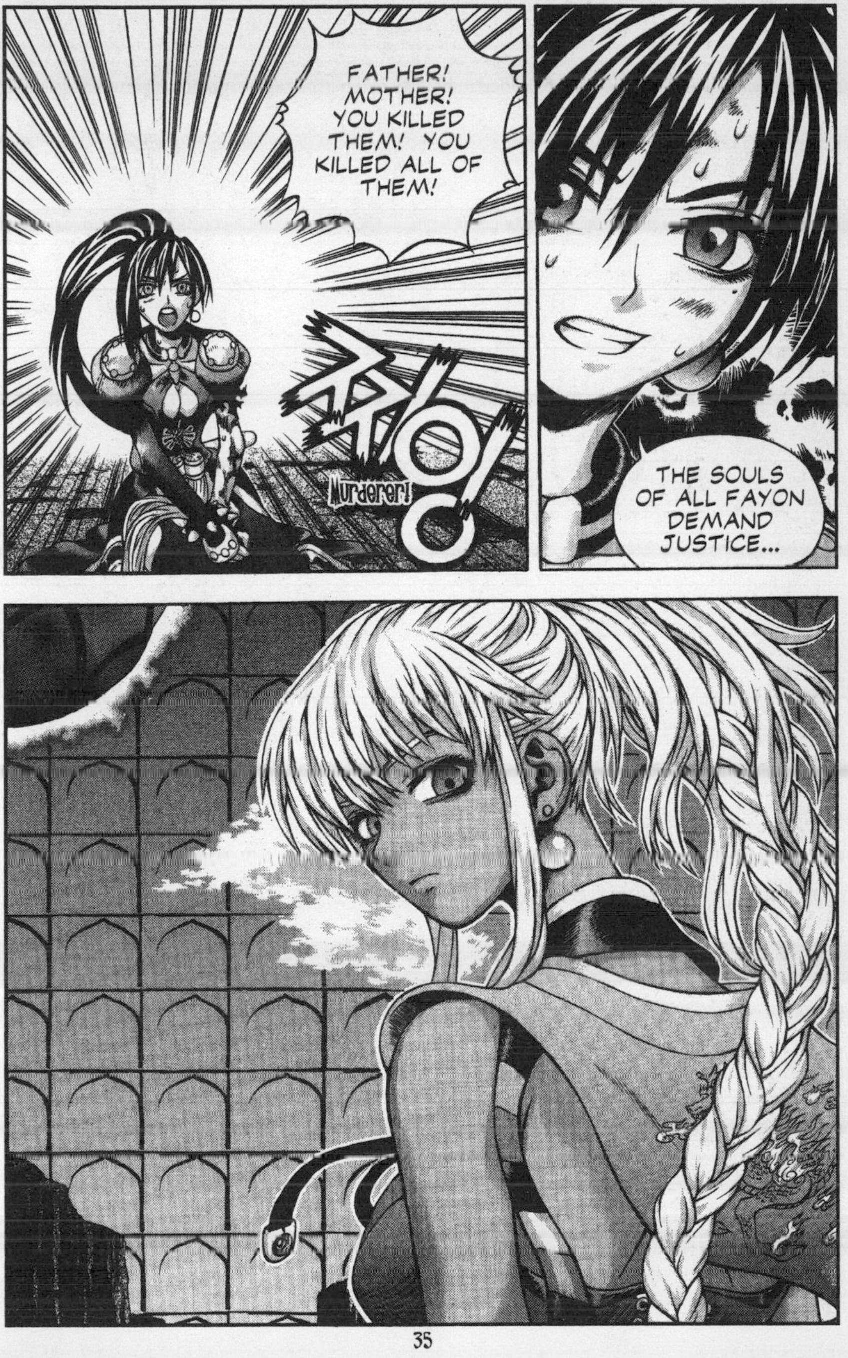
FATHER! MOTHER! YOU KILLED THEM! YOU KILLED ALL OF THEM!
Murderer!
THE SOULS OF ALL FAYON DEMAND JUSTICE...

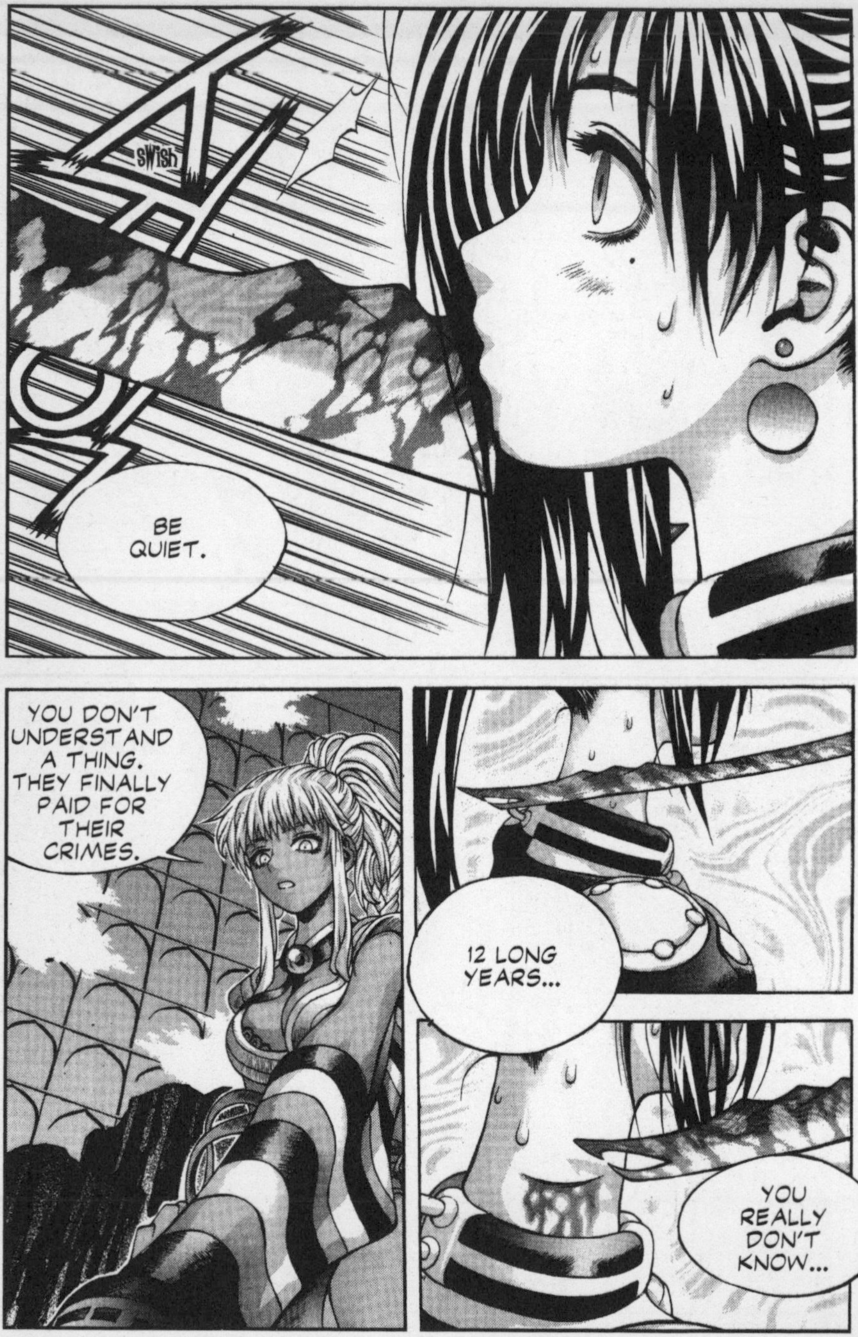
SWISH
BE QUIET.
YOU DON'T UNDERSTAND A THING. THEY FINALLY PAID FOR THEIR CRIMES.
12 LONG YEARS...
YOU REALLY DON'T KNOW...

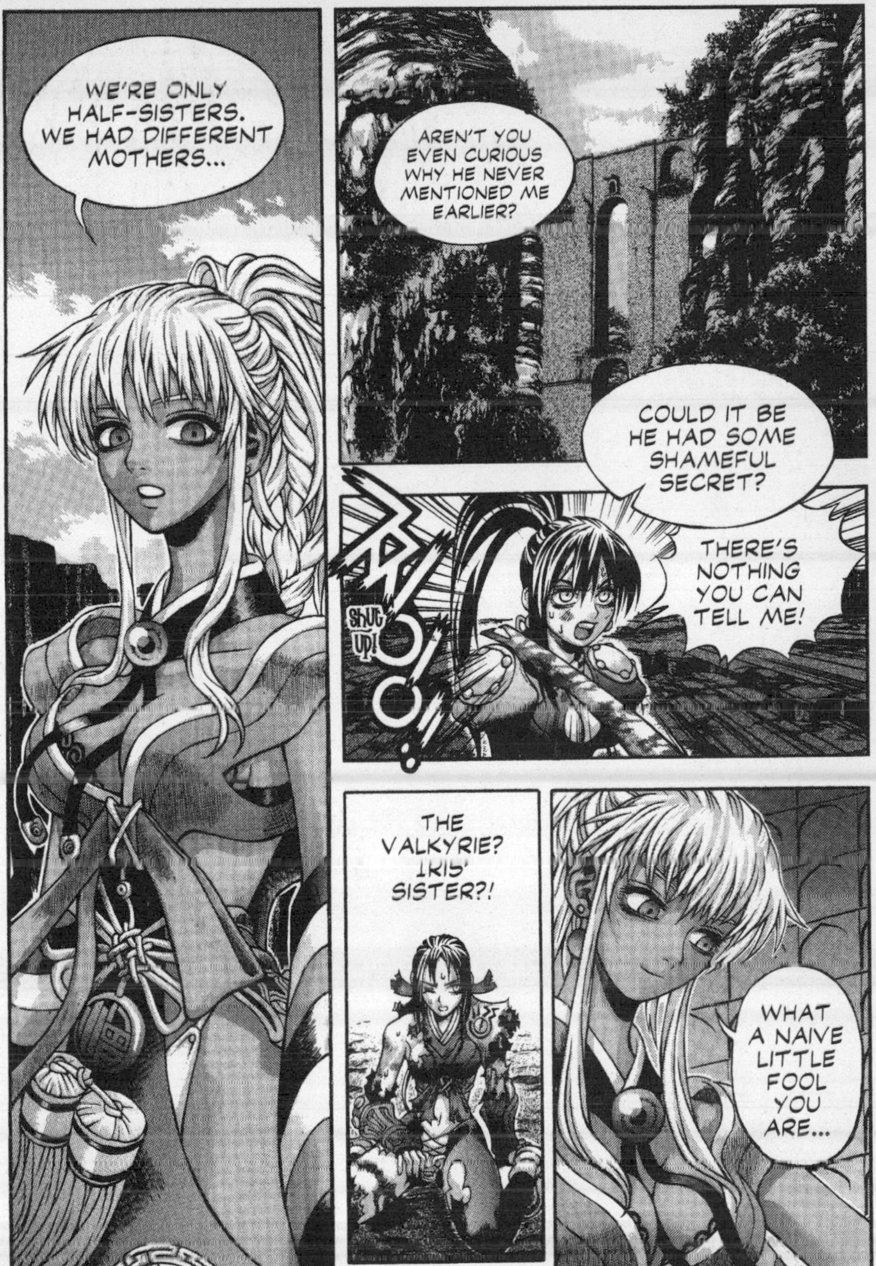
WE'RE ONLY HALF-SISTERS. WE HAD DIFFERENT MOTHERS...
AREN'T YOU EVEN CURIOUS WHY HE NEVER MENTIONED ME EARLIER?
COULD IT BE HE HAD SOME SHAMEFUL SECRET?
SHUT UP!
THERE'S NOTHING YOU CAN TELL ME!
THE VALKYRIE? IRIS' SISTER?!
WHAT A NAIVE LITTLE FOOL YOU ARE...

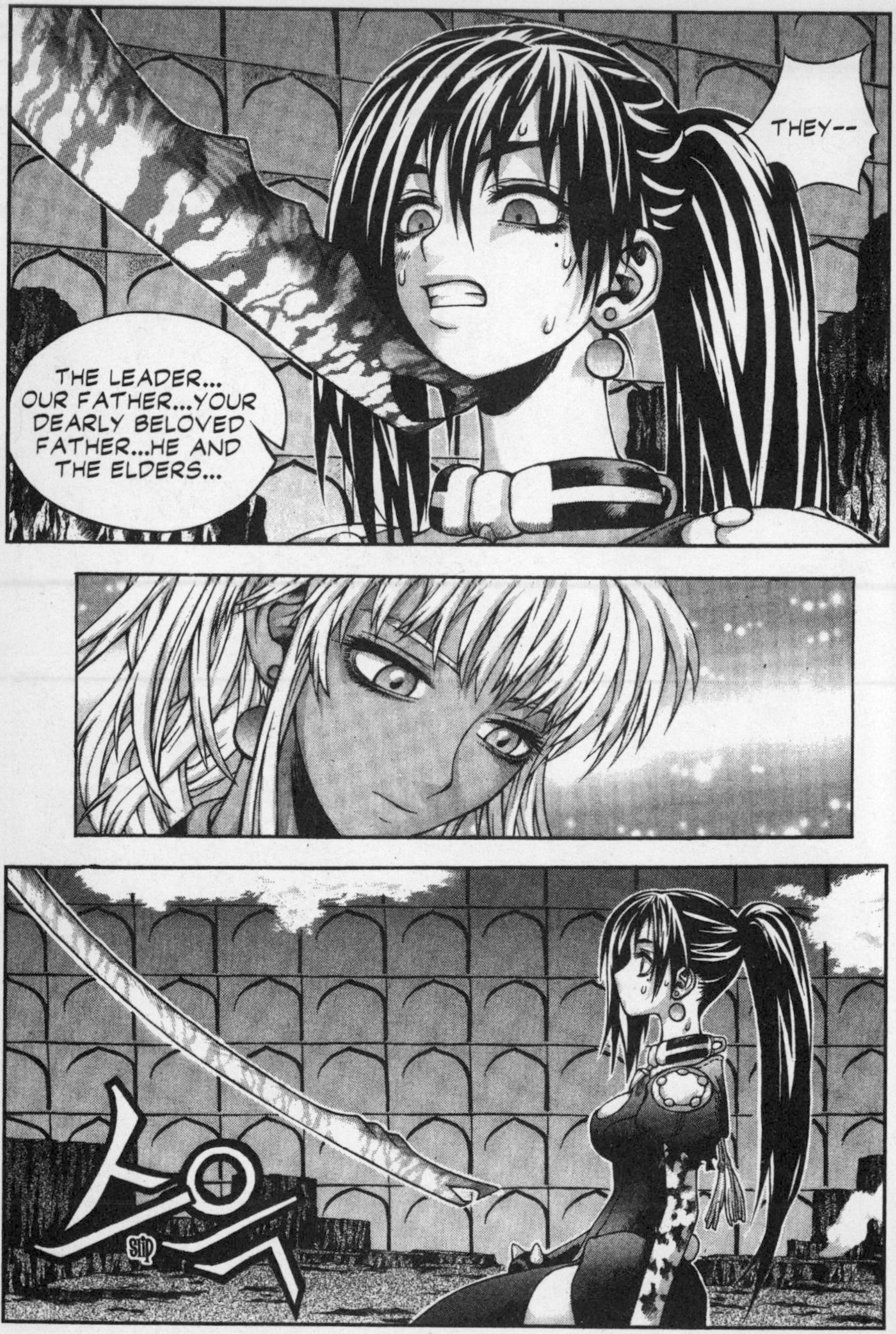
THE LEADER... OUR FATHER...YOUR DEARLY BELOVED FATHER...HE AND THE ELDERS...
THEY--
slip

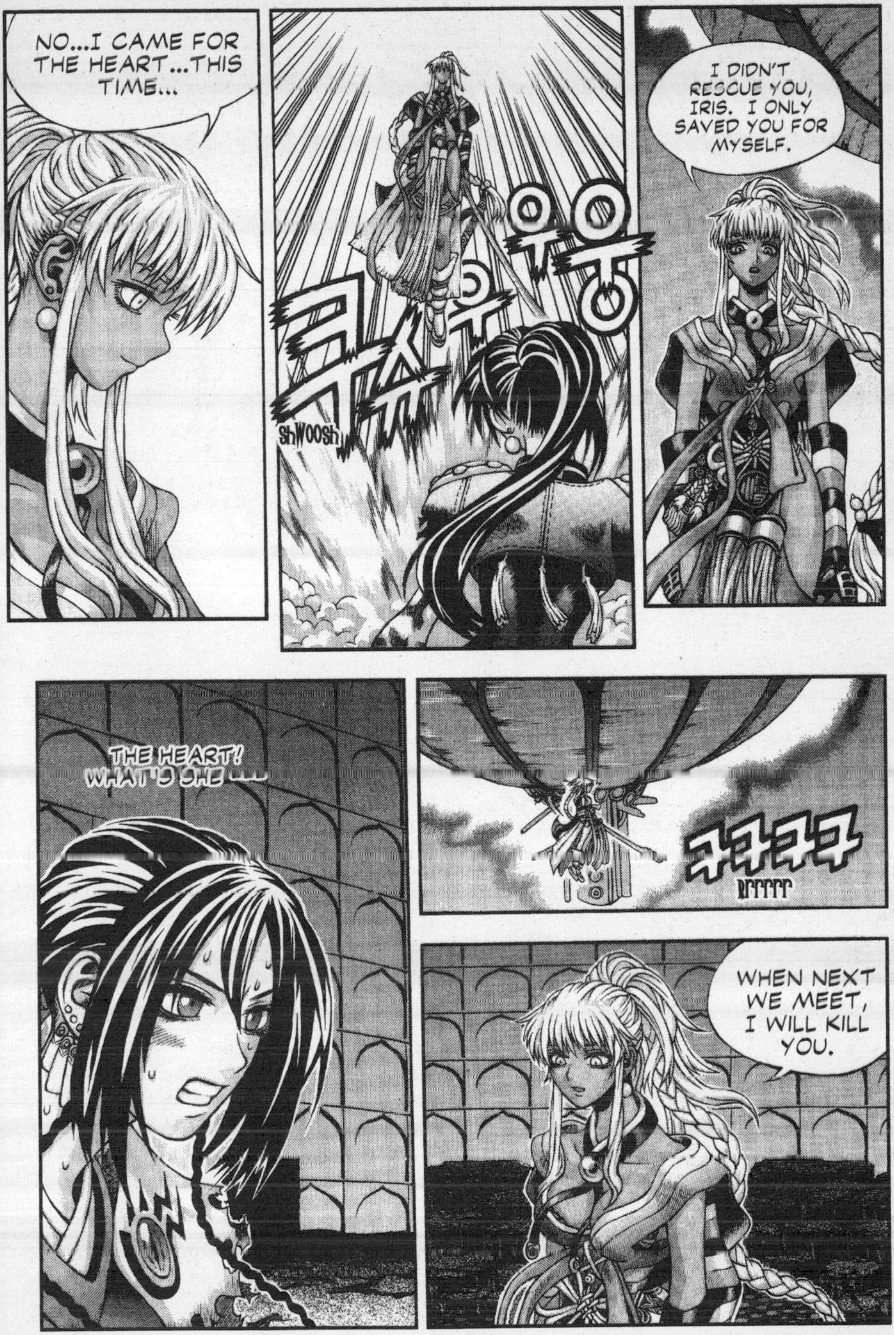
NO...I CAME FOR THE HEART...THIS TIME...
SHWOOSH
I DIDN'T RESCUE YOU, IRIS. I ONLY SAVED YOU FOR MYSELF.
THE HEART! WHAT'S SHE ...
BRRRRR
WHEN NEXT WE MEET, I WILL KILL YOU.

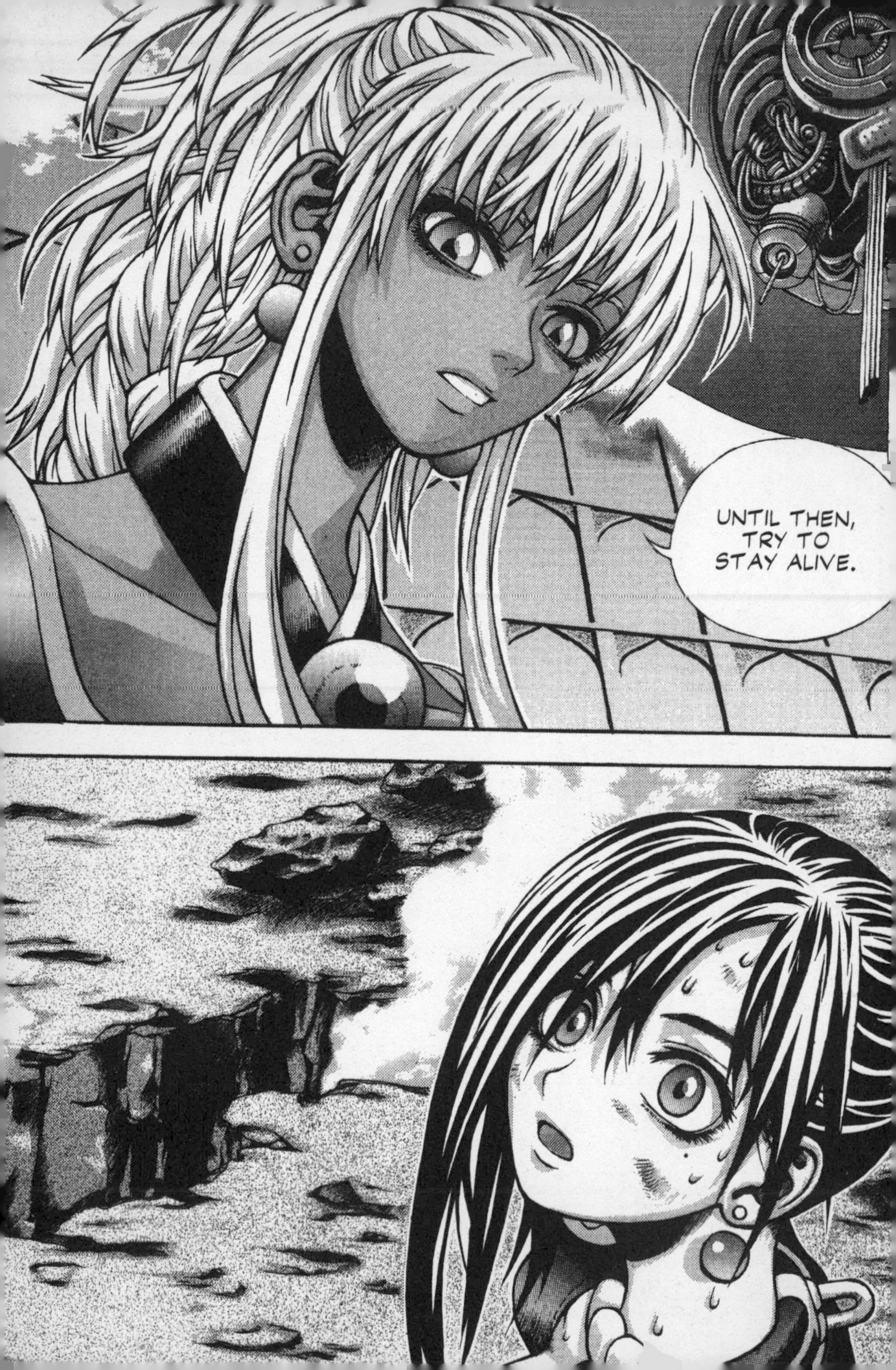
UNTIL THEN, TRY TO STAY ALIVE.

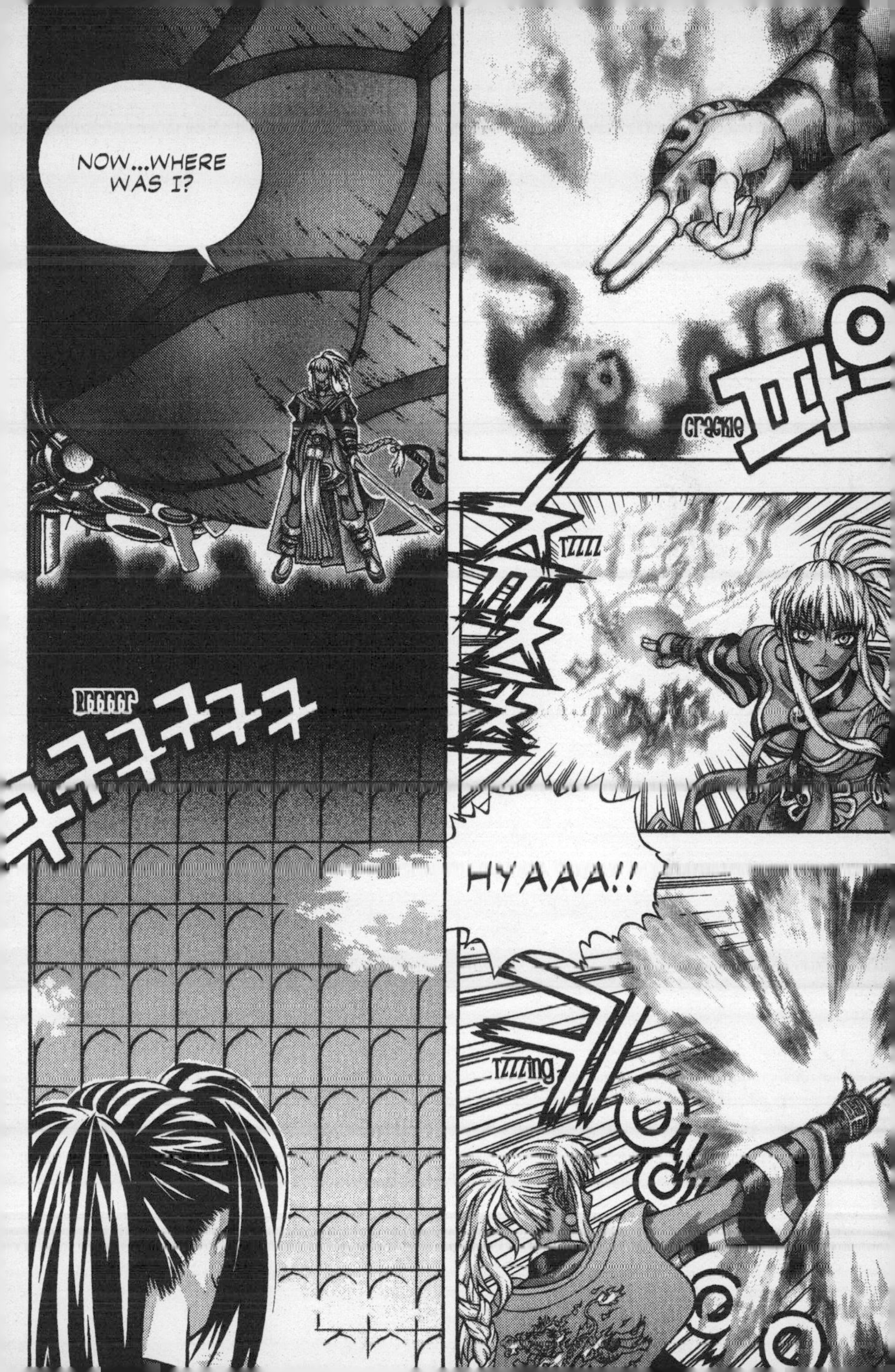
NOW...WHERE WAS I?
crackle
TZZZZ
HYAAA!!
TZZZing

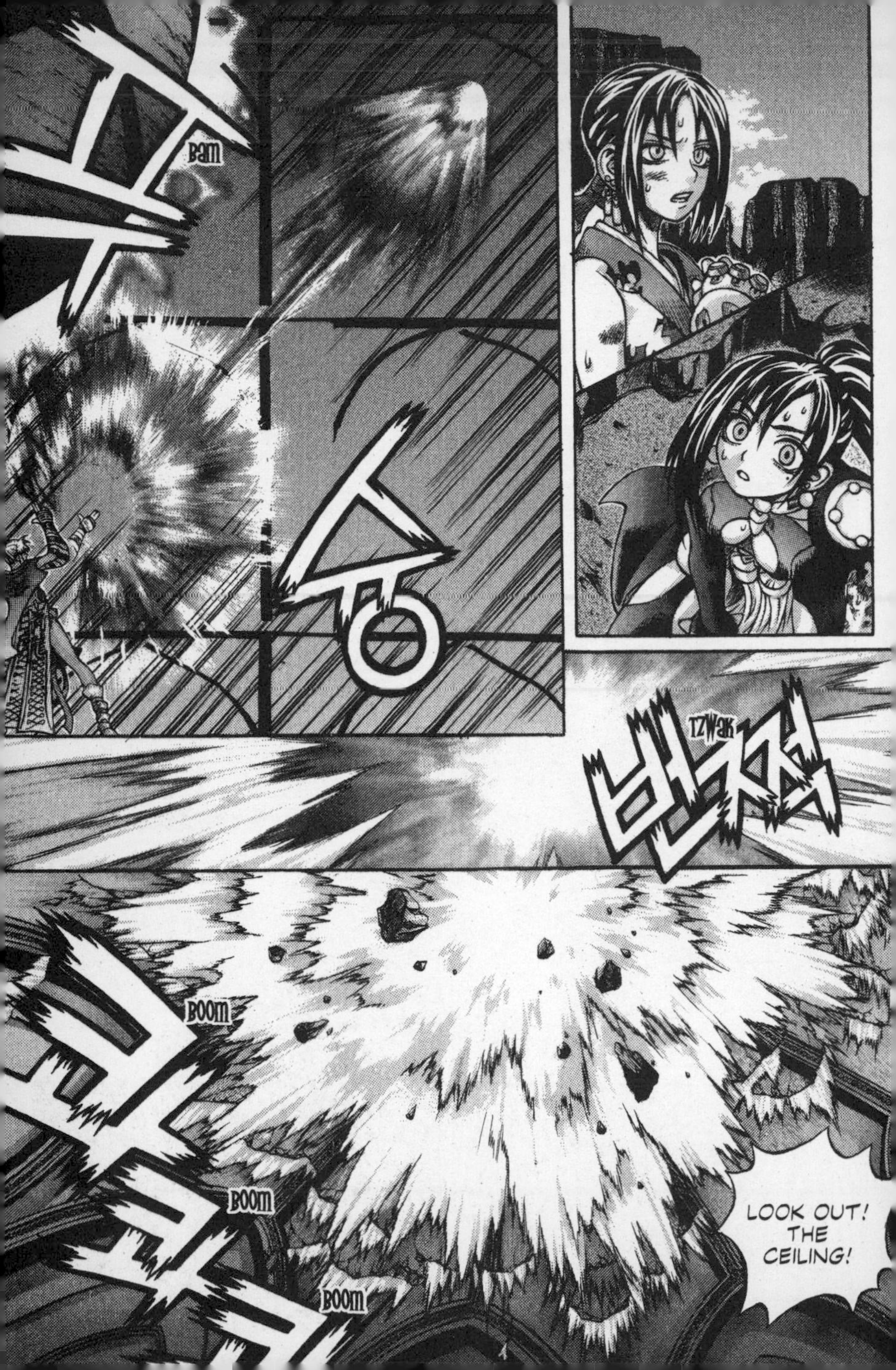
BAM
TZWAK
BOOM
BOOM
BOOM
LOOK OUT! THE CEILING!

RAGNAROK
라그나로크
IN TO THE ABYSS

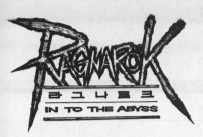

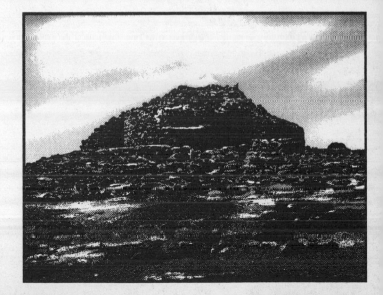

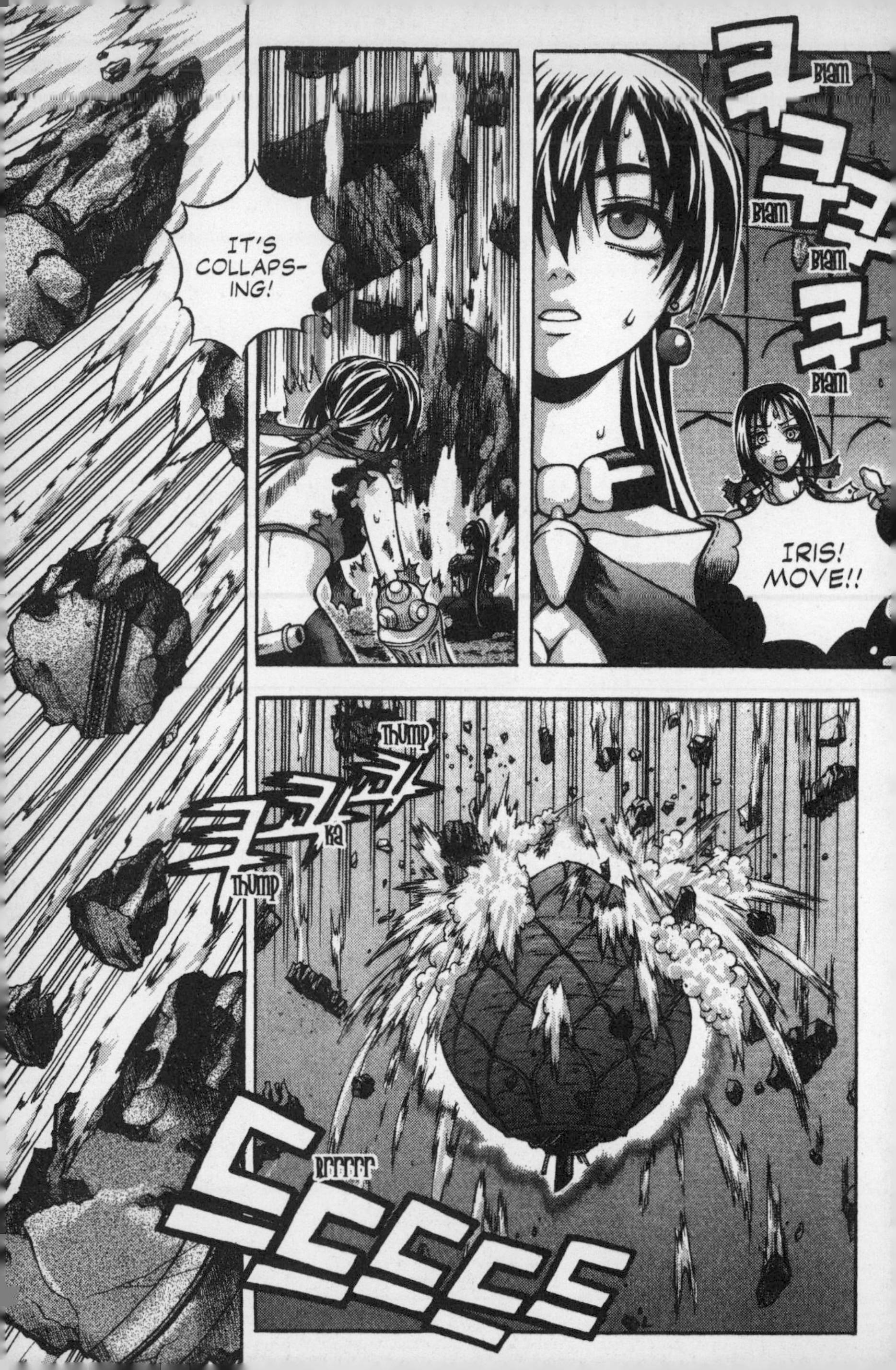
IT'S COLLAPSING!
BLAM
BLAM
BLAM
BLAM
IRIS! MOVE!!
THUMP
KA
THUMP
RRRRRR

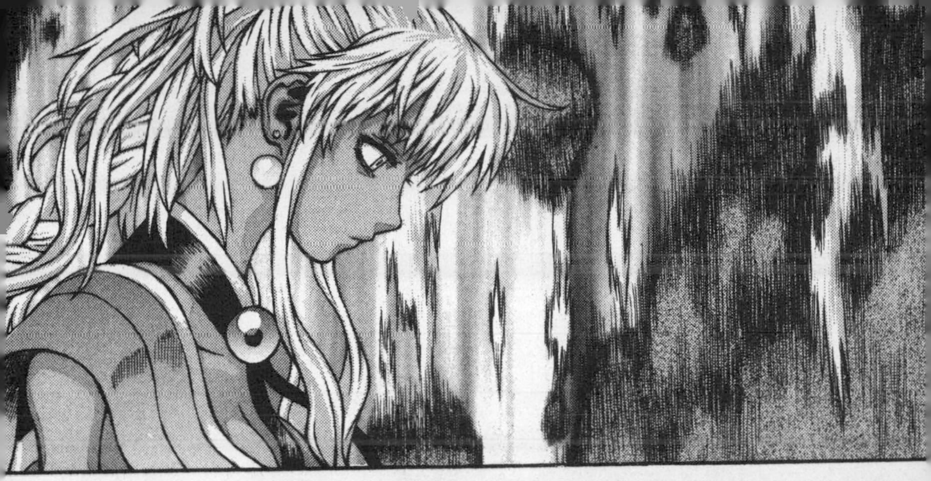
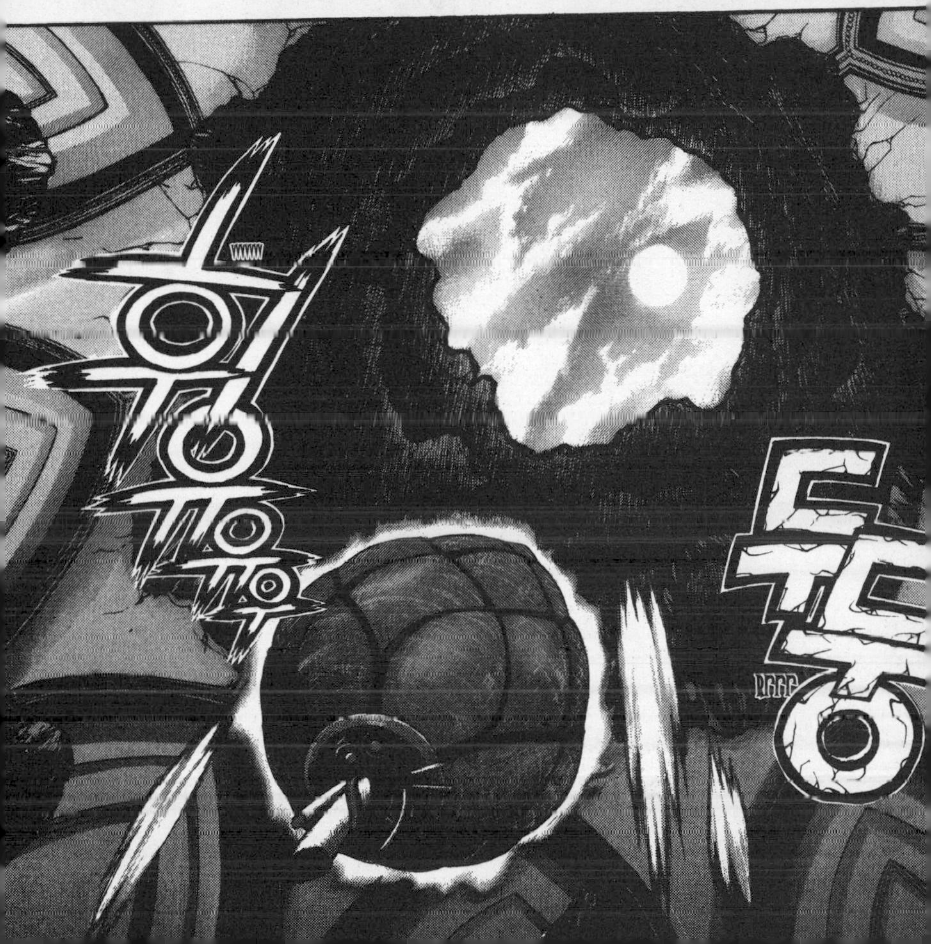

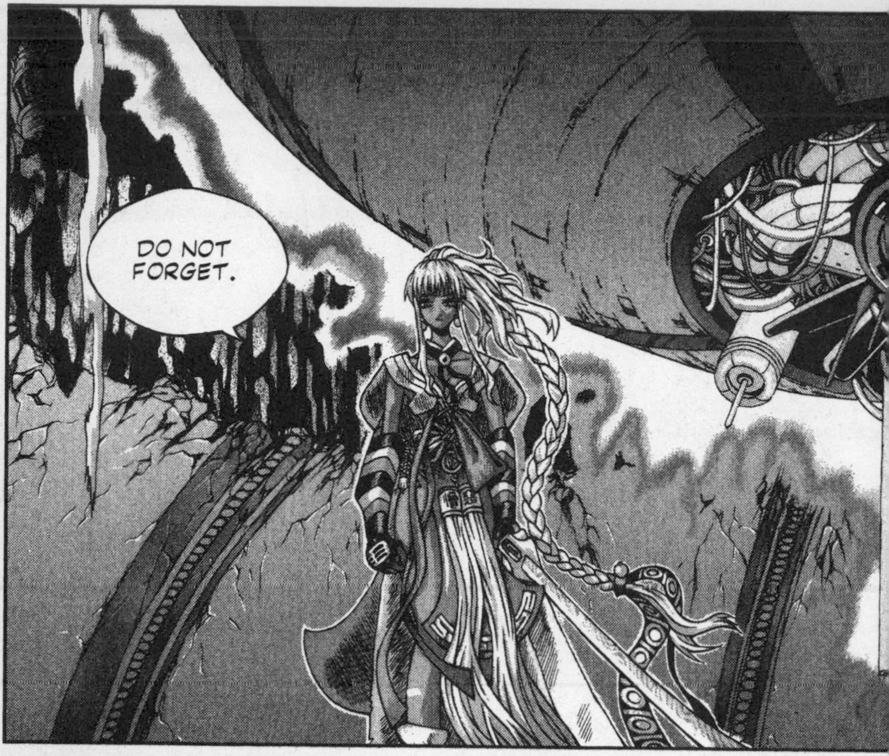
DO NOT FORGET.

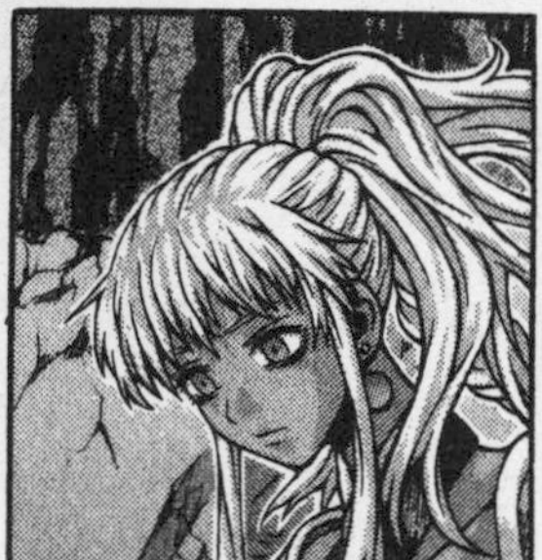
I WILL BE COMING FOR YOU, IRIS...

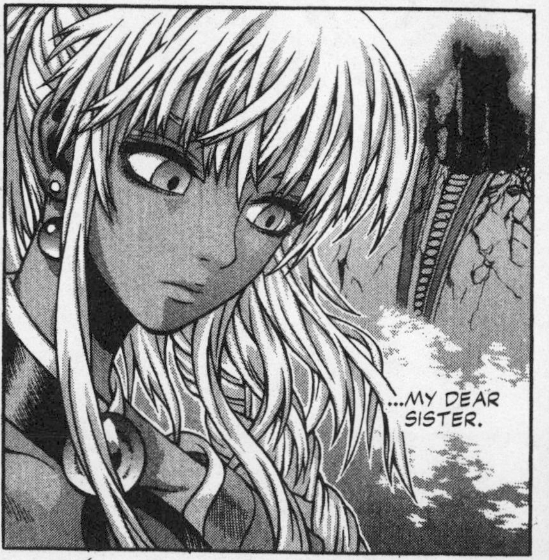
...MY DEAR SISTER.

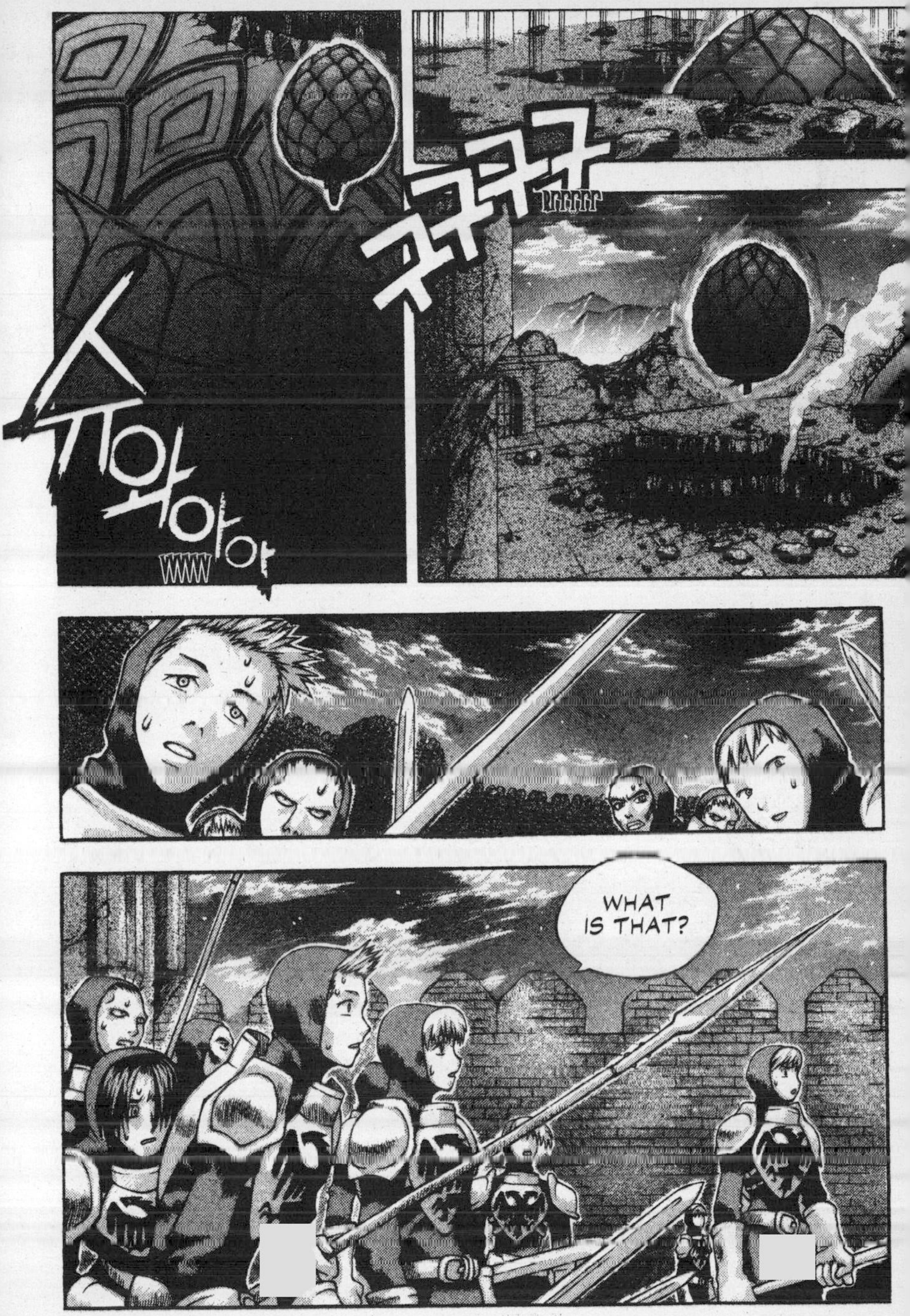
WHAT IS THAT?

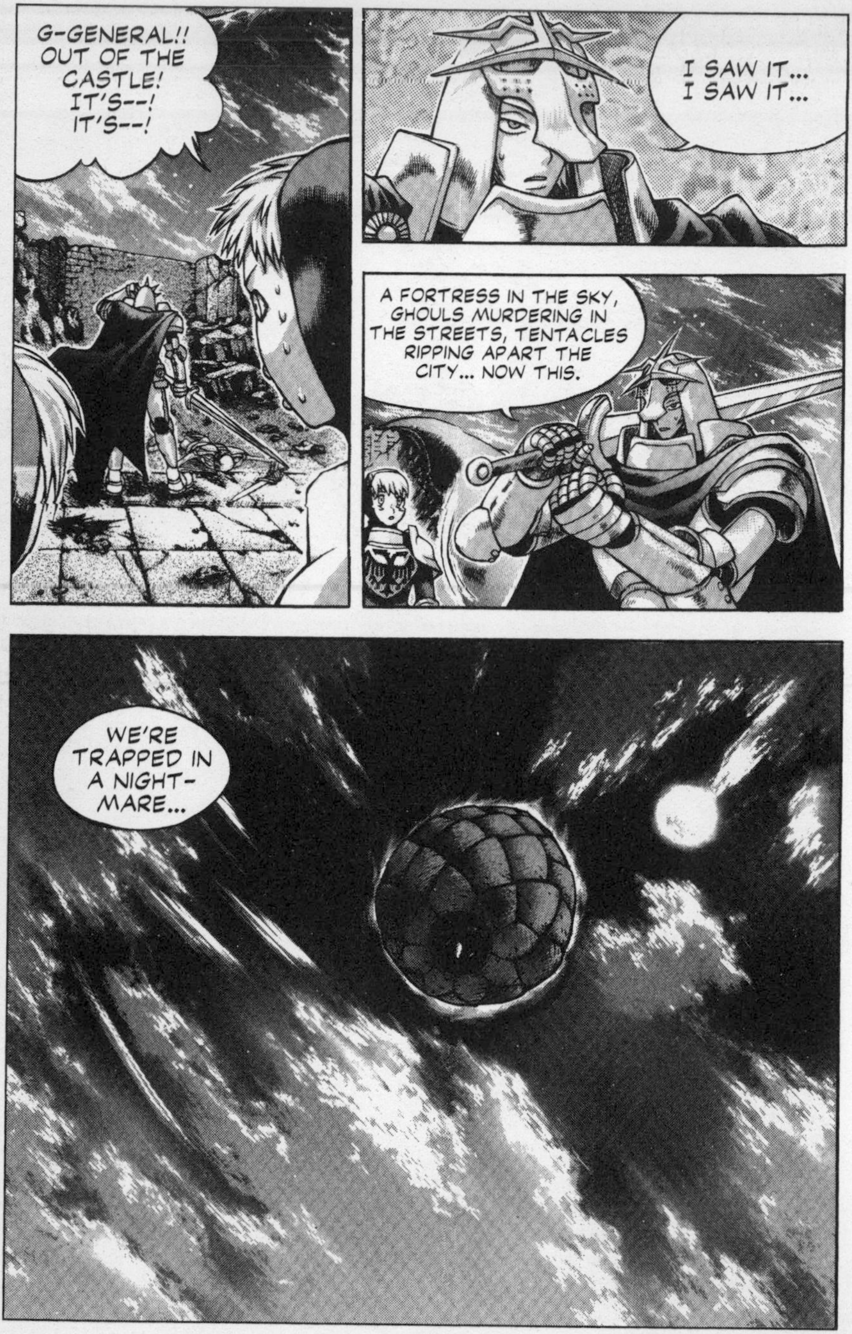
G-GENERAL!! OUT OF THE CASTLE! IT'S--! IT'S--!
I SAW IT... I SAW IT...
A FORTRESS IN THE SKY, GHOULS MURDERING IN THE STREETS, TENTACLES RIPPING APART THE CITY... NOW THIS.
WE'RE TRAPPED IN A NIGHT-MARE...

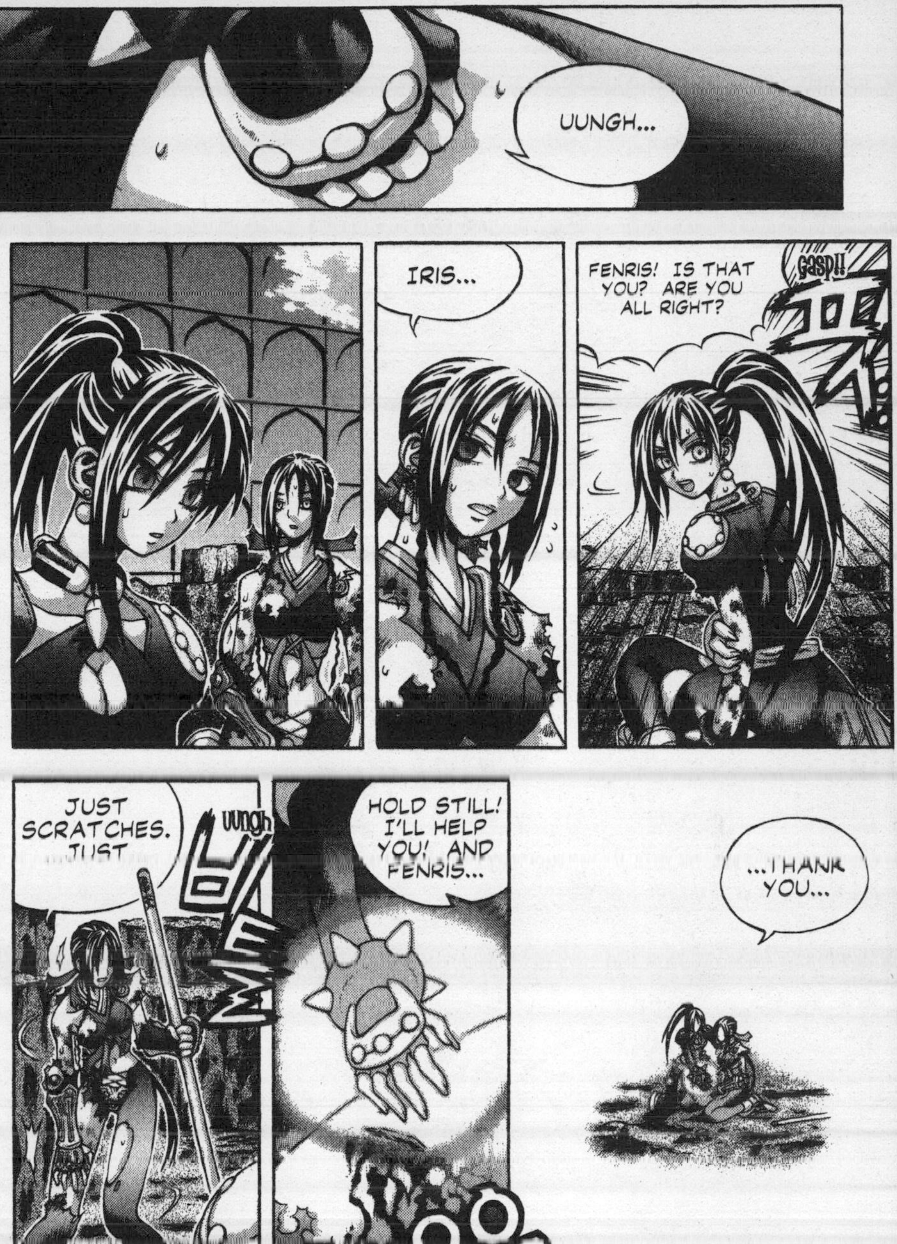
UUNGH...
IRIS...
FENRIS! IS THAT YOU? ARE YOU ALL RIGHT?
GASP!!
JUST SCRATCHES. JUST
UUNGH
HOLD STILL! I'LL HELP YOU! AND FENRIS...
ZZZZ
...THANK YOU...

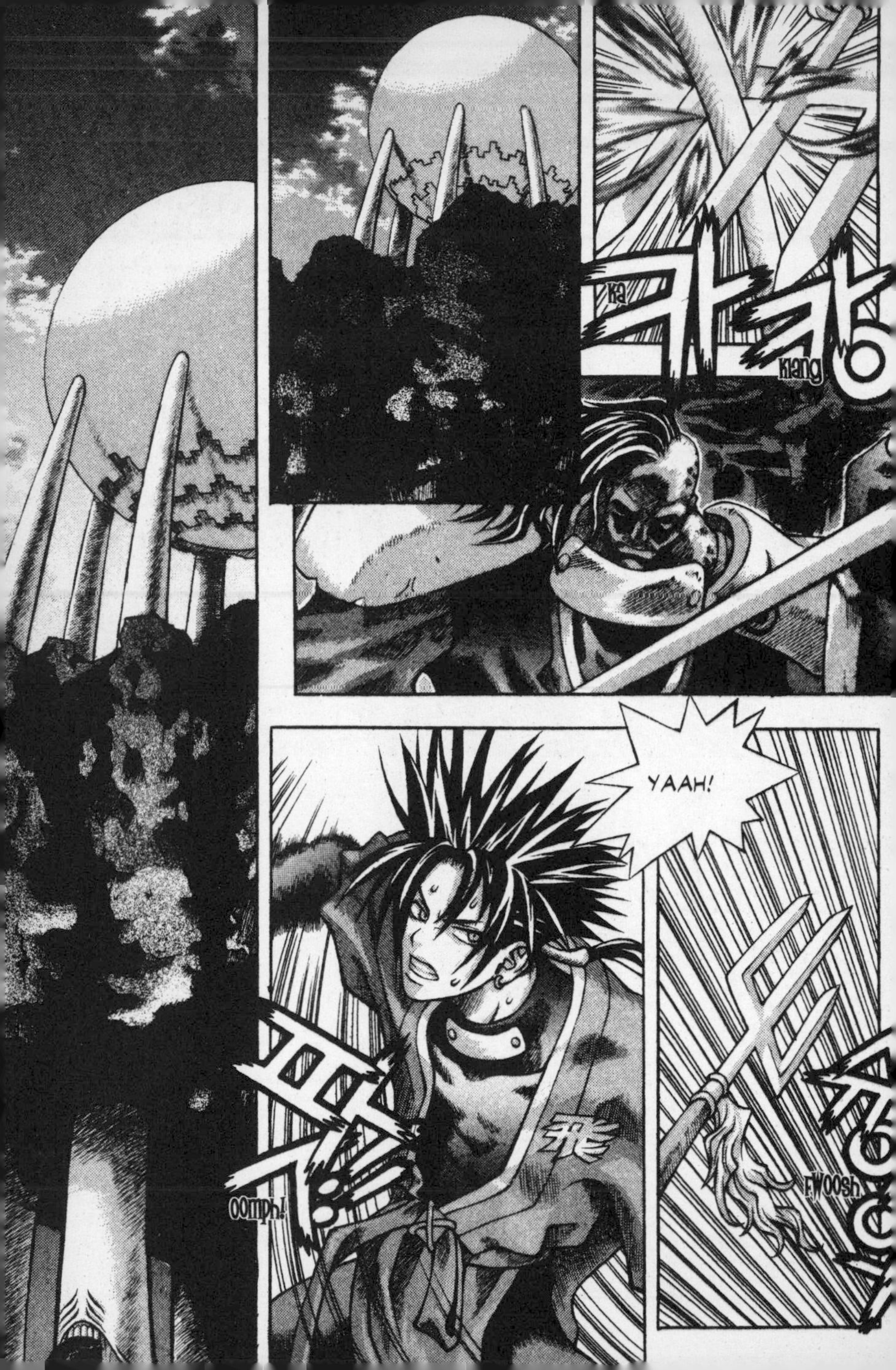
KA
Klang
YAAH!
Oomph!
FWOOSH

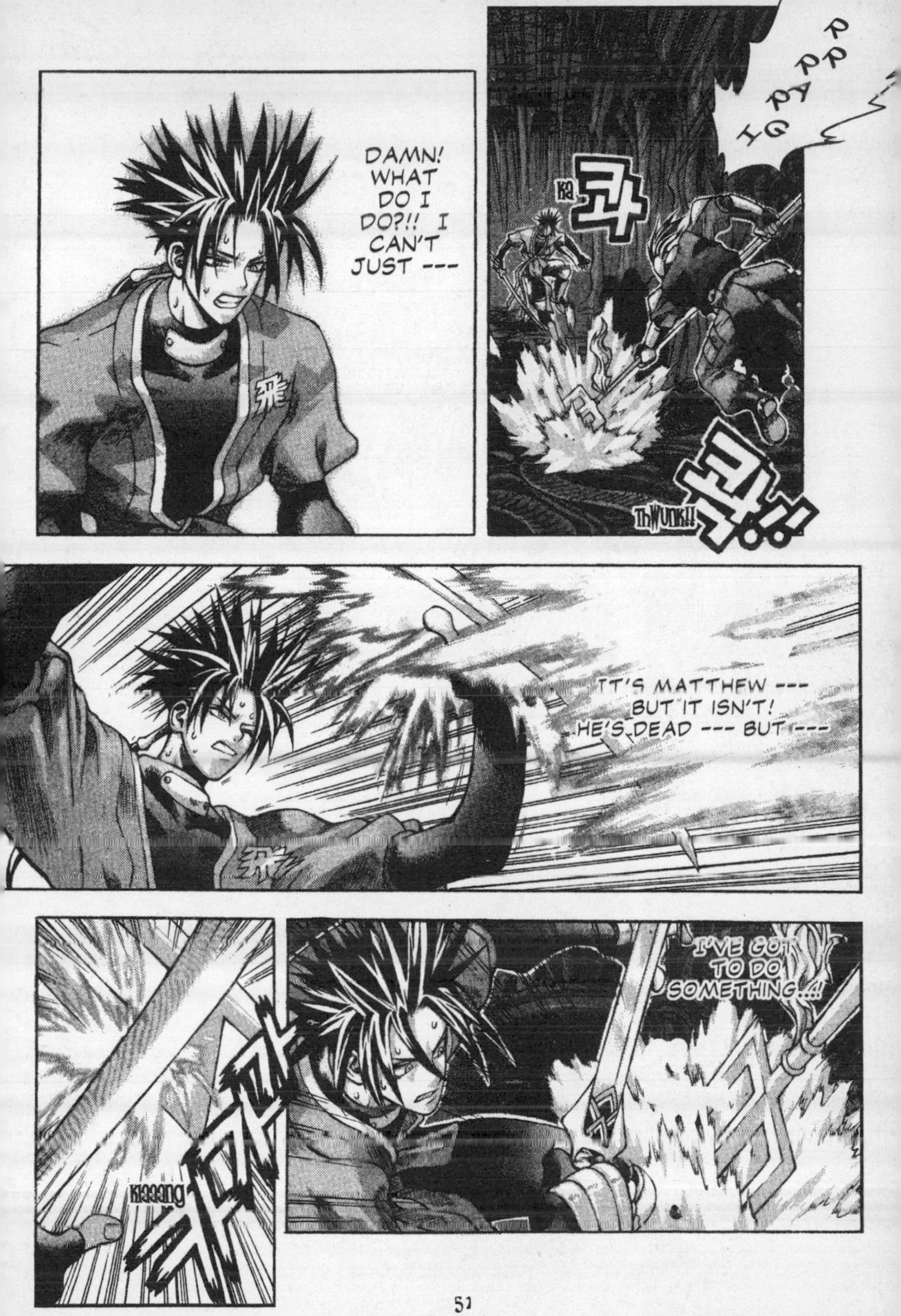
DAMN! WHAT DO I DO?!! I CAN'T JUST ---
KA
THWUNK!!
IT'S MATTHEW --- BUT IT ISN'T! HE'S DEAD --- BUT ---
Kiaaang
I'VE GOT TO DO SOMETHING...!!

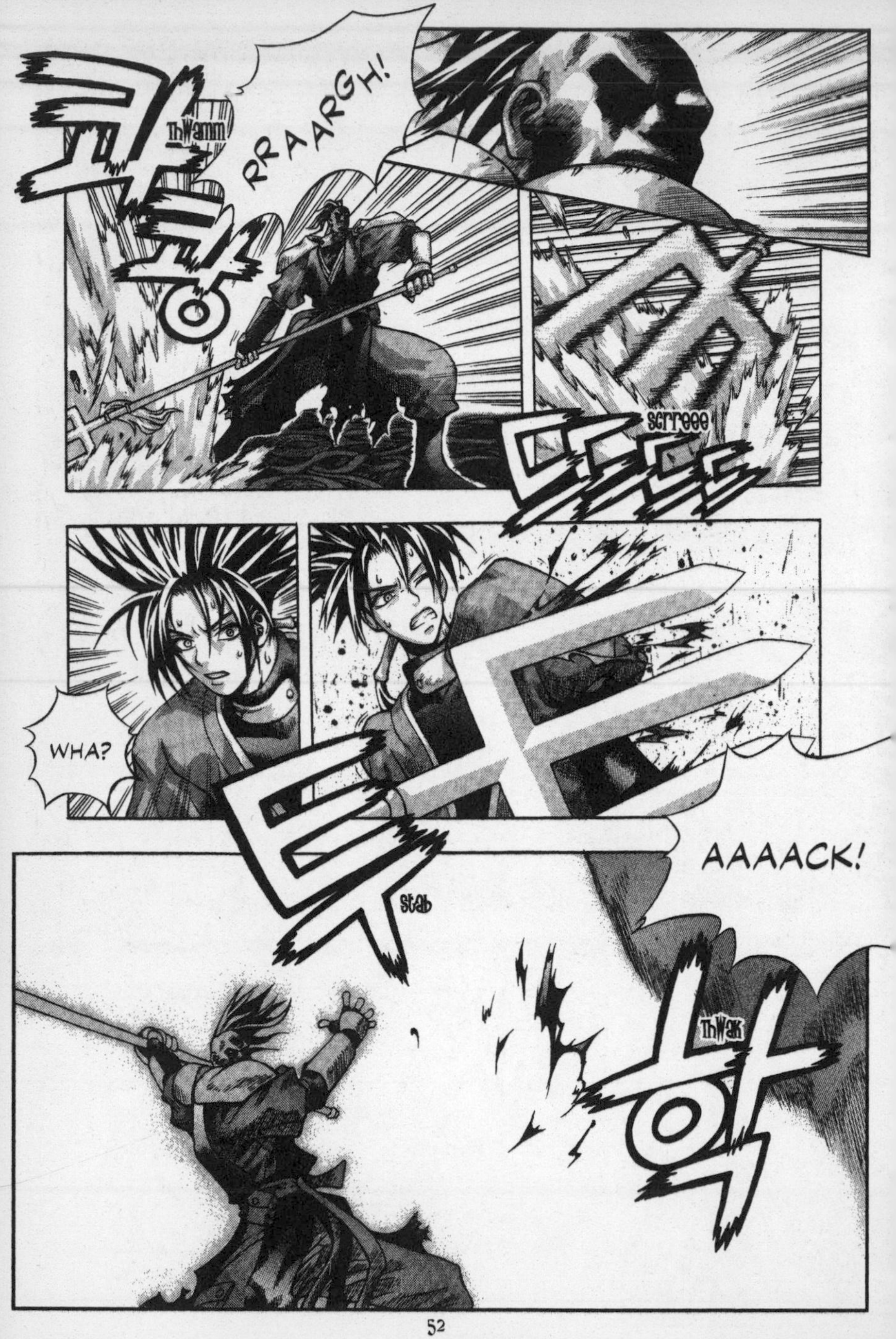
ThWamm
RRAARGH!
scrreee
WHA?
stab
AAAACK!
ThWAK

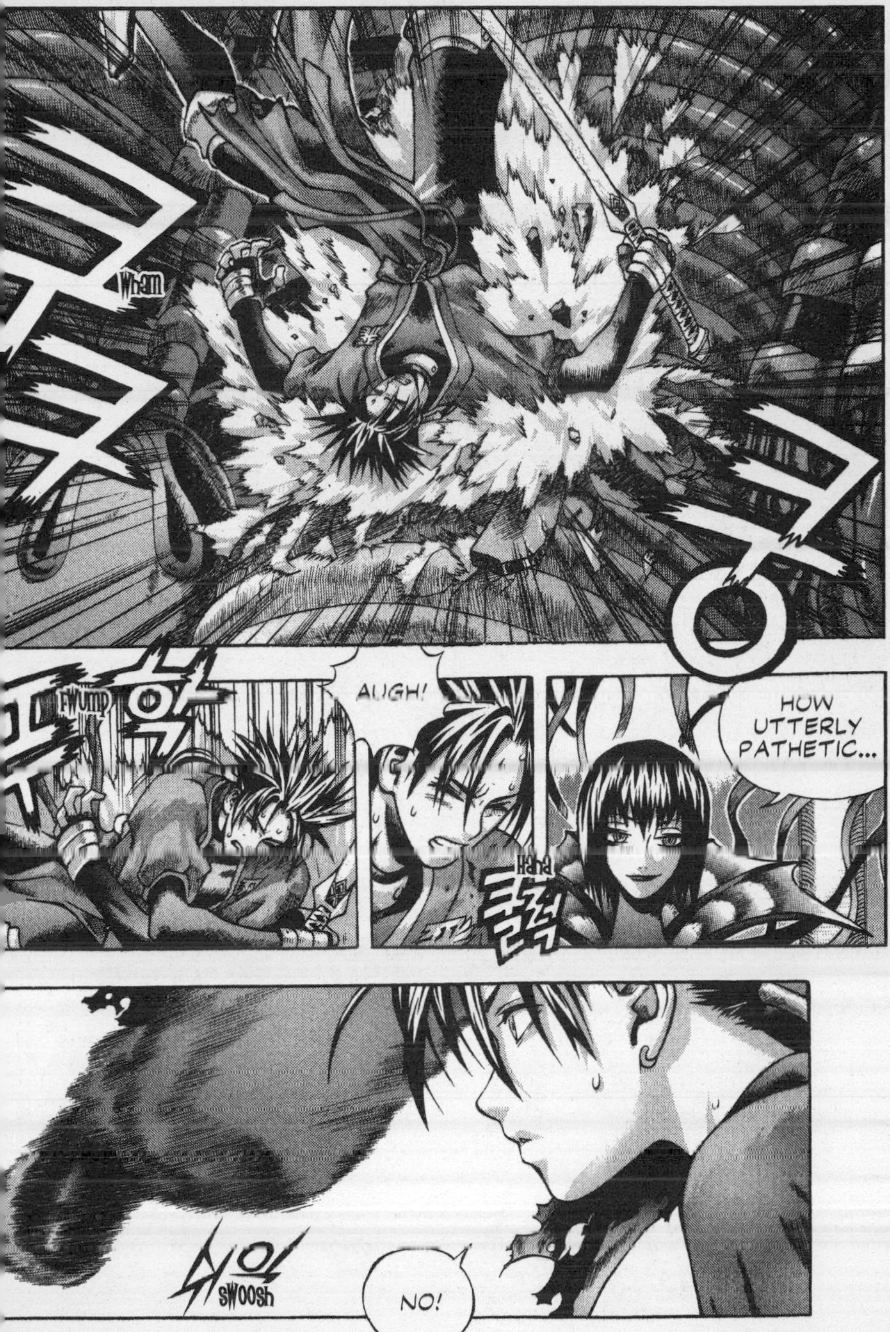

Wham
FWUMP
AUGH!
HOW UTTERLY PATHETIC...
Haha
SWOOSH
NO!

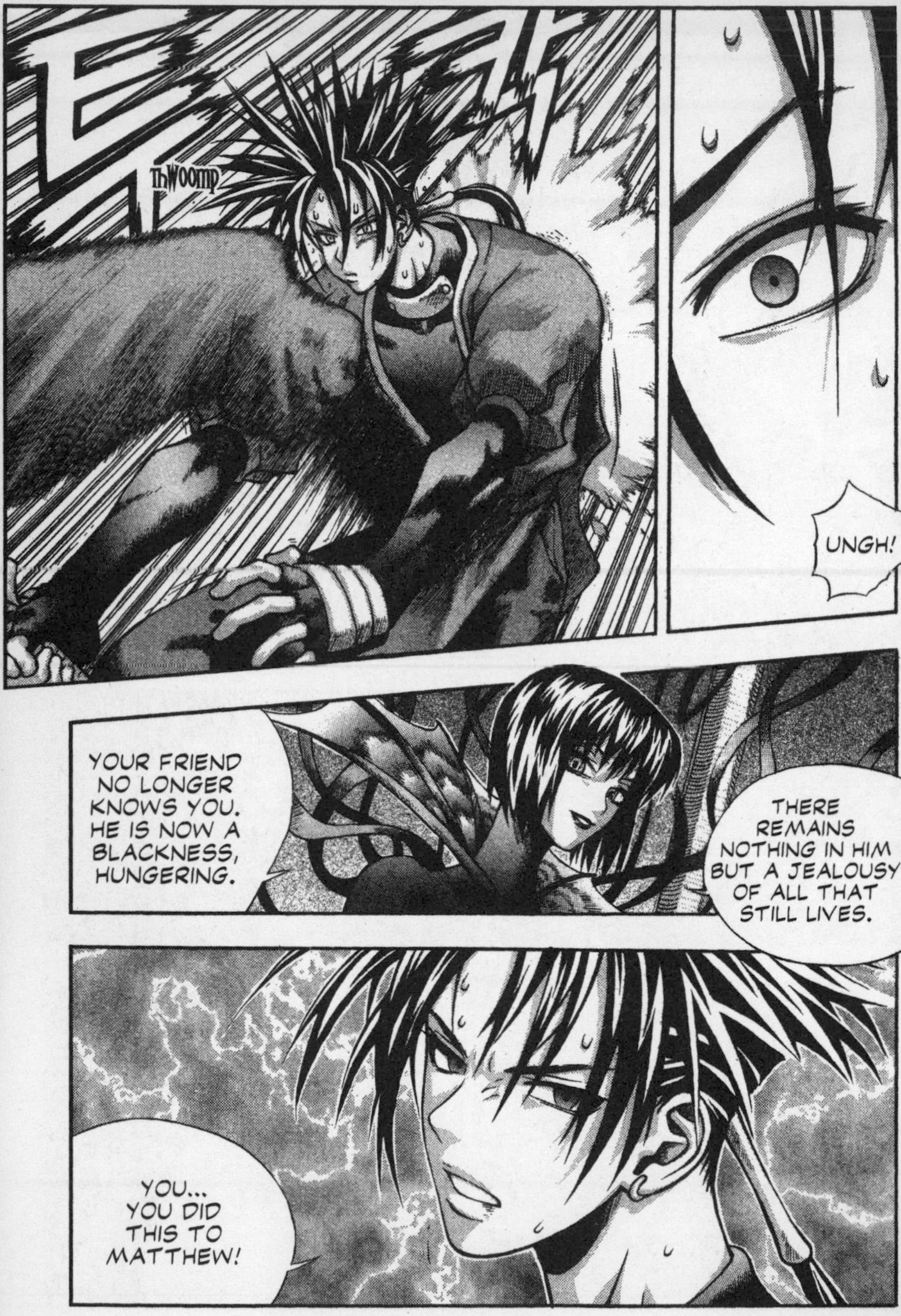
THWOOMP
UNGH!
YOUR FRIEND NO LONGER KNOWS YOU. HE IS NOW A BLACKNESS, HUNGERING.
THERE REMAINS NOTHING IN HIM BUT A JEALOUSY OF ALL THAT STILL LIVES.
YOU... YOU DID THIS TO MATTHEW!

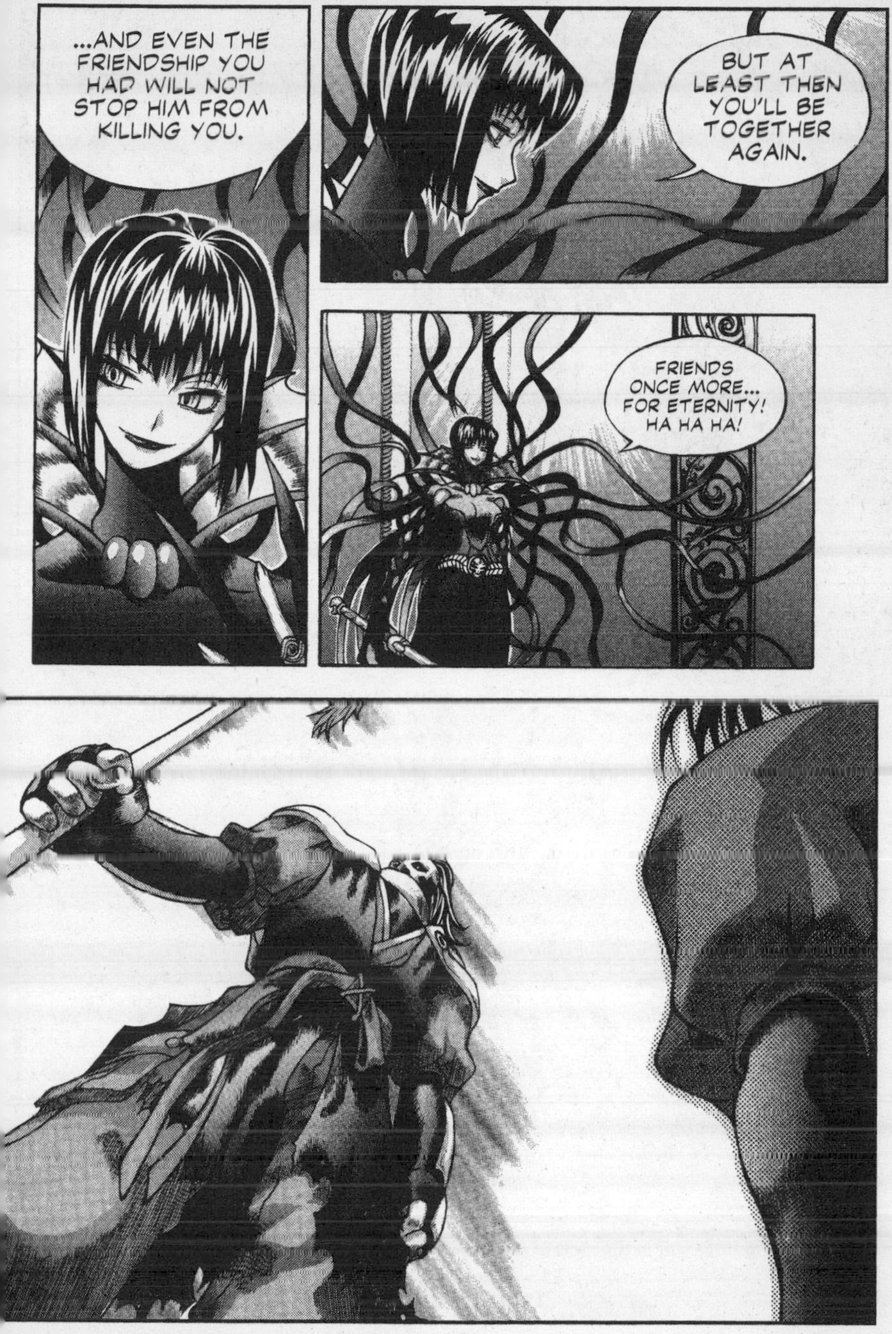
...AND EVEN THE FRIENDSHIP YOU HAD WILL NOT STOP HIM FROM KILLING YOU.
BUT AT LEAST THEN YOU'LL BE TOGETHER AGAIN.
FRIENDS ONCE MORE... FOR ETERNITY! HA HA HA!

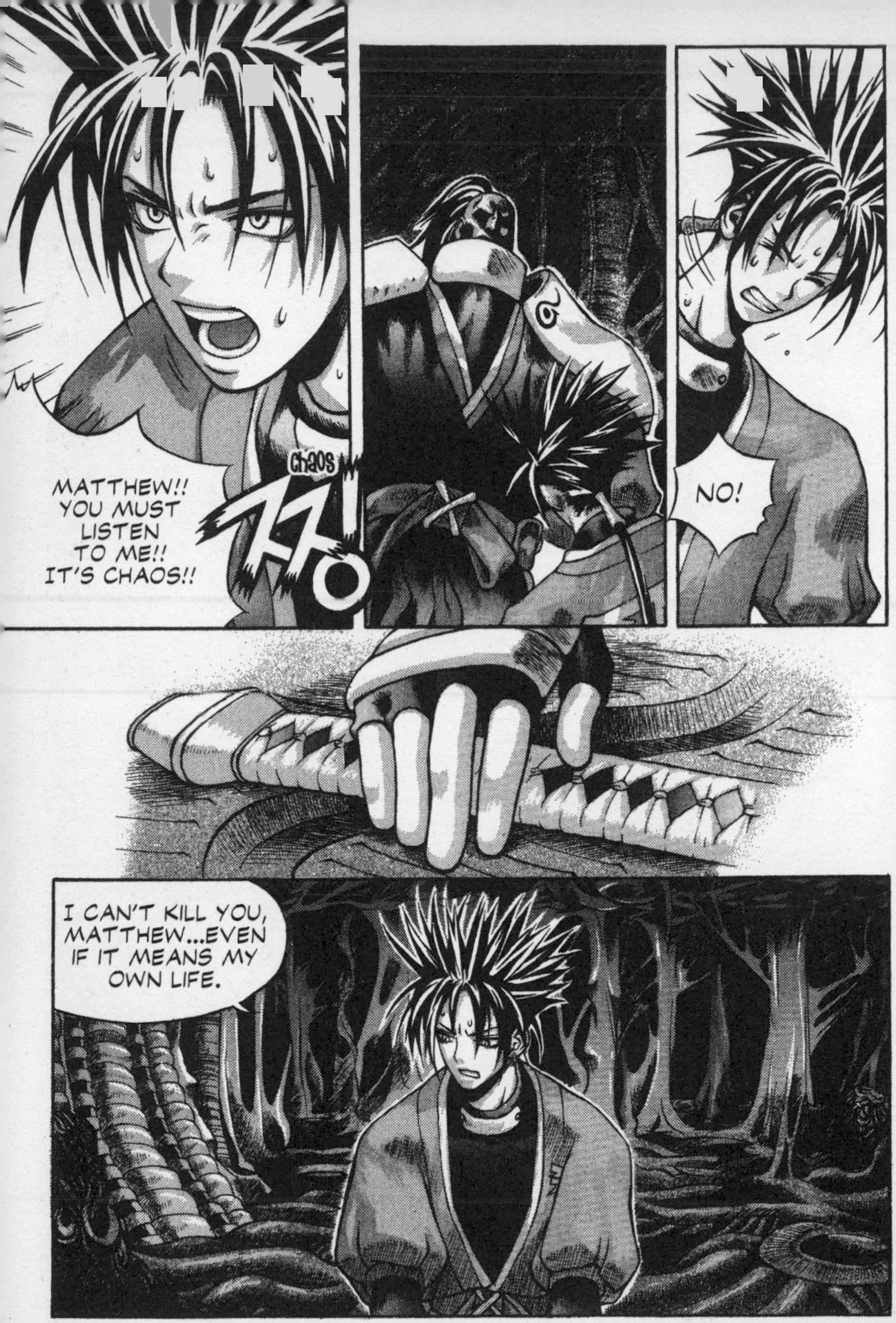
MATTHEW!! YOU MUST LISTEN TO ME!! IT'S CHAOS!!
Chaos
NO!
I CAN'T KILL YOU, MATTHEW...EVEN IF IT MEANS MY OWN LIFE.

RAGNAROK
라그나로크
IN TO THE ABYSS

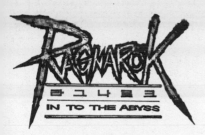

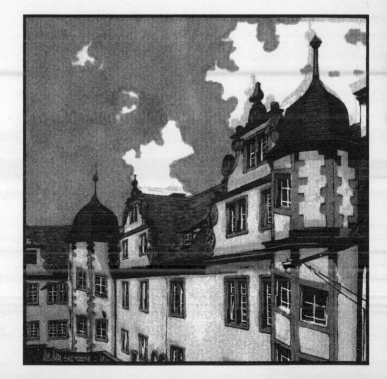

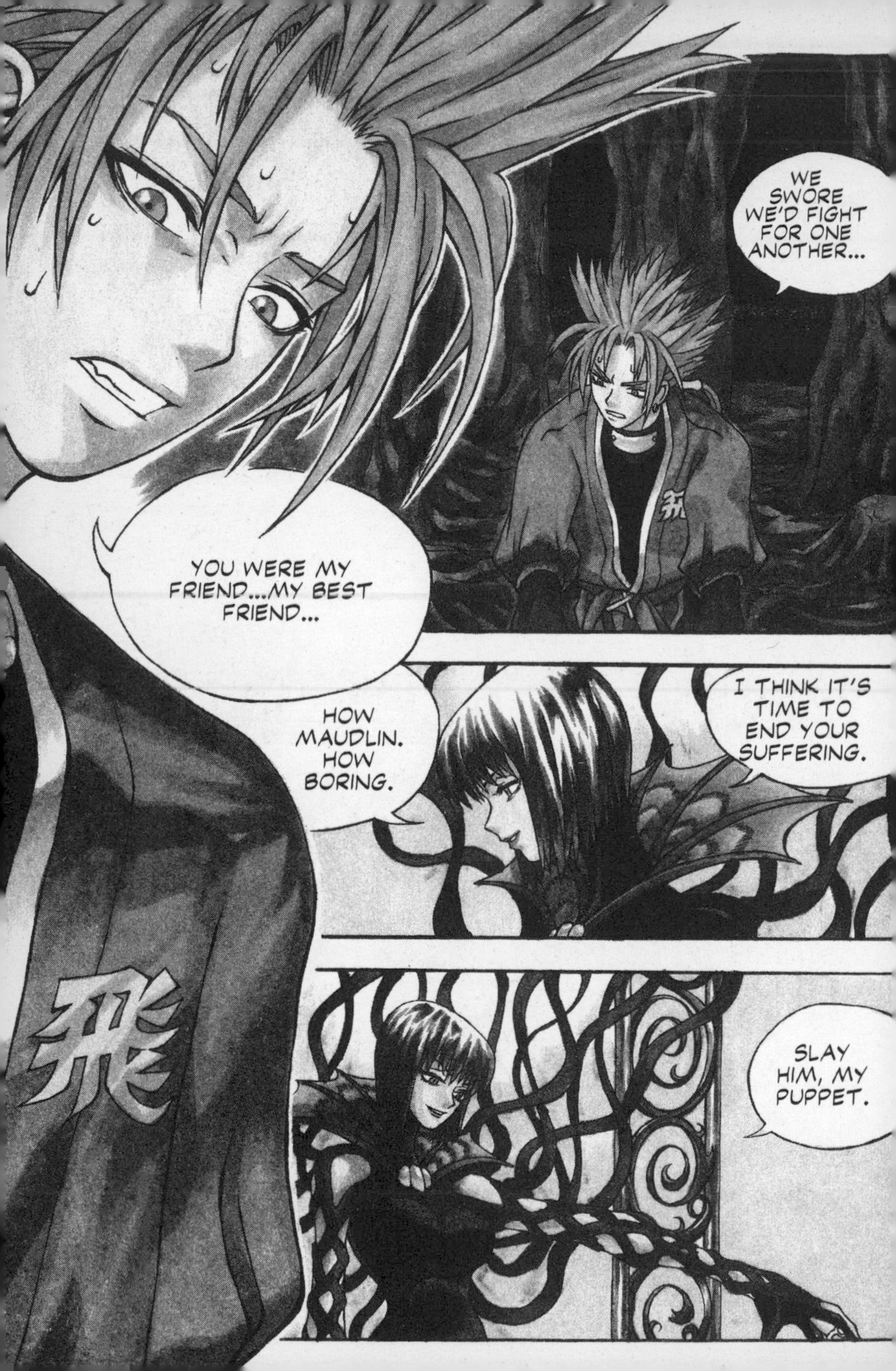
YOU WERE MY FRIEND...MY BEST FRIEND...
WE SWORE WE'D FIGHT FOR ONE ANOTHER...
HOW MAUDLIN. HOW BORING.
I THINK IT'S TIME TO END YOUR SUFFERING.
SLAY HIM, MY PUPPET.

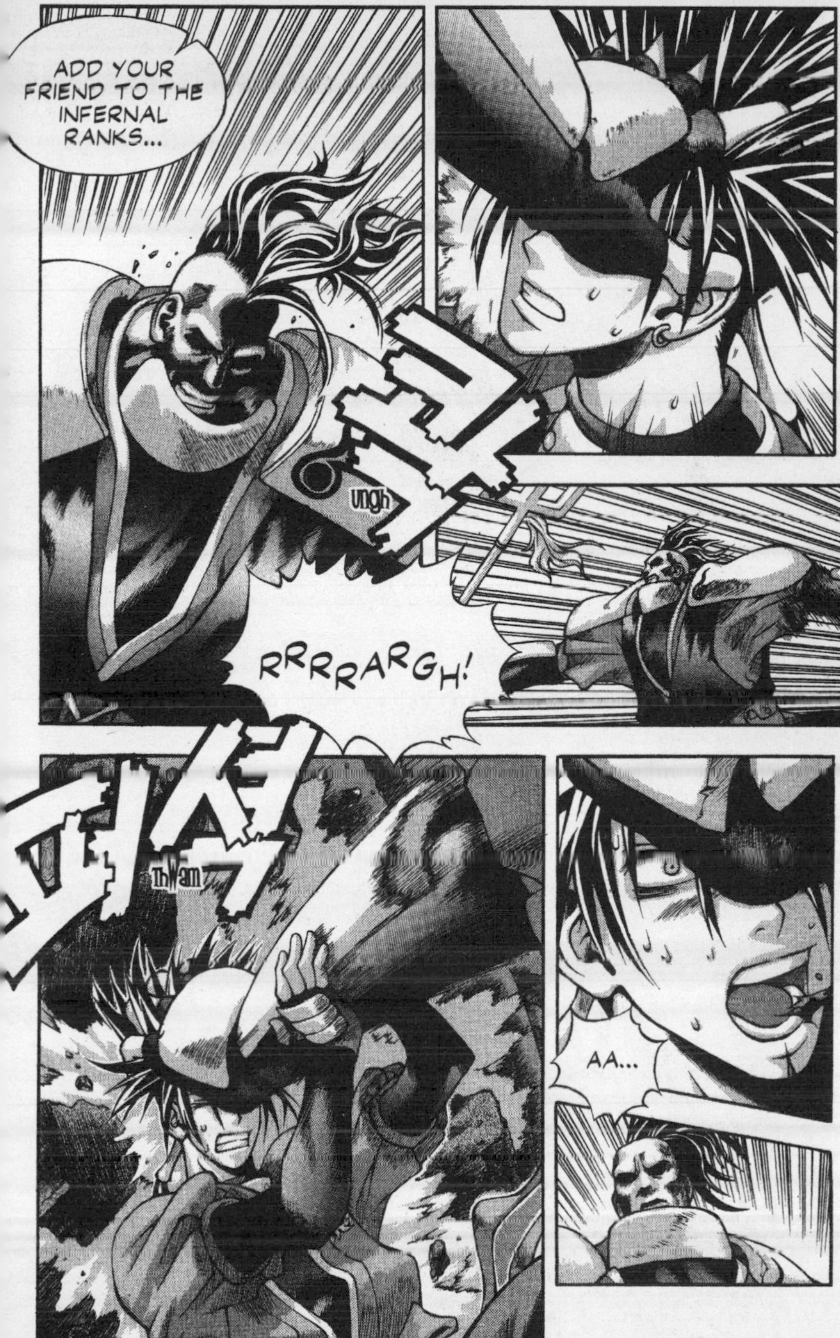
ADD YOUR FRIEND TO THE INFERNAL RANKS...
UNGH
RRRRRARGH!
THWAM
AA...

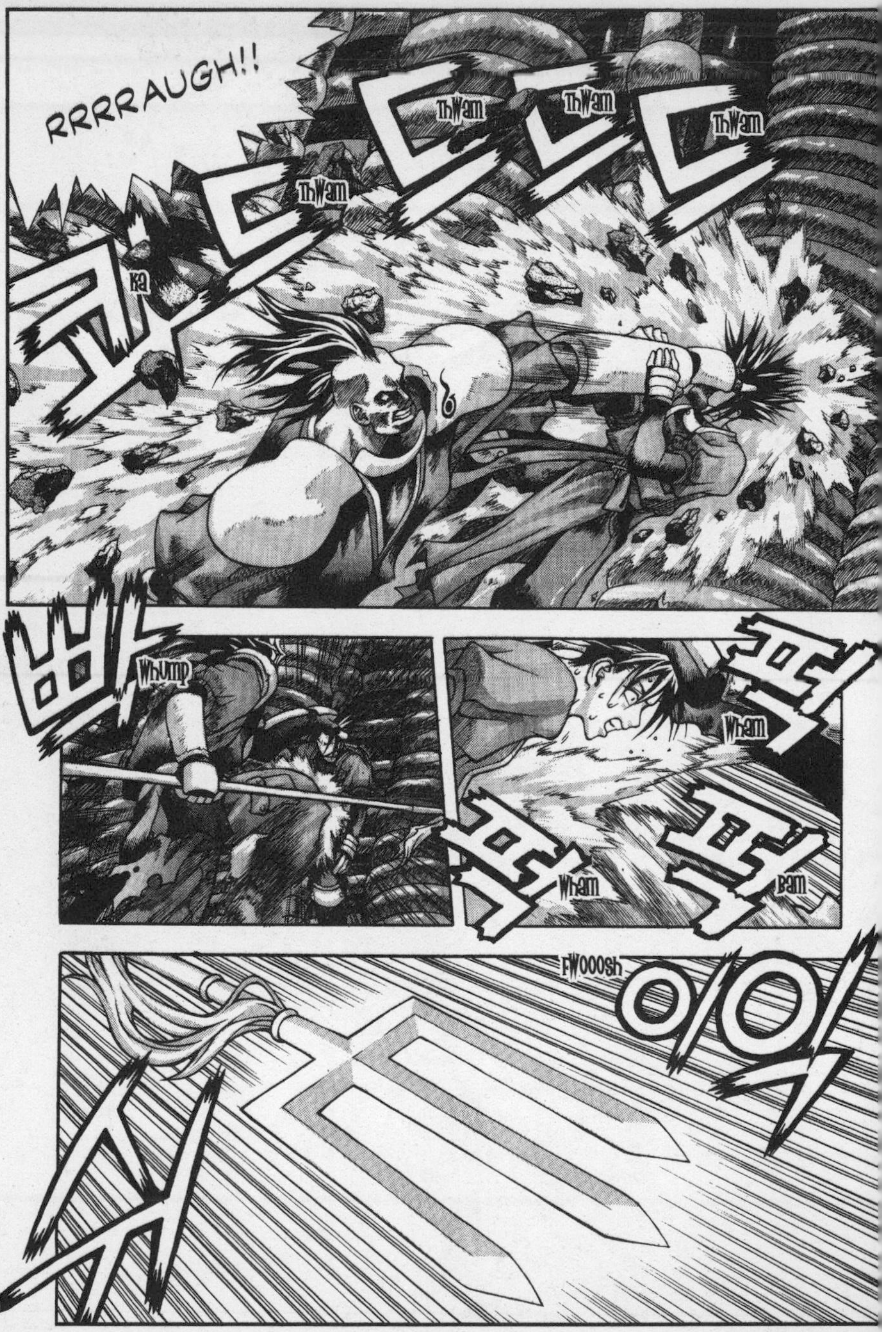
RRRRAUGH!!
Ka
ThWam
ThWam
ThWam
ThWam
Whump
Wham
Wham
Bam
FWOOOsh

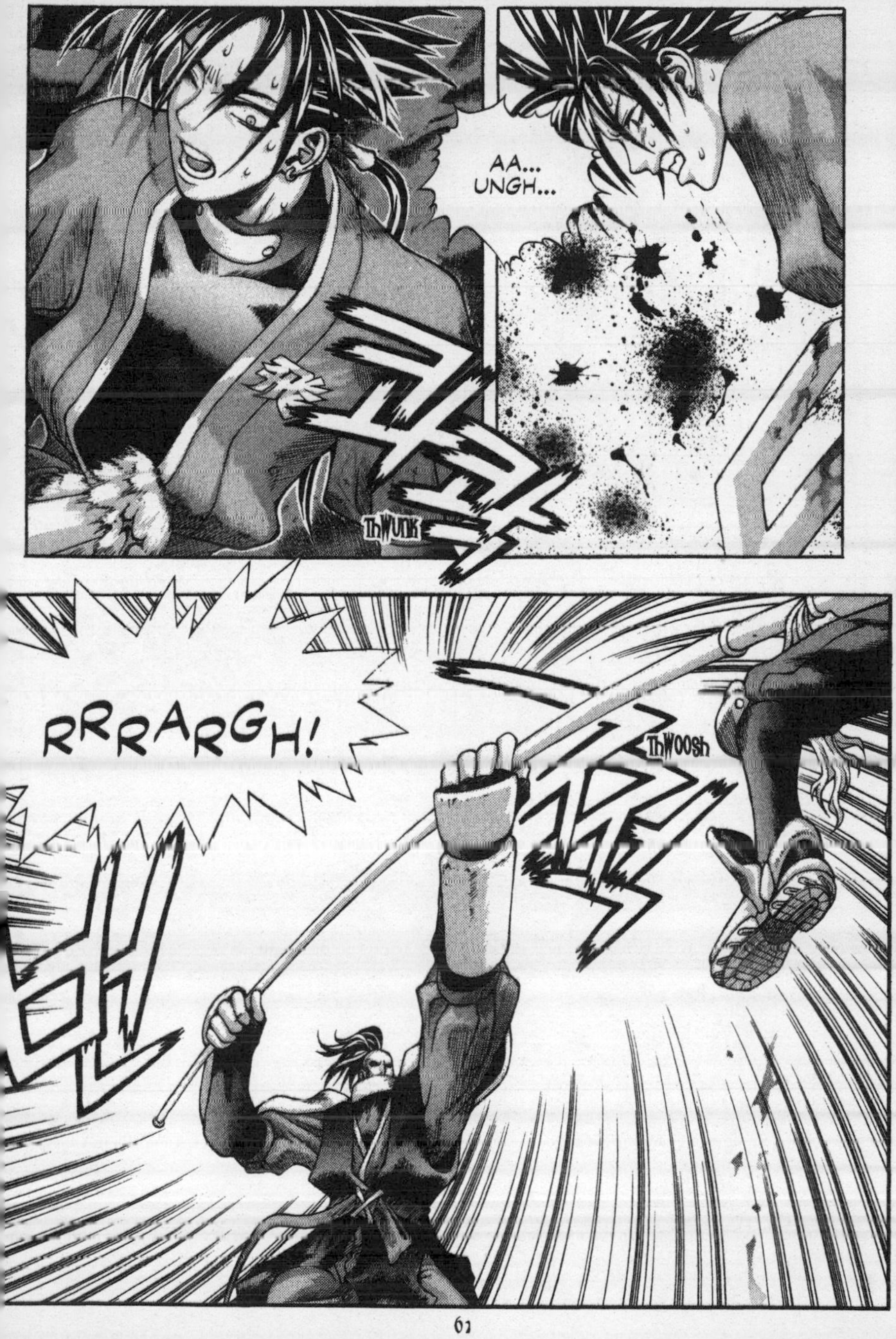
ThWUNK
AA...
UNGH...
RRRARGH!
ThWOOSH

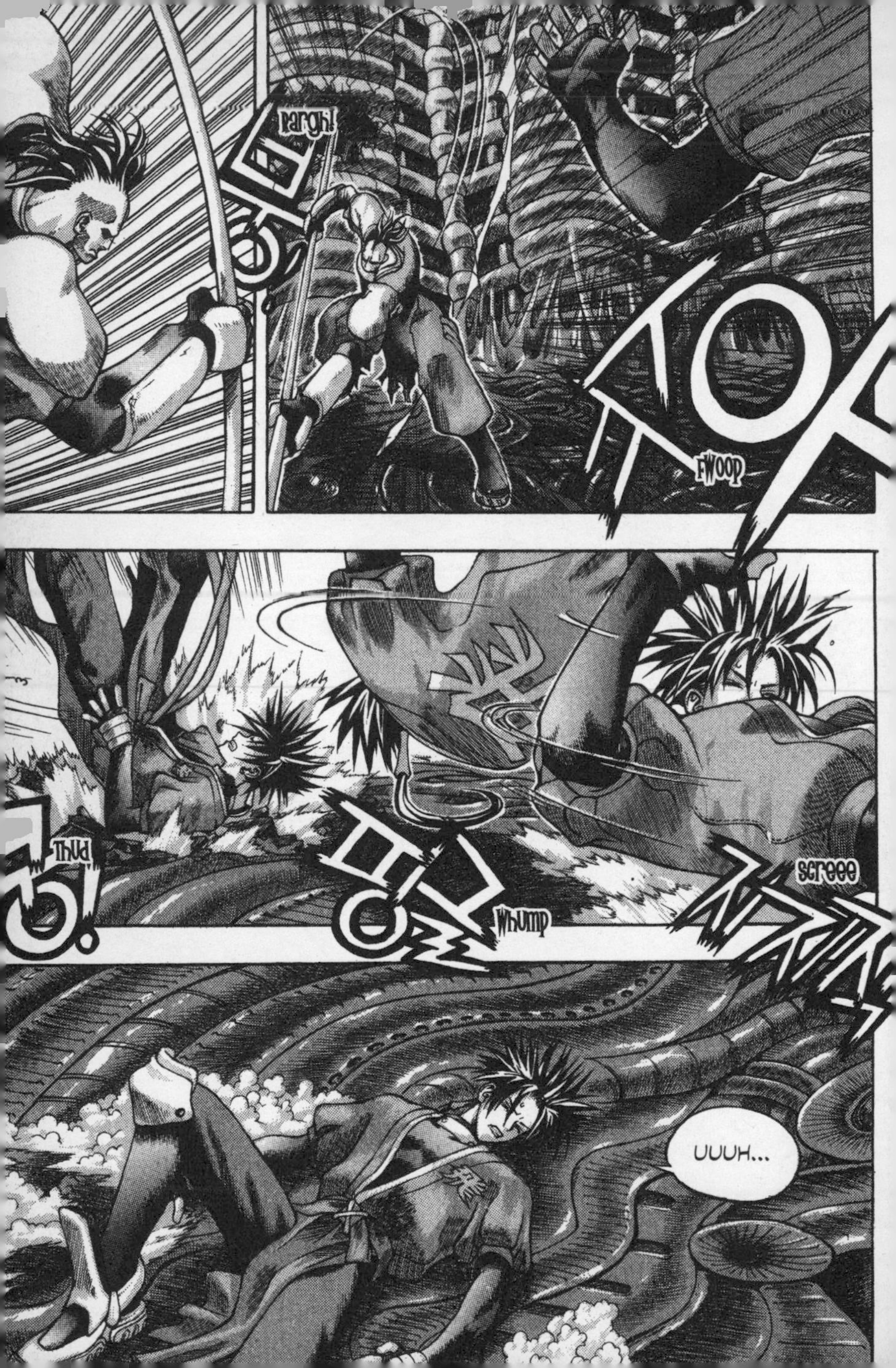

RARGH!
FWOOP
THUD
WHUMP
SCREEE
UUUH...

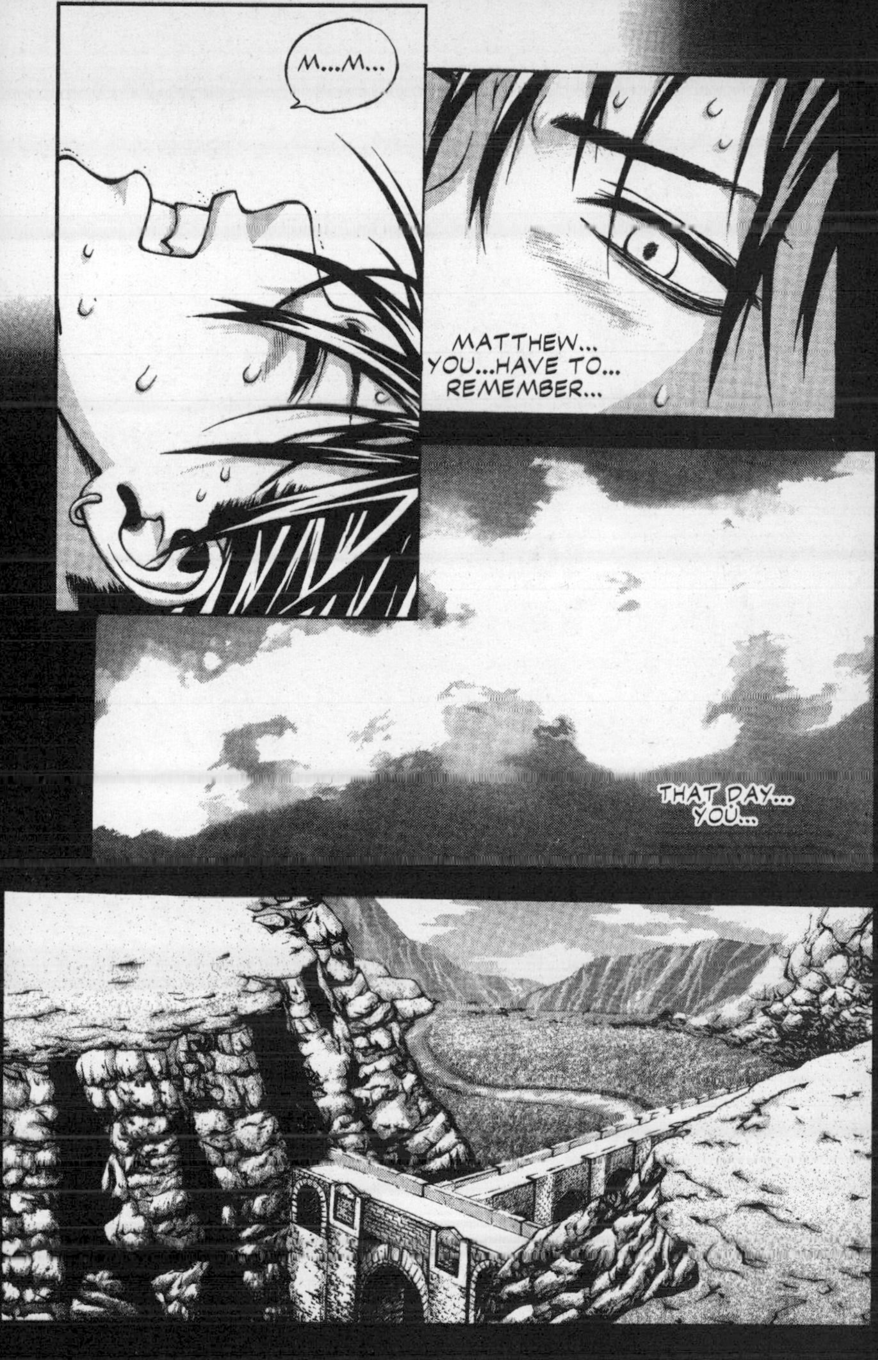
M...M...
MATTHEW... YOU...HAVE TO... REMEMBER...
THAT DAY... YOU...

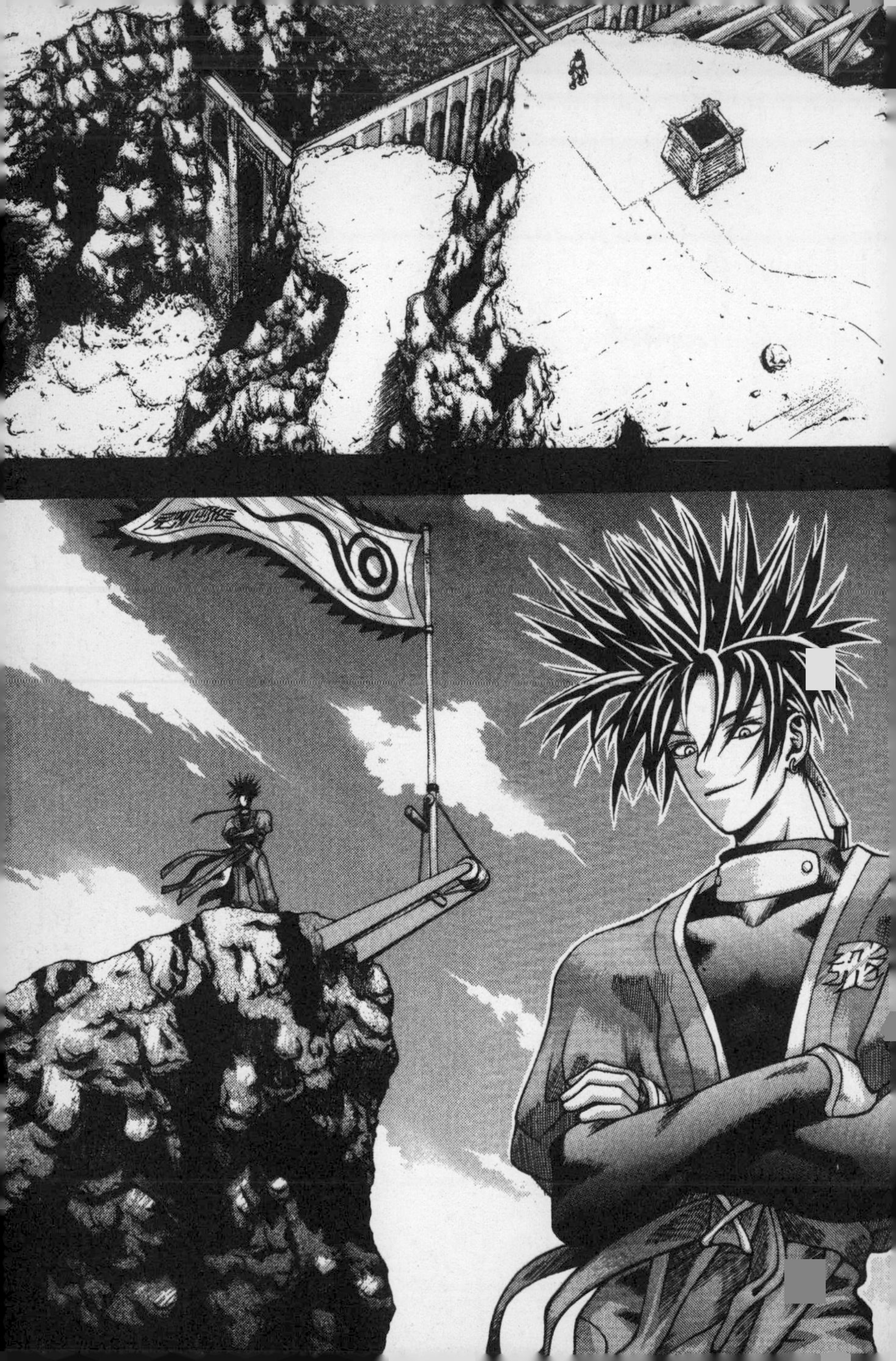

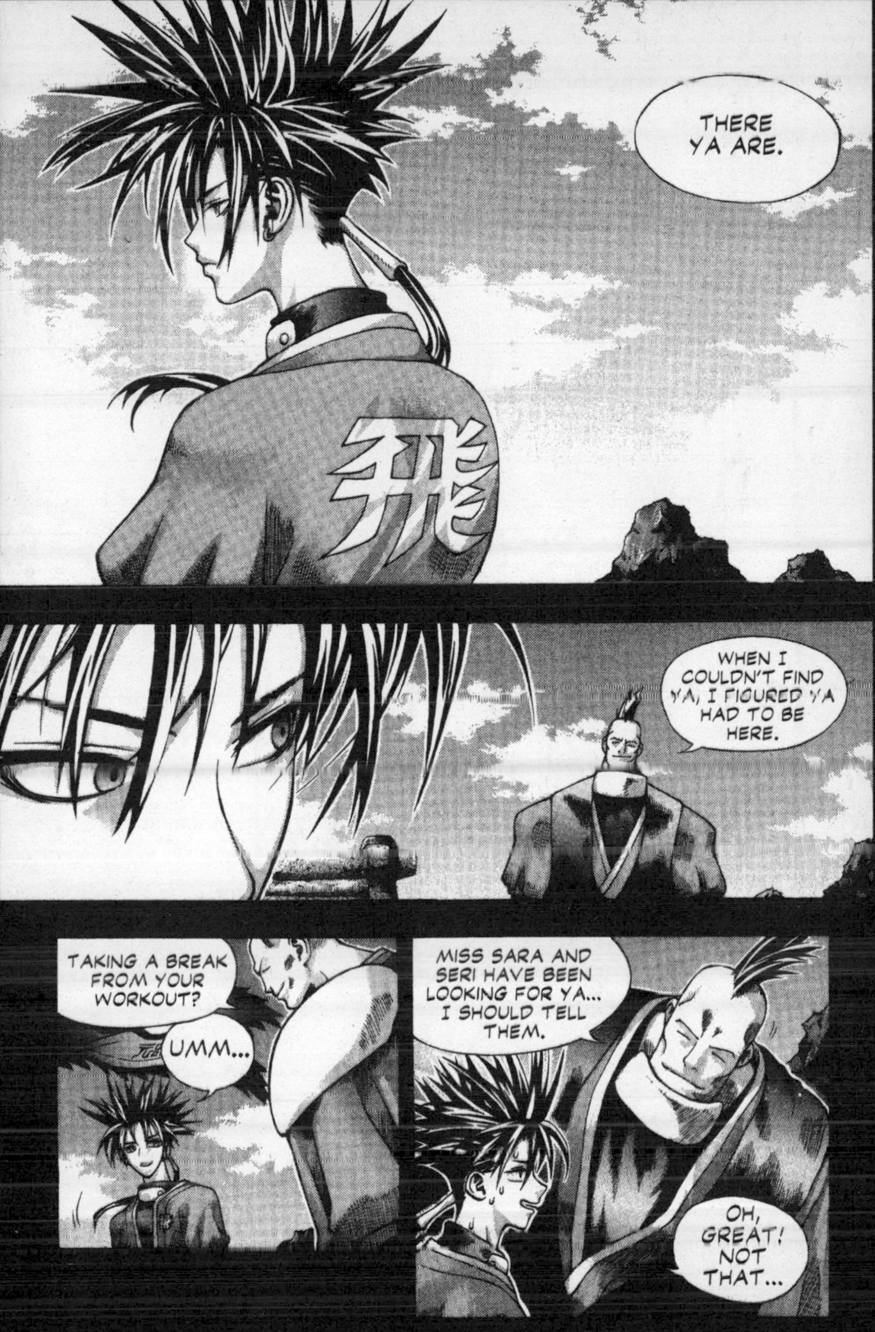
THERE YA ARE.
WHEN I COULDN'T FIND YA, I FIGURED YA HAD TO BE HERE.
TAKING A BREAK FROM YOUR WORKOUT?
UMM...
MISS SARA AND SERI HAVE BEEN LOOKING FOR YA... I SHOULD TELL THEM.
OH, GREAT! NOT THAT...

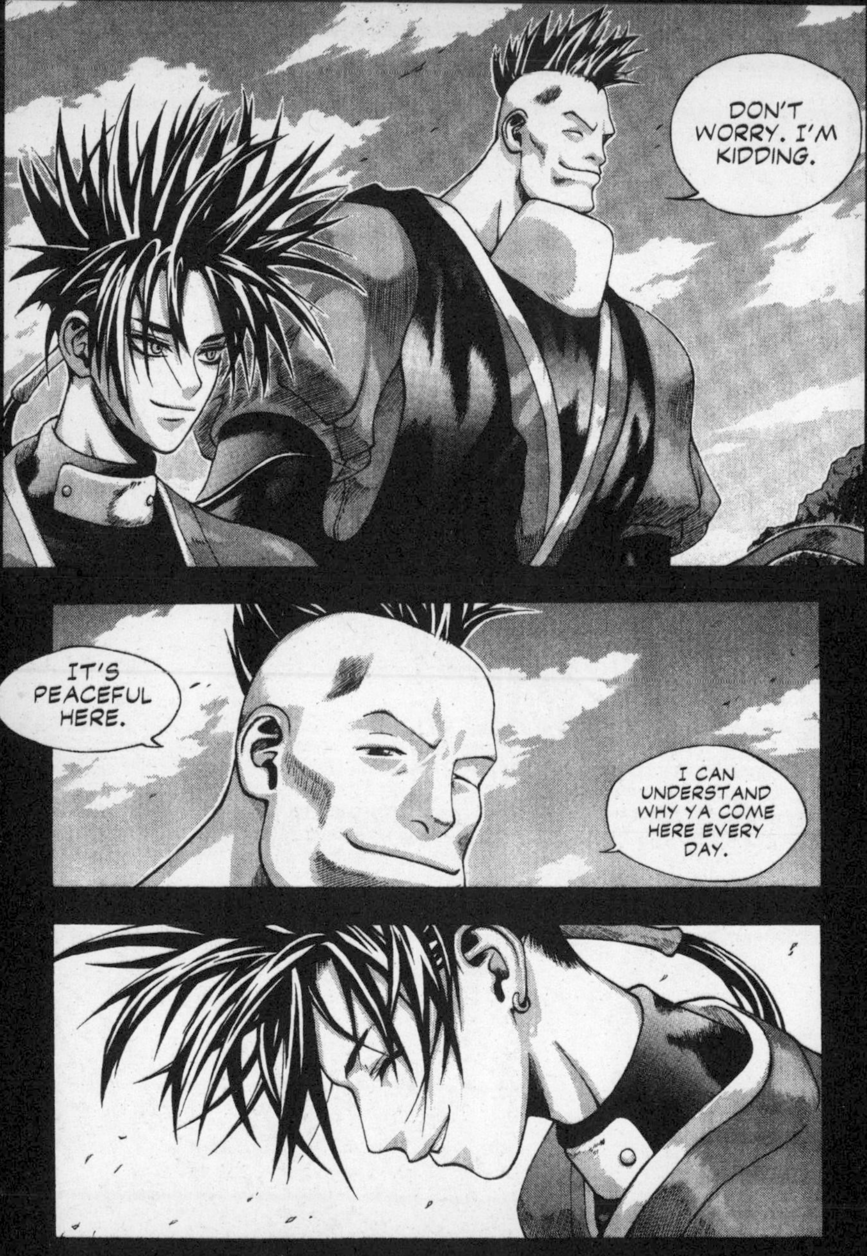
DON'T WORRY. I'M KIDDING.
IT'S PEACEFUL HERE.
I CAN UNDERSTAND WHY YA COME HERE EVERY DAY.

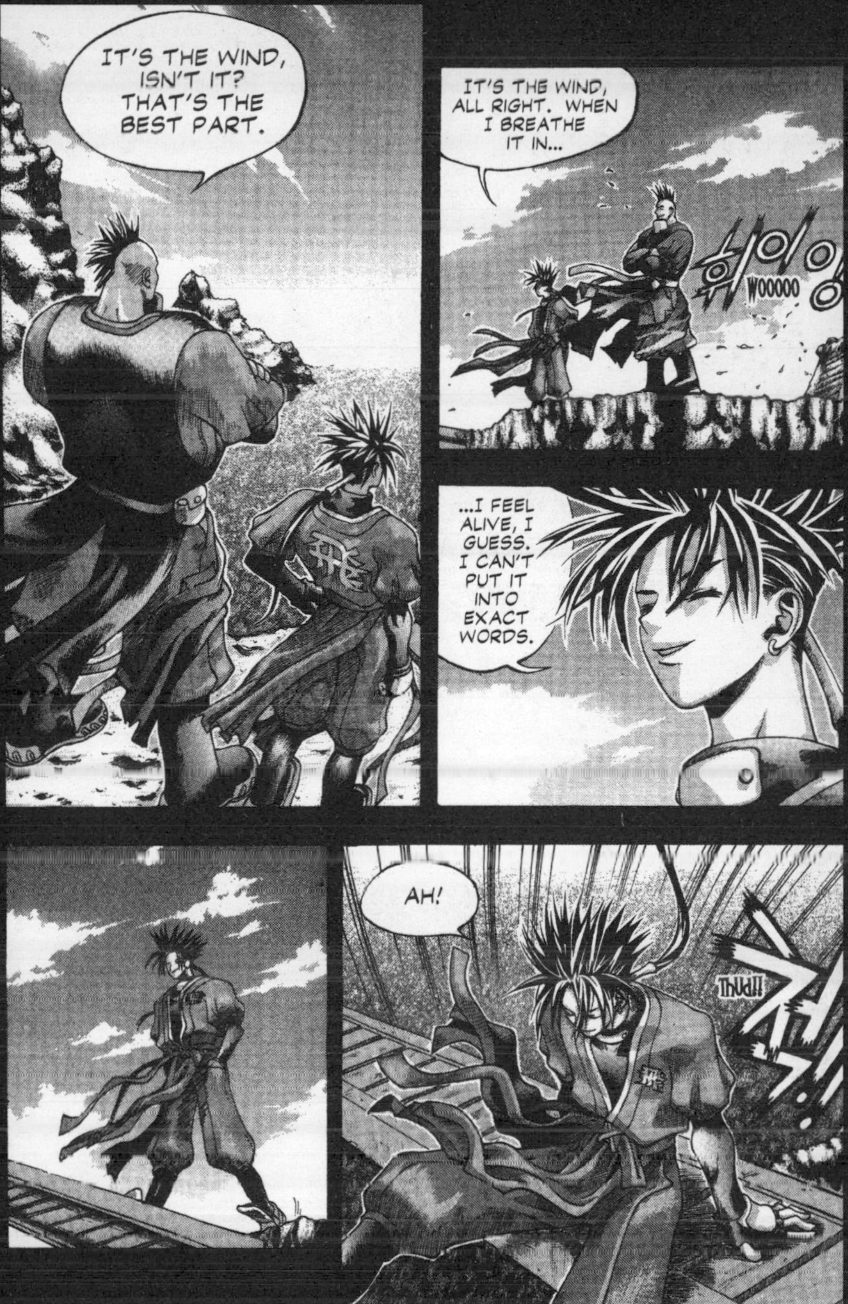
IT'S THE WIND, ISN'T IT? THAT'S THE BEST PART.
IT'S THE WIND, ALL RIGHT. WHEN I BREATHE IT IN...
WOOOOO
...I FEEL ALIVE, I GUESS. I CAN'T PUT IT INTO EXACT WORDS.
AH!
THUD!!

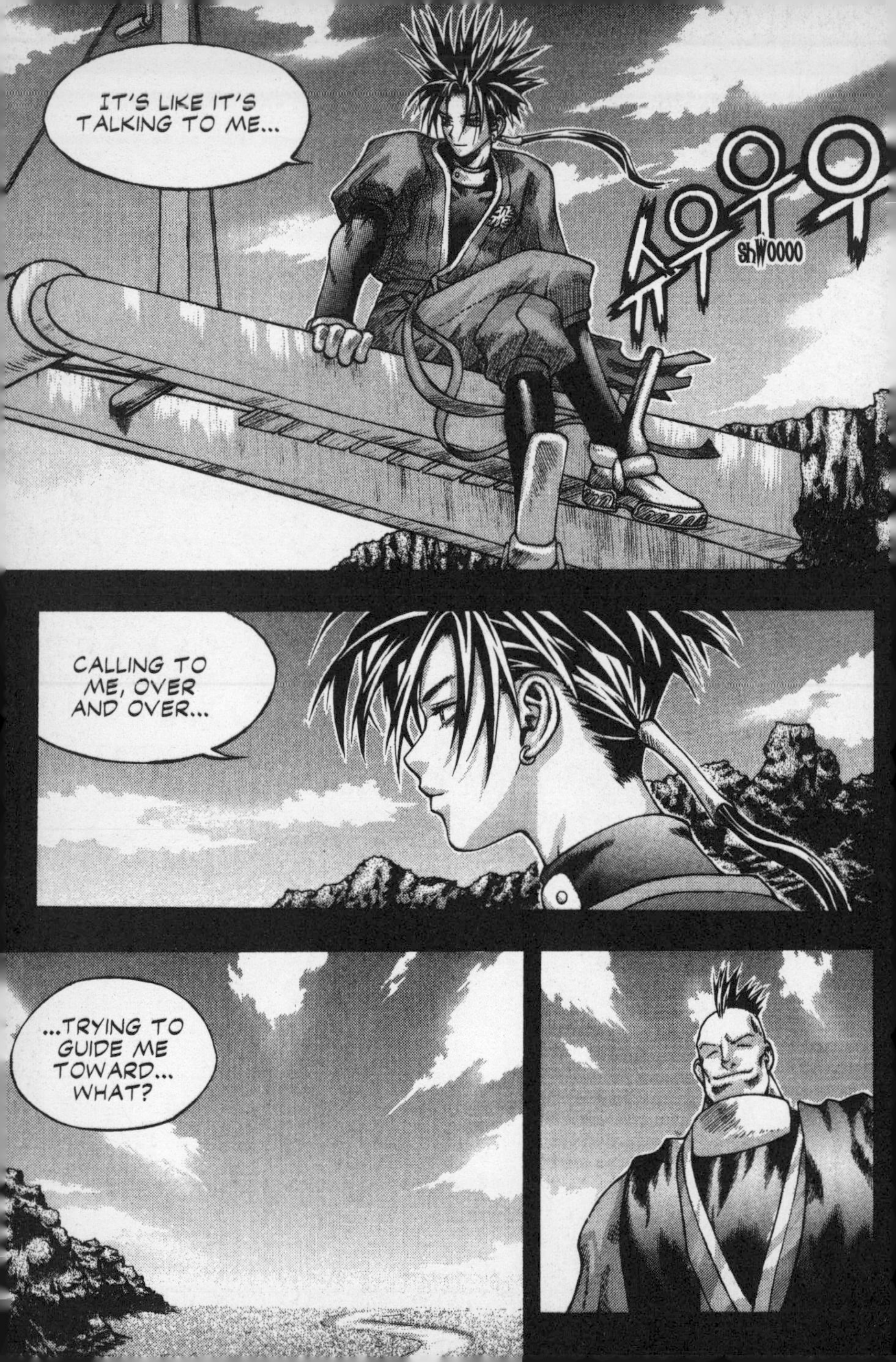
IT'S LIKE IT'S TALKING TO ME...
슈우우우
ShWOOOO
CALLING TO ME, OVER AND OVER...
...TRYING TO GUIDE ME TOWARD... WHAT?

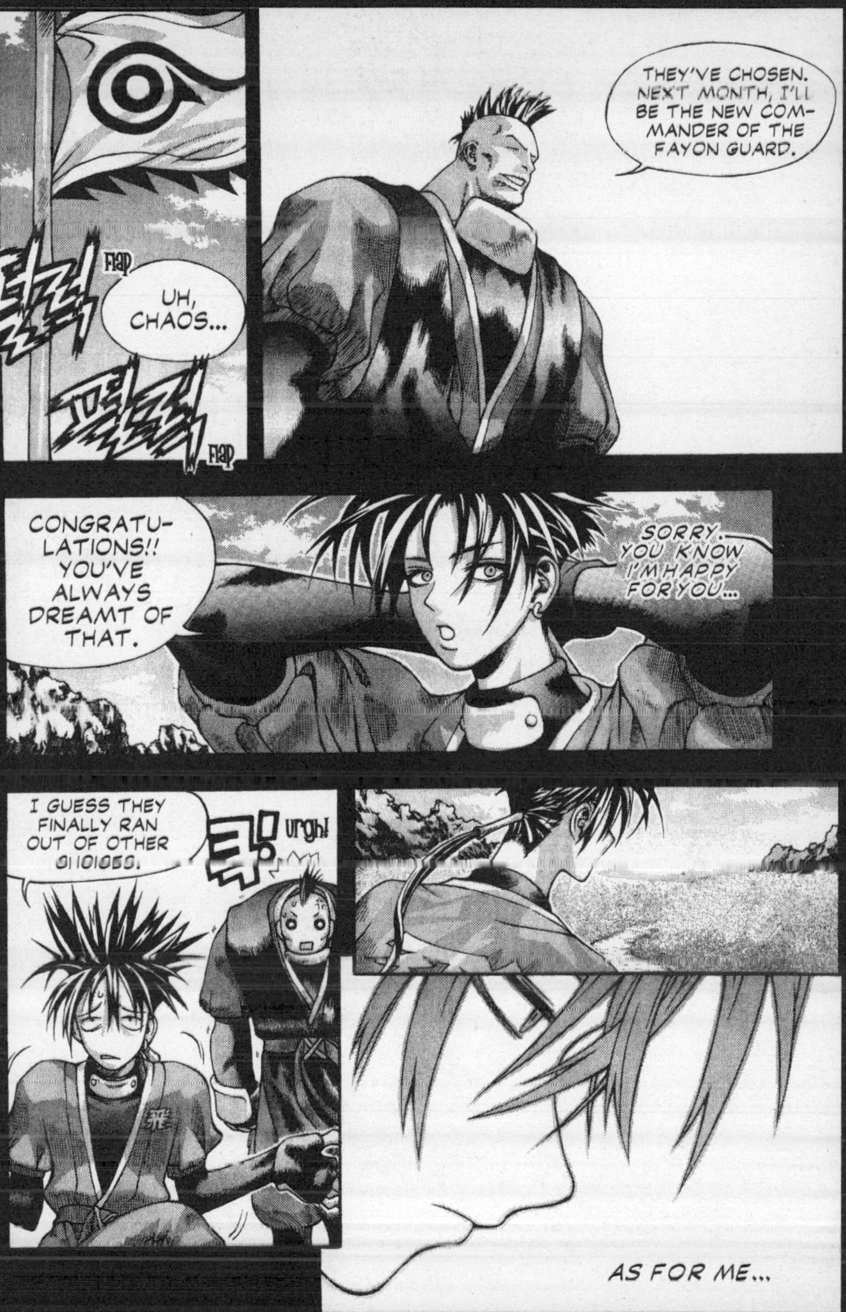
FLAP
UH, CHAOS...
FLAP
THEY'VE CHOSEN. NEXT MONTH, I'LL BE THE NEW COMMANDER OF THE FAYON GUARD.
CONGRATULATIONS!! YOU'VE ALWAYS DREAMT OF THAT.
SORRY. YOU KNOW I'M HAPPY FOR YOU...
I GUESS THEY FINALLY RAN OUT OF OTHER
URGH!
AS FOR ME...

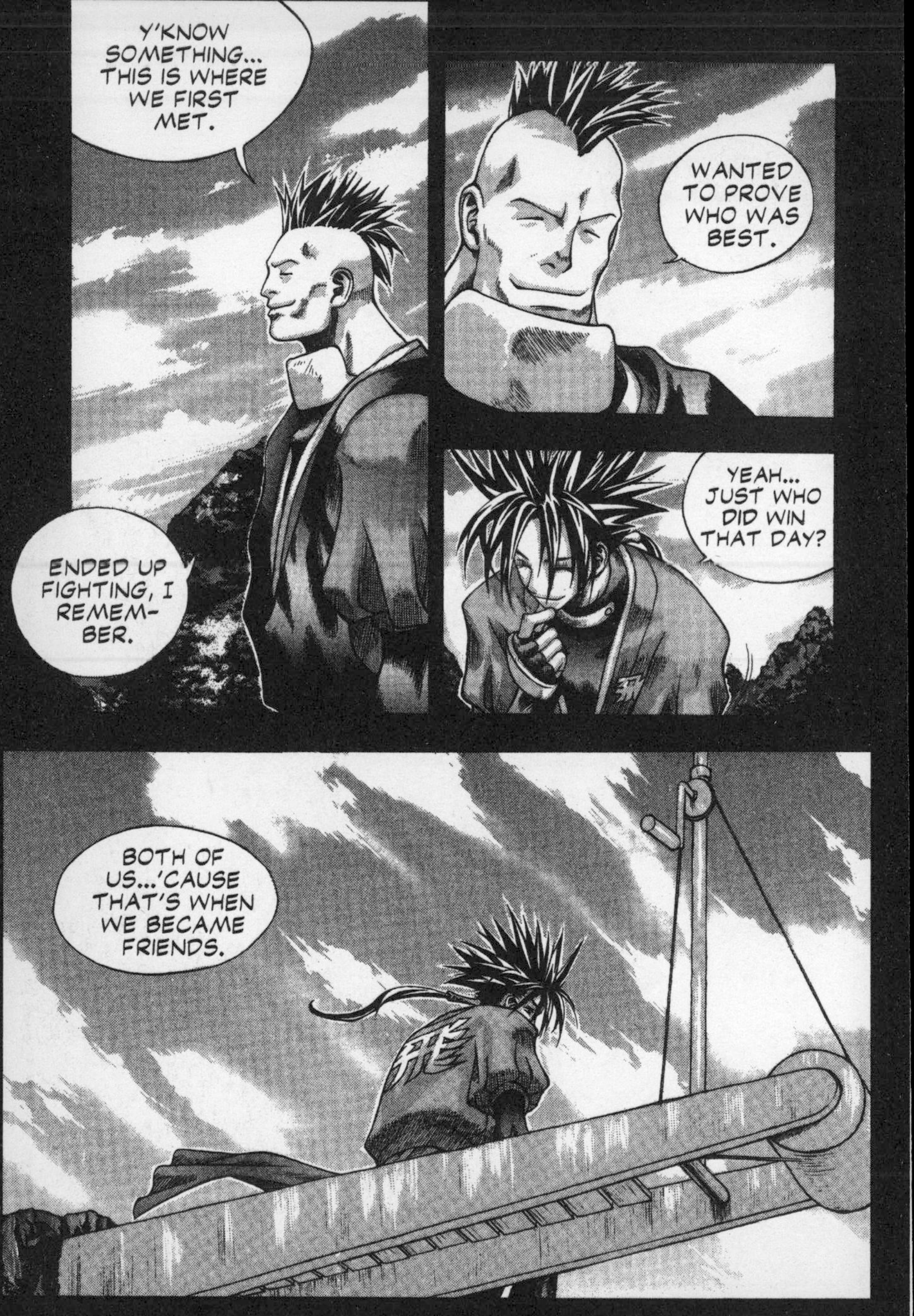
Y'KNOW SOMETHING... THIS IS WHERE WE FIRST MET.
ENDED UP FIGHTING, I REMEM-BER.
WANTED TO PROVE WHO WAS BEST.
YEAH... JUST WHO DID WIN THAT DAY?
BOTH OF US...'CAUSE THAT'S WHEN WE BECAME FRIENDS.

RAGNAROK
라그나로크
IN TO THE ABYSS

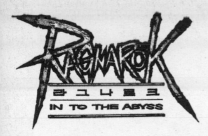

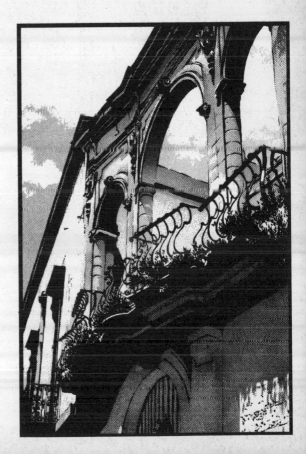

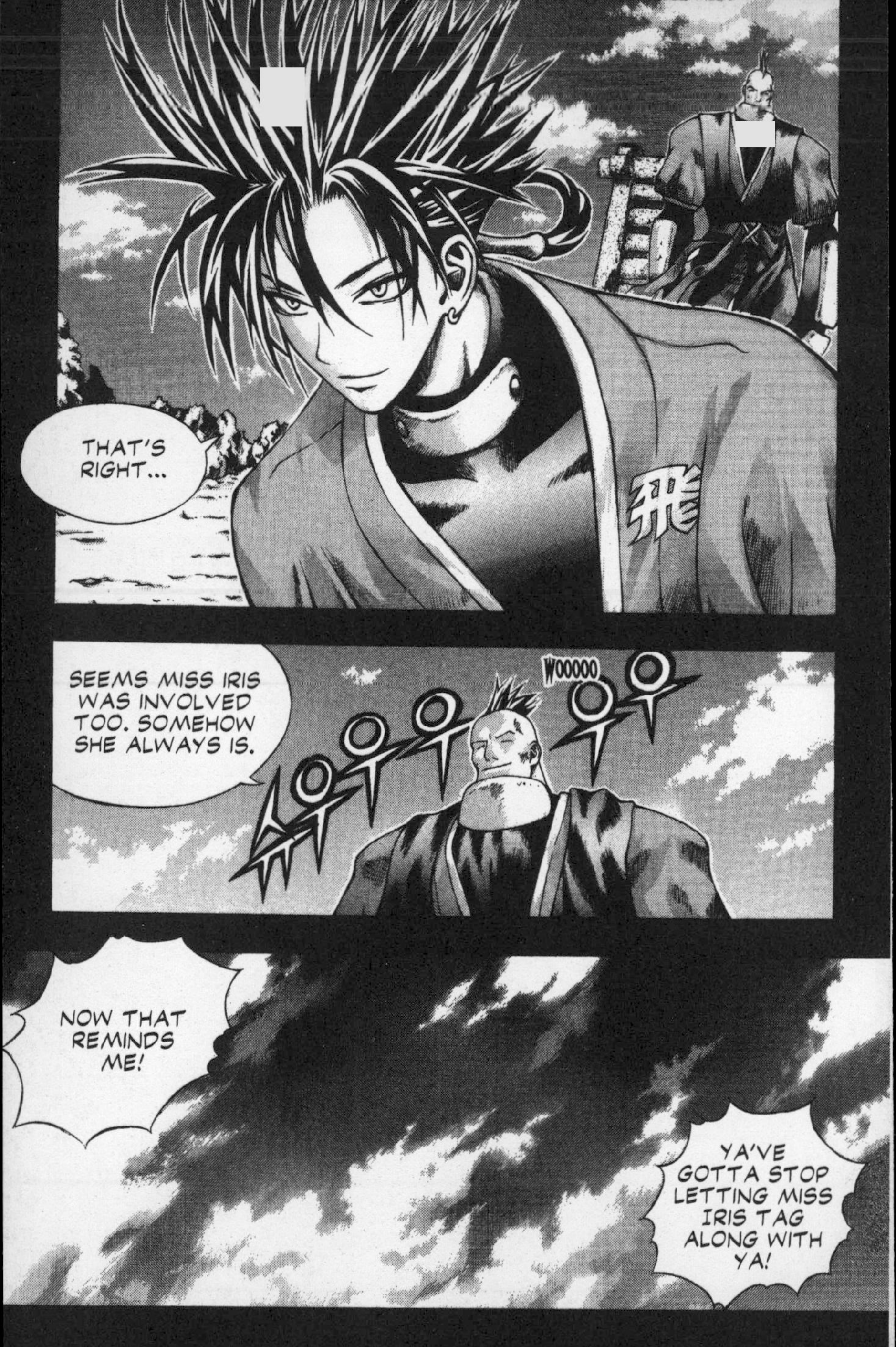

THAT'S RIGHT...
飛
SEEMS MISS IRIS WAS INVOLVED TOO. SOMEHOW SHE ALWAYS IS.
WOOOOO
NOW THAT REMINDS ME!
YA'VE GOTTA STOP LETTING MISS IRIS TAG ALONG WITH YA!

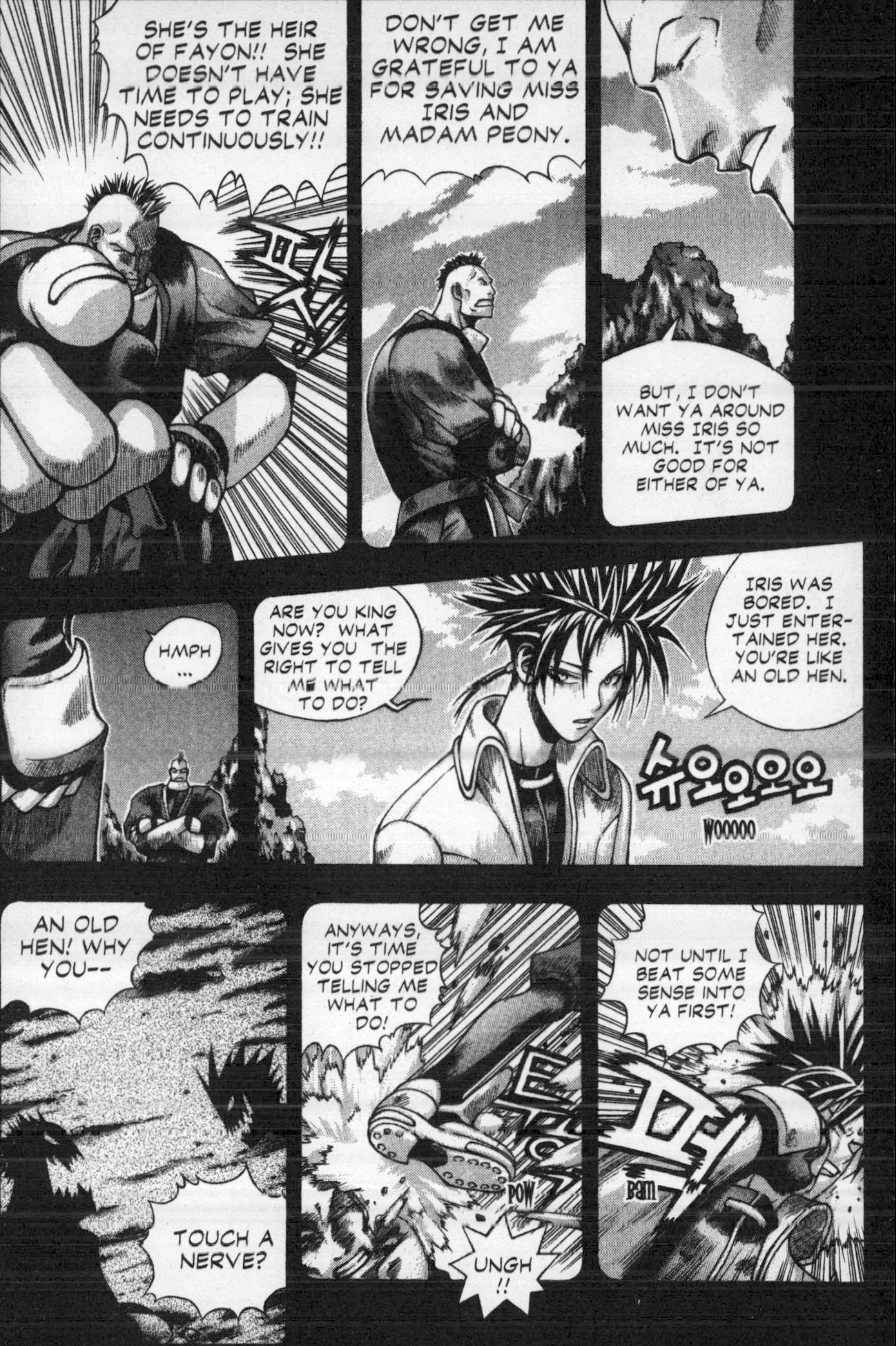

SHE'S THE HEIR OF FAYON!! SHE DOESN'T HAVE TIME TO PLAY; SHE NEEDS TO TRAIN CONTINUOUSLY!!
DON'T GET ME WRONG, I AM GRATEFUL TO YA FOR SAVING MISS IRIS AND MADAM PEONY.
BUT, I DON'T WANT YA AROUND MISS IRIS SO MUCH. IT'S NOT GOOD FOR EITHER OF YA.
HMPH ...
ARE YOU KING NOW? WHAT GIVES YOU THE RIGHT TO TELL ME WHAT TO DO?
IRIS WAS BORED. I JUST ENTERTAINED HER. YOU'RE LIKE AN OLD HEN.
슈오오오오
WOOOOO
AN OLD HEN! WHY YOU--
TOUCH A NERVE?
ANYWAYS, IT'S TIME YOU STOPPED TELLING ME WHAT TO DO!
POW
UNGH !!
NOT UNTIL I BEAT SOME SENSE INTO YA FIRST!
BAM

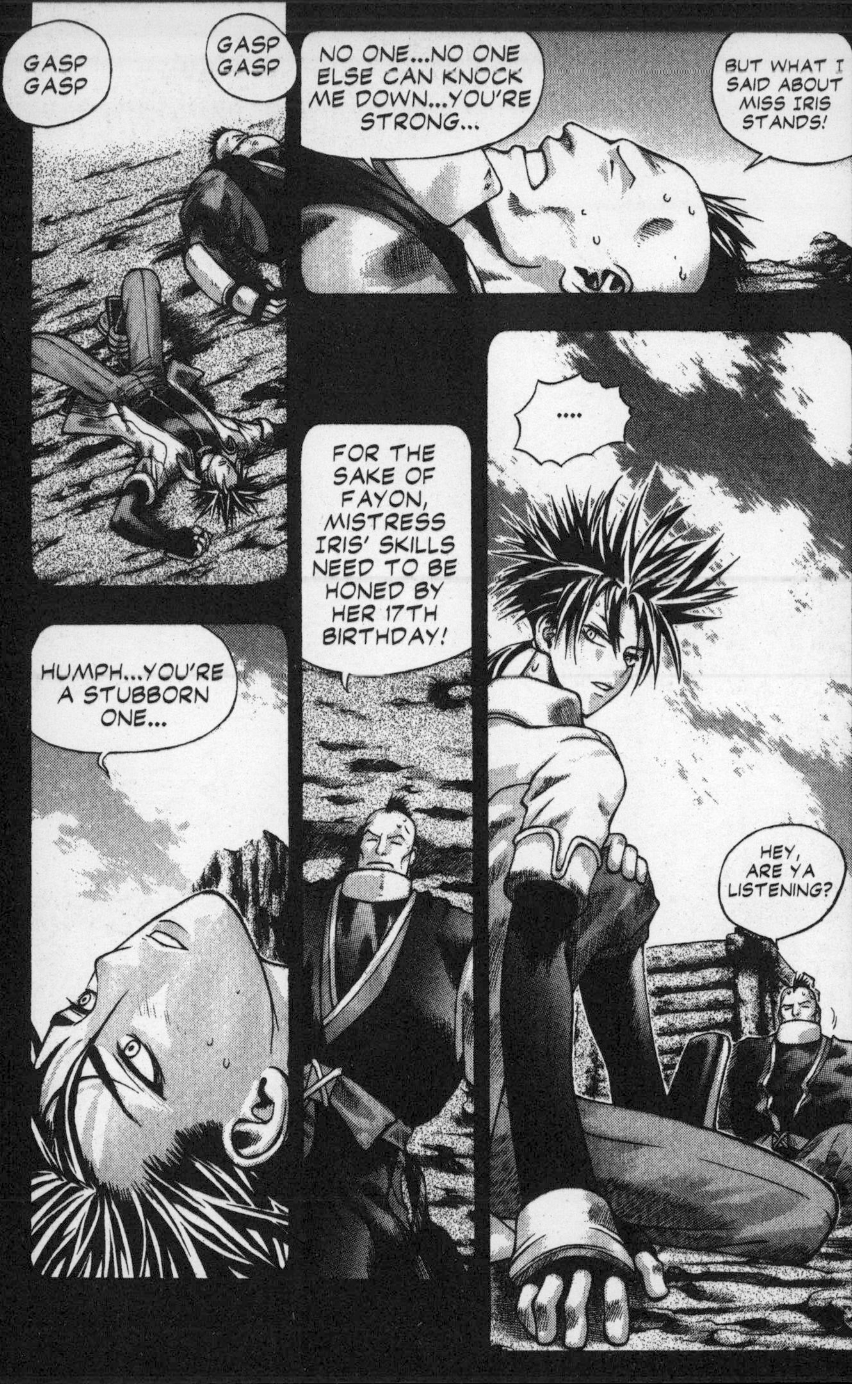
GASP GASP
GASP GASP
NO ONE...NO ONE ELSE CAN KNOCK ME DOWN...YOU'RE STRONG...
BUT WHAT I SAID ABOUT MISS IRIS STANDS!
HUMPH...YOU'RE A STUBBORN ONE...
FOR THE SAKE OF FAYON, MISTRESS IRIS' SKILLS NEED TO BE HONED BY HER 17TH BIRTHDAY!
....
HEY, ARE YA LISTENING?

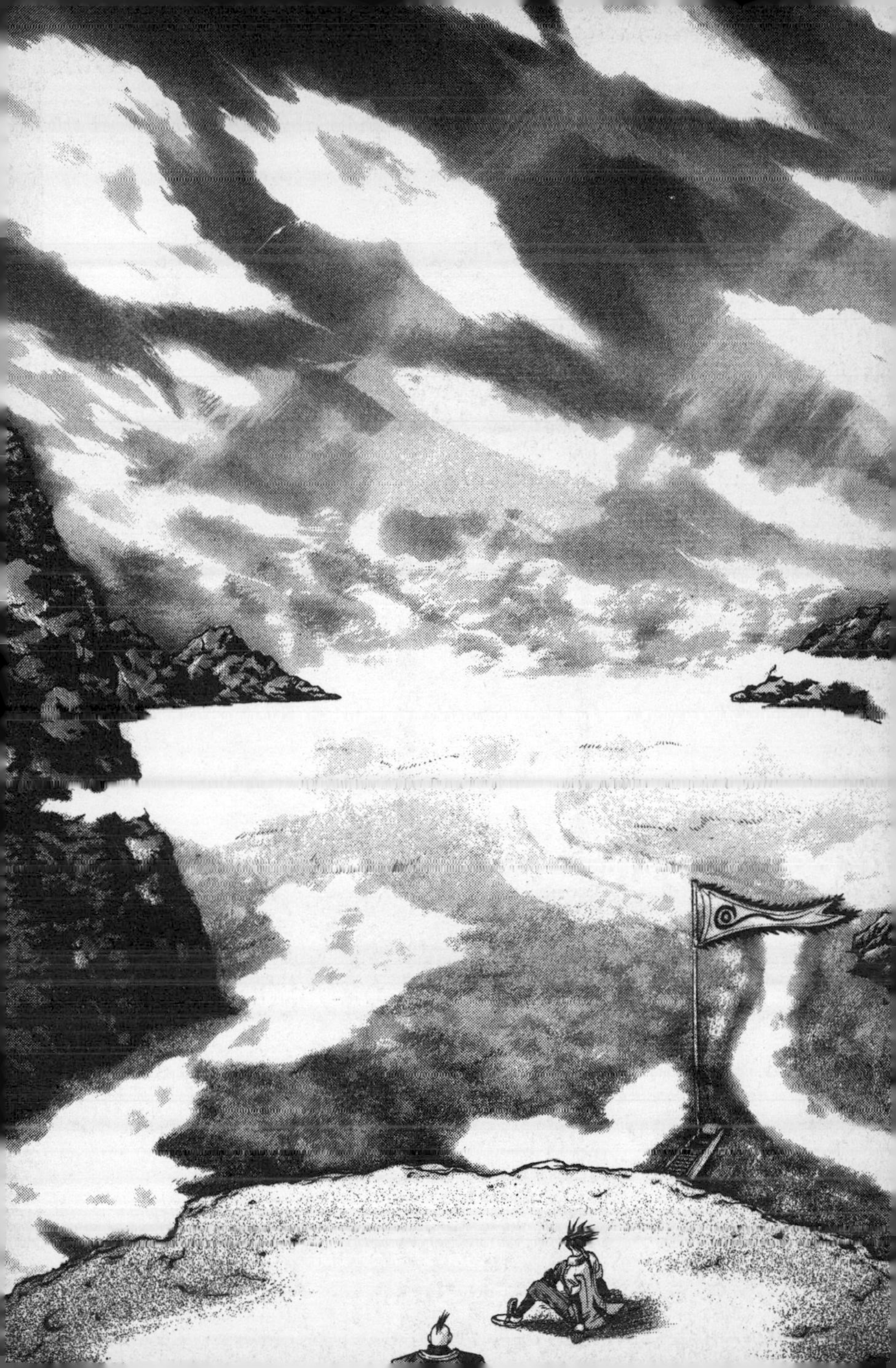

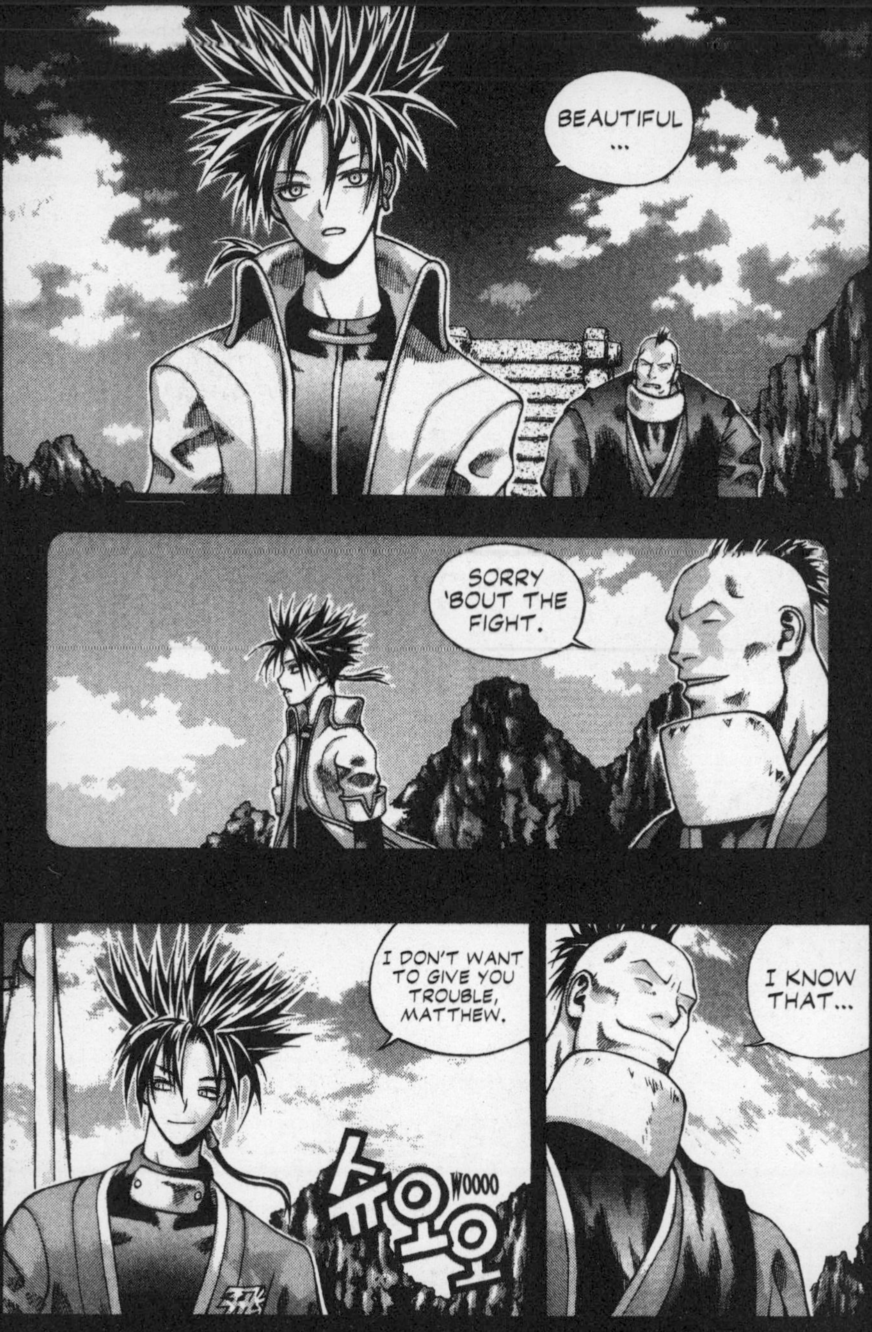
BEAUTIFUL ...
SORRY 'BOUT THE FIGHT.
I DON'T WANT TO GIVE YOU TROUBLE, MATTHEW.
WOOOO
I KNOW THAT...

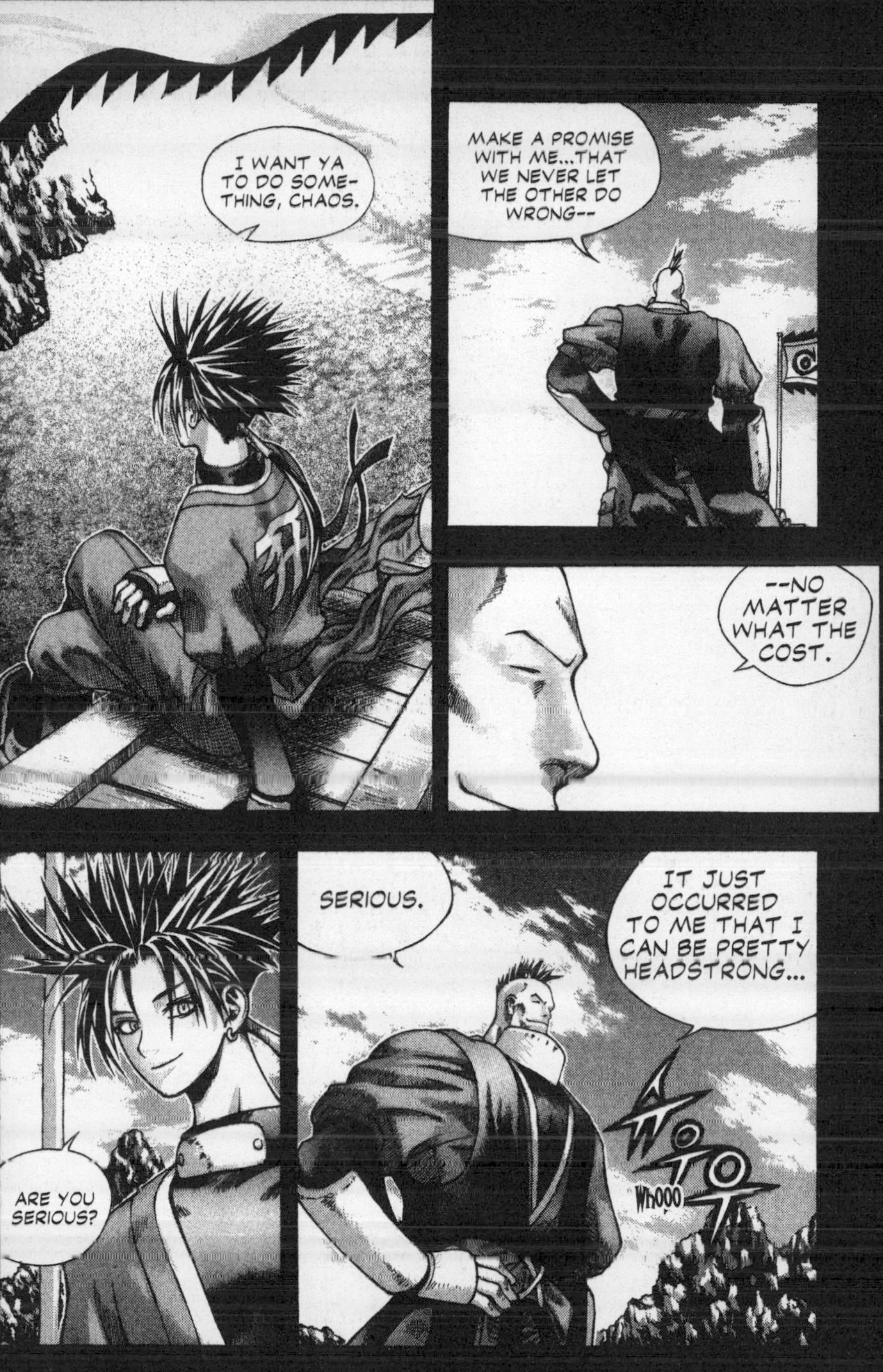
I WANT YA TO DO SOME-THING, CHAOS.
MAKE A PROMISE WITH ME...THAT WE NEVER LET THE OTHER DO WRONG--
--NO MATTER WHAT THE COST.
ARE YOU SERIOUS?
SERIOUS.
IT JUST OCCURRED TO ME THAT I CAN BE PRETTY HEADSTRONG...
WHOOO

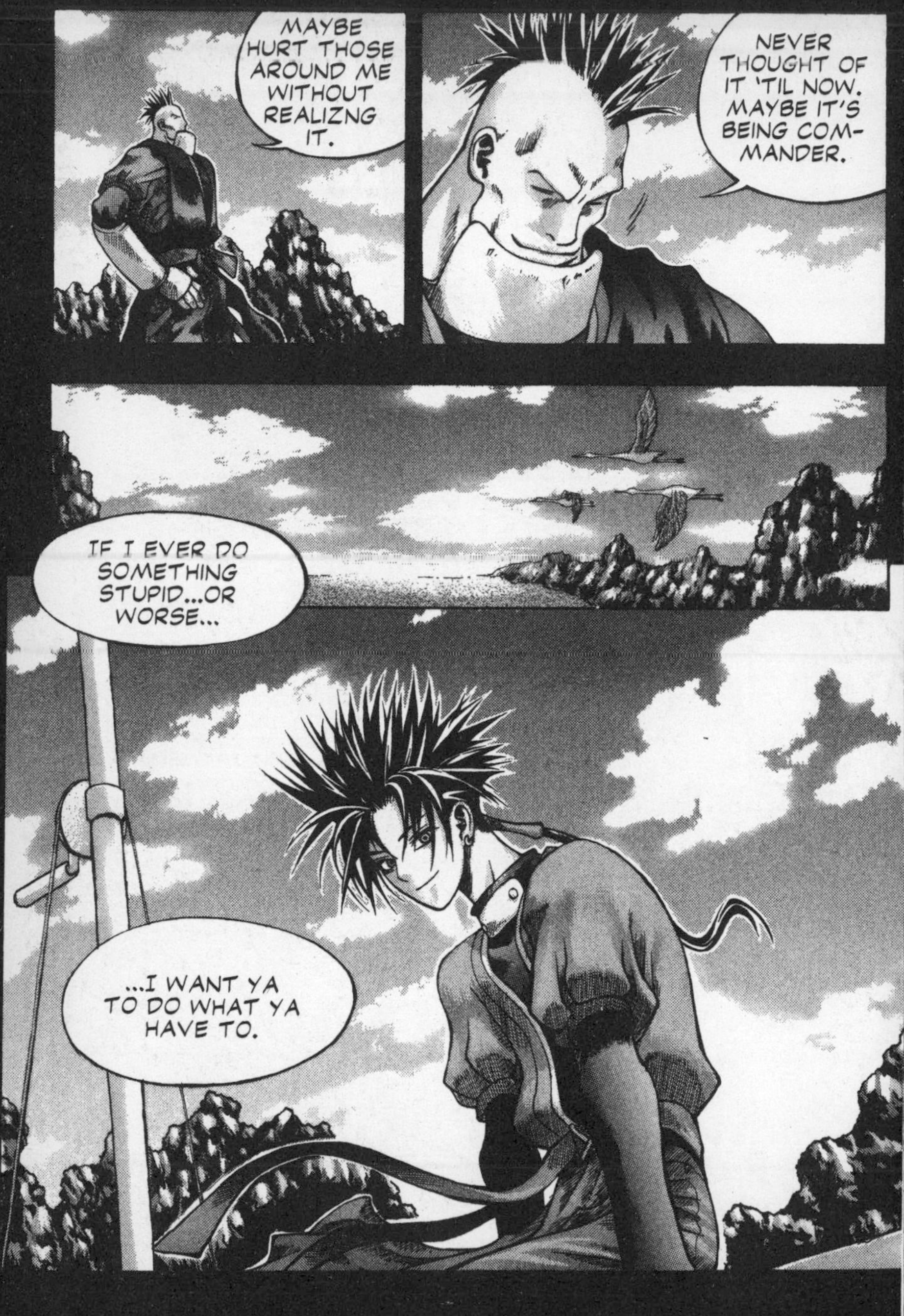
MAYBE HURT THOSE AROUND ME WITHOUT REALIZNG IT.
NEVER THOUGHT OF IT 'TIL NOW. MAYBE IT'S BEING COM-MANDER.
IF I EVER DO SOMETHING STUPID...OR WORSE...
...I WANT YA TO DO WHAT YA HAVE TO.

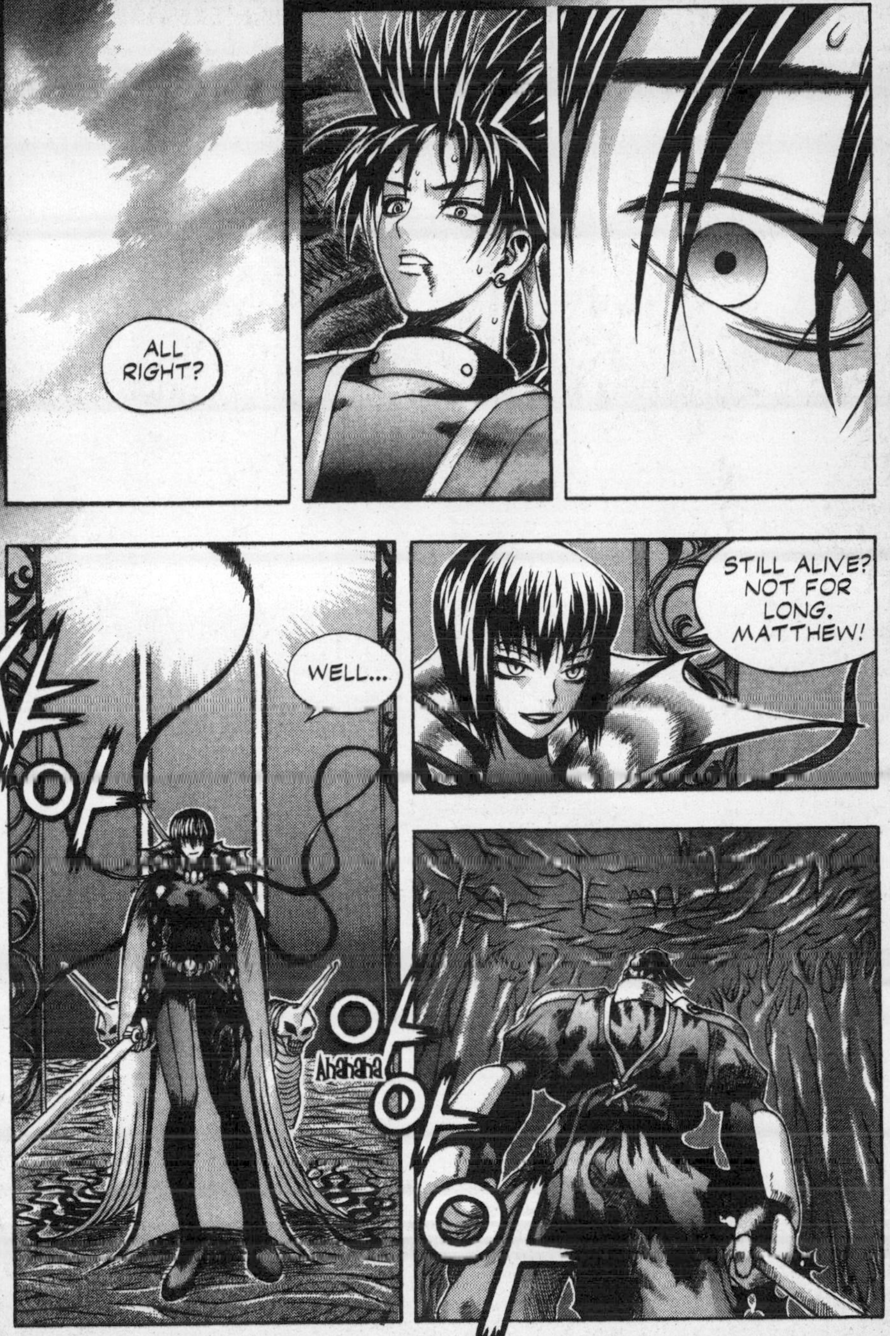
ALL RIGHT?
WELL...
Ahahaha
STILL ALIVE? NOT FOR LONG. MATTHEW!

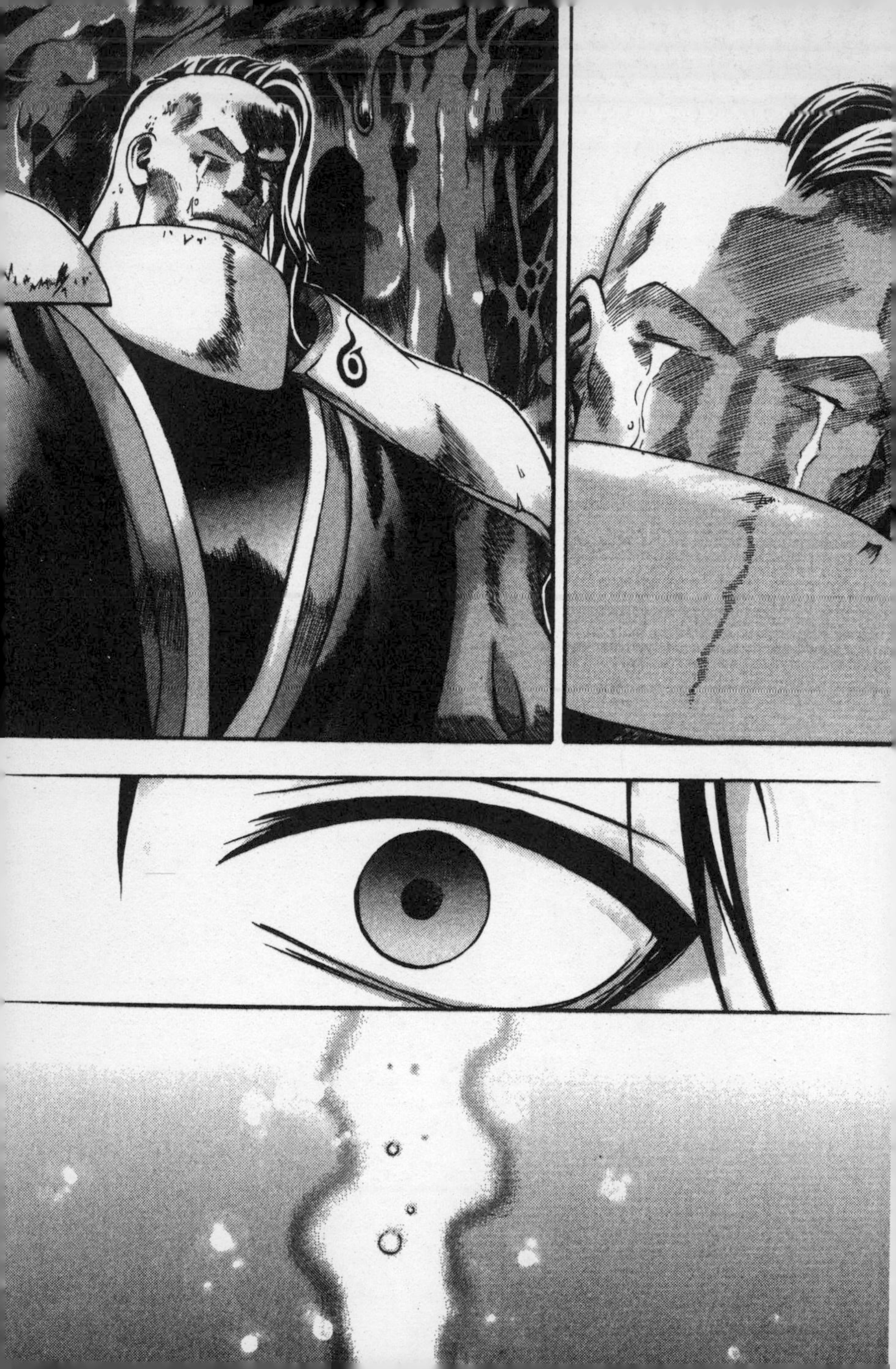

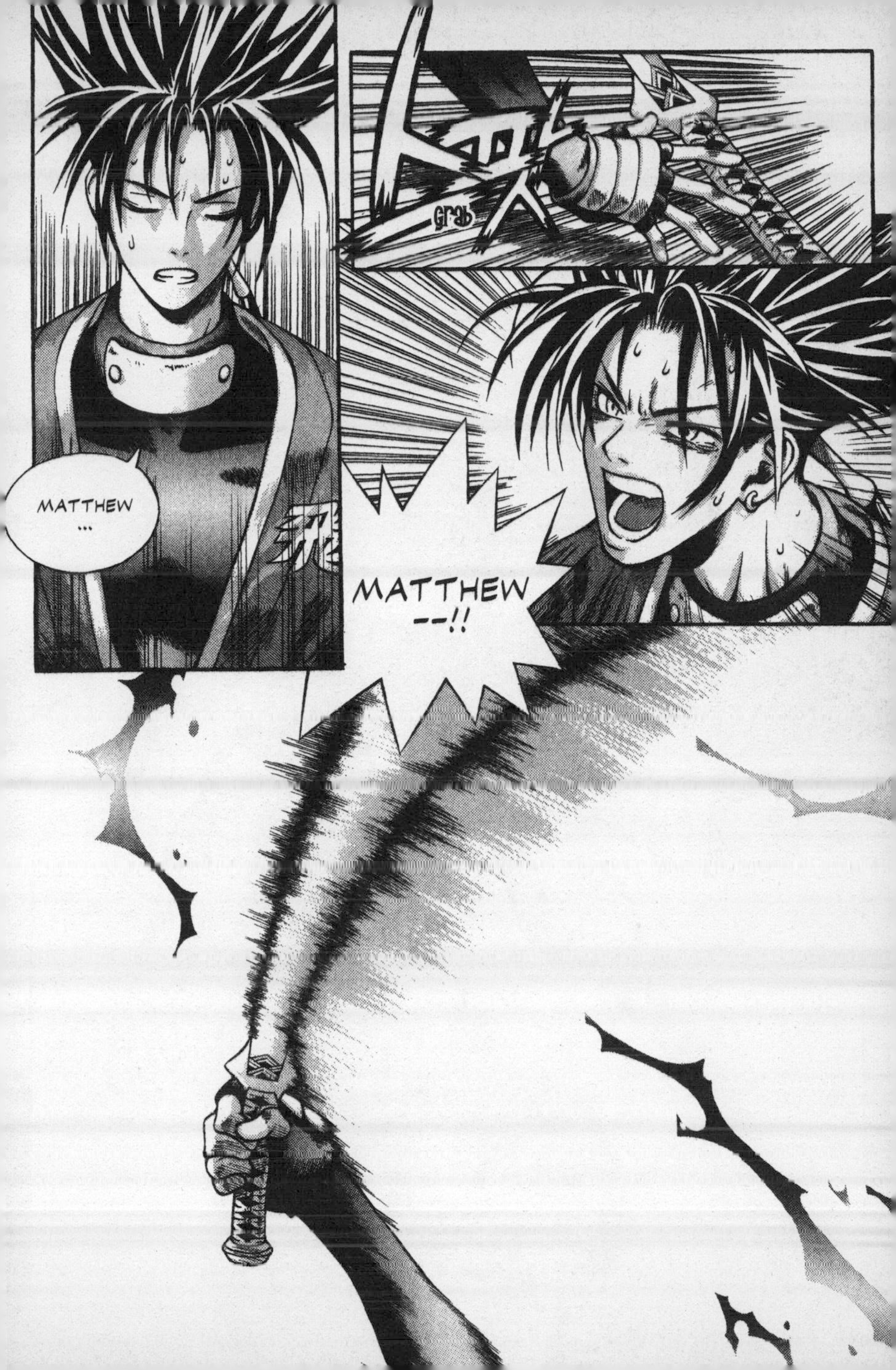
MATTHEW
...
Grab
MATTHEW
--!!

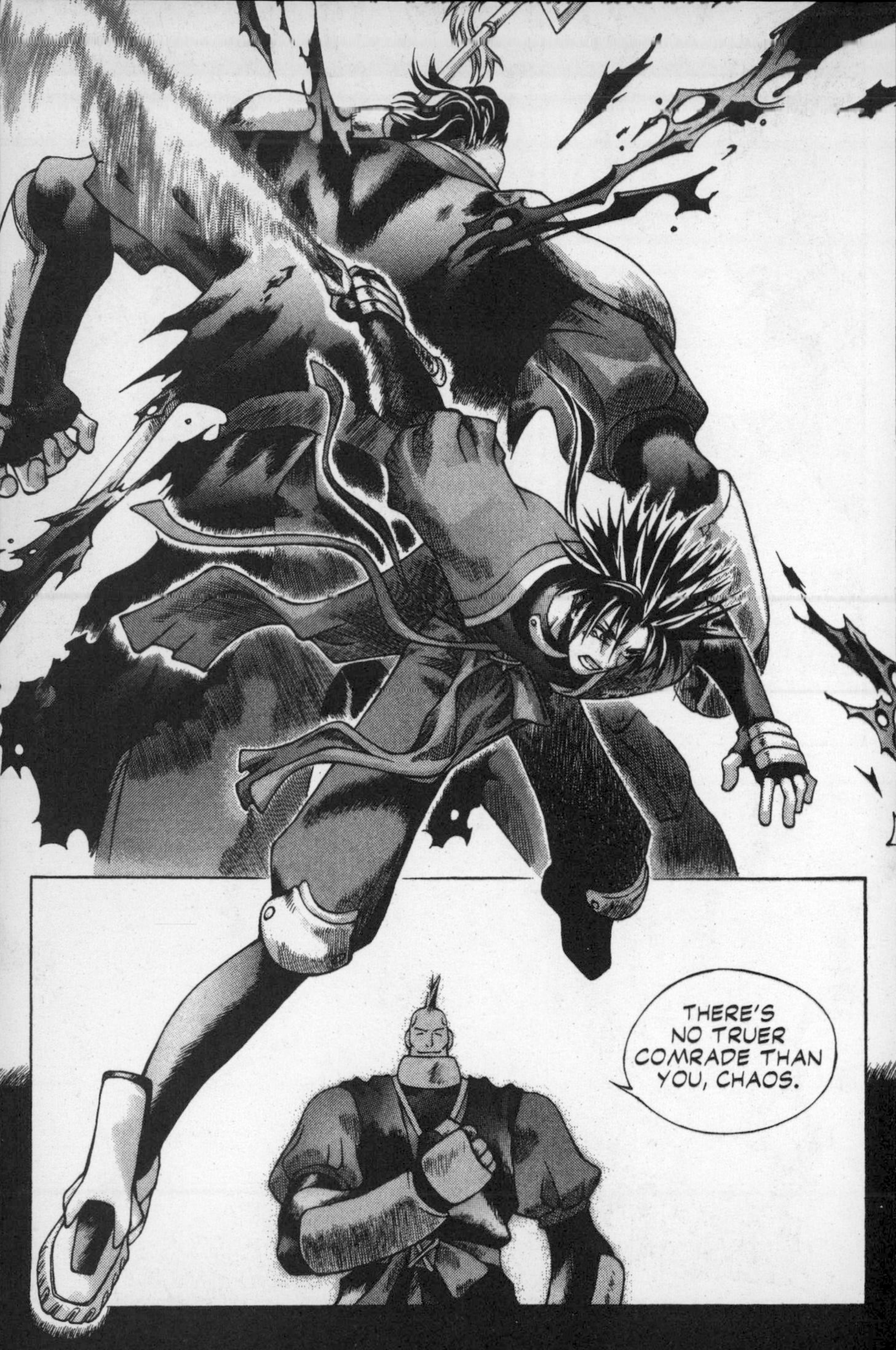
THERE'S NO TRUER COMRADE THAN YOU, CHAOS.

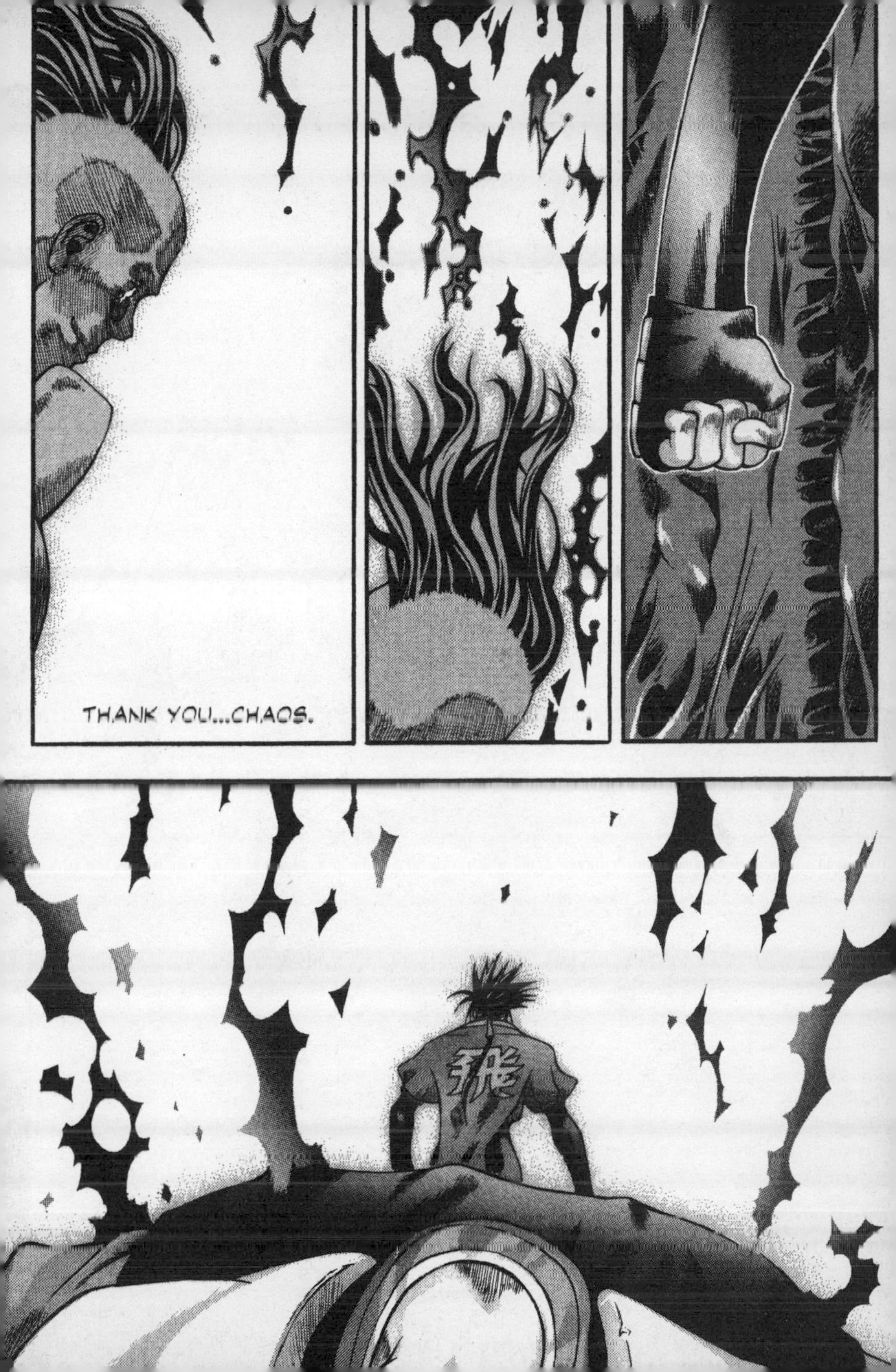
THANK YOU...CHAOS.
飛

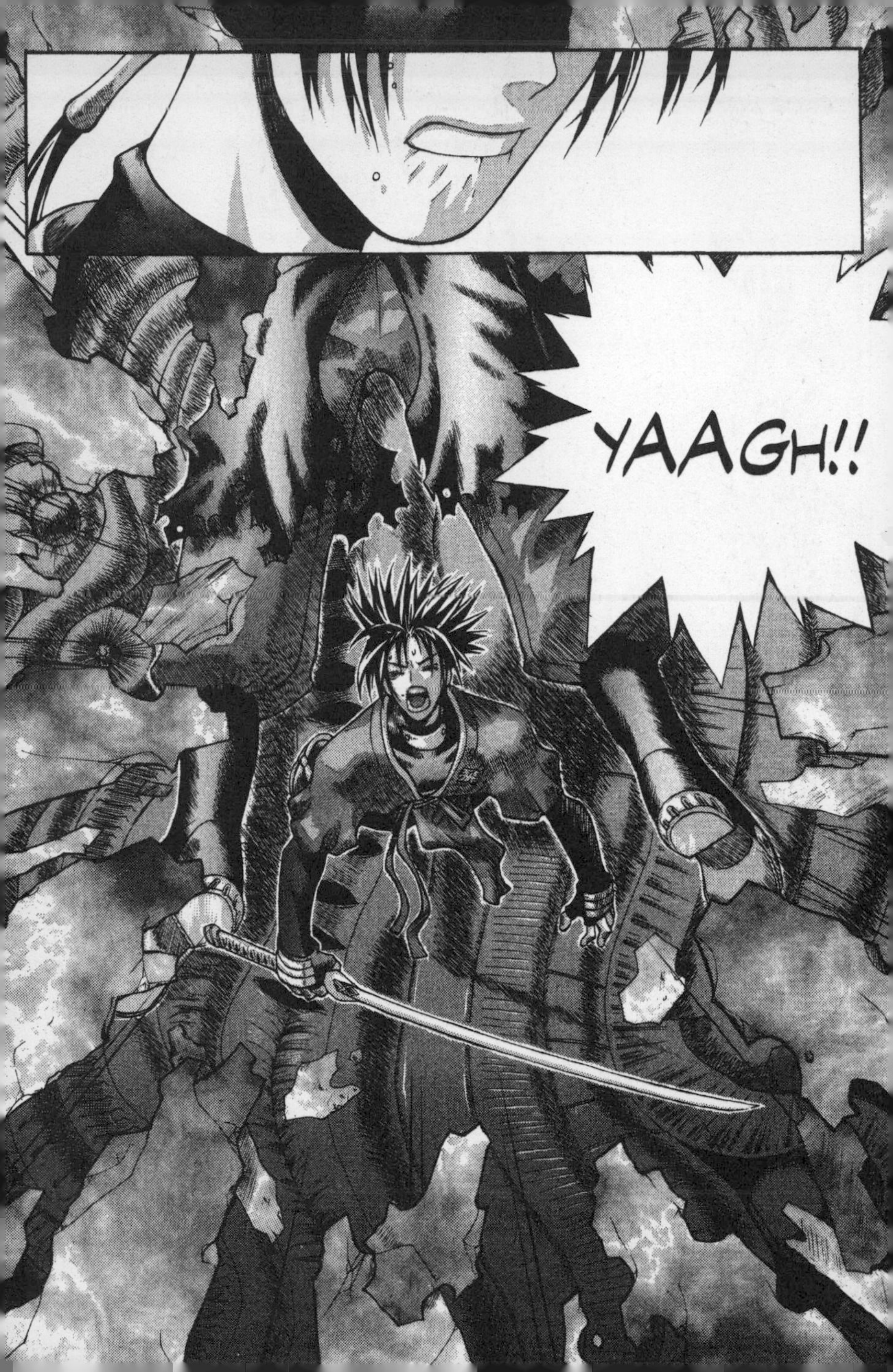
YAAGH!!

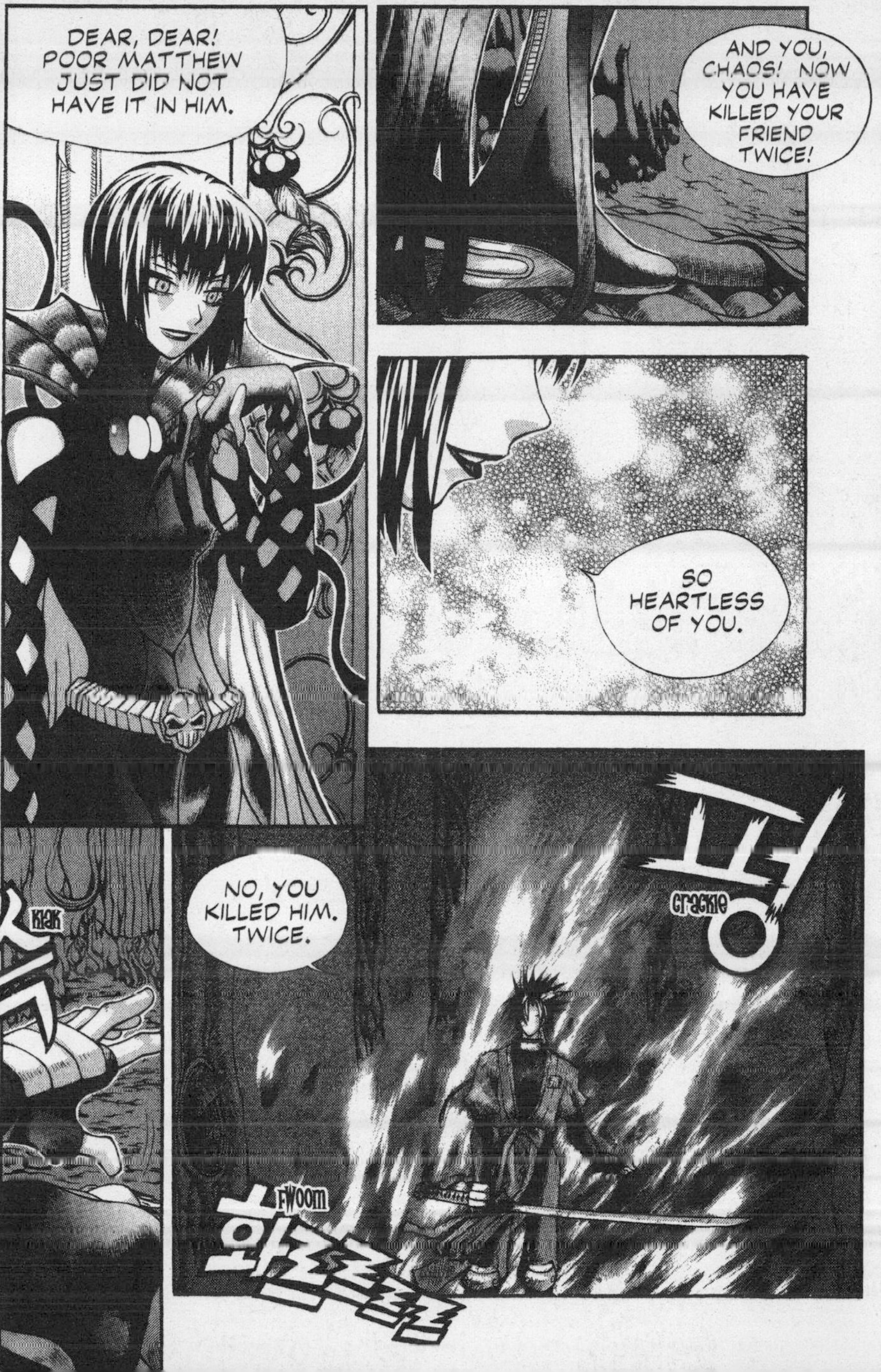
DEAR, DEAR! POOR MATTHEW JUST DID NOT HAVE IT IN HIM.
AND YOU, CHAOS! NOW YOU HAVE KILLED YOUR FRIEND TWICE!
SO HEARTLESS OF YOU.
KLAK
NO, YOU KILLED HIM. TWICE.
CRACKLE
FWOOM

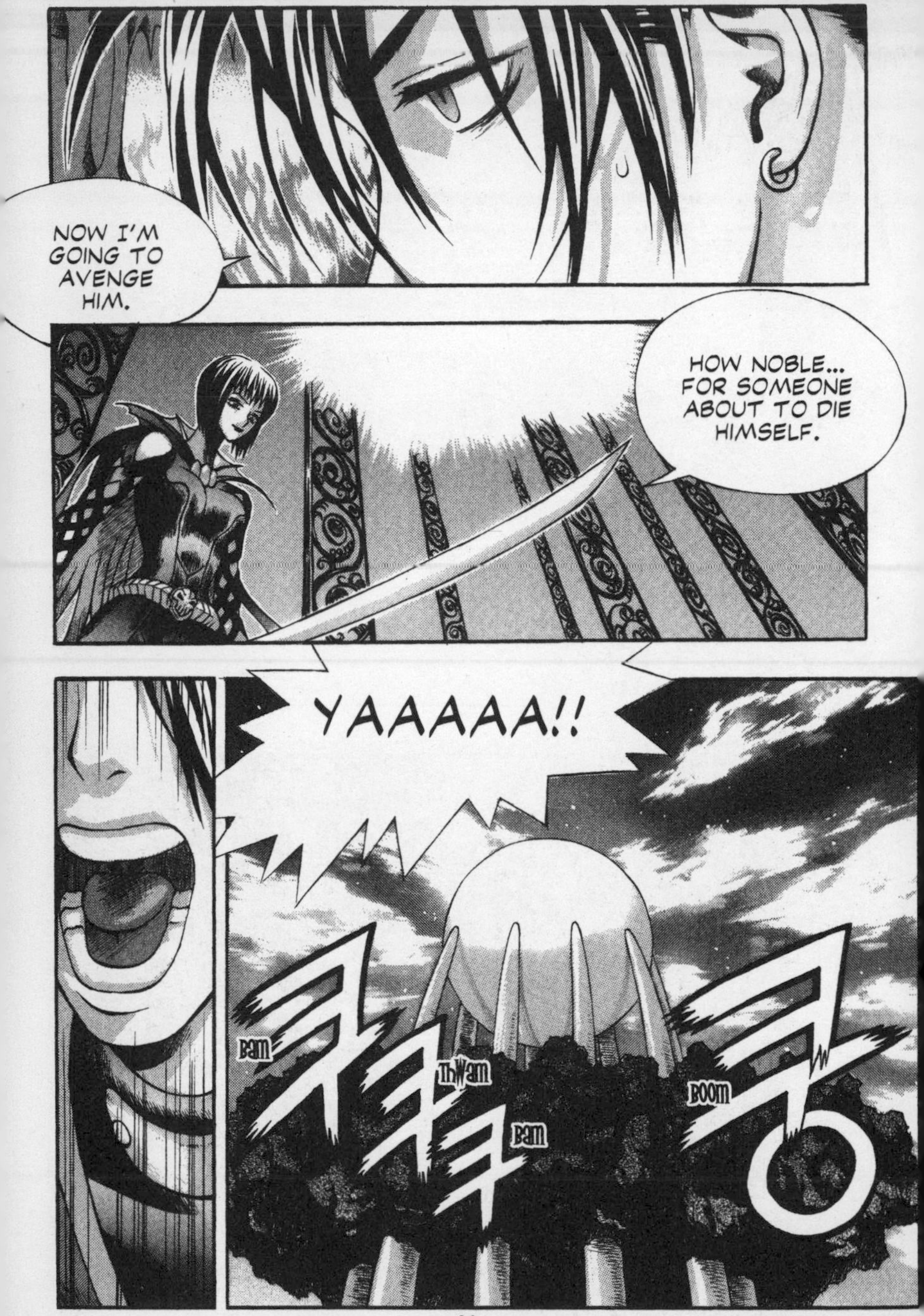
NOW I'M GOING TO AVENGE HIM.
HOW NOBLE... FOR SOMEONE ABOUT TO DIE HIMSELF.
YAAAAA!!
BAM
THWAM
BAM
BOOM

RAGNAROK
라그나로크
IN TO THE ABYSS

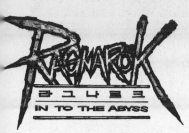

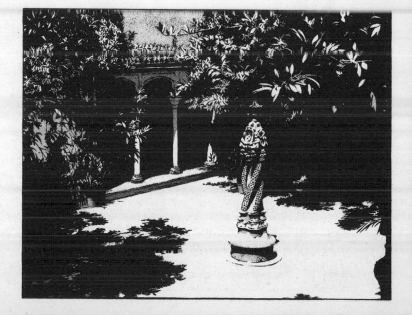

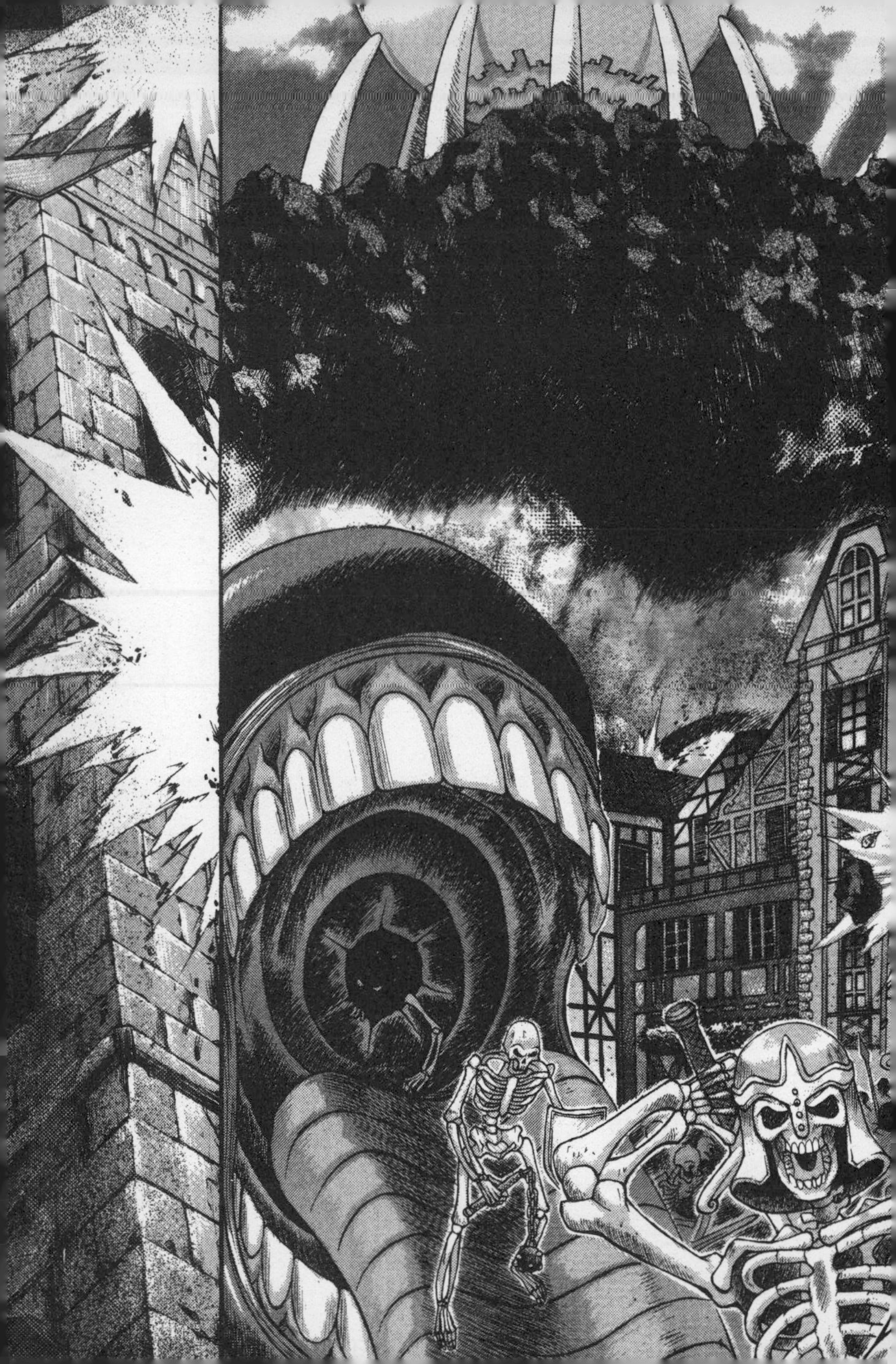

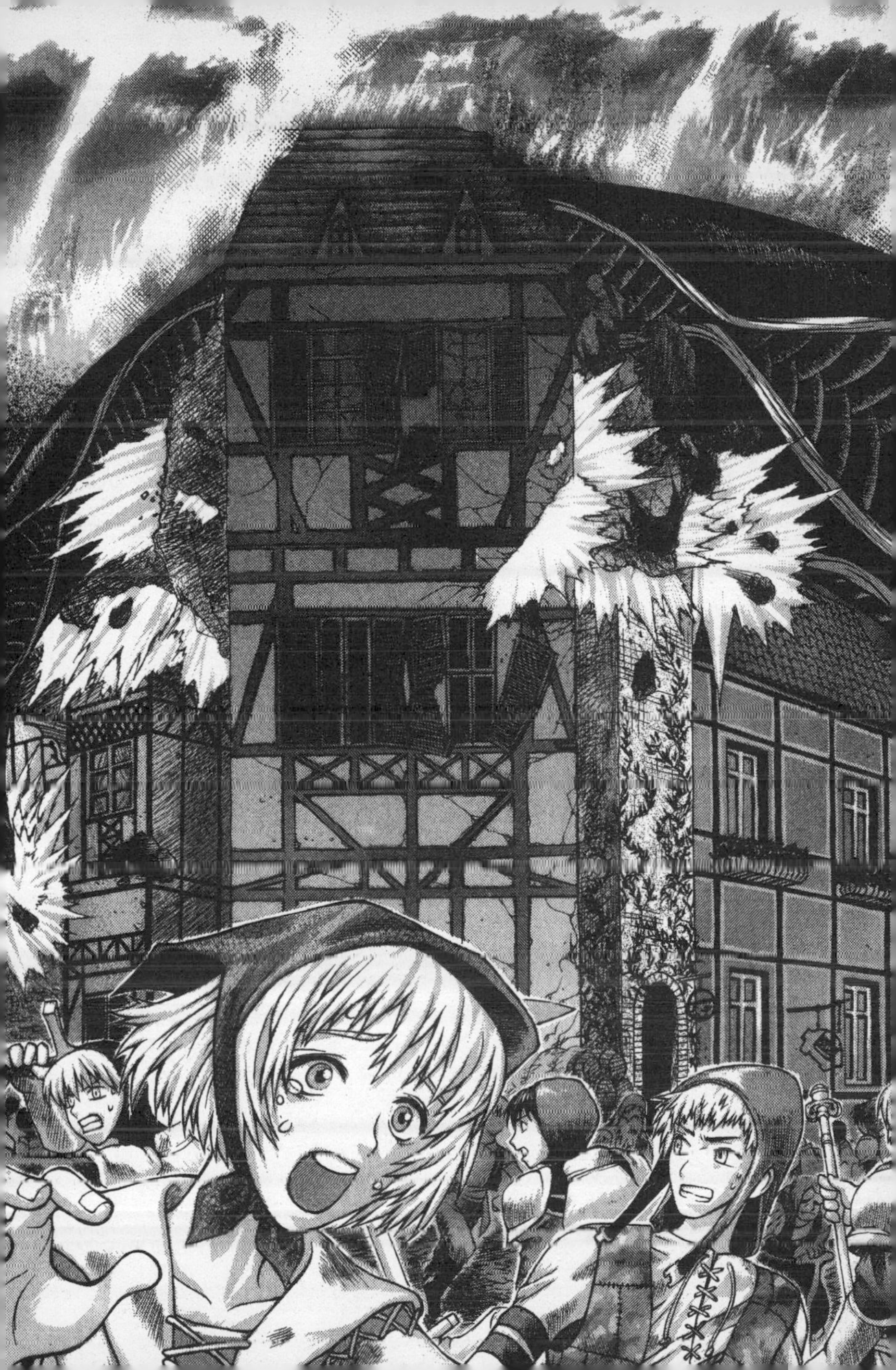

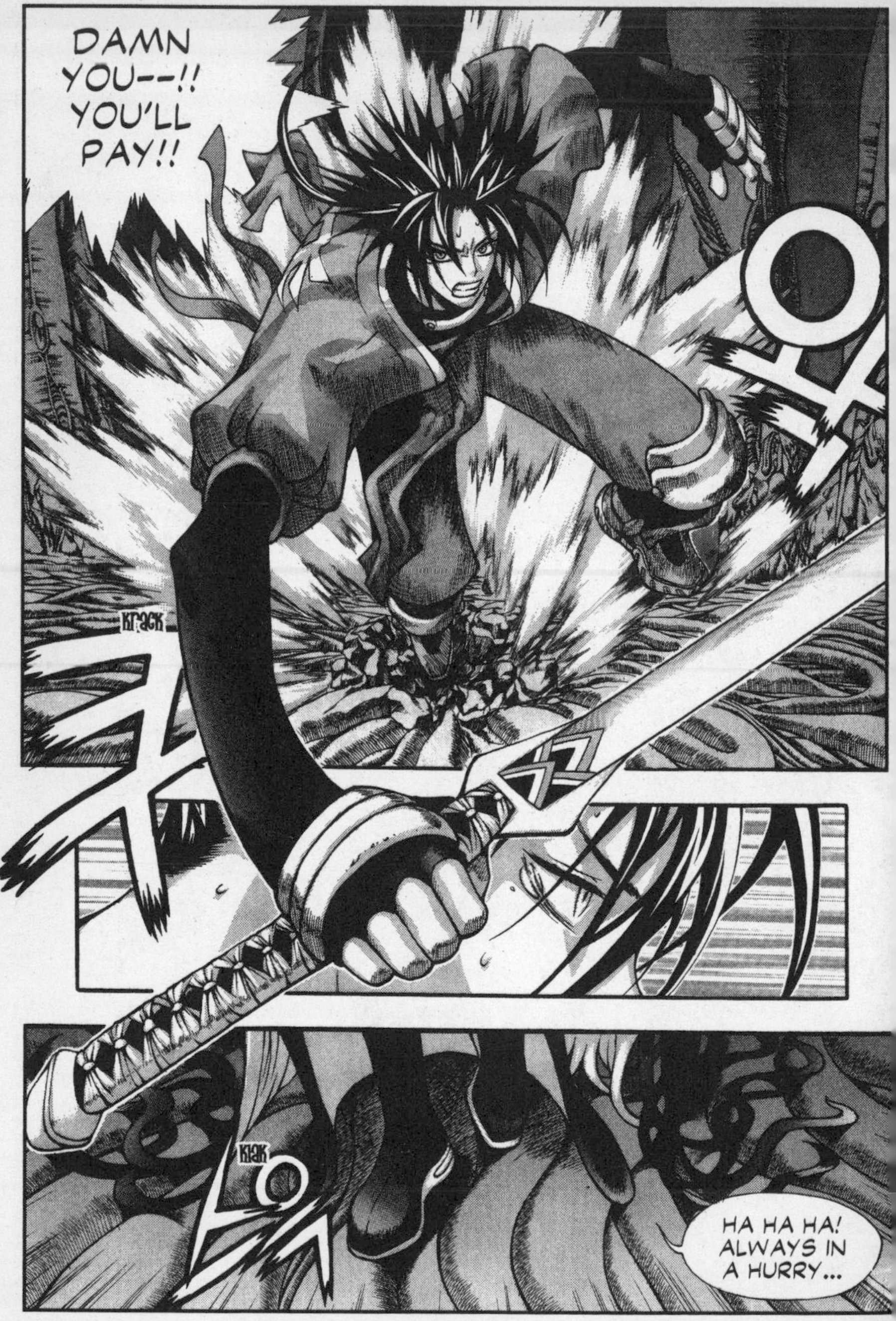
DAMN YOU--!! YOU'LL PAY!!
KRACK
KLAK
HA HA HA! ALWAYS IN A HURRY...

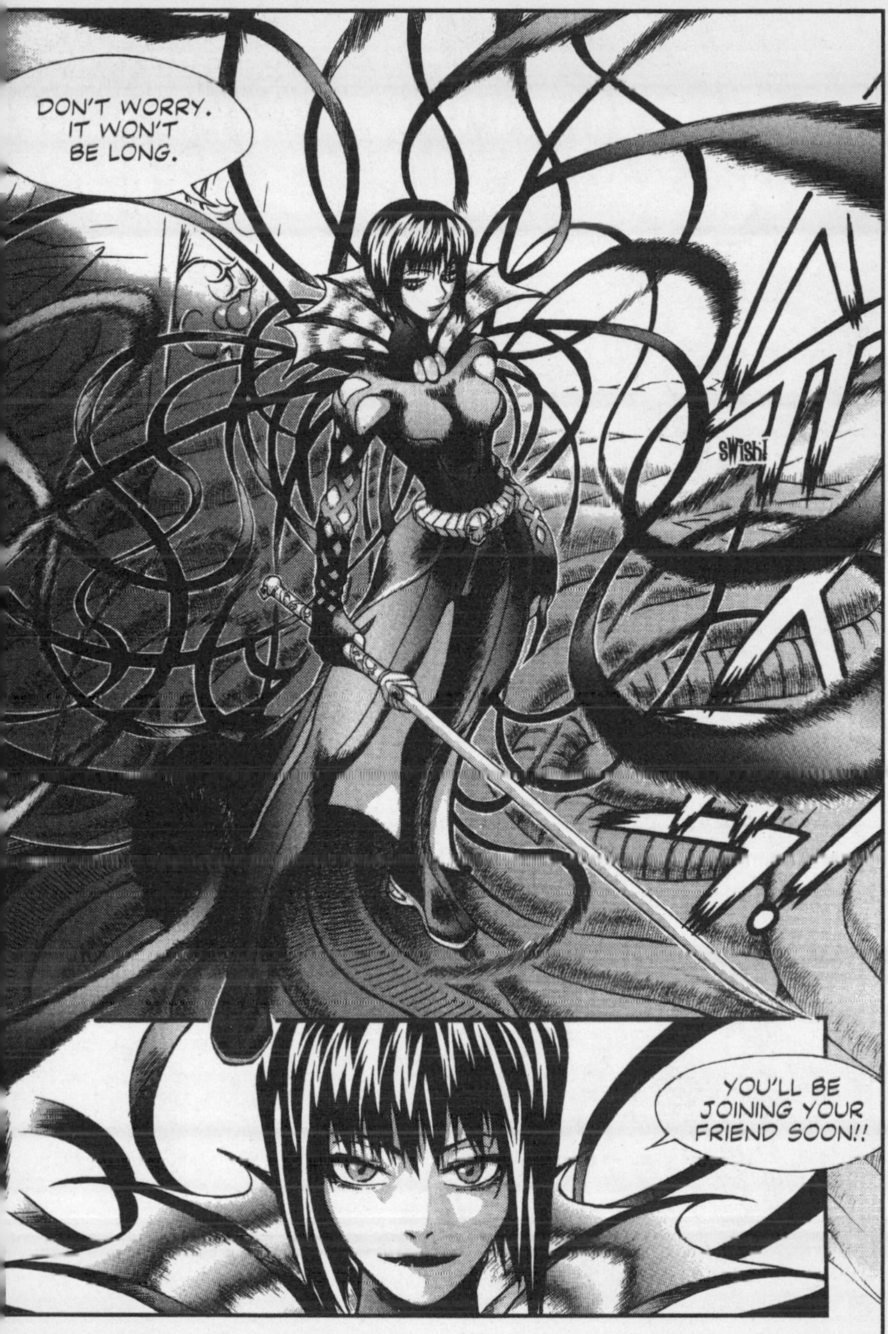
DON'T WORRY. IT WON'T BE LONG.
SWISH!
YOU'LL BE JOINING YOUR FRIEND SOON!!

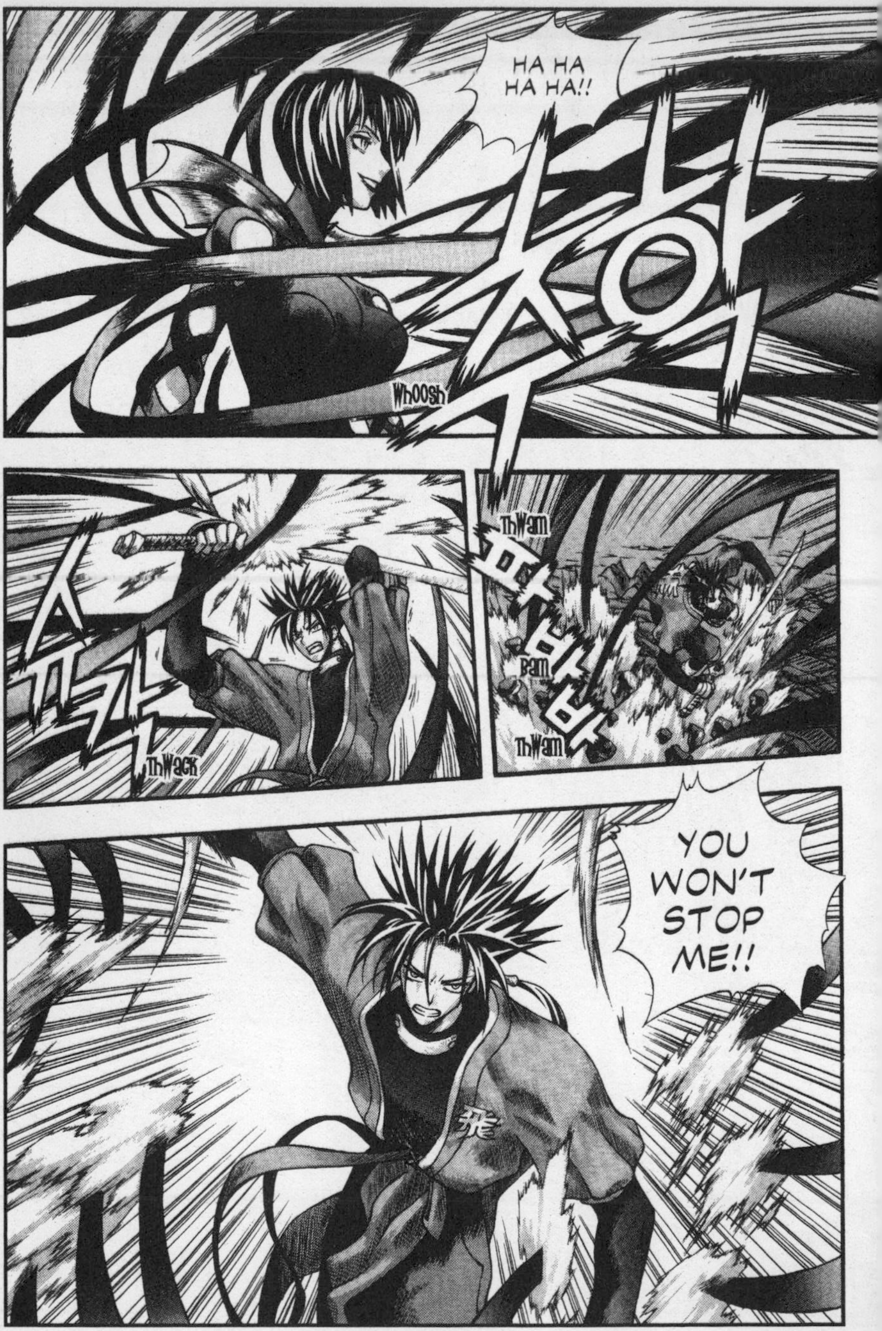

HA HA HA HA!!
Whoosh
Thwack
Thwam
Bam
Thwam
YOU WON'T STOP ME!!

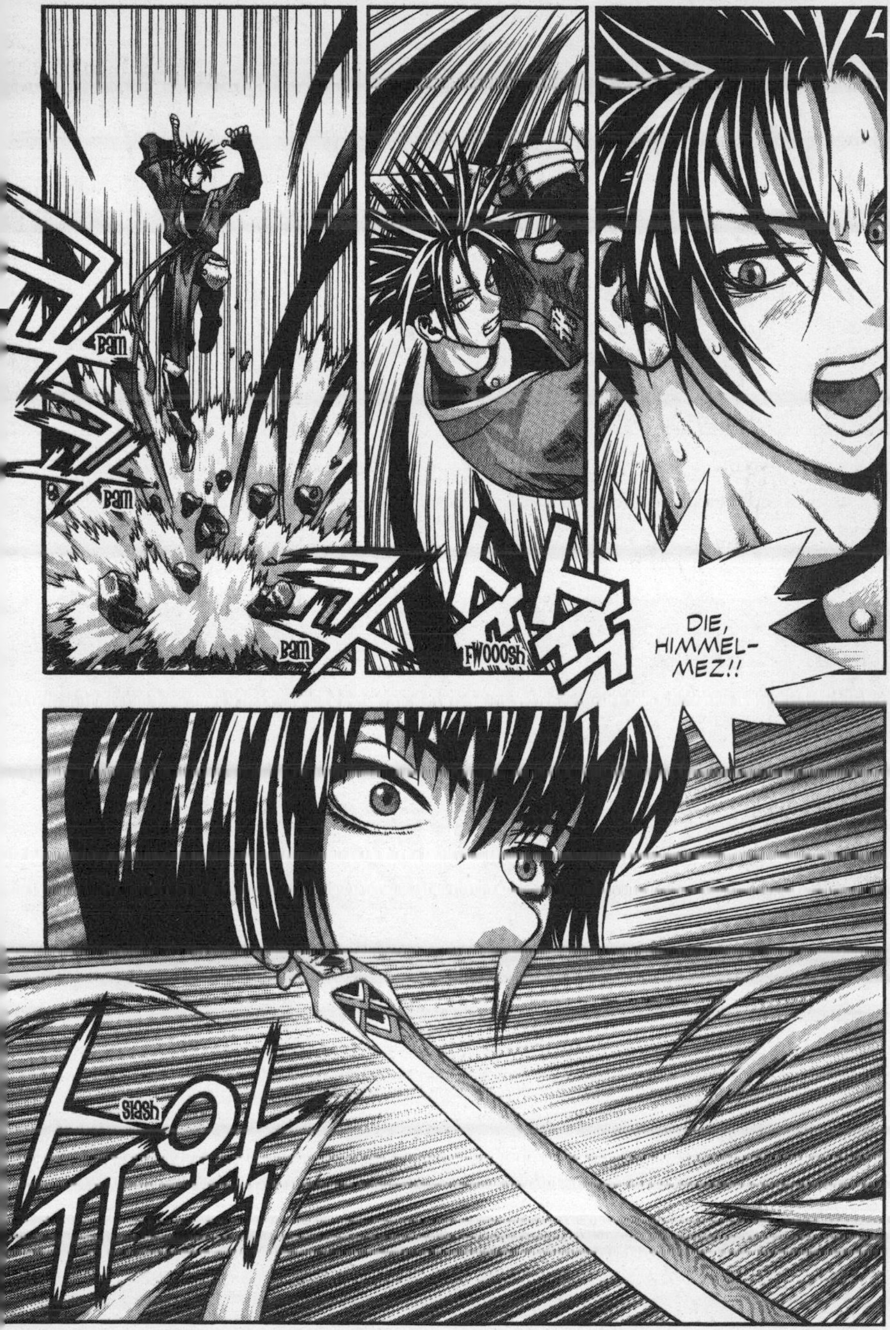
Bam
Bam
Bam
FWOOOSH
DIE, HIMMEL-MEZ!!
SLASH

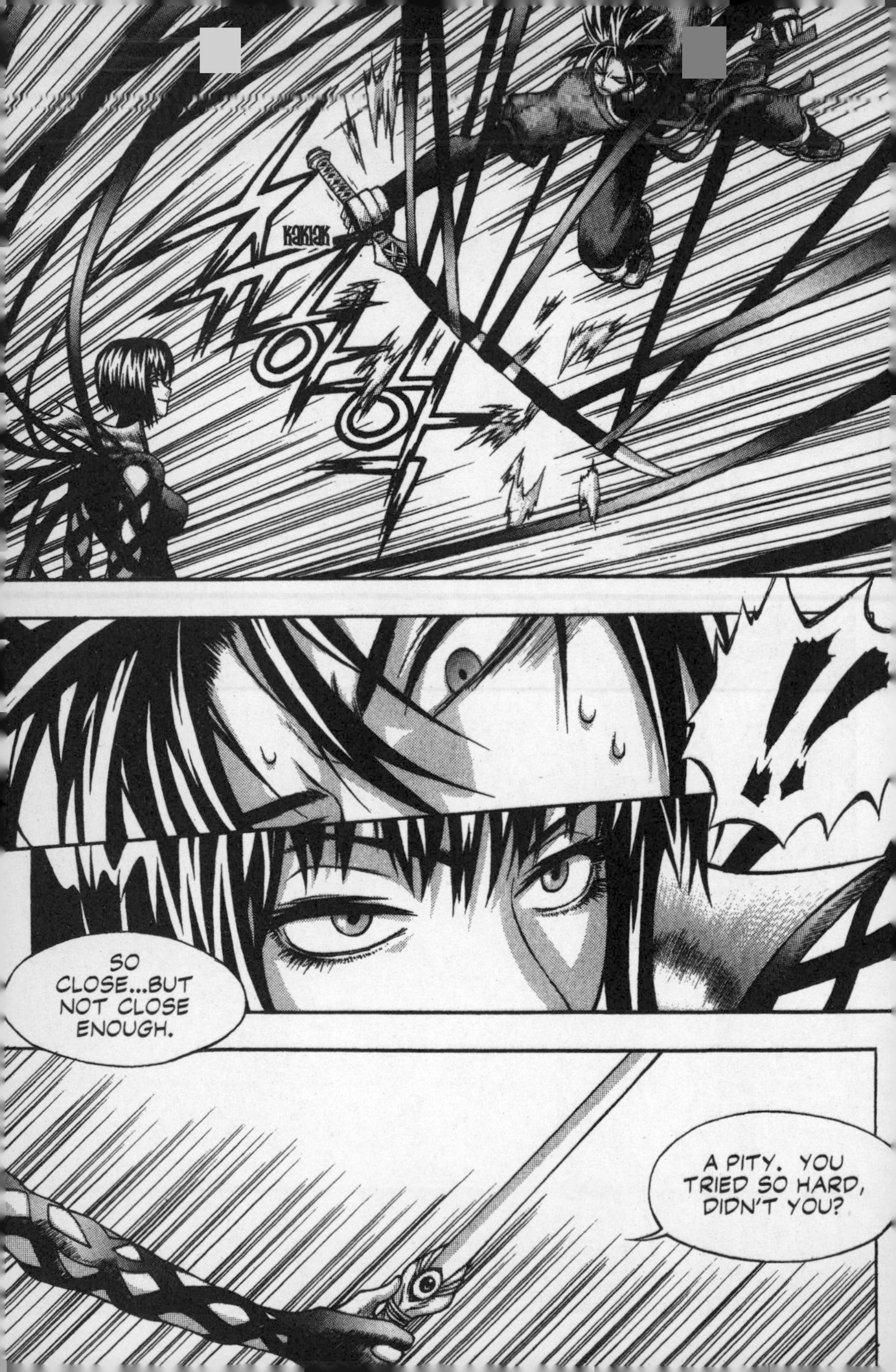
KAKIAK
SO CLOSE...BUT NOT CLOSE ENOUGH.
A PITY. YOU TRIED SO HARD, DIDN'T YOU?

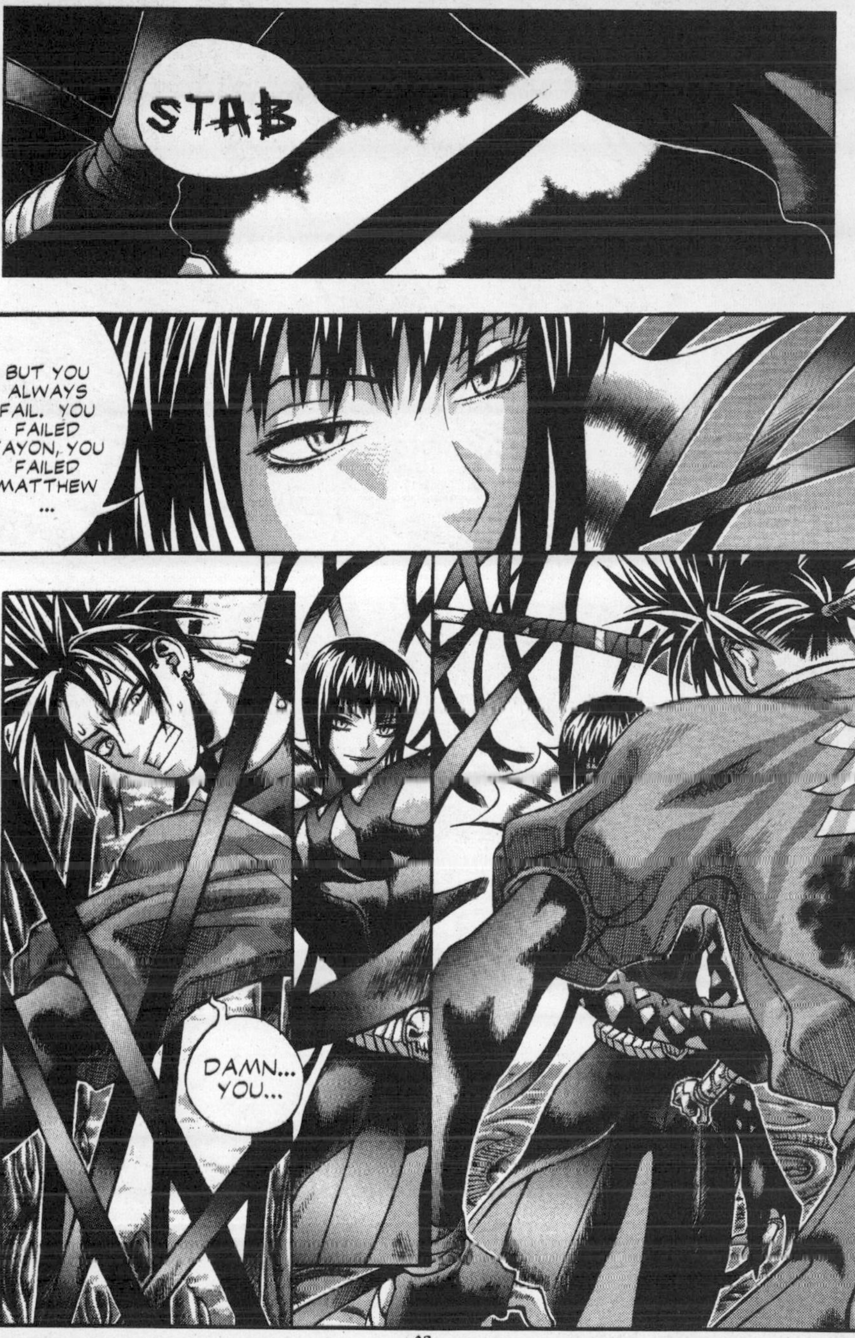
STAB
BUT YOU ALWAYS FAIL. YOU FAILED FAYON, YOU FAILED MATTHEW ...
DAMN... YOU...

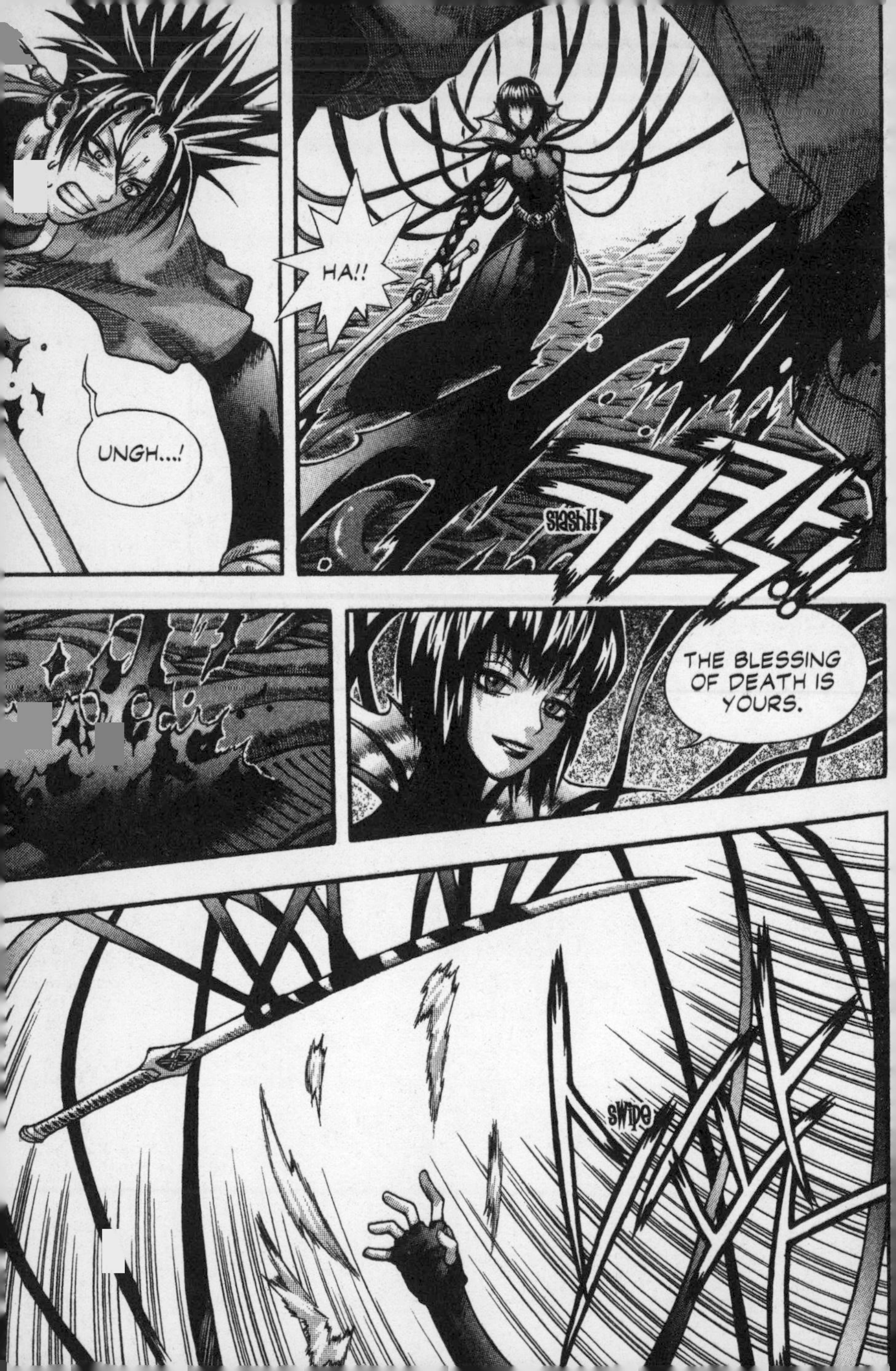
UNGH...!
HA!!
SLASH!!
THE BLESSING OF DEATH IS YOURS.
SWIPE

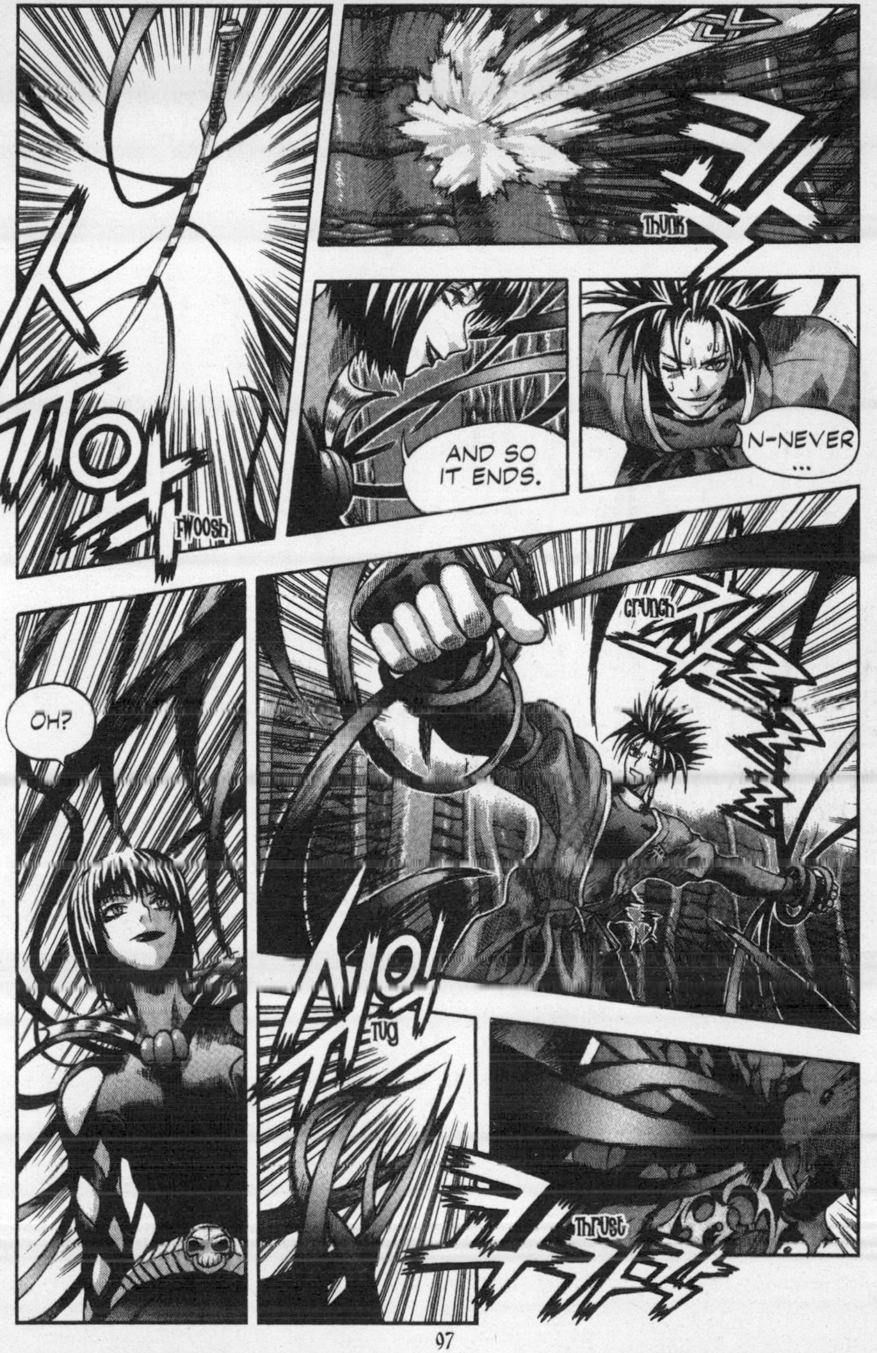
PWOOSH
THUNK
AND SO IT ENDS.
N-NEVER ...
OH?
CRUNCH
TUG
THRUST

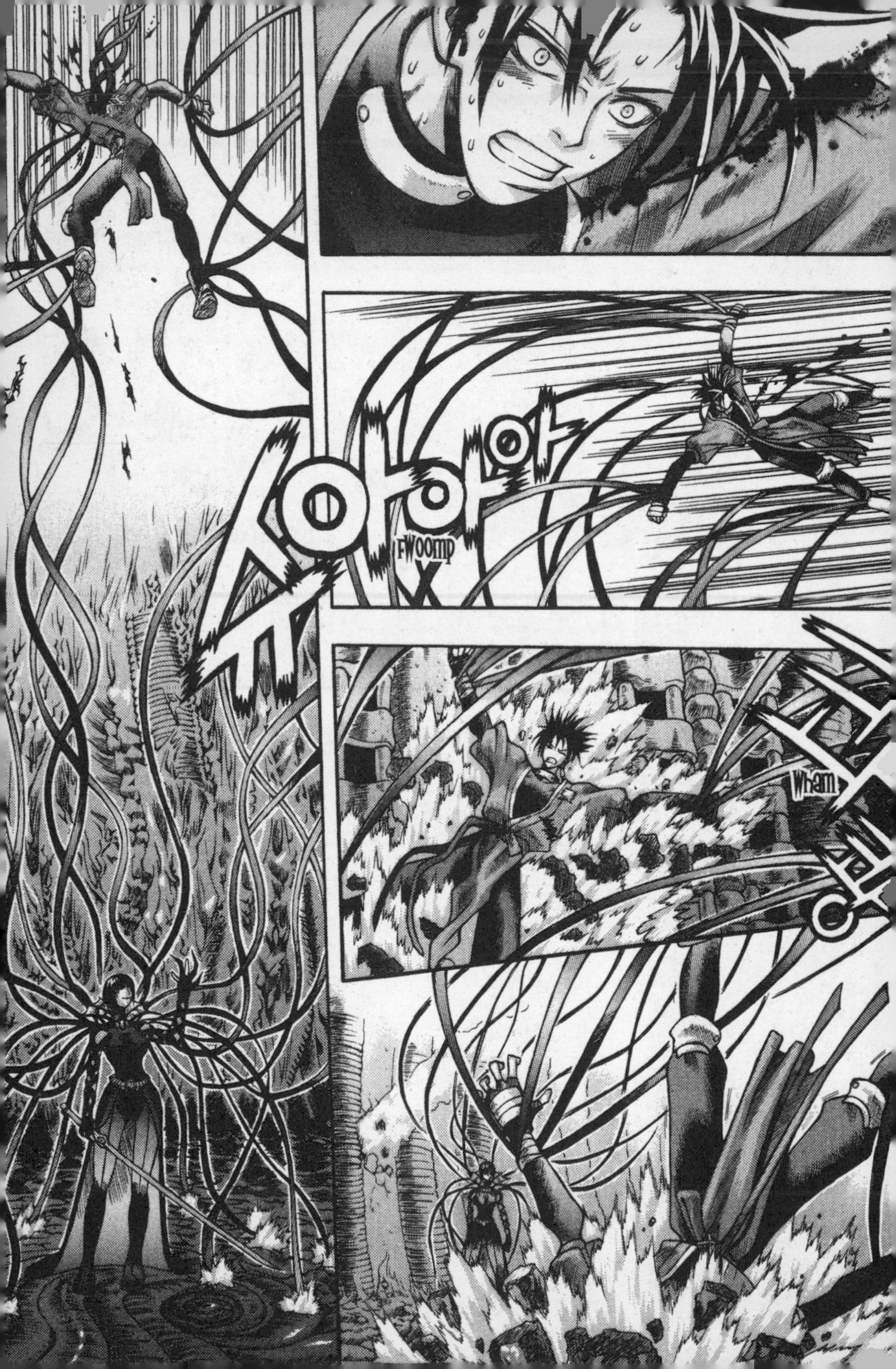
FWOOMP
Wham

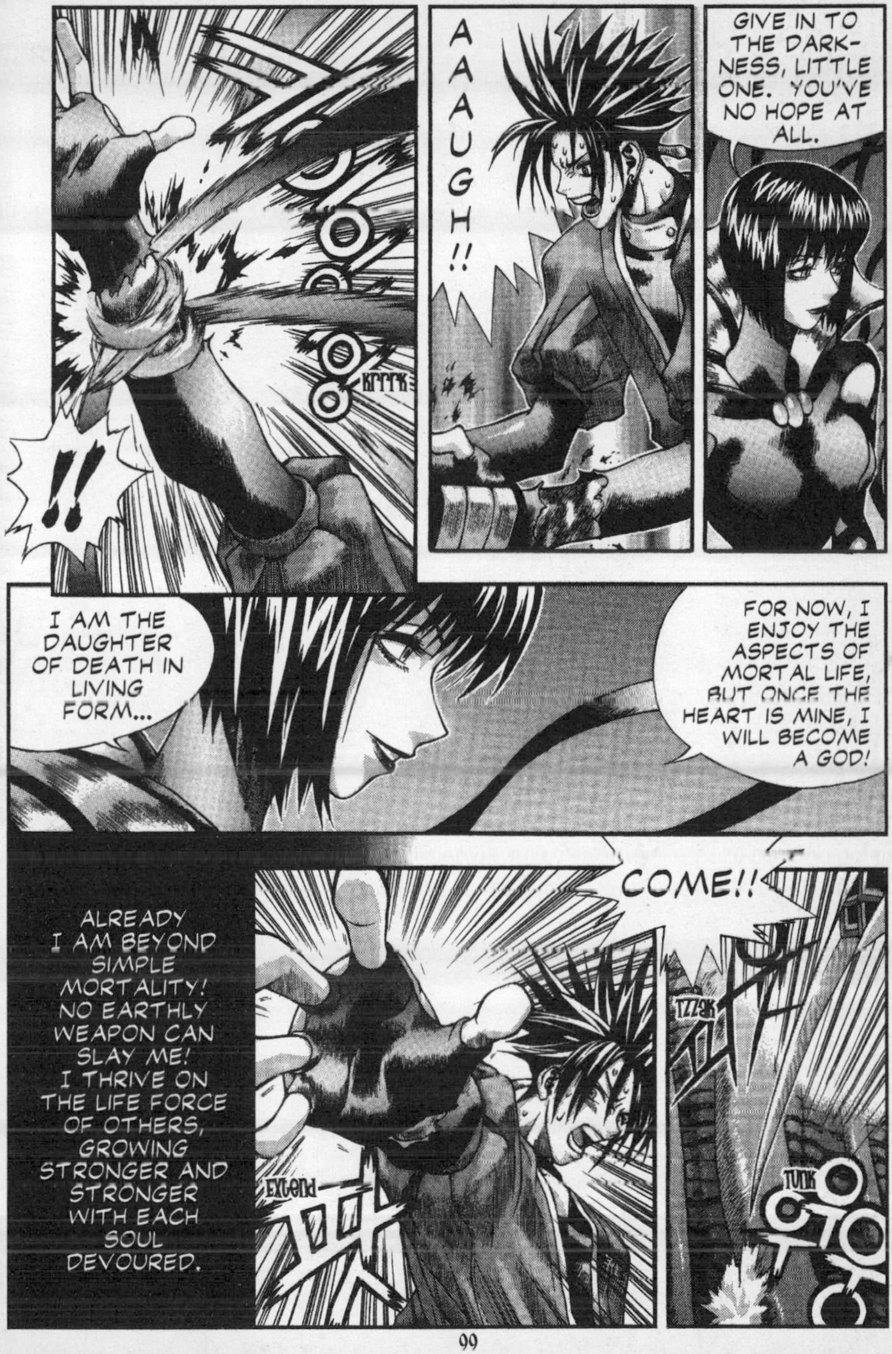
KRRRK
!!
AAAUGH!!
GIVE IN TO THE DARKNESS, LITTLE ONE. YOU'VE NO HOPE AT ALL.
I AM THE DAUGHTER OF DEATH IN LIVING FORM...
FOR NOW, I ENJOY THE ASPECTS OF MORTAL LIFE, BUT ONCE THE HEART IS MINE, I WILL BECOME A GOD!
ALREADY I AM BEYOND SIMPLE MORTALITY! NO EARTHLY WEAPON CAN SLAY ME! I THRIVE ON THE LIFE FORCE OF OTHERS, GROWING STRONGER AND STRONGER WITH EACH SOUL DEVOURED.
COME!!
EXTEND
TZZAK
TUNK

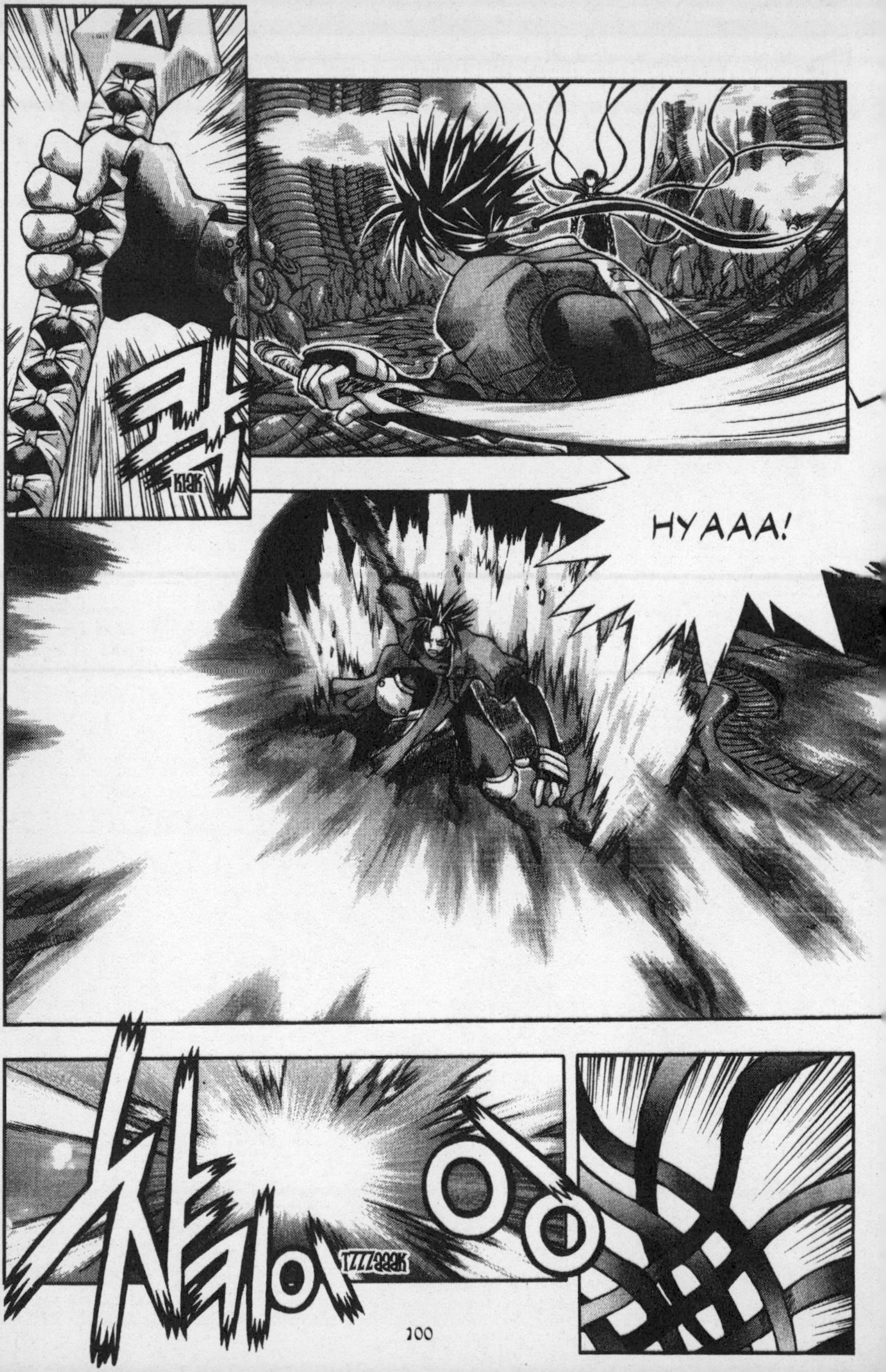
KIGAK
HYAAA!
TZZZGGGK

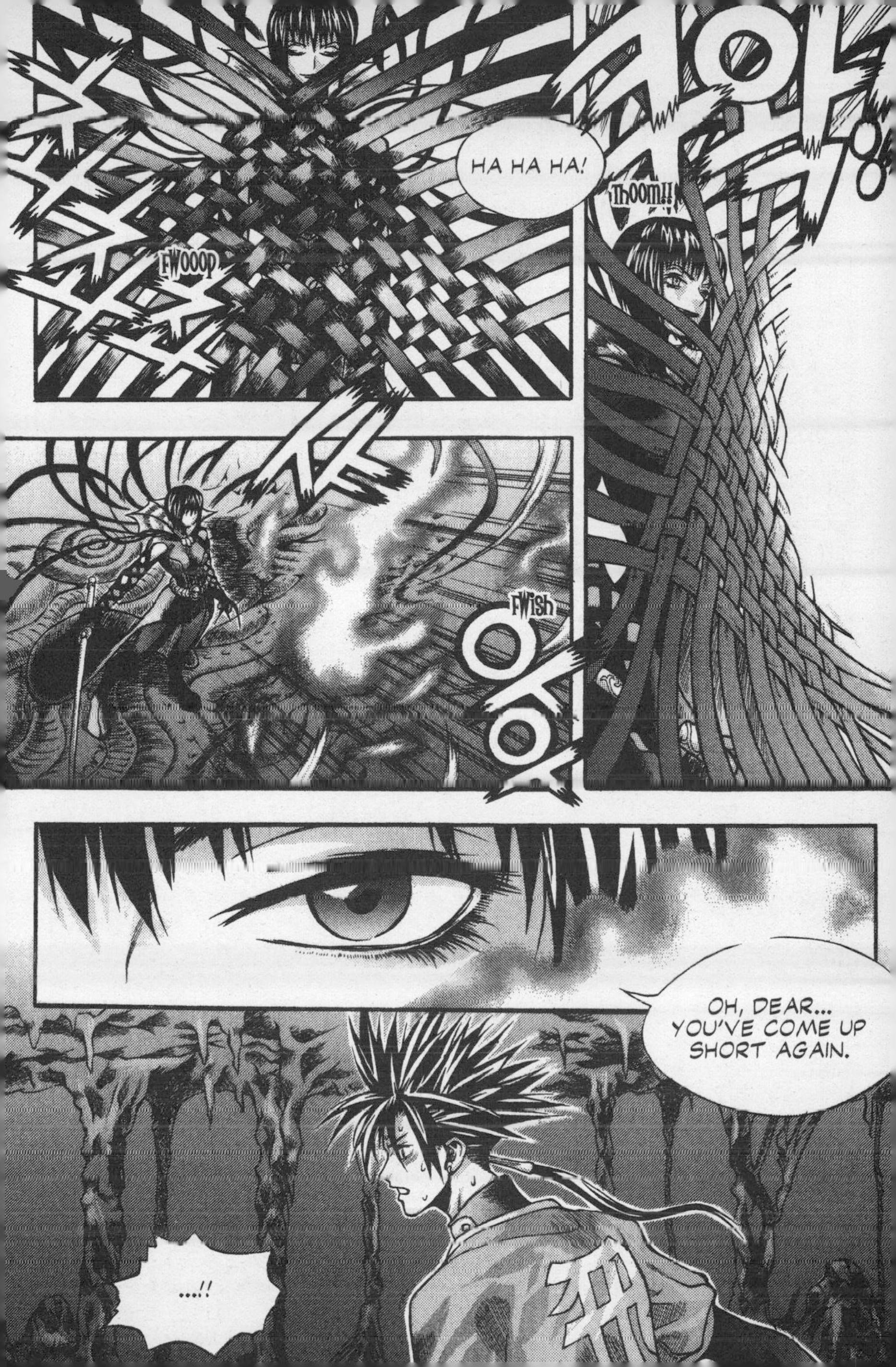
HA HA HA!
FWOOOP
FWISH
THOOM!!
OH, DEAR... YOU'VE COME UP SHORT AGAIN.
...!!

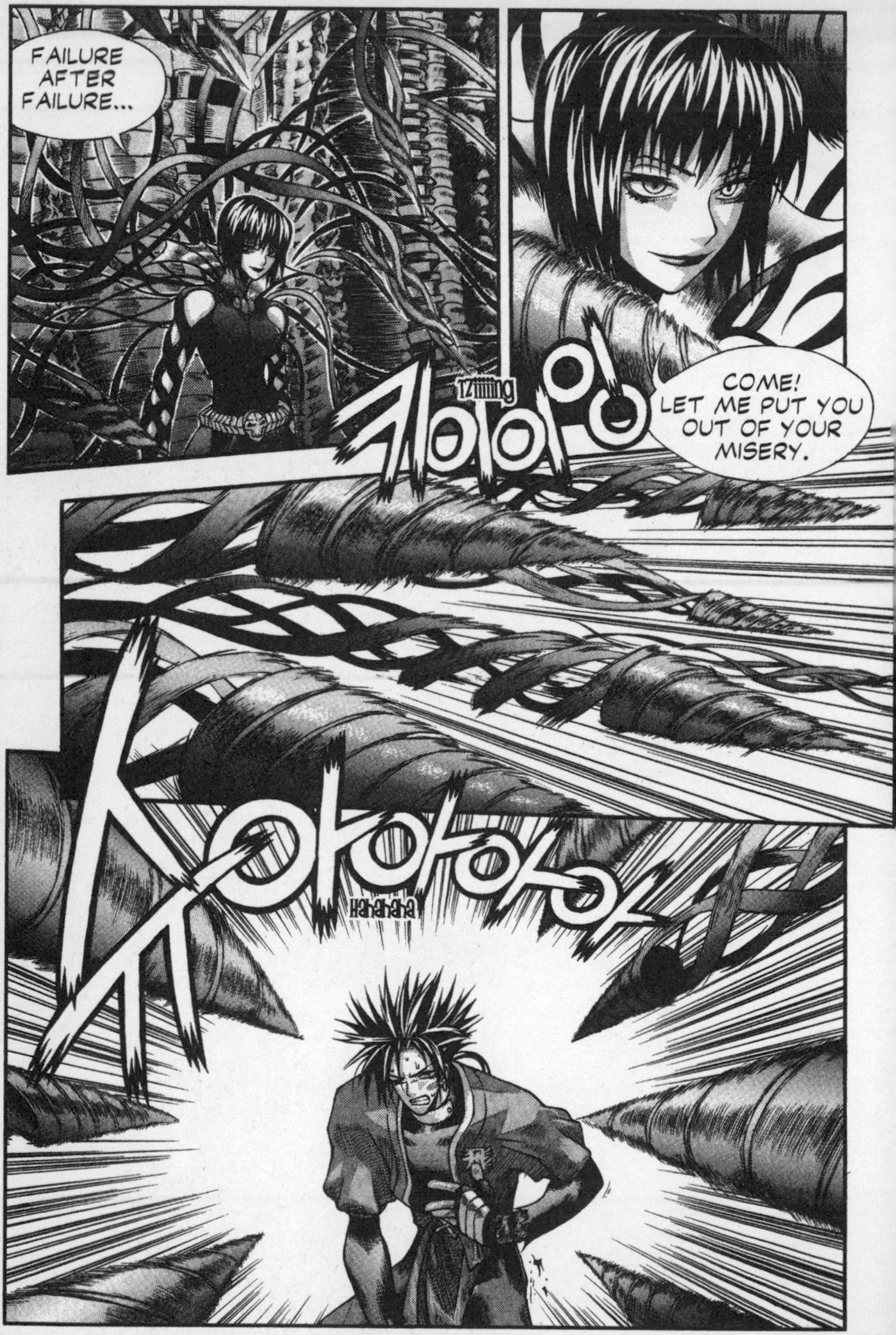
FAILURE AFTER FAILURE...
TZiiiiing
COME! LET ME PUT YOU OUT OF YOUR MISERY.
HaHaHaHa

RAGNAROK
라그나로크
IN TO THE ABYSS

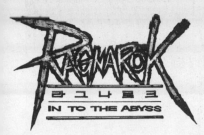

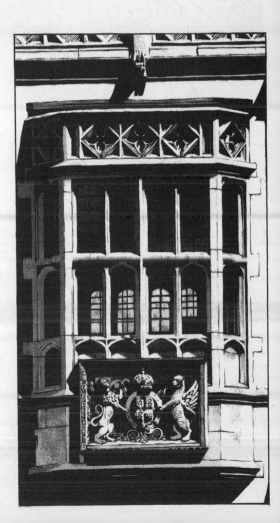

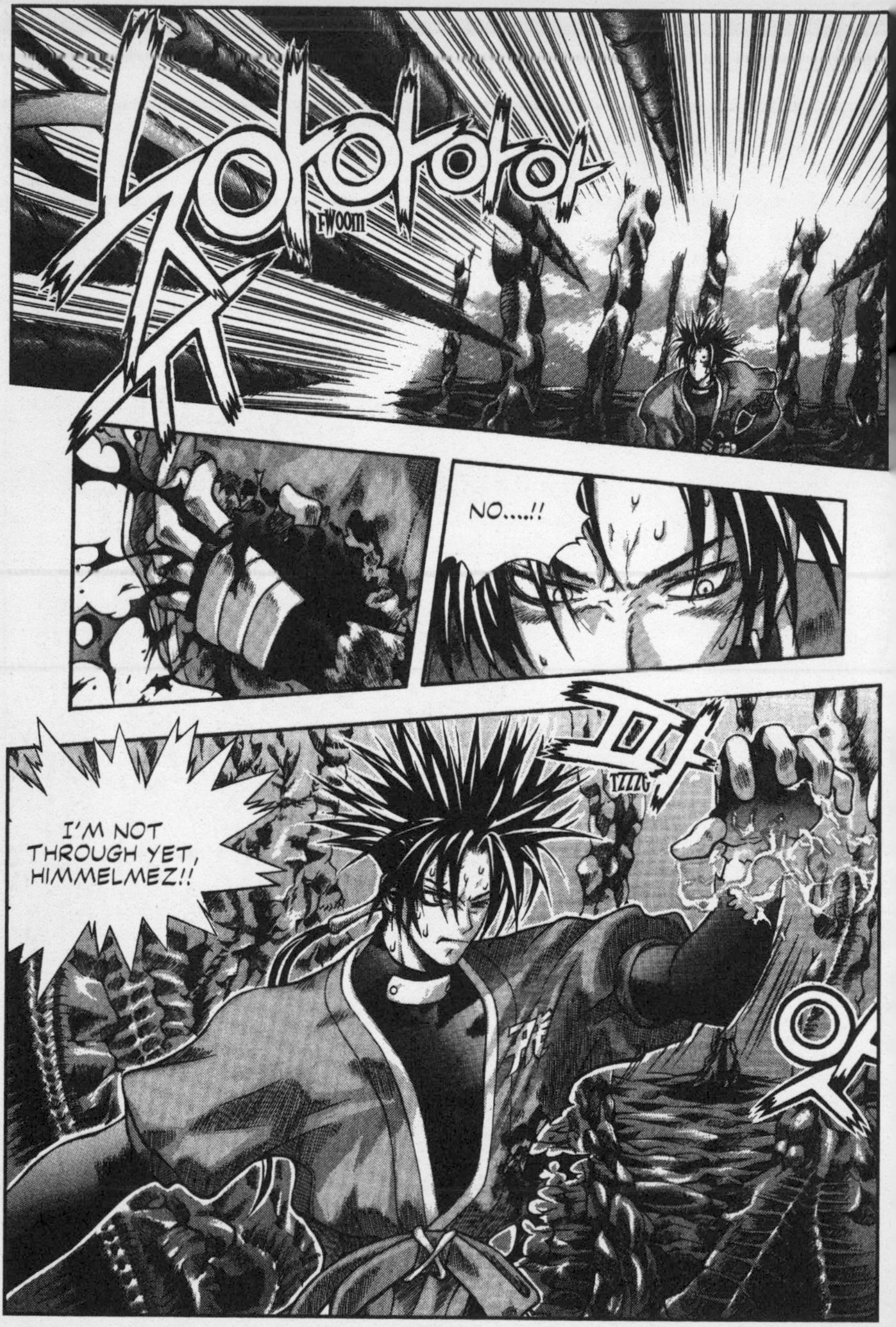
FWOOM
NO....!!
I'M NOT THROUGH YET, HIMMELMEZ!!
TZZZG

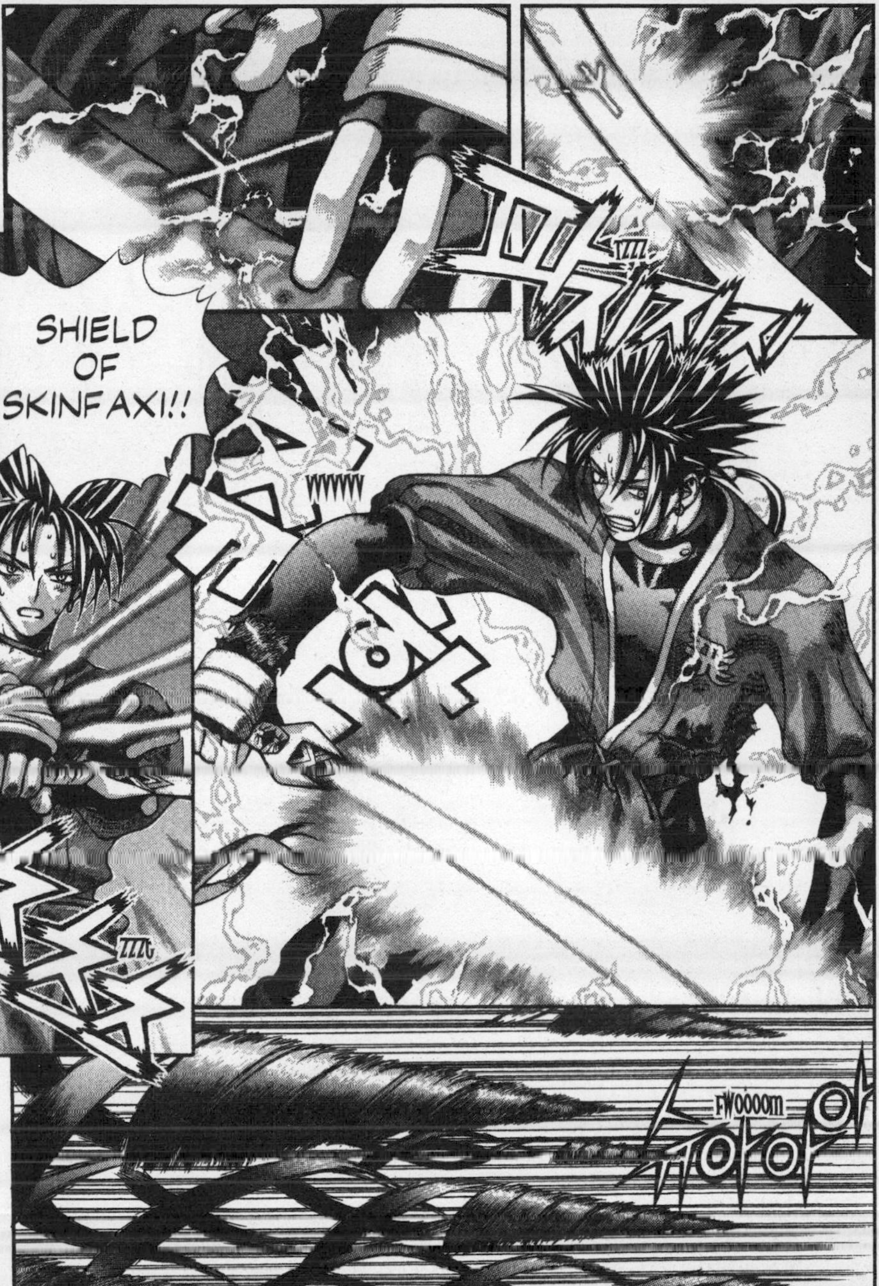
SHIELD OF SKINFAXI!!
fwoooom

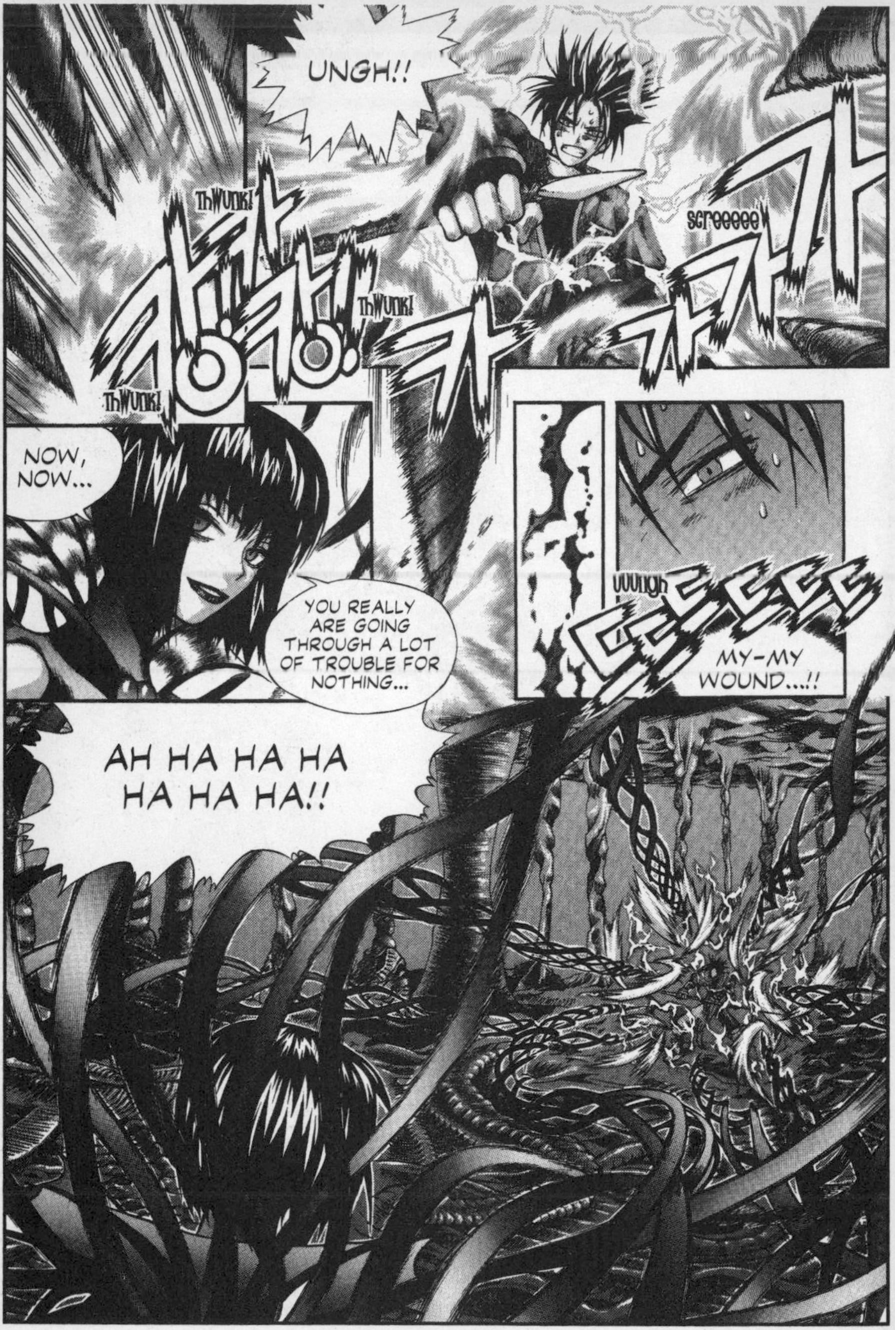
UNGH!!
ThWUNK!
ThWUNK!
ThWUNK!
screeeeee
NOW, NOW...
YOU REALLY ARE GOING THROUGH A LOT OF TROUBLE FOR NOTHING...
uuugh
MY-MY WOUND...!!
AH HA HA HA HA HA HA!!

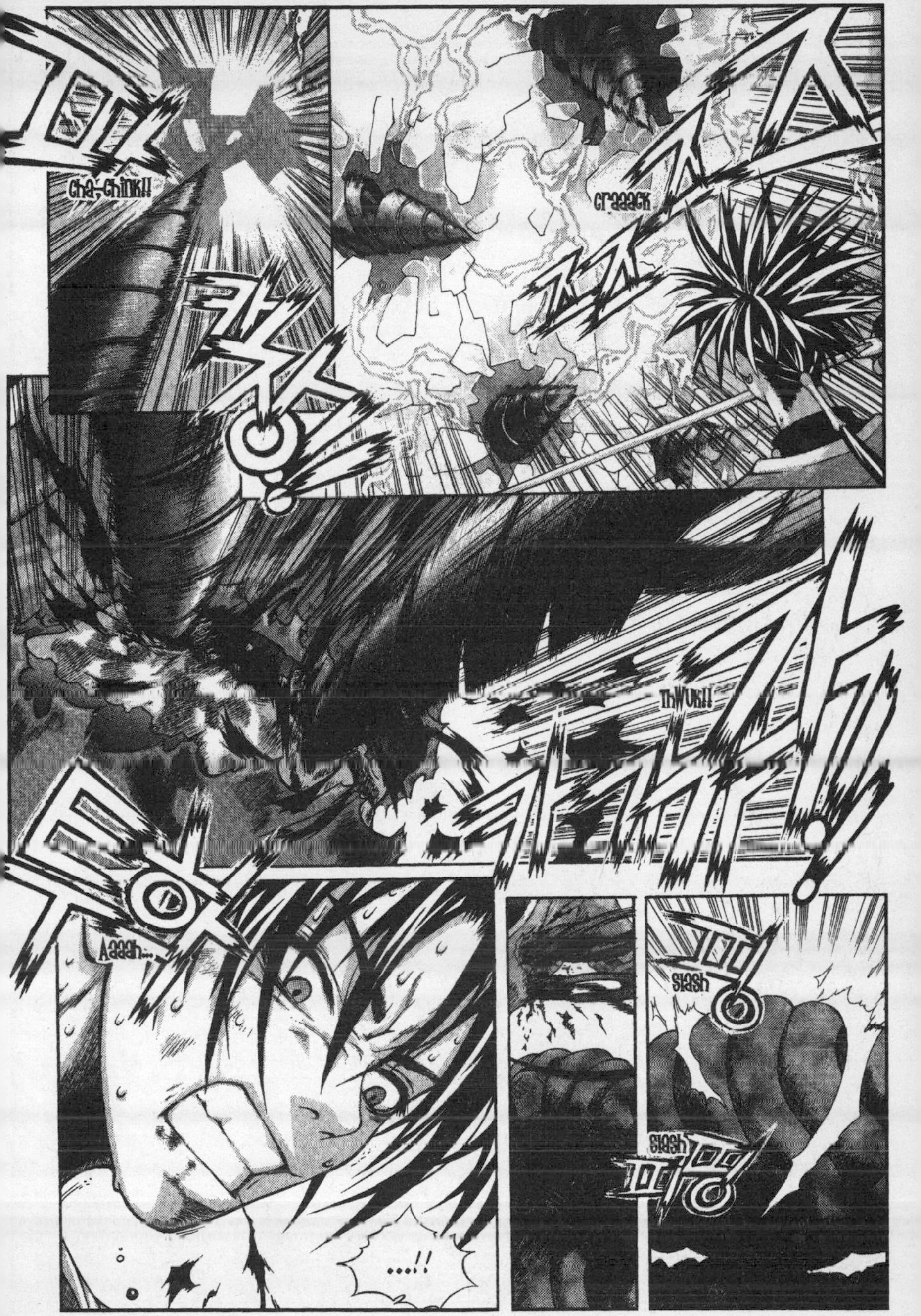
Cha-chink!!
craaack
Thwuk!!
Aaaah...
...!!
Slash
Slash

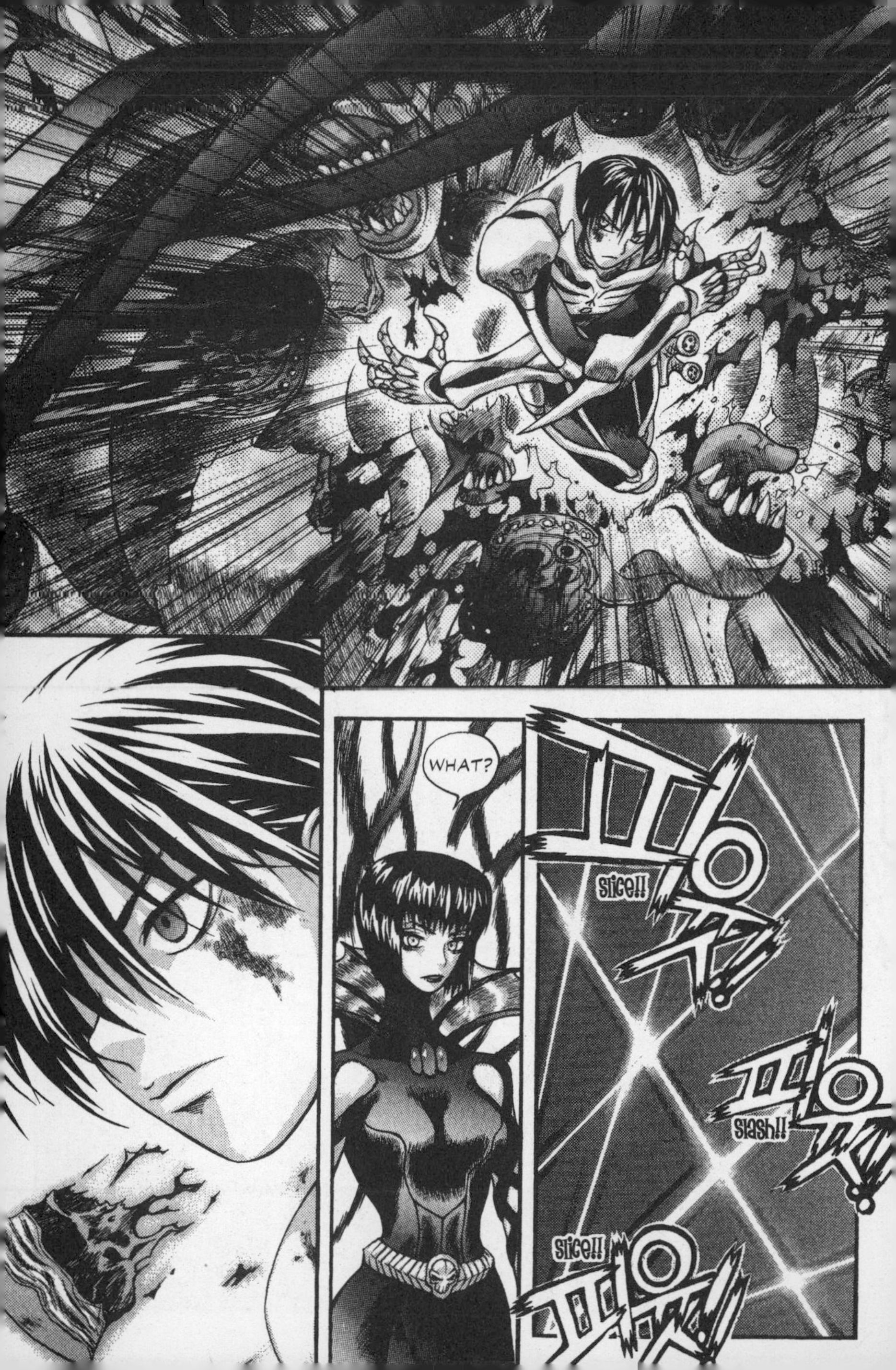
WHAT?
slice!!
slash!!
slice!!

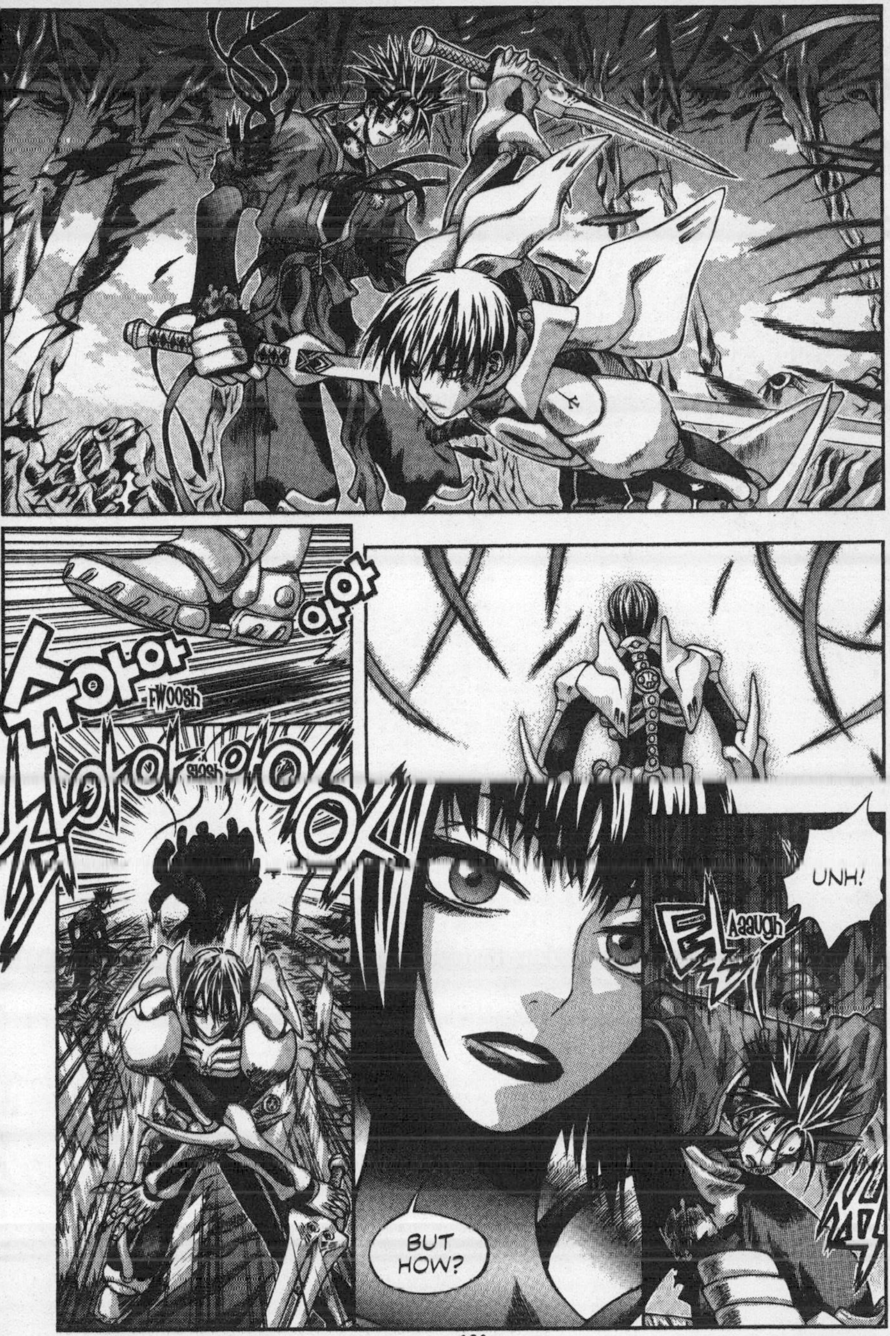
FWOOSH
SLOSH
BUT HOW?
UNH!
Aaaugh

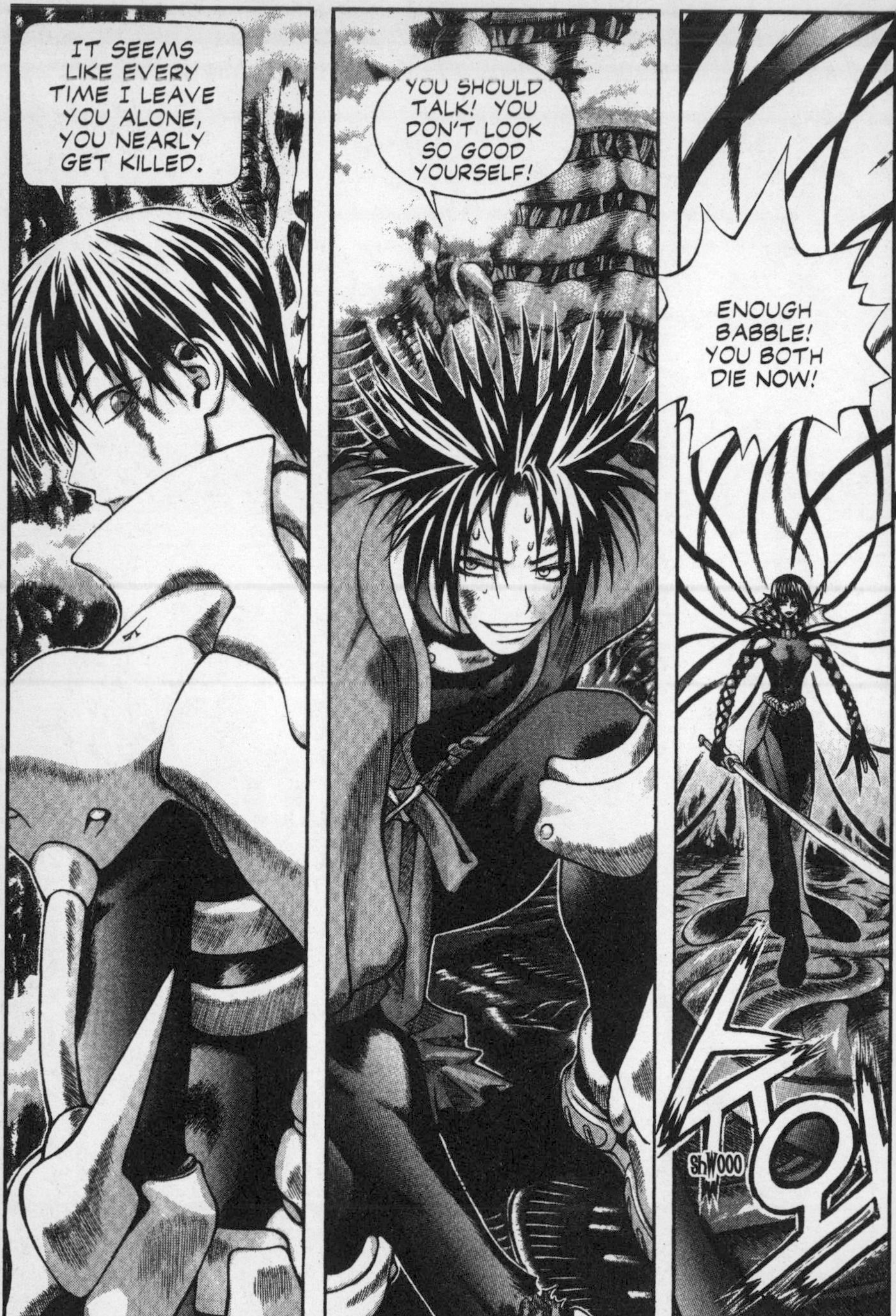
IT SEEMS LIKE EVERY TIME I LEAVE YOU ALONE, YOU NEARLY GET KILLED.
YOU SHOULD TALK! YOU DON'T LOOK SO GOOD YOURSELF!
ENOUGH BABBLE! YOU BOTH DIE NOW!
ShWOOO

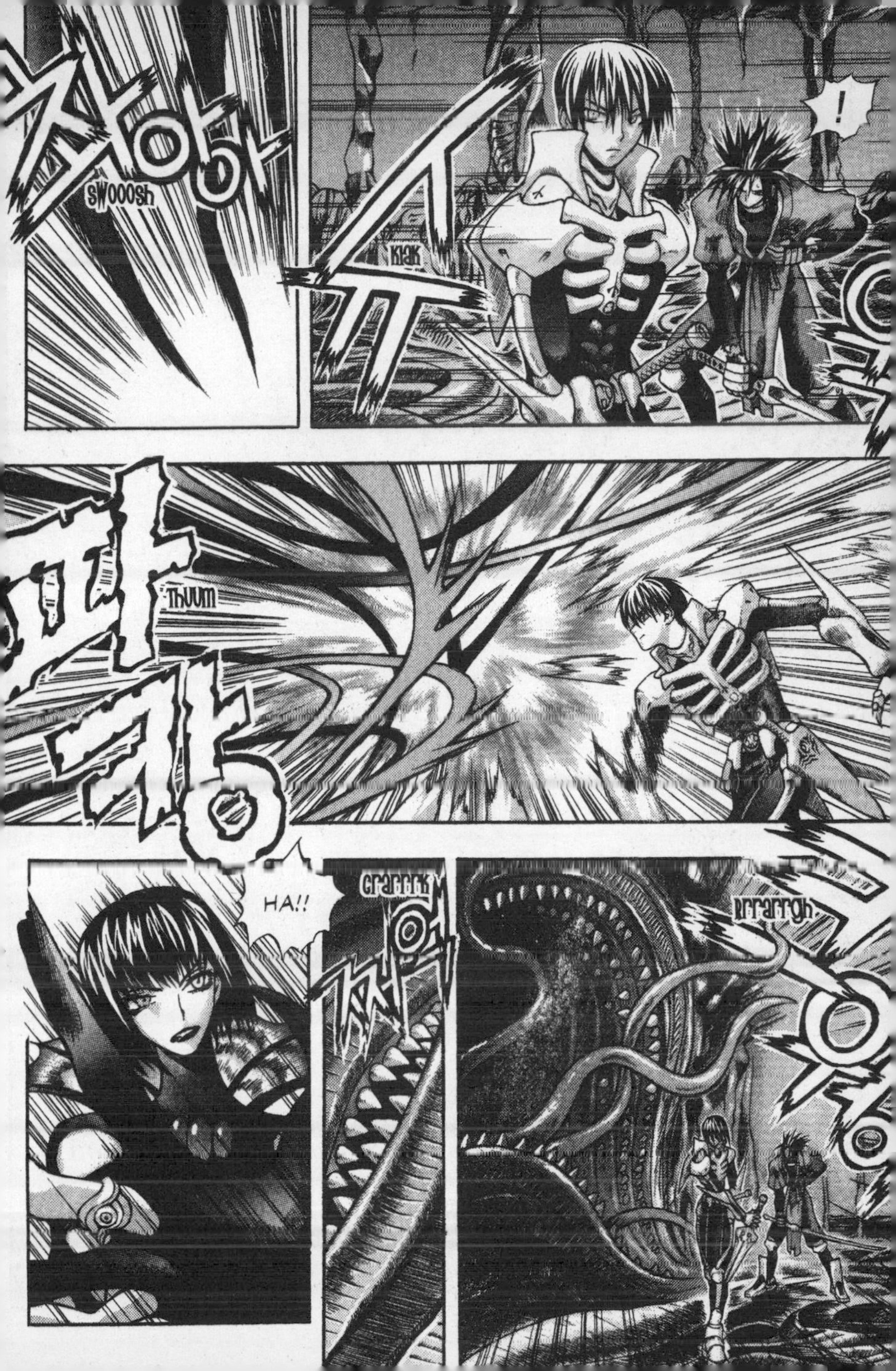
SWOOOSH
KLAK
!
THUUM
HA!!
CRARRRK
RRRARRGH

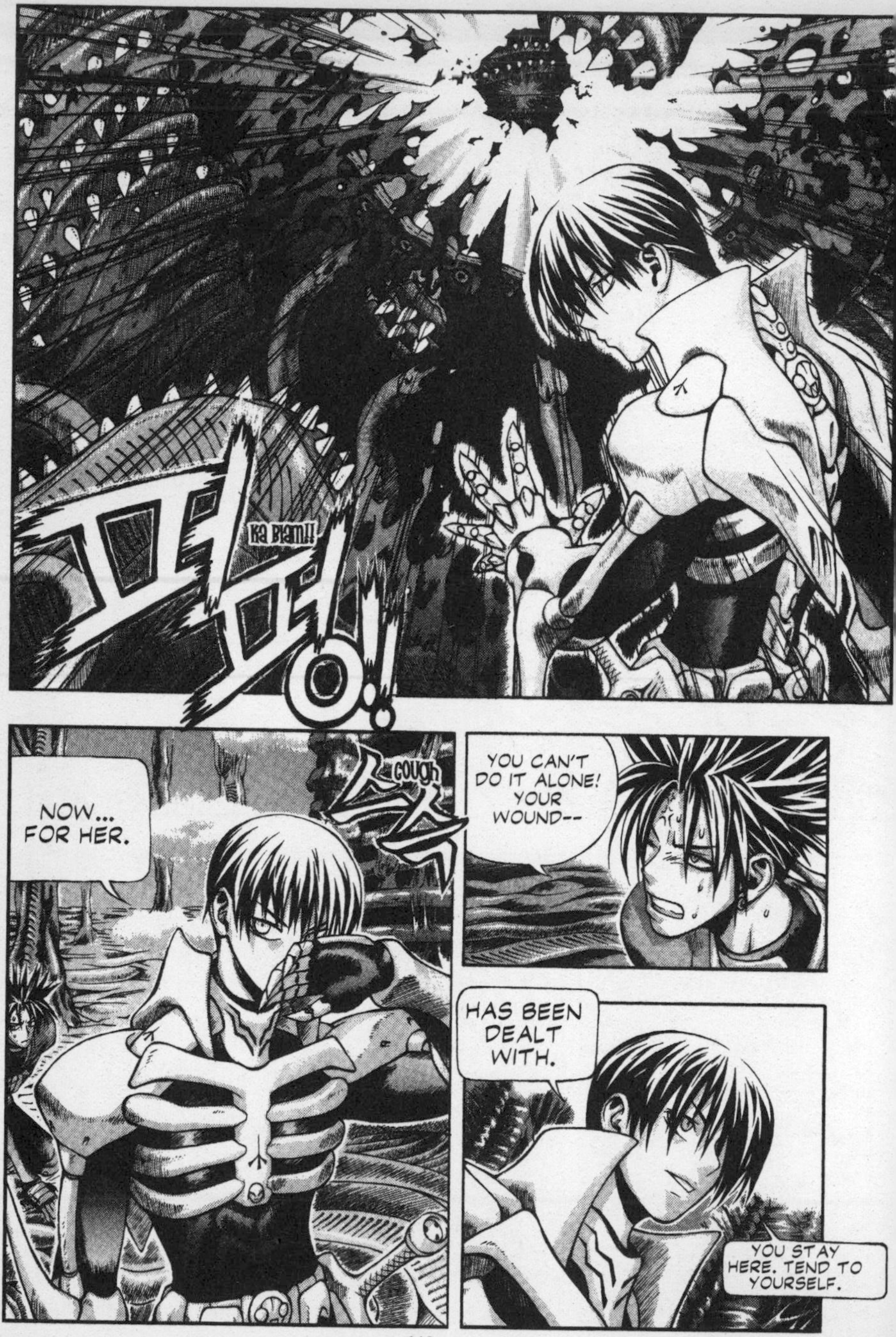
KA BLAM!!
NOW... FOR HER.
cough
YOU CAN'T DO IT ALONE! YOUR WOUND--
HAS BEEN DEALT WITH.
YOU STAY HERE. TEND TO YOURSELF.

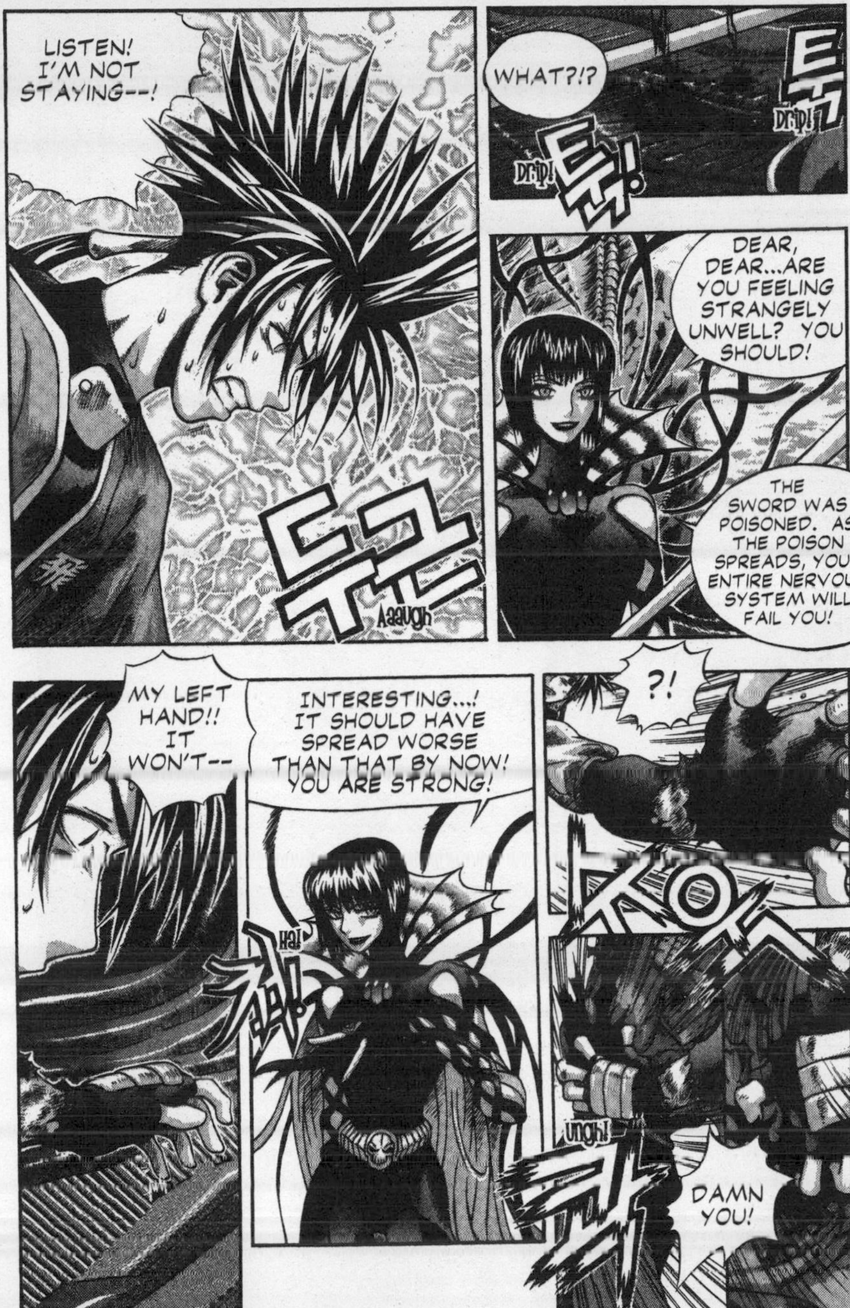
LISTEN! I'M NOT STAYING--!
Aaaugh
WHAT?!?
Drip!
Drip!
DEAR, DEAR...ARE YOU FEELING STRANGELY UNWELL? YOU SHOULD!
THE SWORD WAS POISONED. AS THE POISON SPREADS, YOUR ENTIRE NERVOUS SYSTEM WILL FAIL YOU!
MY LEFT HAND!! IT WON'T--
INTERESTING...! IT SHOULD HAVE SPREAD WORSE THAN THAT BY NOW! YOU ARE STRONG!
Ha!
?!
Ungh!
DAMN YOU!

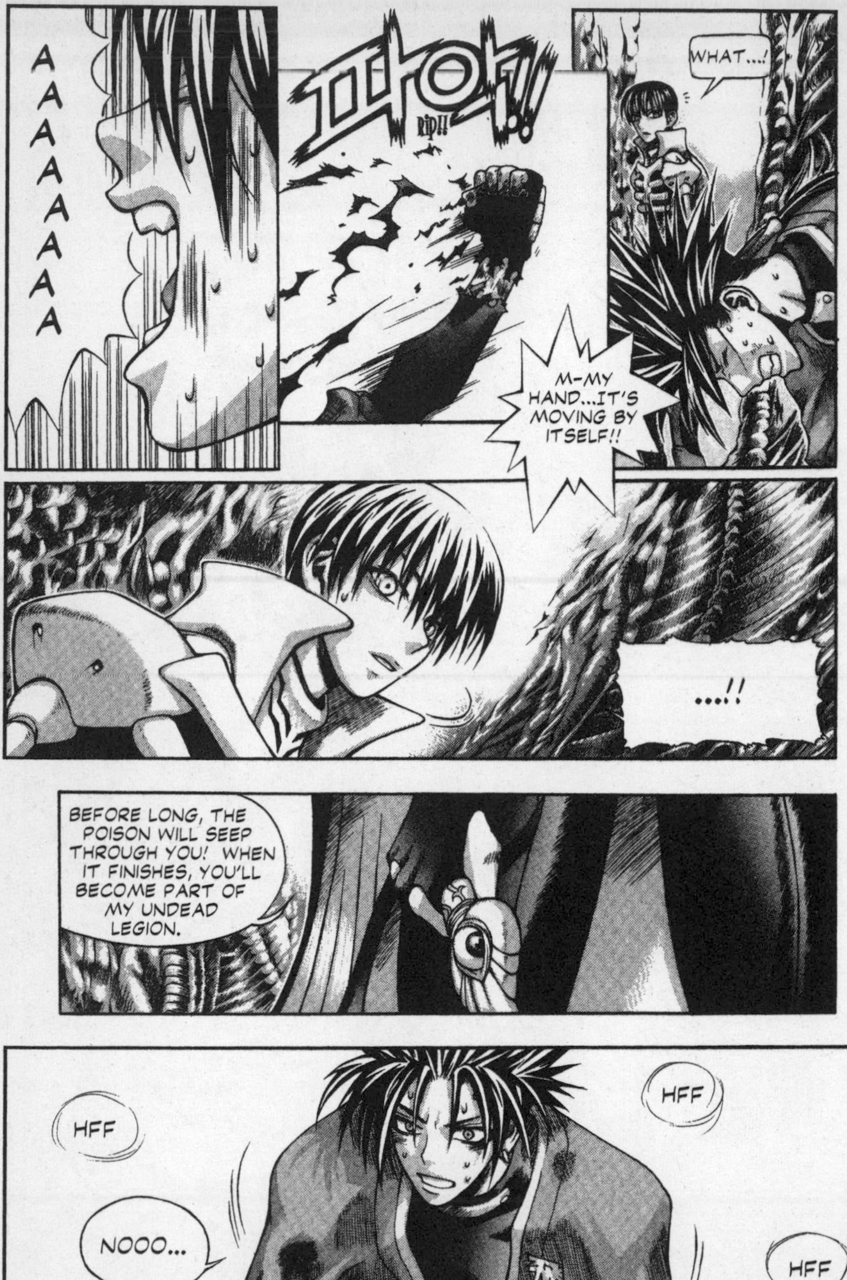

AAAAAAAAA
RIP!!
WHAT...!
M-MY HAND...IT'S MOVING BY ITSELF!!
...!!
BEFORE LONG, THE POISON WILL SEEP THROUGH YOU! WHEN IT FINISHES, YOU'LL BECOME PART OF MY UNDEAD LEGION.
HFF
HFF
NOOO...
HFF

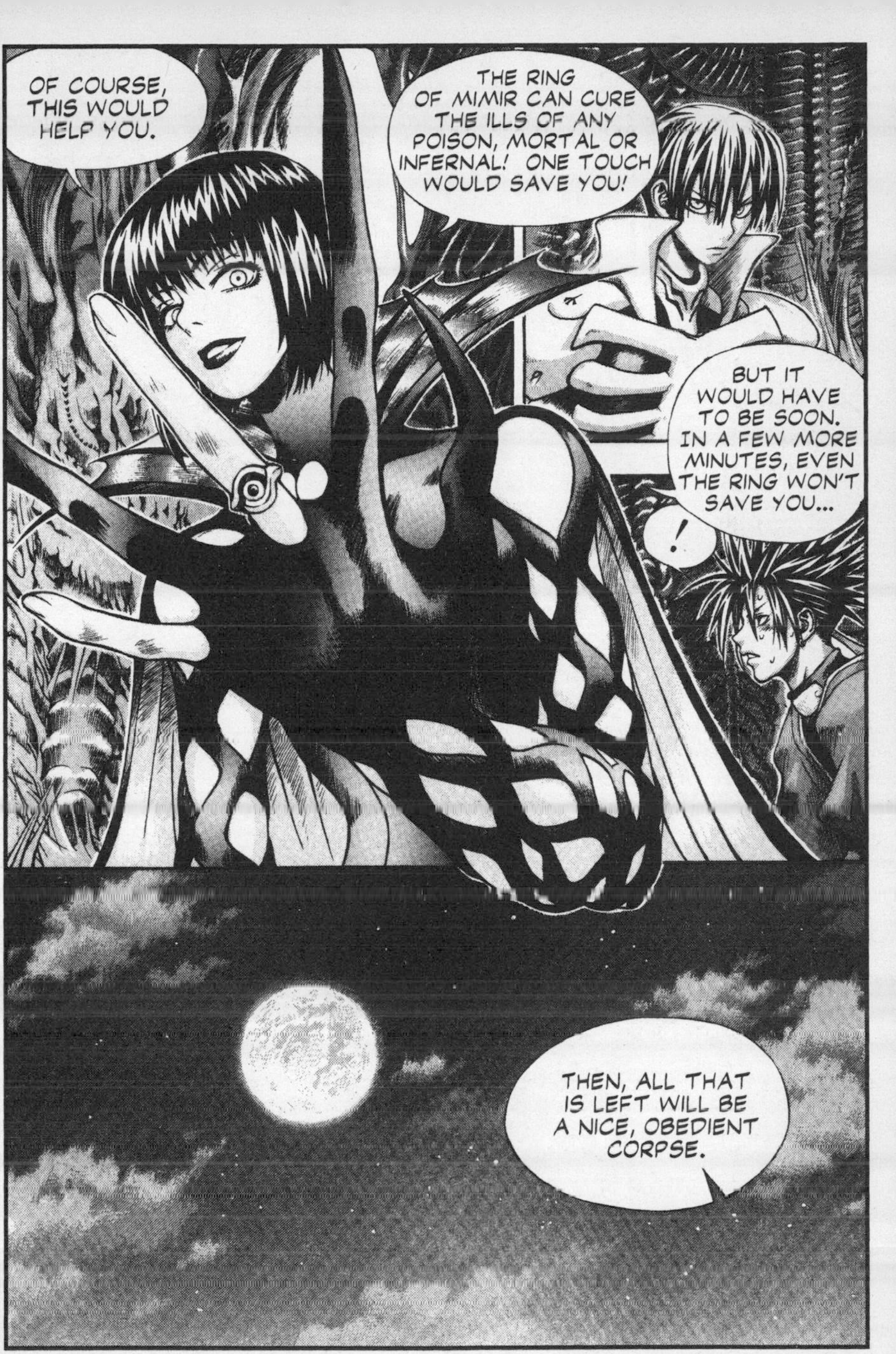
OF COURSE, THIS WOULD HELP YOU.
THE RING OF MIMIR CAN CURE THE ILLS OF ANY POISON, MORTAL OR INFERNAL! ONE TOUCH WOULD SAVE YOU!
BUT IT WOULD HAVE TO BE SOON. IN A FEW MORE MINUTES, EVEN THE RING WON'T SAVE YOU...
!
THEN, ALL THAT IS LEFT WILL BE A NICE, OBEDIENT CORPSE.

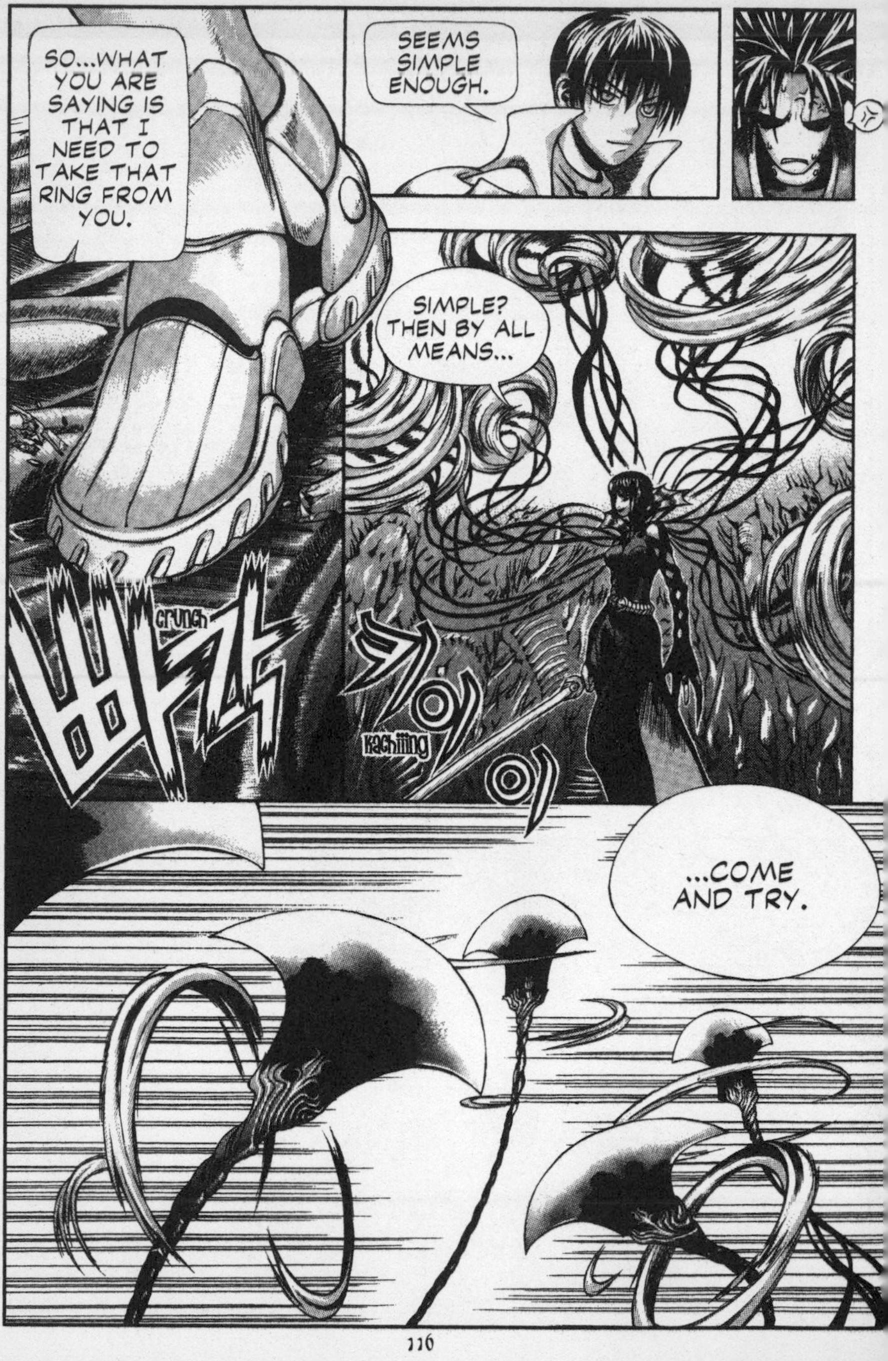
SO...WHAT YOU ARE SAYING IS THAT I NEED TO TAKE THAT RING FROM YOU.
SEEMS SIMPLE ENOUGH.
crunch
SIMPLE? THEN BY ALL MEANS...
kachiiing
...COME AND TRY.

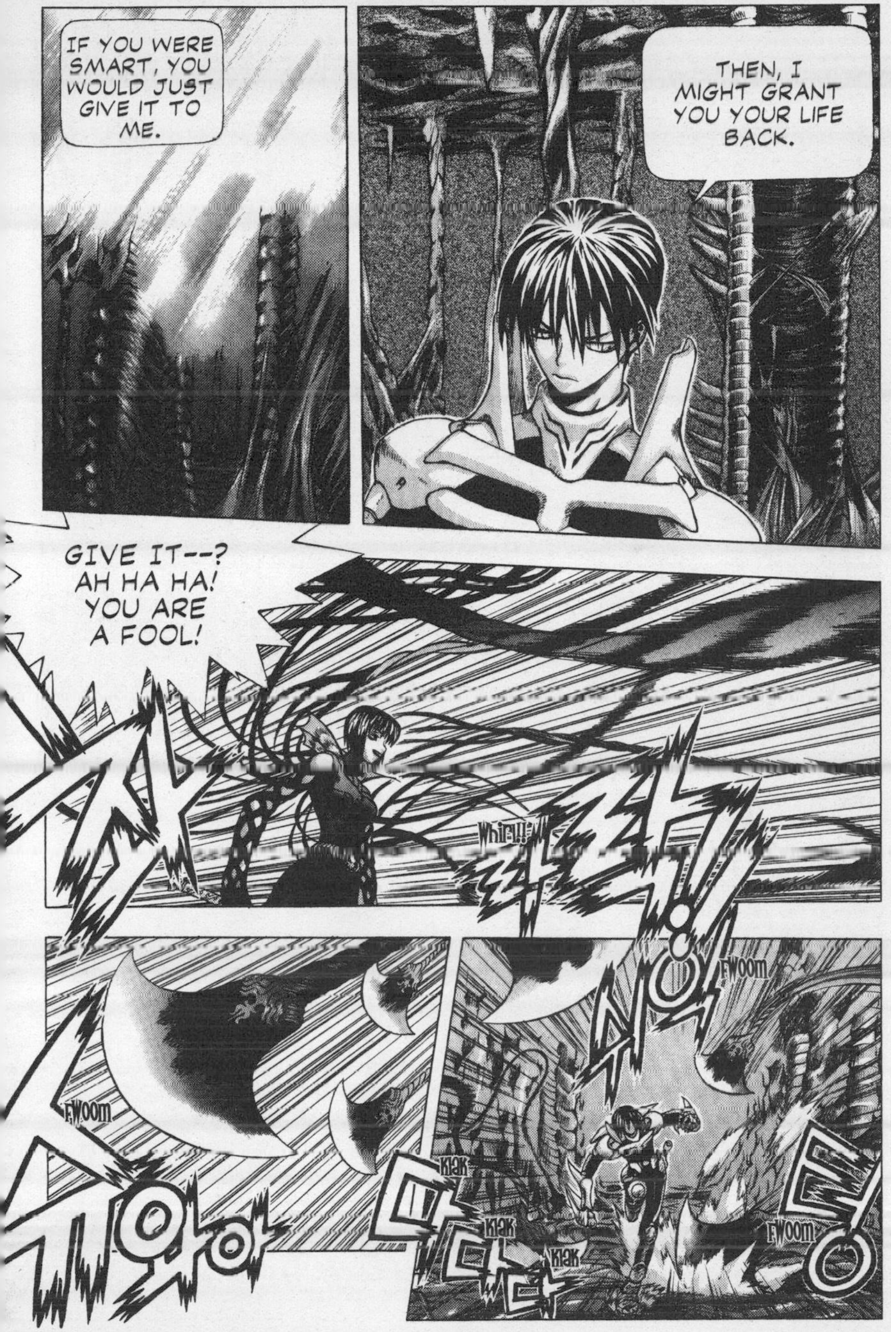
IF YOU WERE SMART, YOU WOULD JUST GIVE IT TO ME.
THEN, I MIGHT GRANT YOU YOUR LIFE BACK.
GIVE IT--? AH HA HA! YOU ARE A FOOL!
Whirl!!
FWOOM
FWOOM
Klak
Klak
Klak
FWOOM

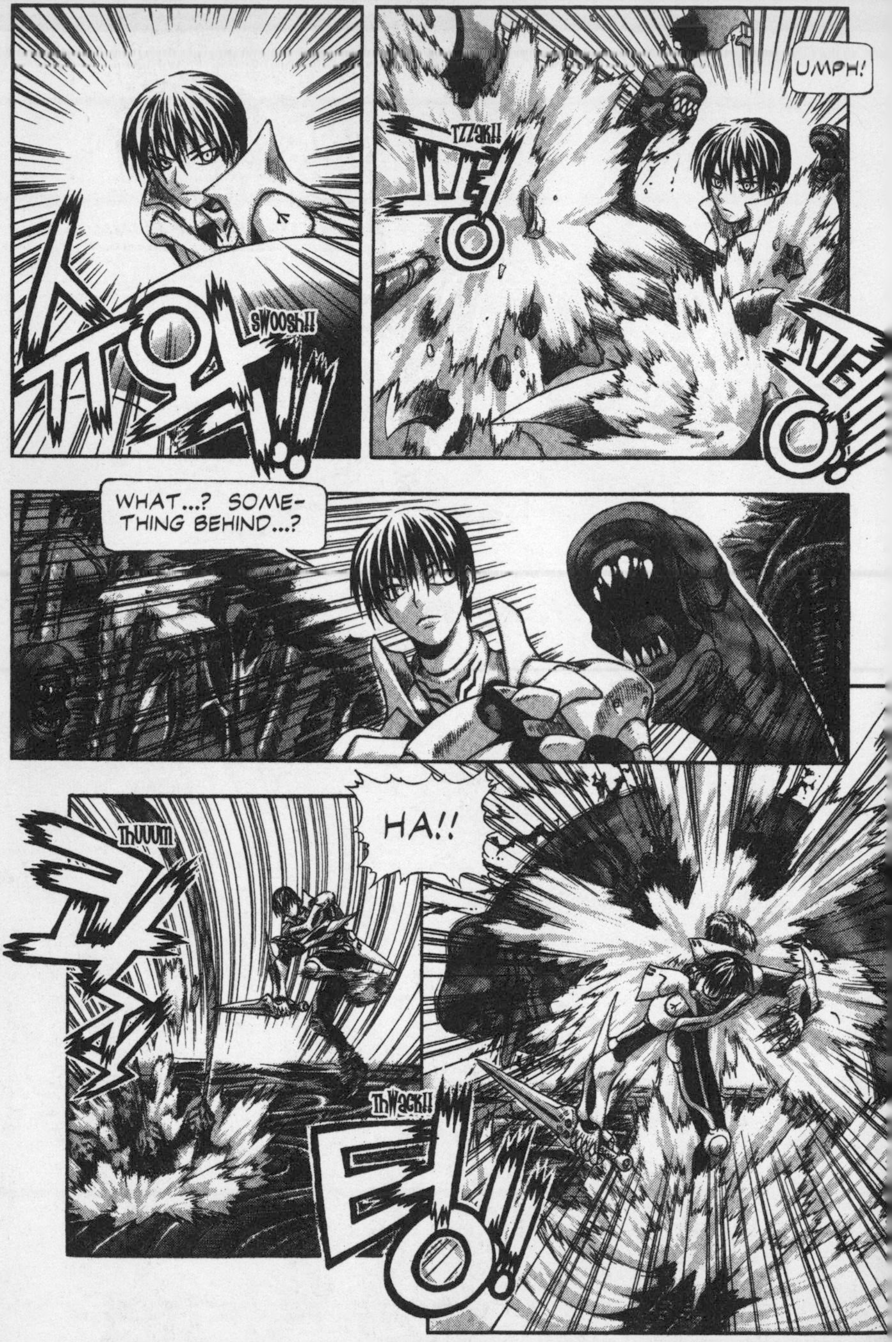
SWOOSH!!
TZZAK!!
UMPH!
WHAT...? SOME-
THING BEHIND...?
THUUUM
HA!!
THWACK!!

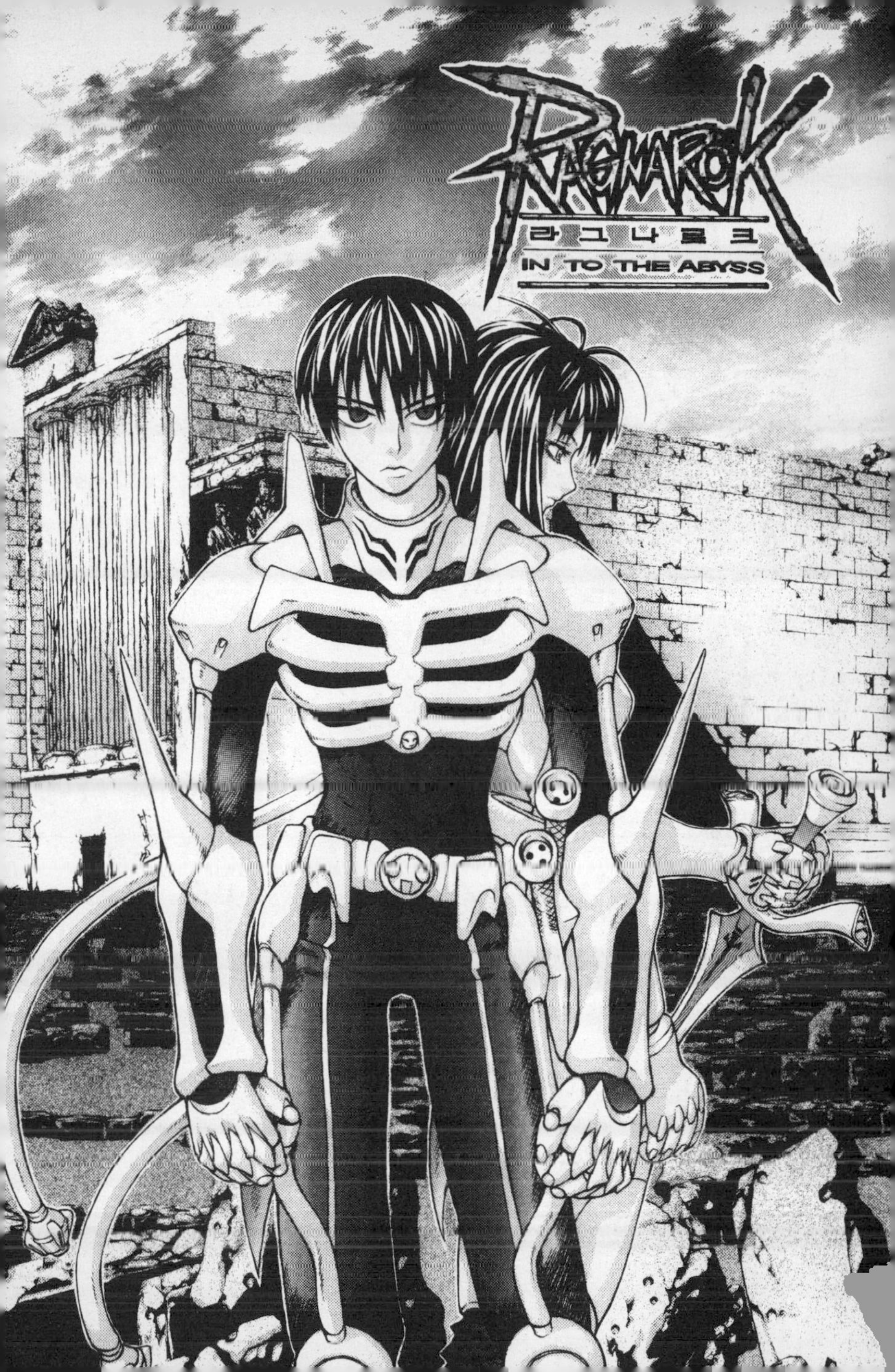
RAGNAROK
라그나로크
IN TO THE ABYSS

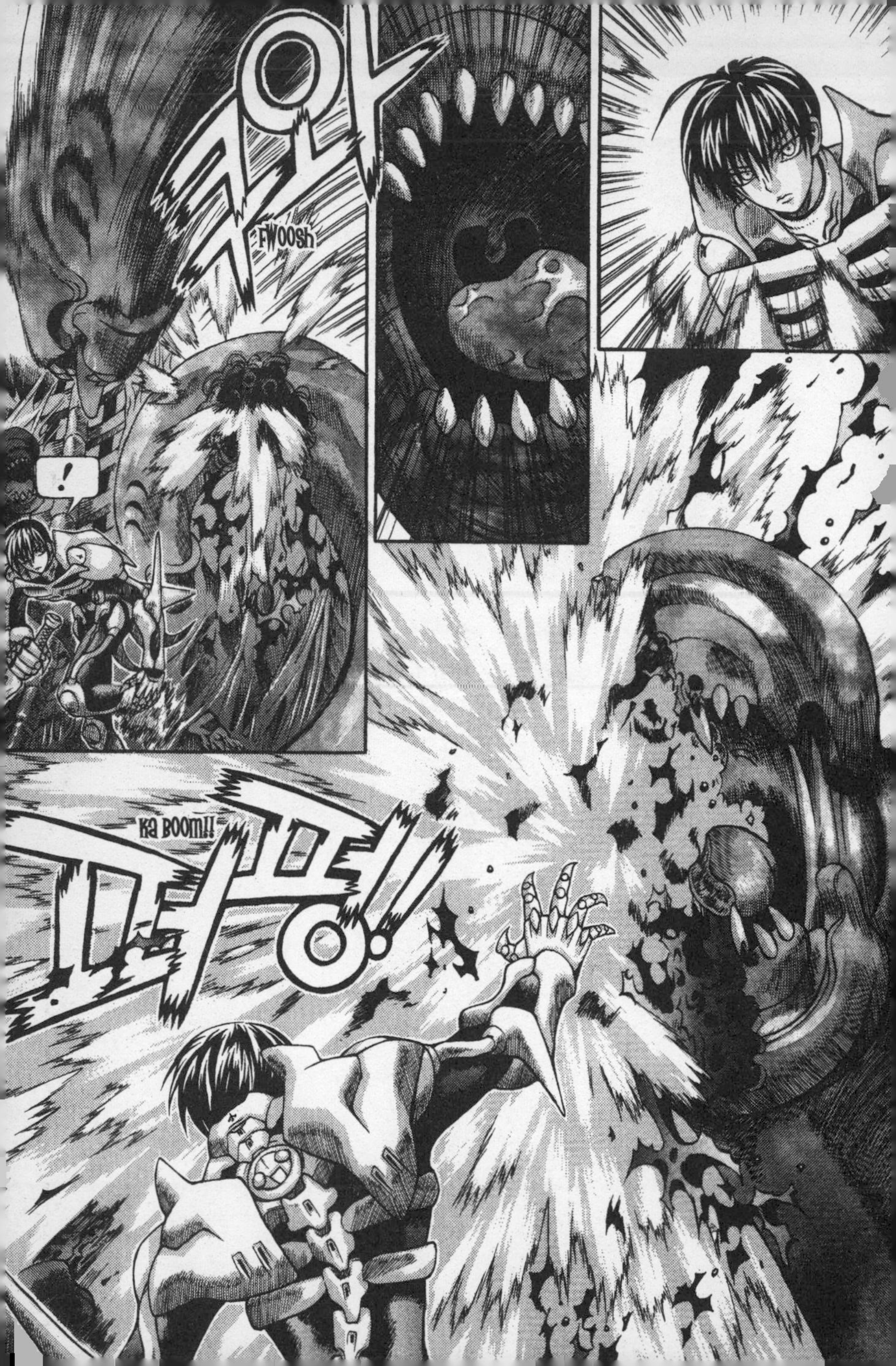
FWOOSH
!
KA BOOM!!

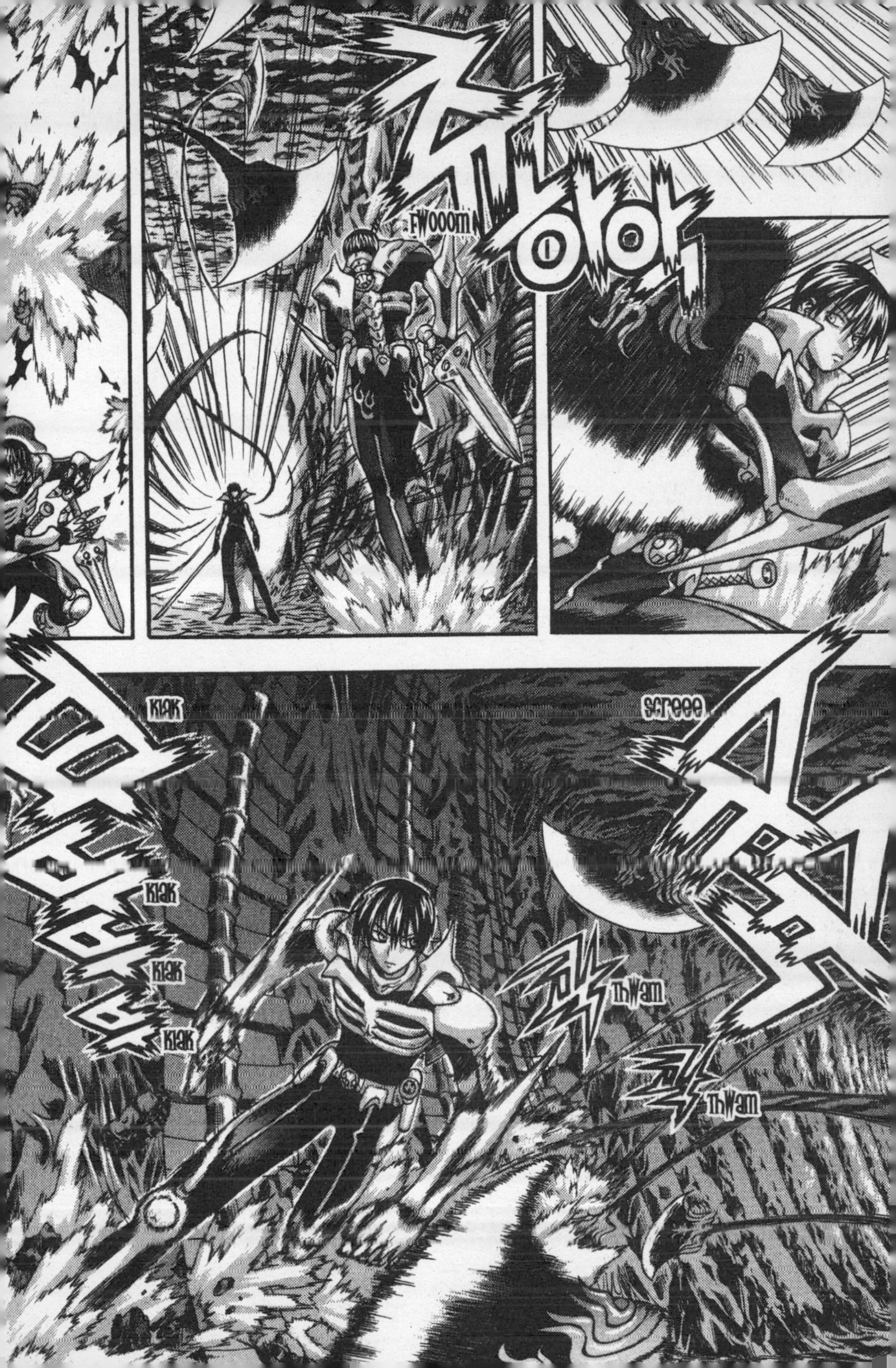
FWOOOM
KLAK
SCREEE
KLAK
KLAK
THWAM
KLAK
THWAM

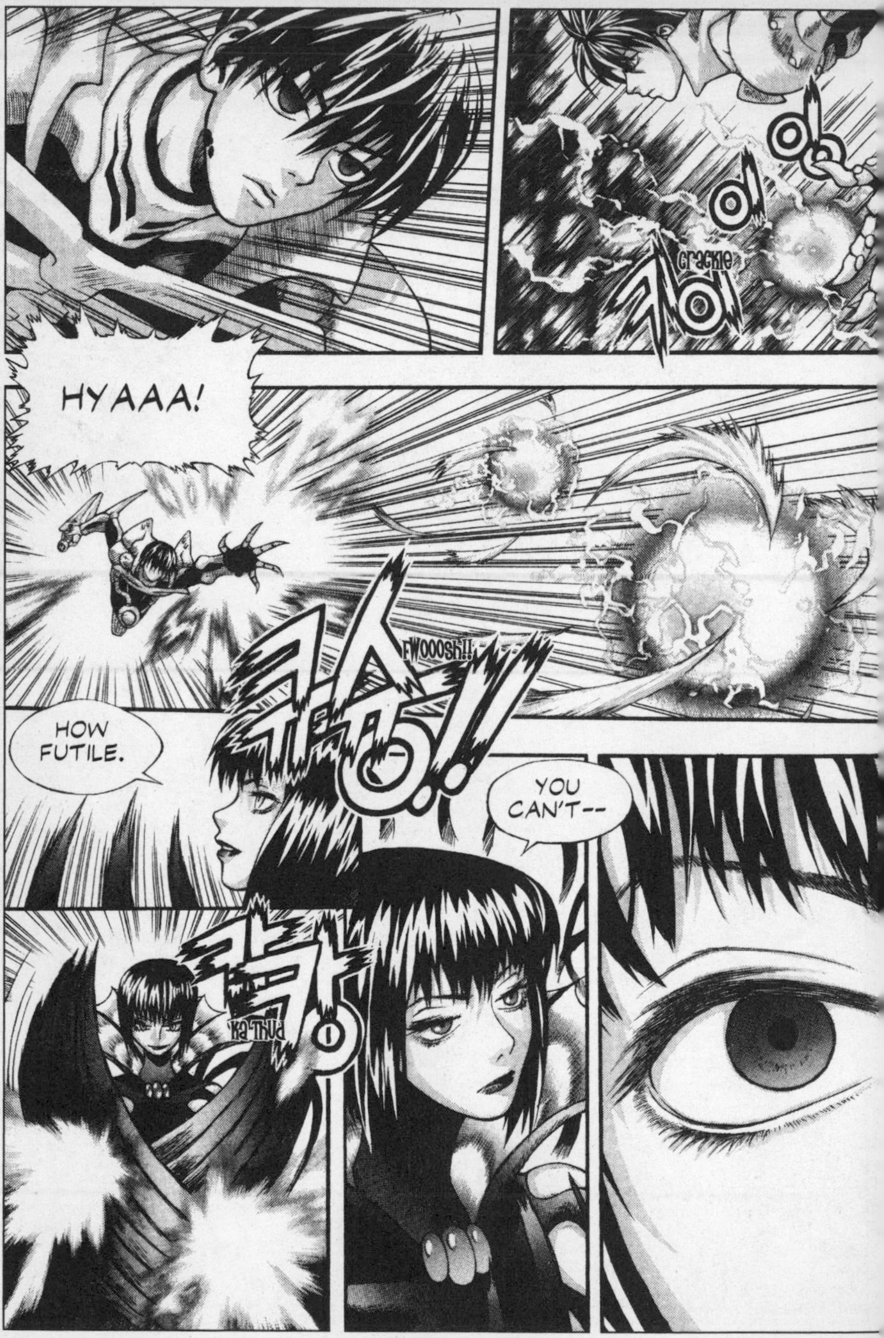
crackle
HYAAA!
FWOOOSH!!
HOW FUTILE.
YOU CAN'T--
KA-THUD

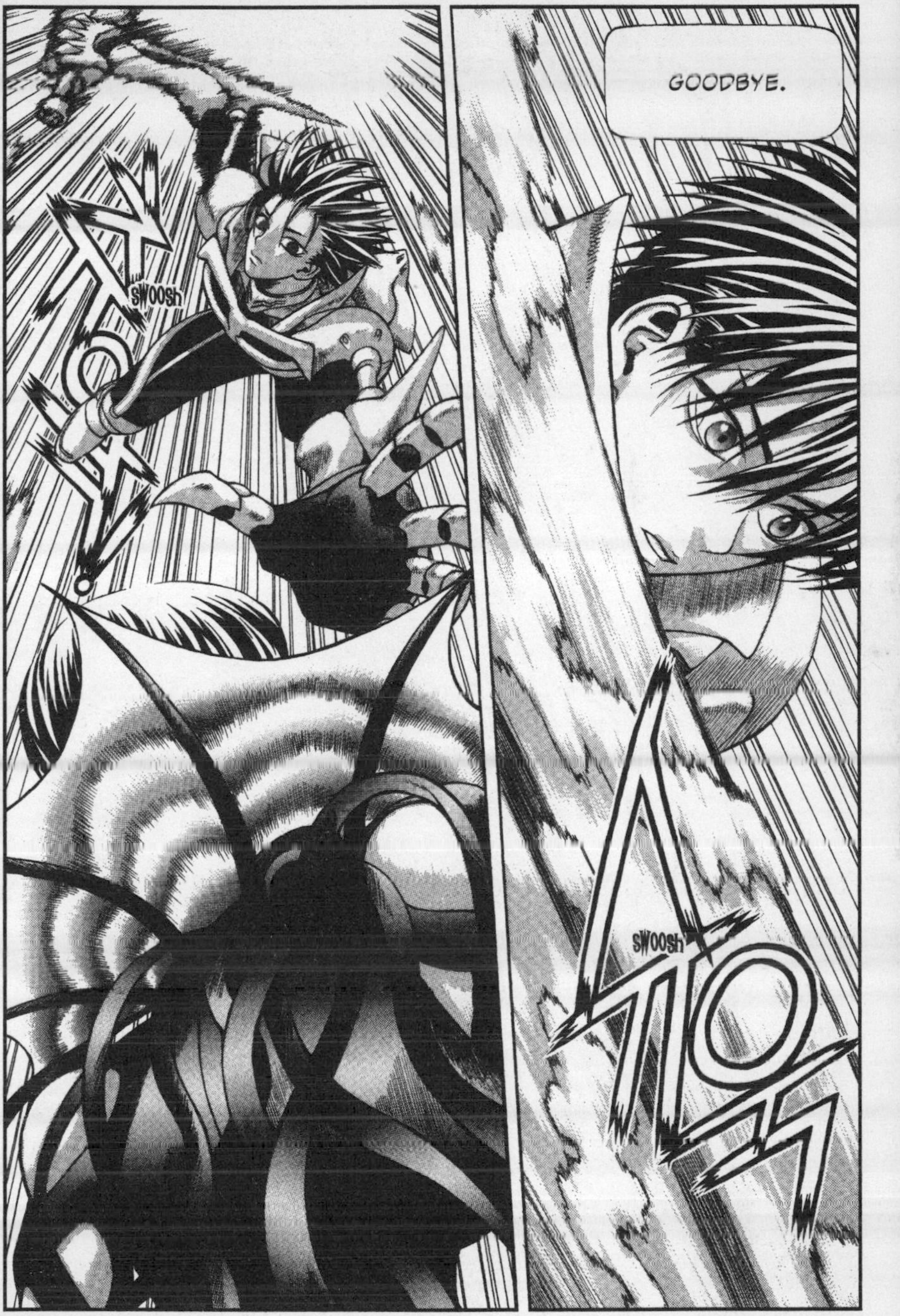
SWOOSH
GOODBYE.
SWOOSH

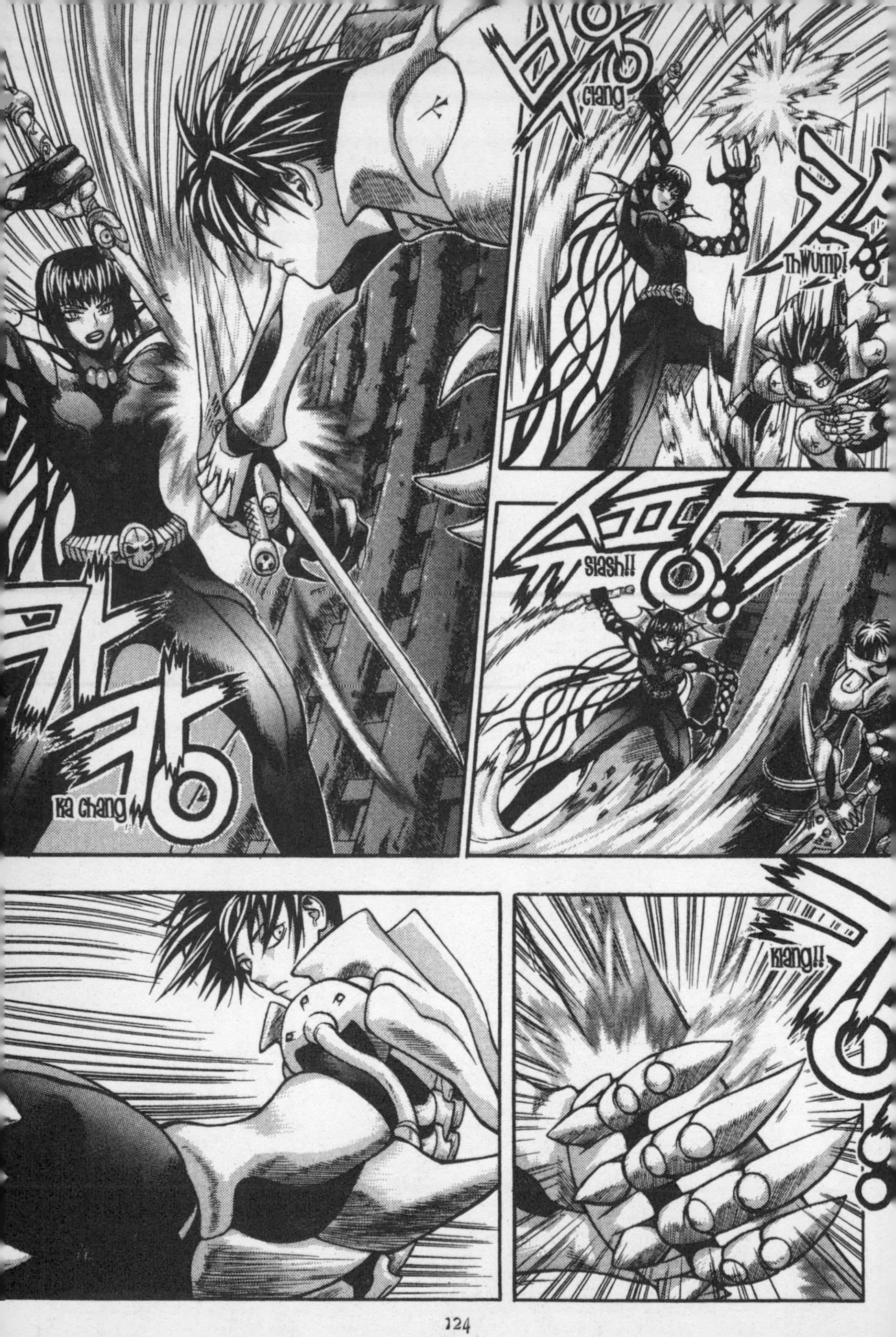
Ka Chang
Clang
ThWump!
Slash!!
Klang!!

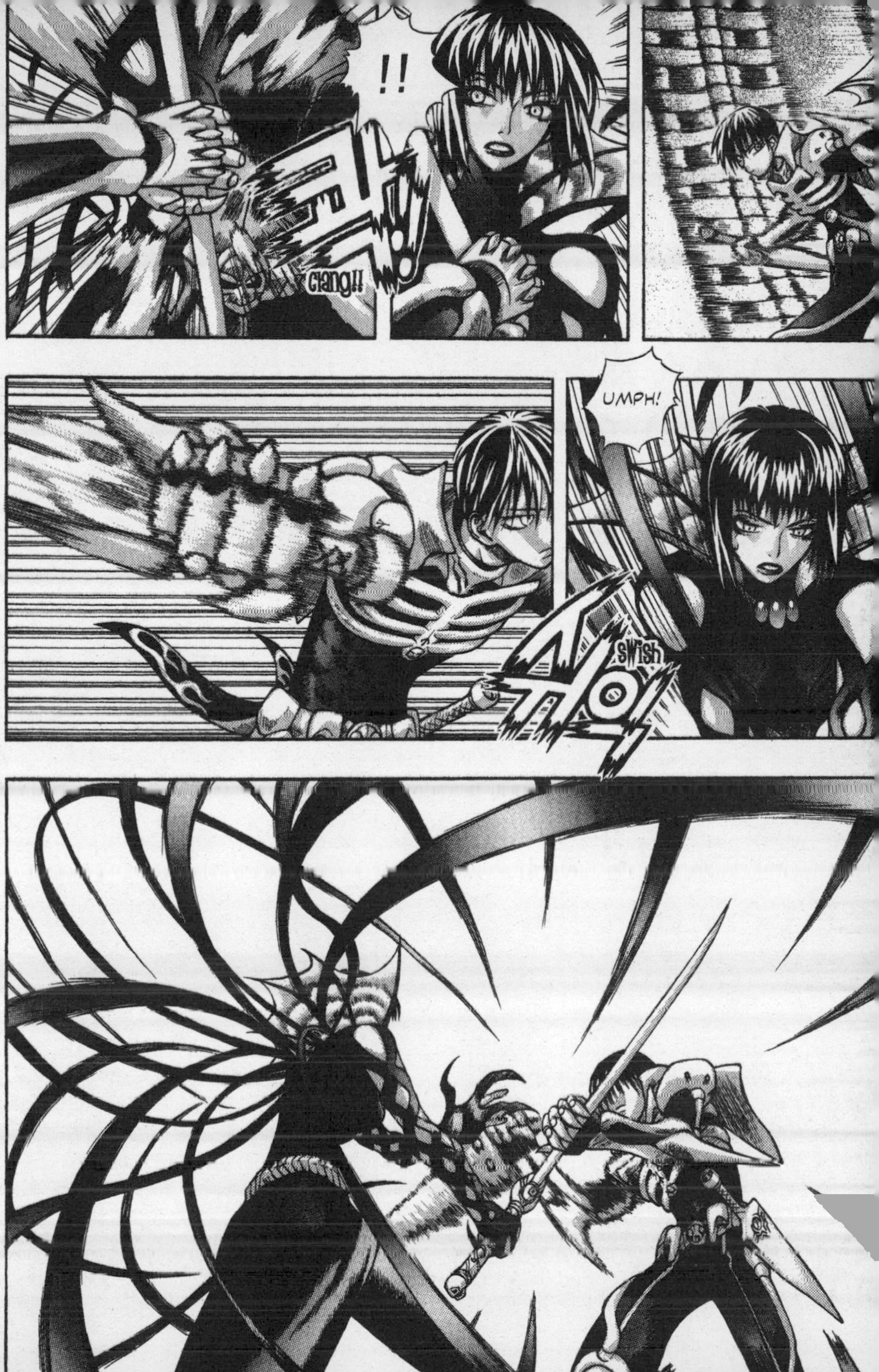
!!
CLANG!!
UMPH!
SWISH

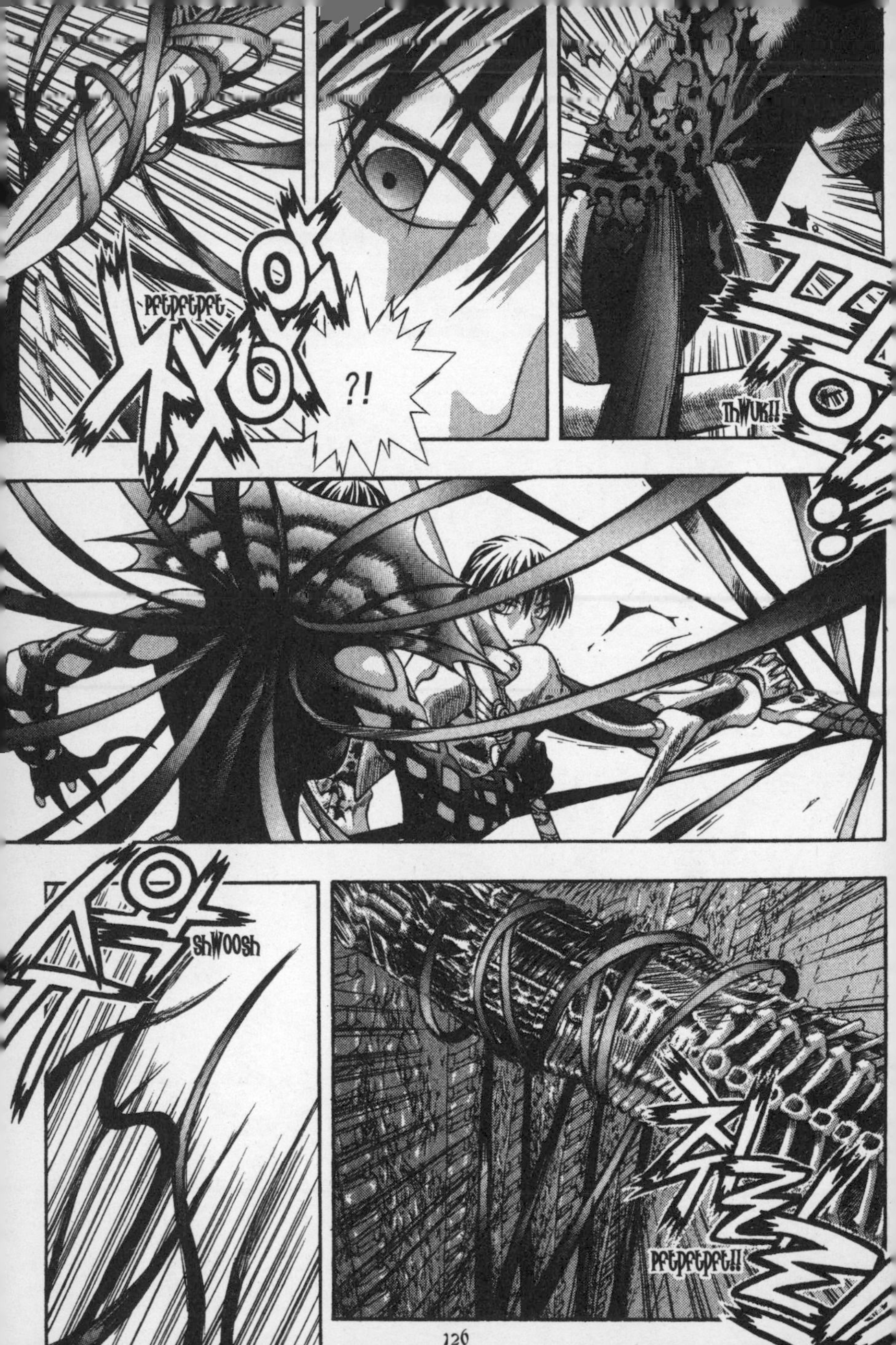
PFtPFtPFt
?!
ThWUK!!
ShWOOSh
PFtPFtPFt!!

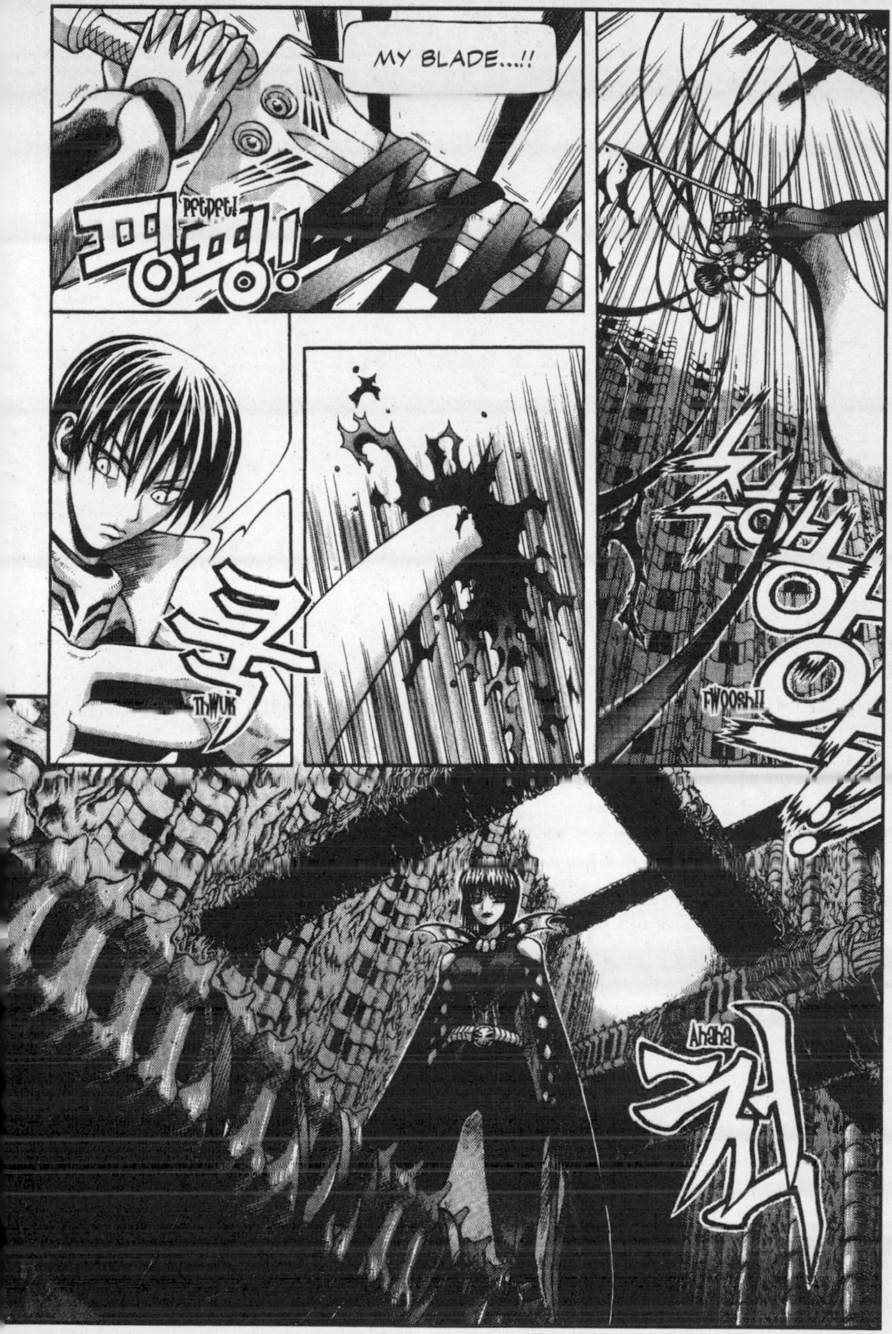
MY BLADE...!!
PFtDFt!
ThWUK
FWOOSh!!
Ahaha

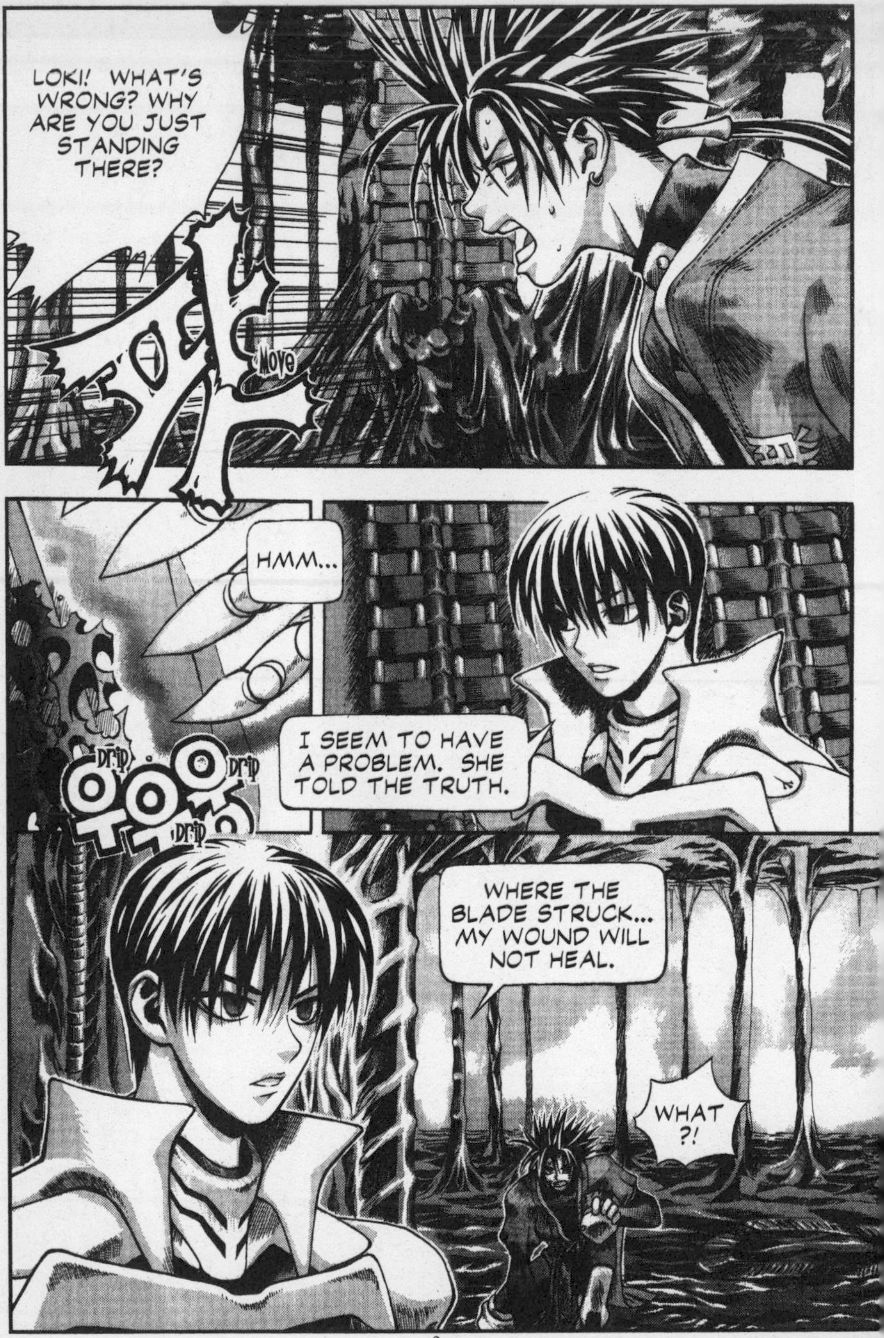
LOKI! WHAT'S WRONG? WHY ARE YOU JUST STANDING THERE?
Move
HMM...
Drip
Drip
Drip
I SEEM TO HAVE A PROBLEM. SHE TOLD THE TRUTH.
WHERE THE BLADE STRUCK... MY WOUND WILL NOT HEAL.
WHAT?!

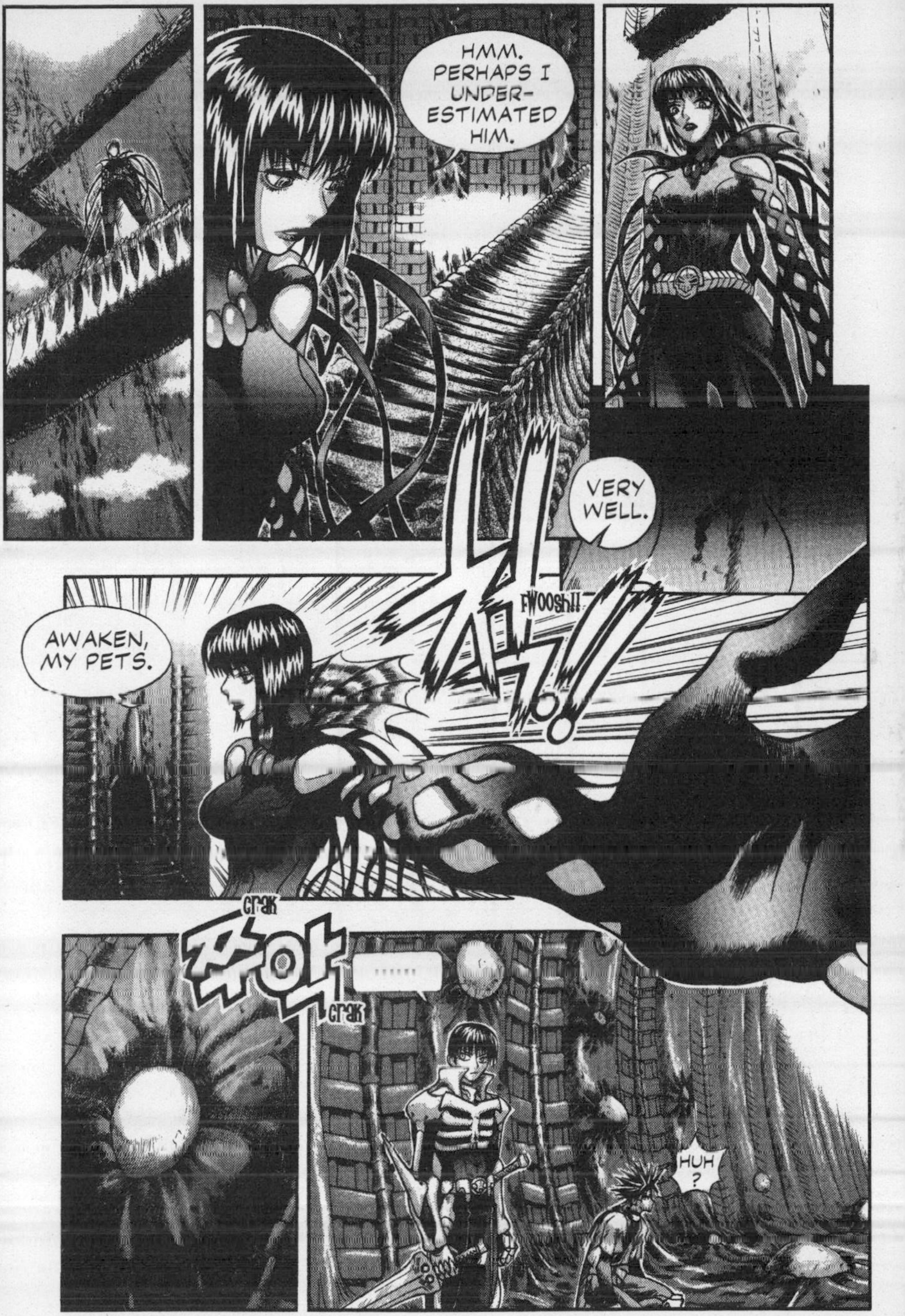
HMM. PERHAPS I UNDER-ESTIMATED HIM.
VERY WELL.
AWAKEN, MY PETS.
FWOOSH!!
CRAK
CRAK
......
HUH ?

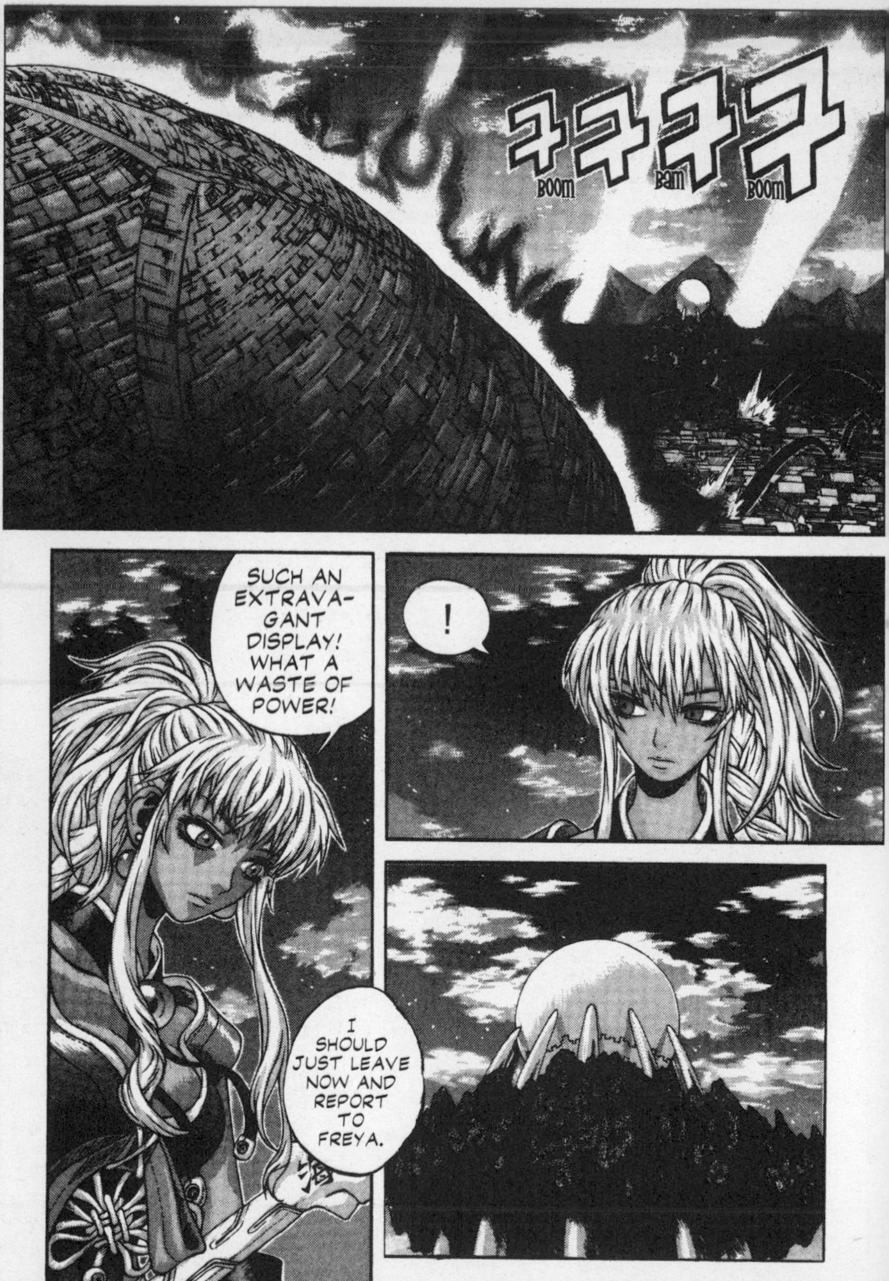
BOOM
BAM
BOOM
SUCH AN EXTRAVA-GANT DISPLAY! WHAT A WASTE OF POWER!
I SHOULD JUST LEAVE NOW AND REPORT TO FREYA.
!

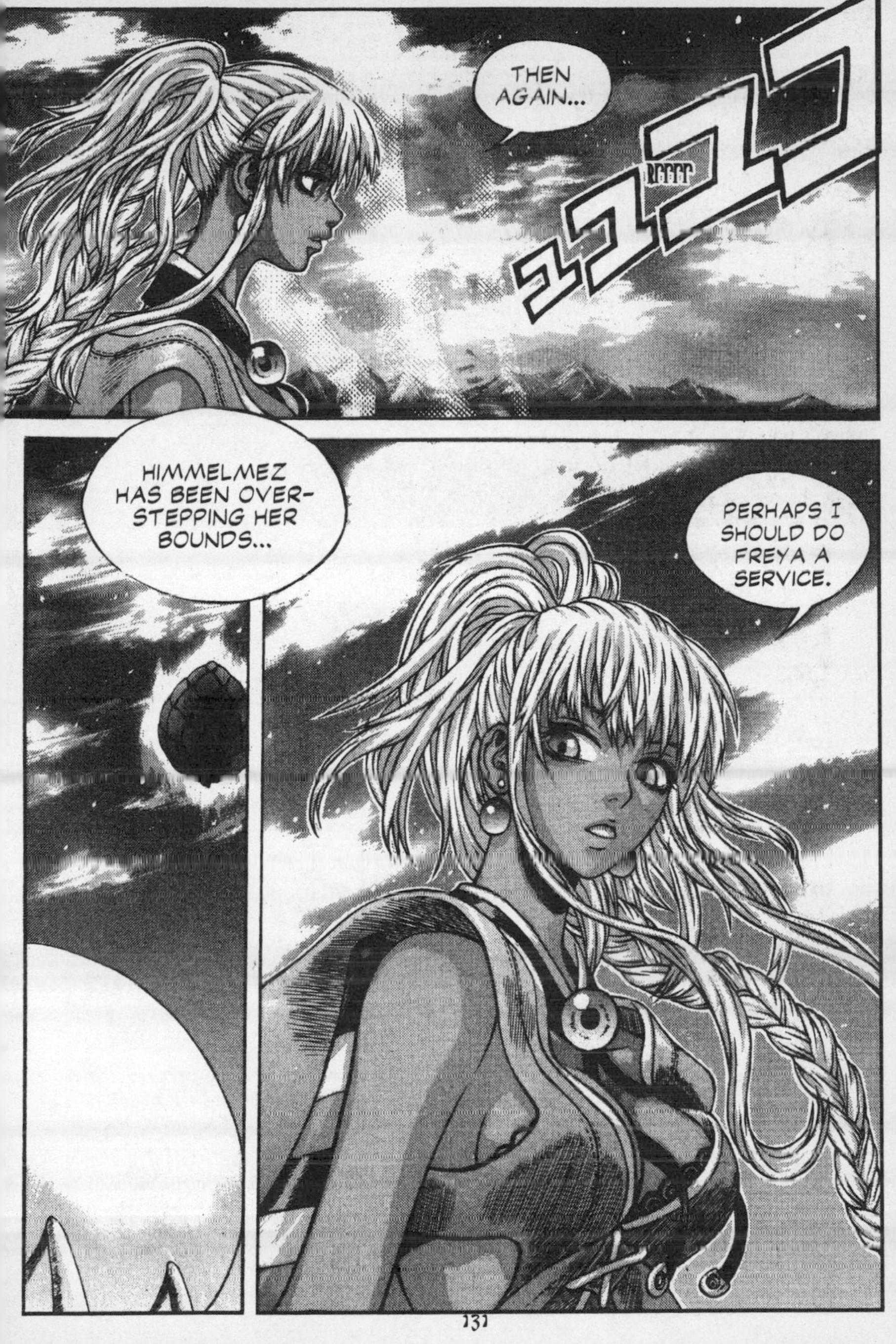
THEN AGAIN...
HIMMELMEZ HAS BEEN OVER-STEPPING HER BOUNDS...
PERHAPS I SHOULD DO FREYA A SERVICE.

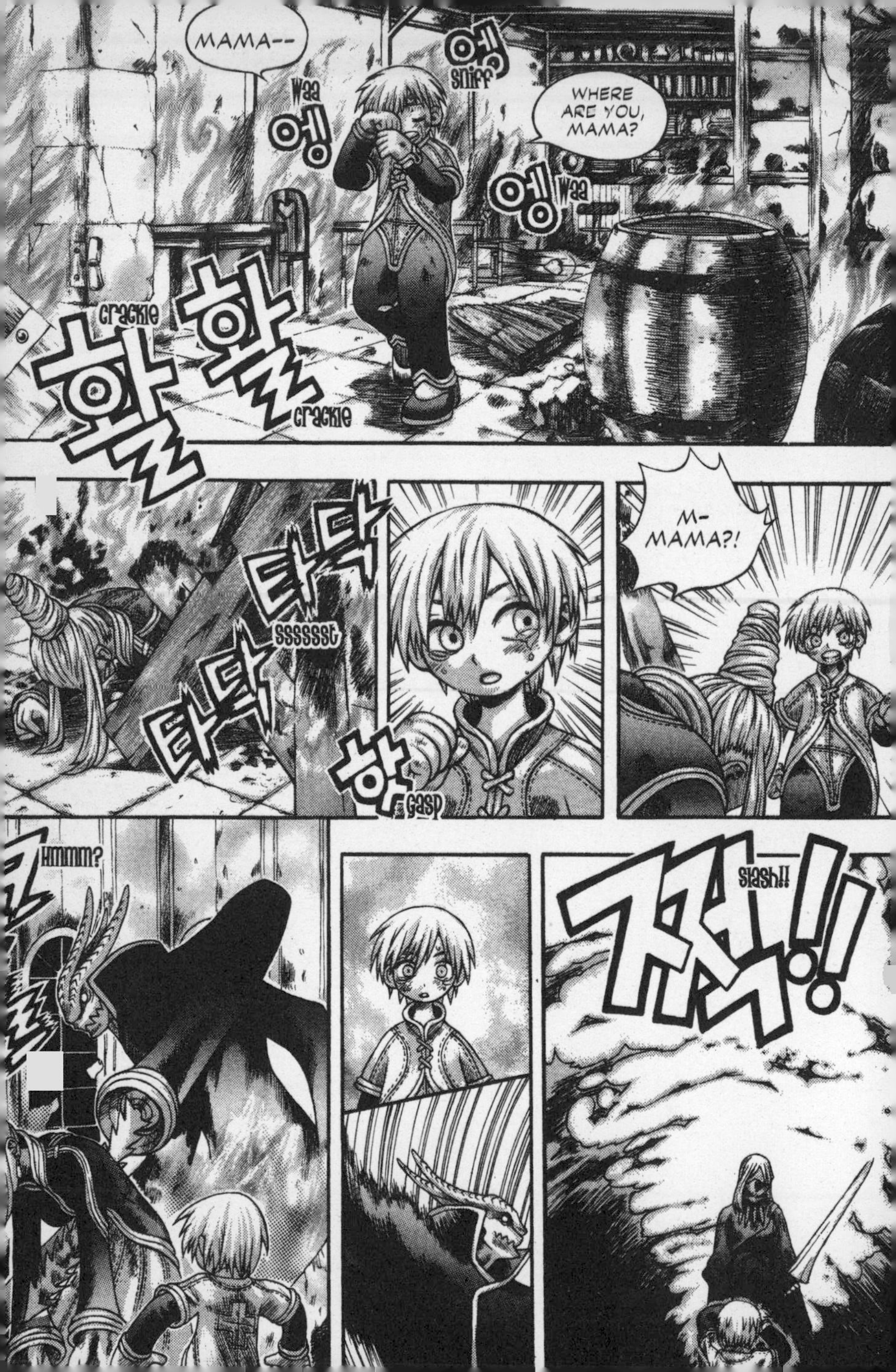
MAMA--
엥
Waa
Sniff
WHERE ARE YOU, MAMA?
엥
Waa
crackle
crackle
타닥
타닥
sssssst
헉
gasp
M- MAMA?!
Hmmm?
slash!!

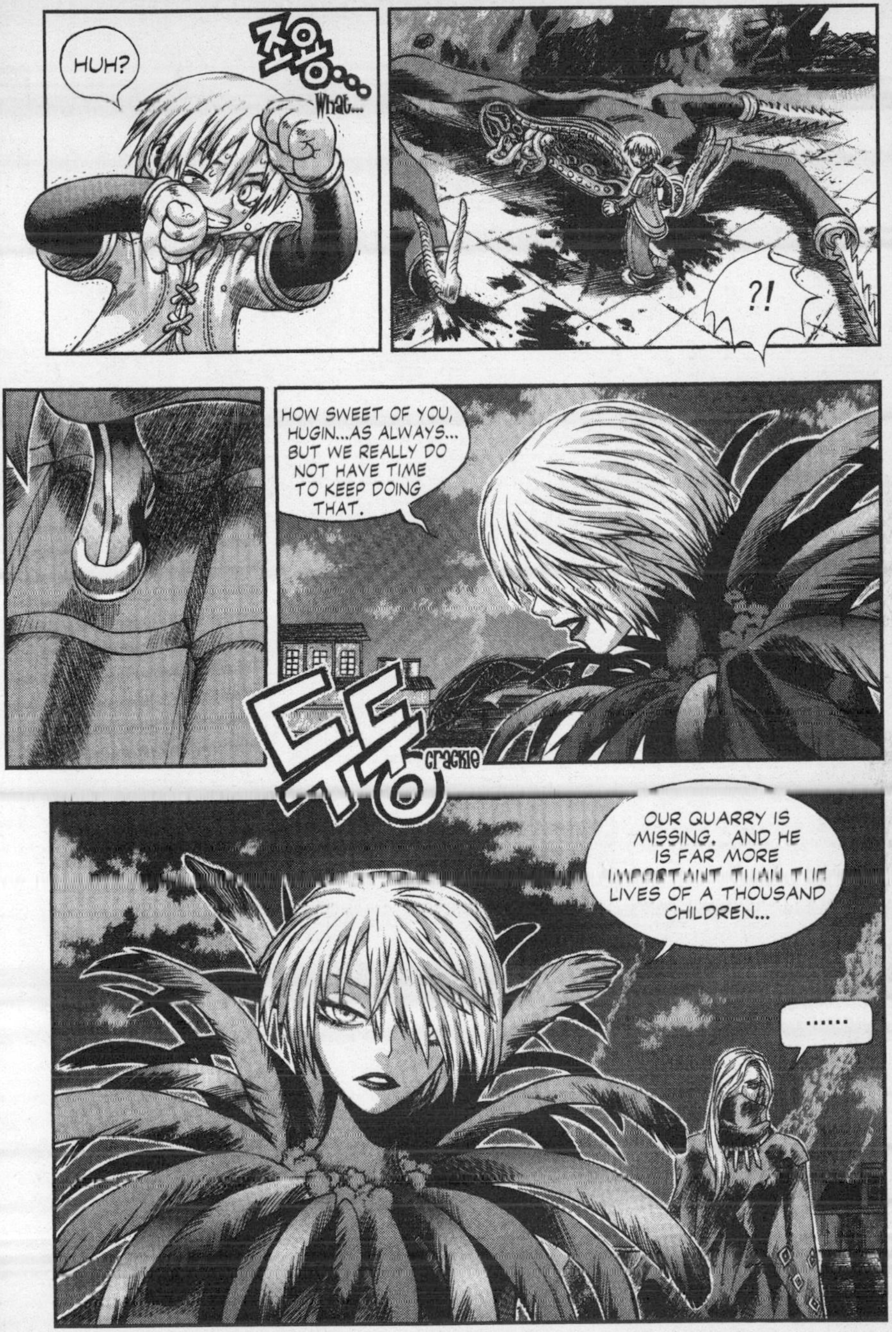
HUH?
What...
?!
HOW SWEET OF YOU, HUGIN...AS ALWAYS... BUT WE REALLY DO NOT HAVE TIME TO KEEP DOING THAT.
crackle
OUR QUARRY IS MISSING. AND HE IS FAR MORE IMPORTANT THAN THE LIVES OF A THOUSAND CHILDREN...
......

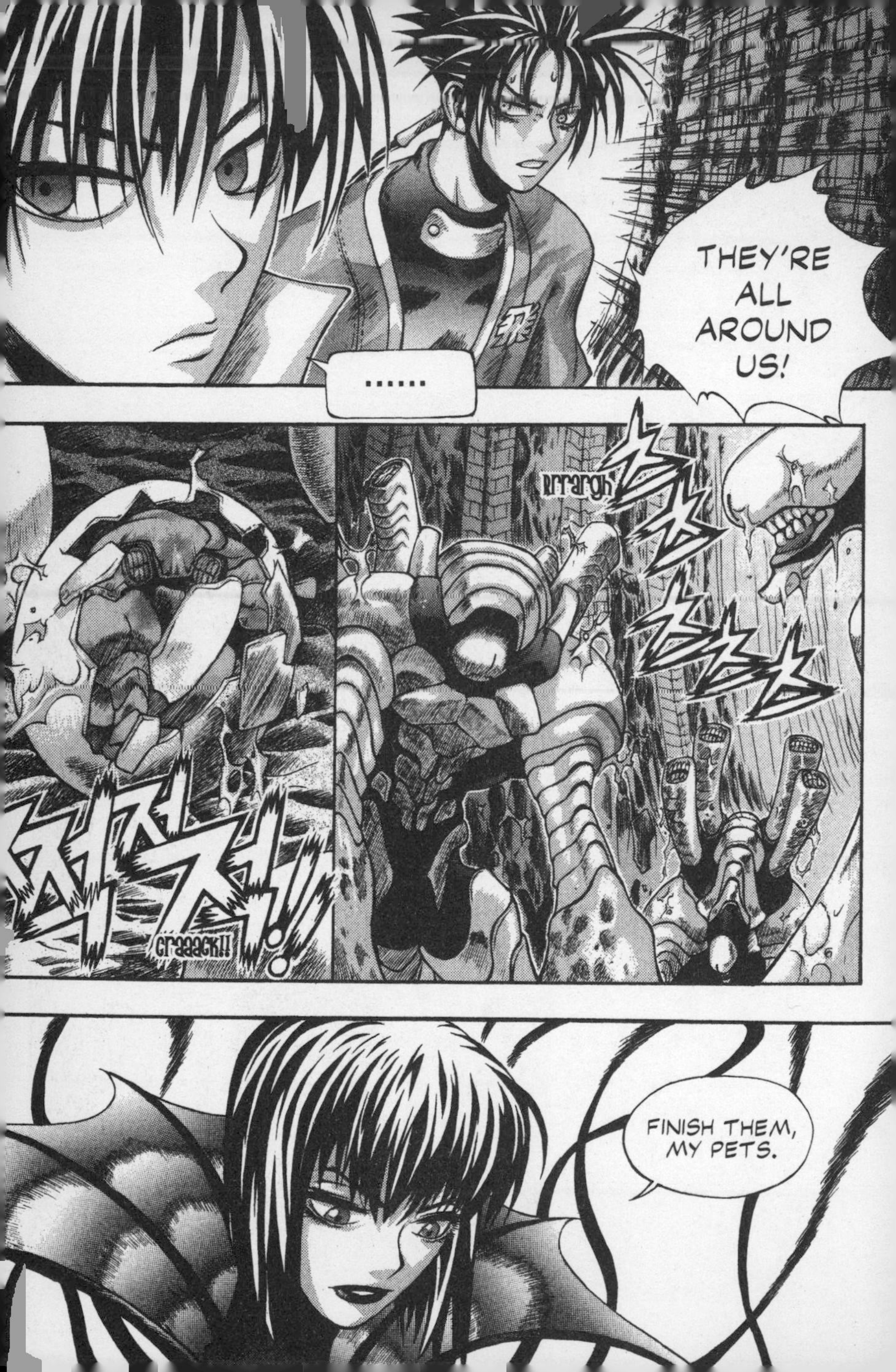
THEY'RE ALL AROUND US!
......
Craaack!!
Rrrargh
FINISH THEM, MY PETS.

RAGNAROK
라그나로크
IN TO THE ABYSS

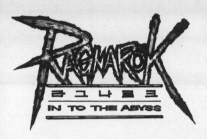

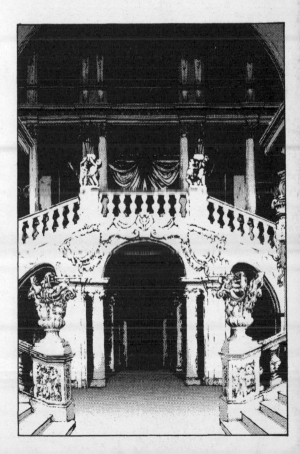

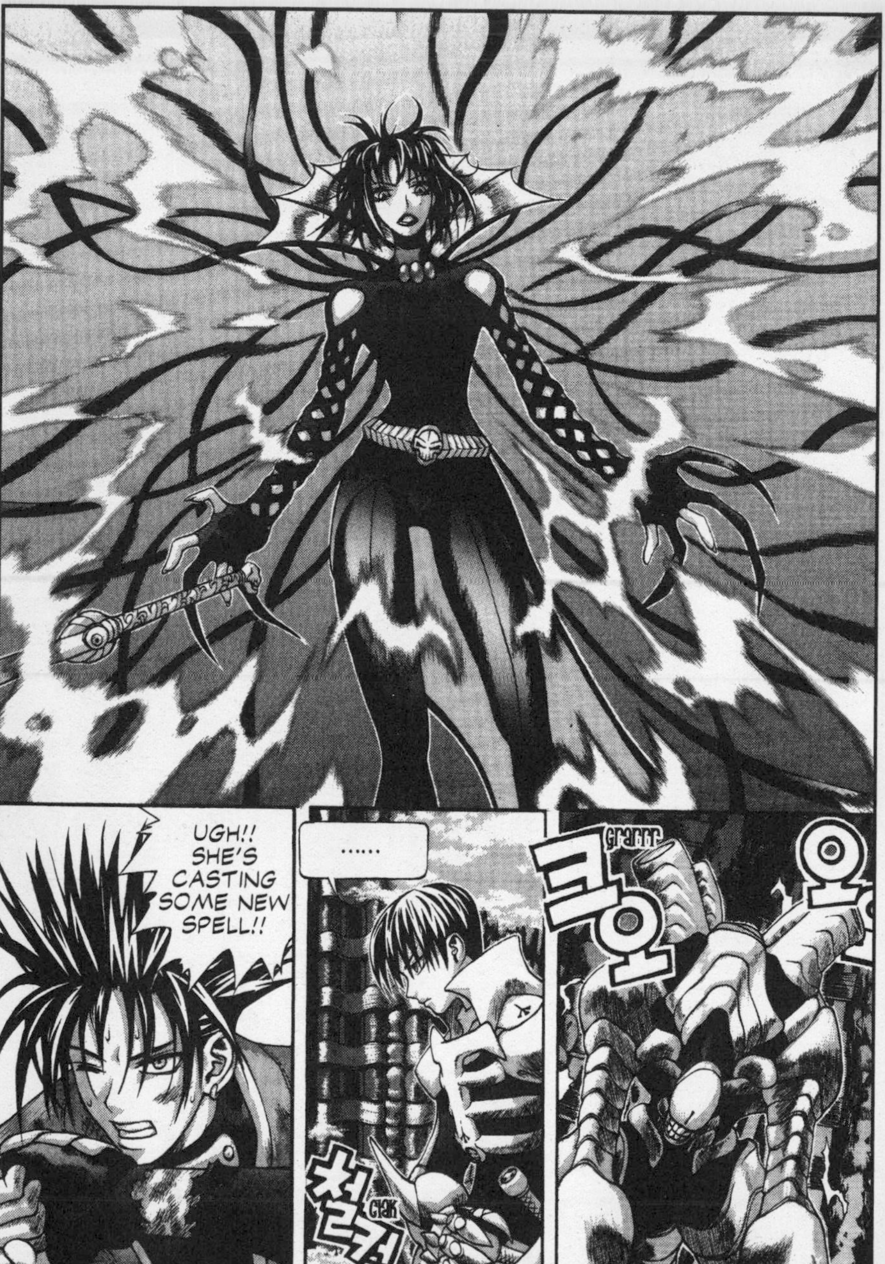
UGH!! SHE'S CASTING SOME NEW SPELL!!
......
CLAK
GRARRR

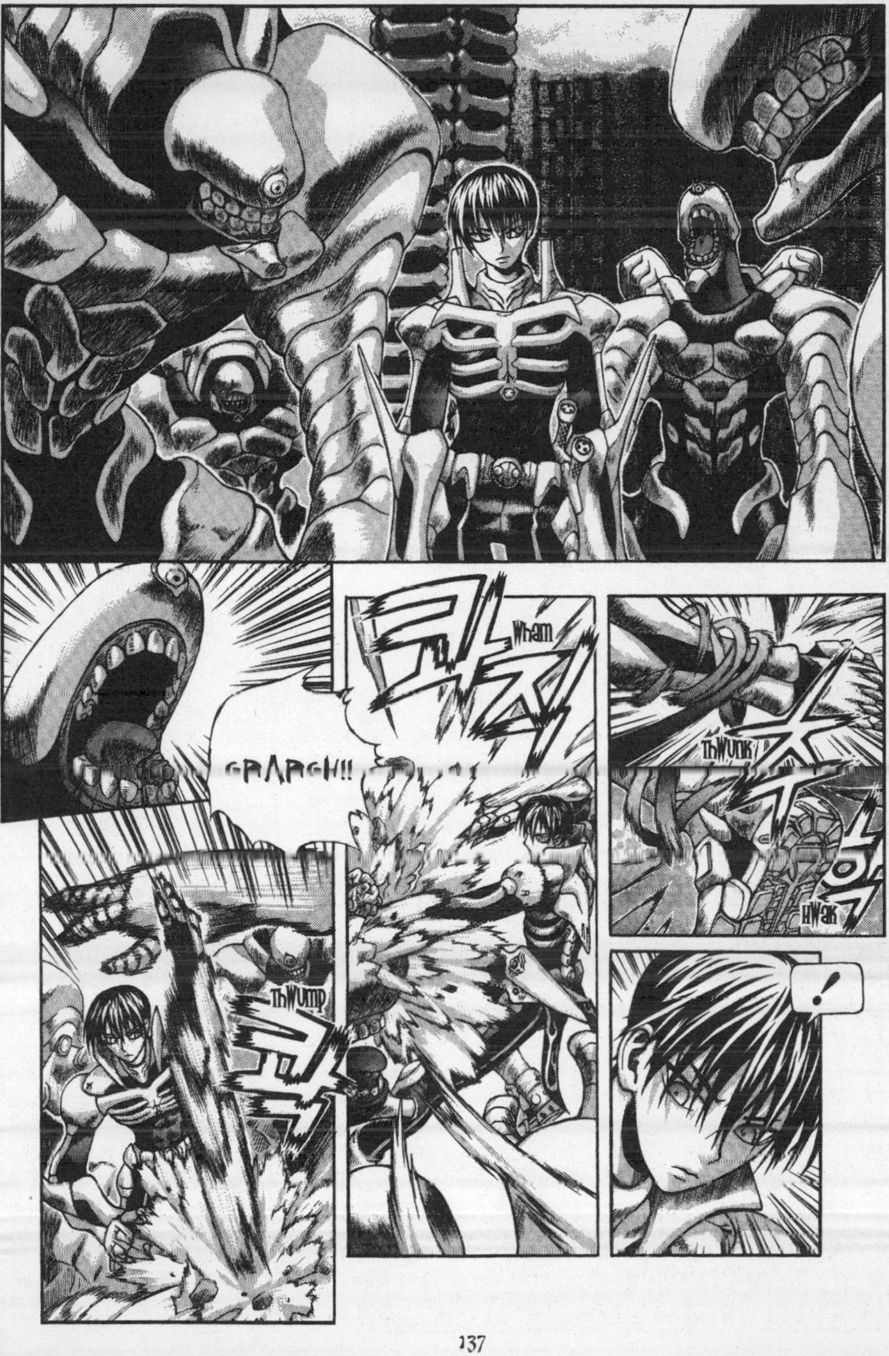

Wham
GRARGH!!
ThWUNK
HWak
ThWUmp
!

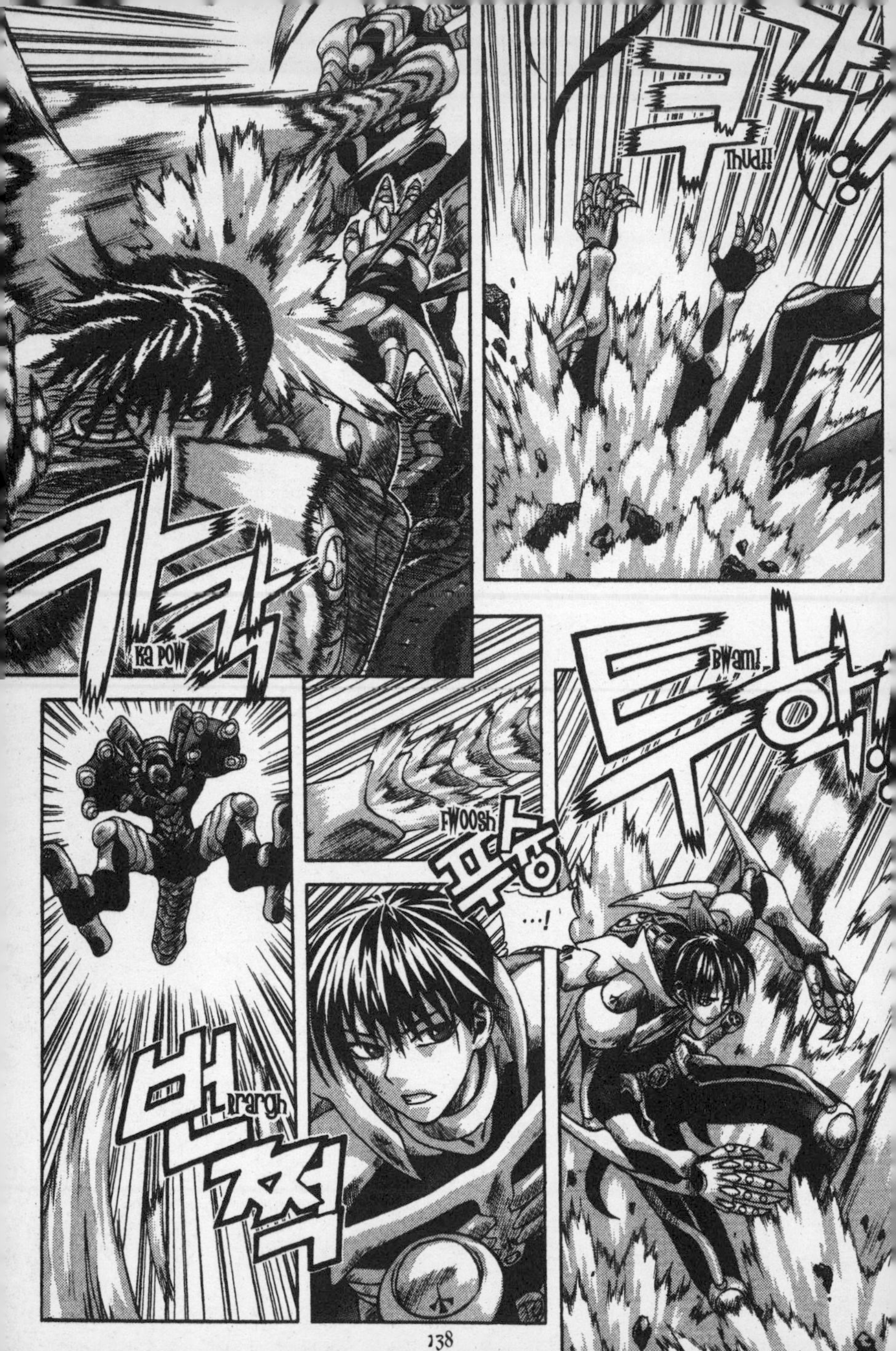
KA POW
THUD!!
BRARGH
FWOOSH
...!
BWAM!

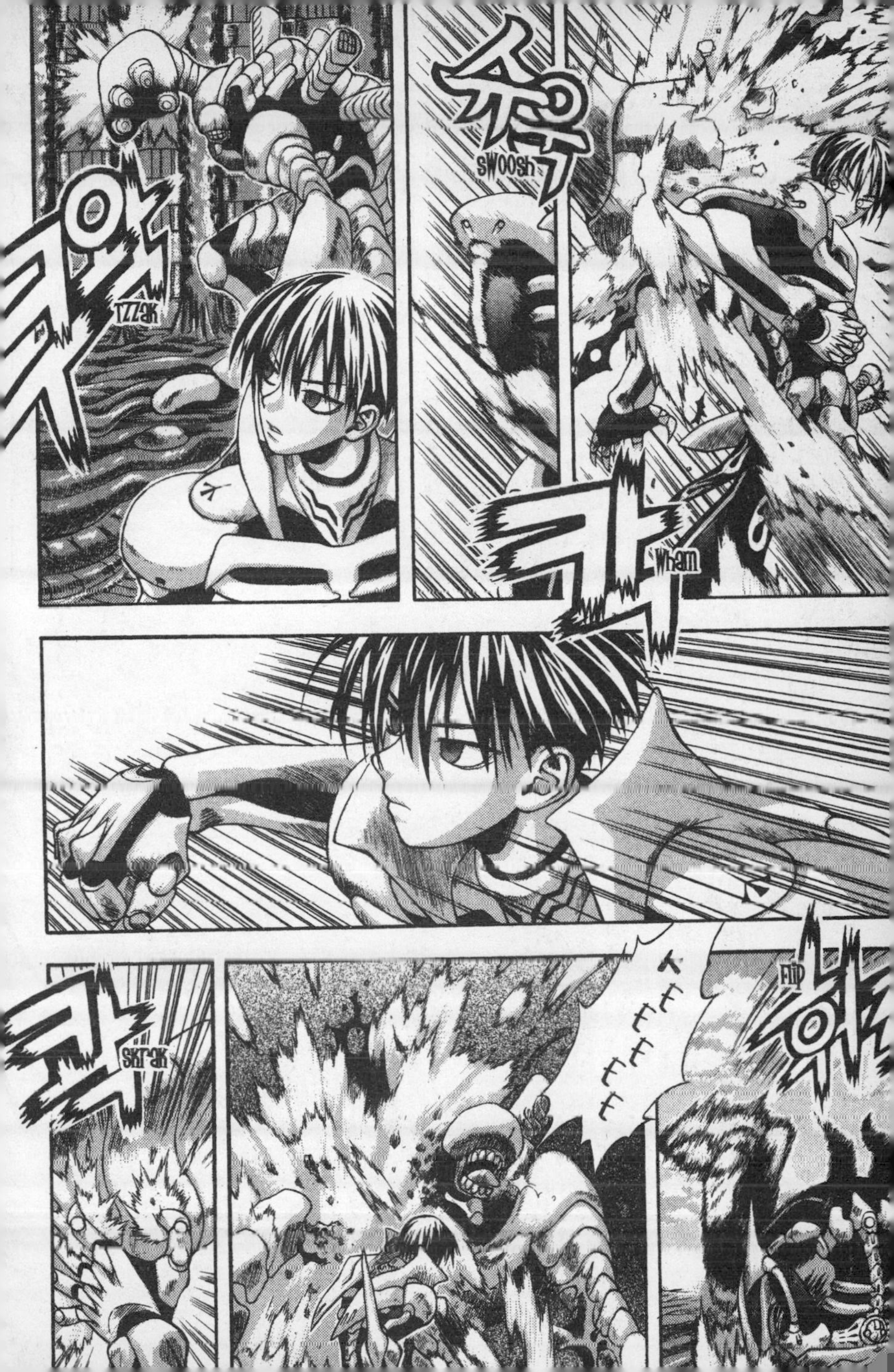
TZZAK
SWOOSH
Wham
SKRAK
Flip

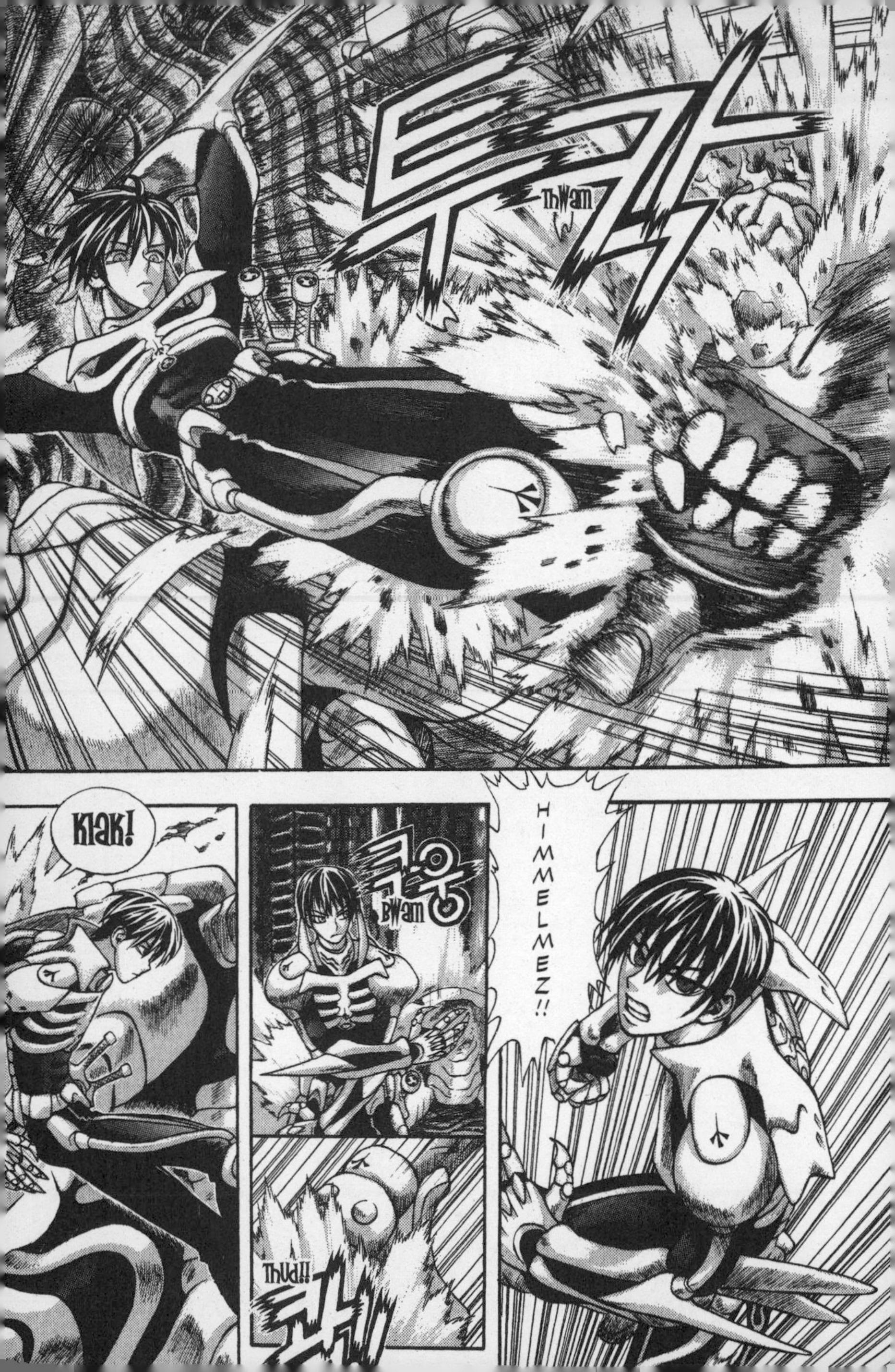

THWAM
KLAK!
BWAM
HIMMELMMEZ!!
THUD!!

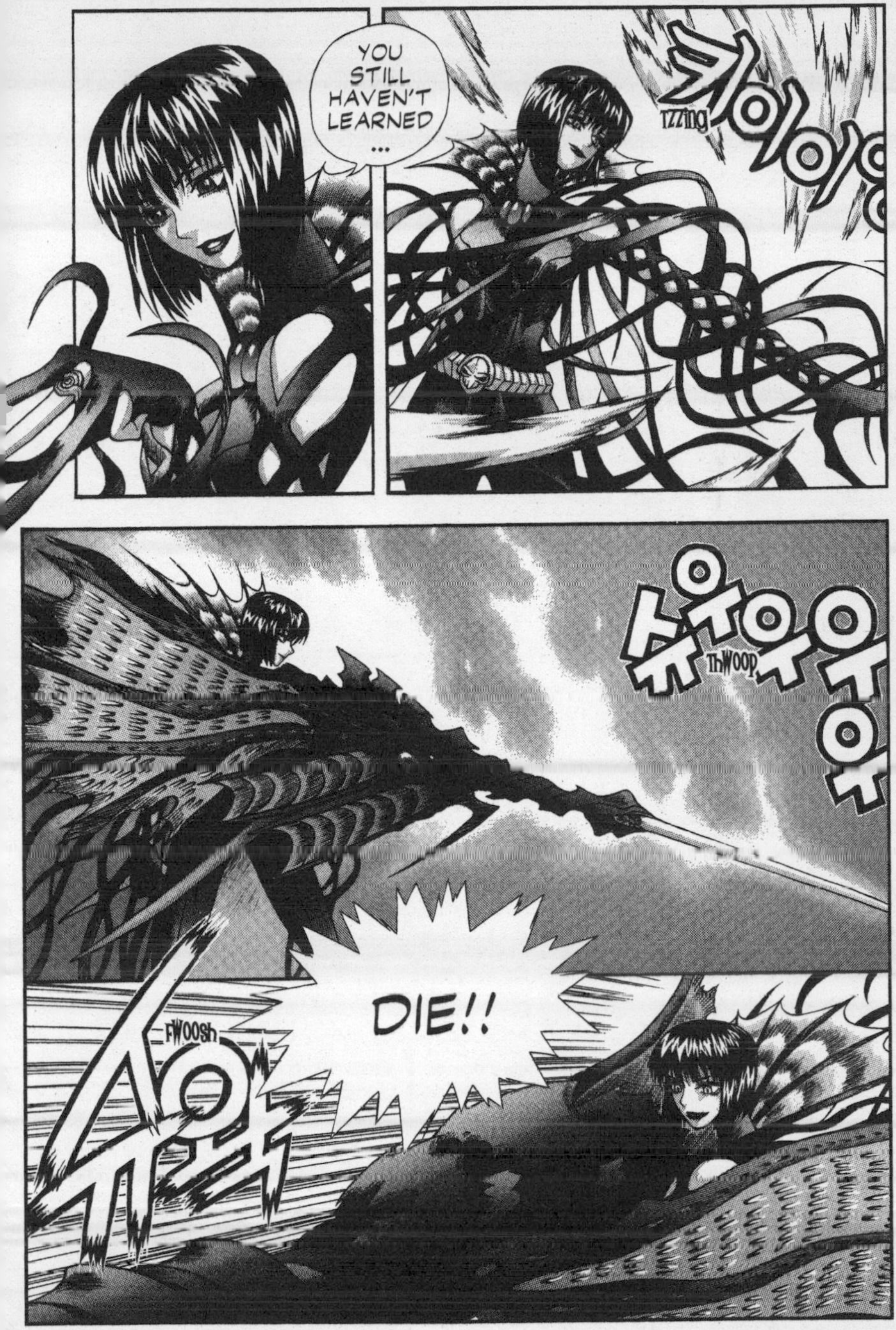

YOU STILL HAVEN'T LEARNED ...
TZZing
ThWOOP
DIE!!
FWOOSh

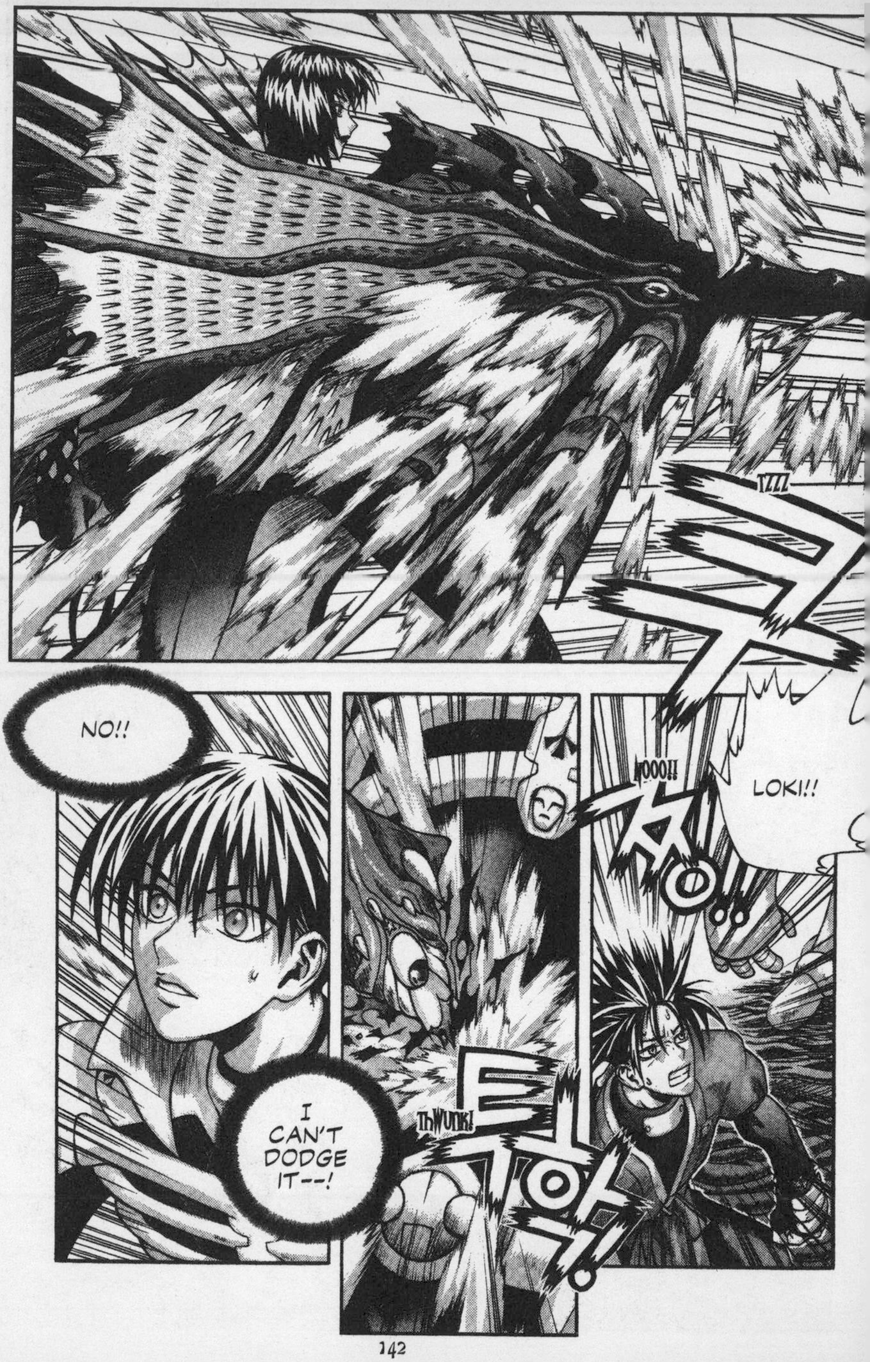
TZZZ
NO!!
I CAN'T DODGE IT--!
THWUNK!
NOOO!!
LOKI!!

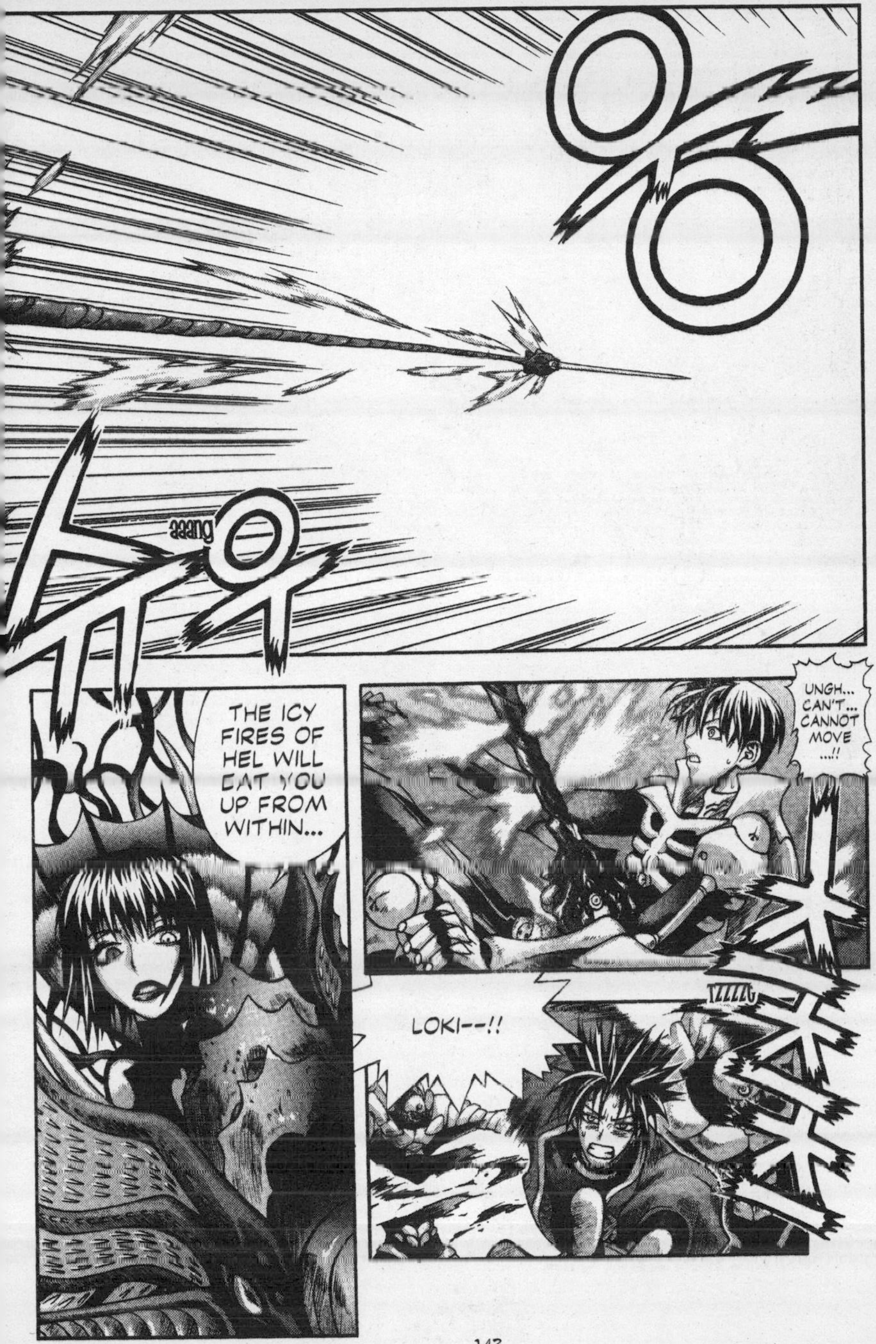
aaang
THE ICY FIRES OF HEL WILL EAT YOU UP FROM WITHIN...
UNGH... CAN'T... CANNOT MOVE ...!!
LOKI--!!
TZZZZG

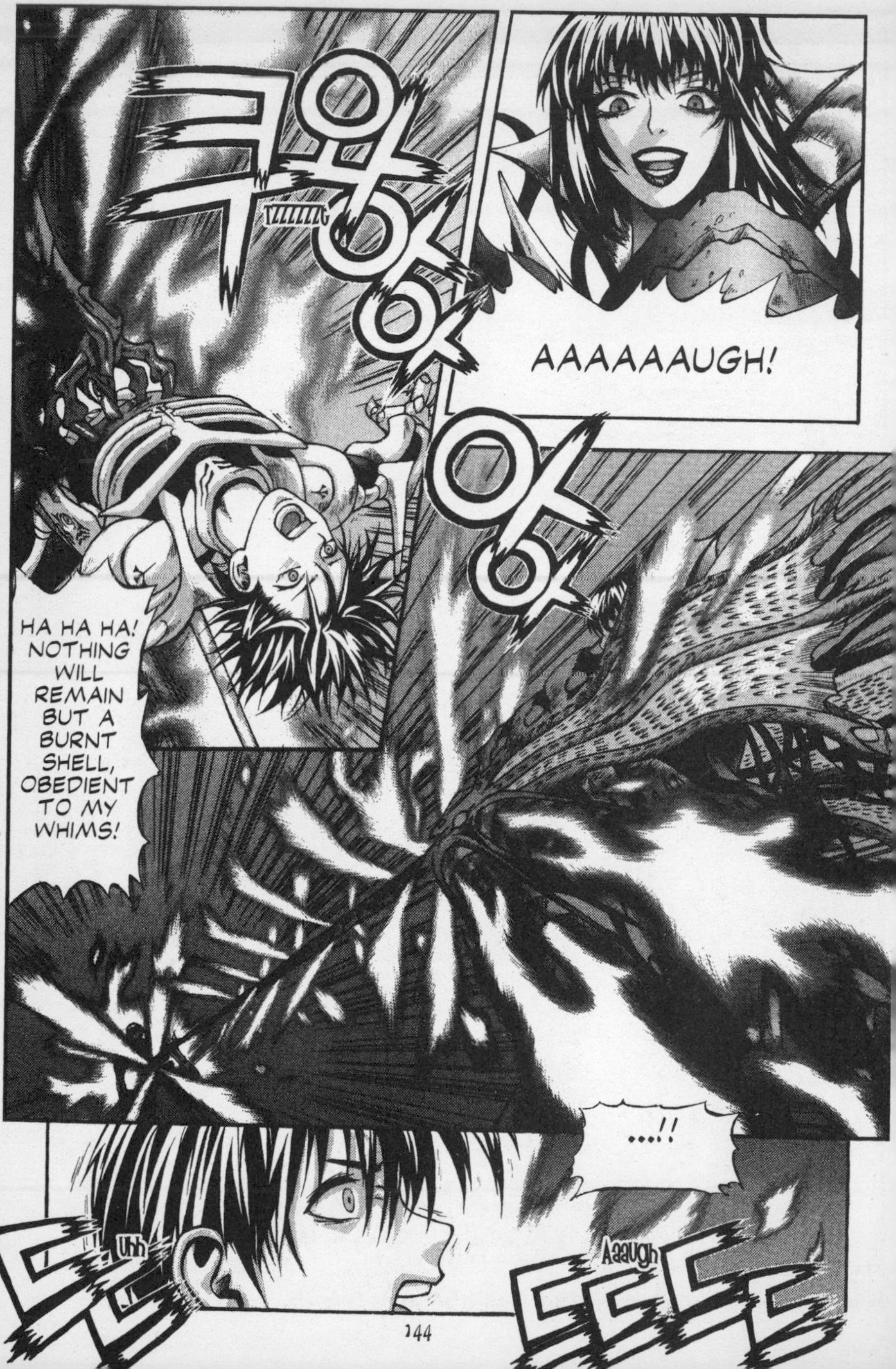
TZZZZZZG
AAAAAAAUGH!
HA HA HA! NOTHING WILL REMAIN BUT A BURNT SHELL, OBEDIENT TO MY WHIMS!
...!!
Uhh
Aaaugh

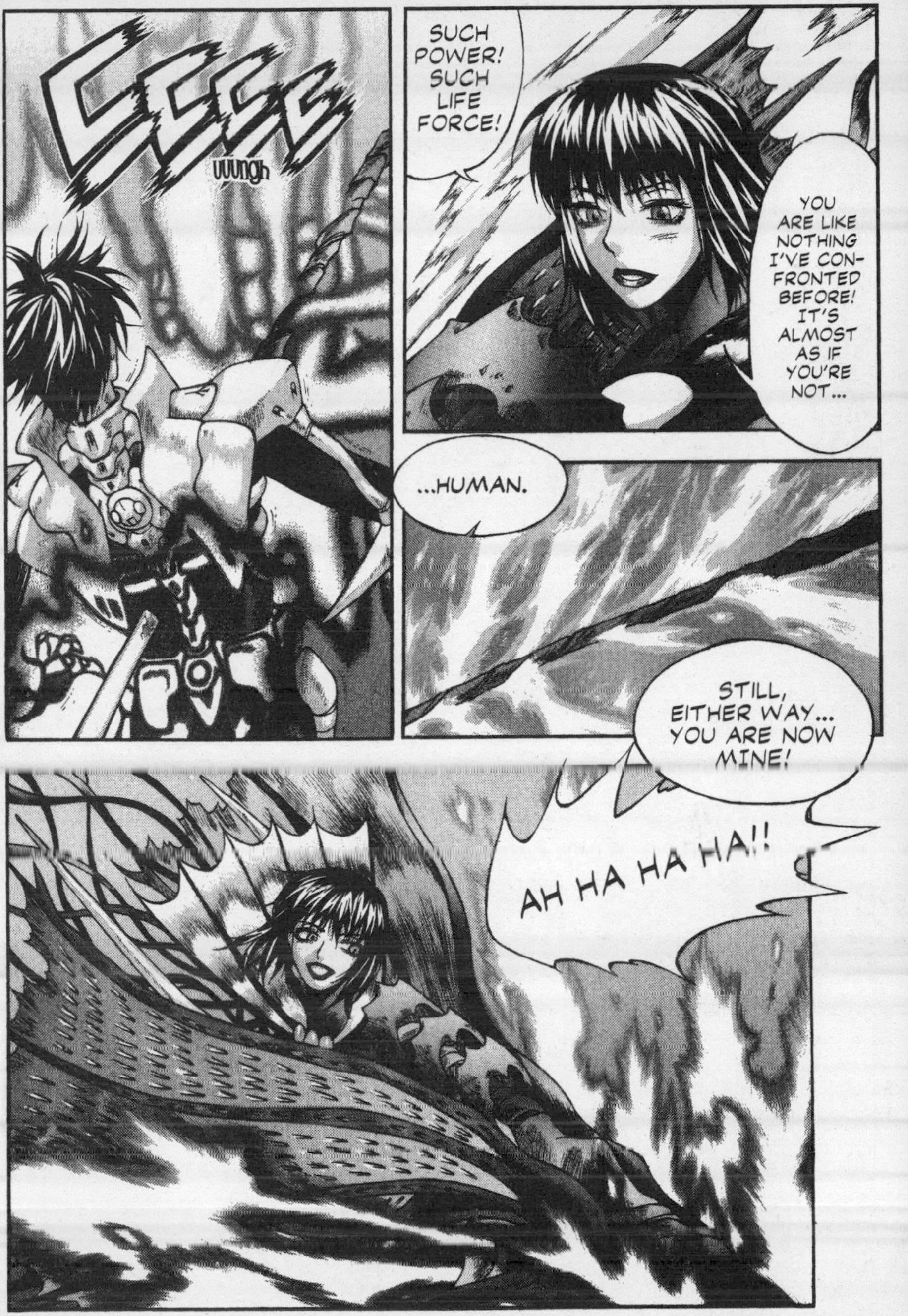
CCCG
vvungh
SUCH POWER! SUCH LIFE FORCE!
YOU ARE LIKE NOTHING I'VE CON-FRONTED BEFORE! IT'S ALMOST AS IF YOU'RE NOT...
...HUMAN.
STILL, EITHER WAY... YOU ARE NOW MINE!
AH HA HA HA!!

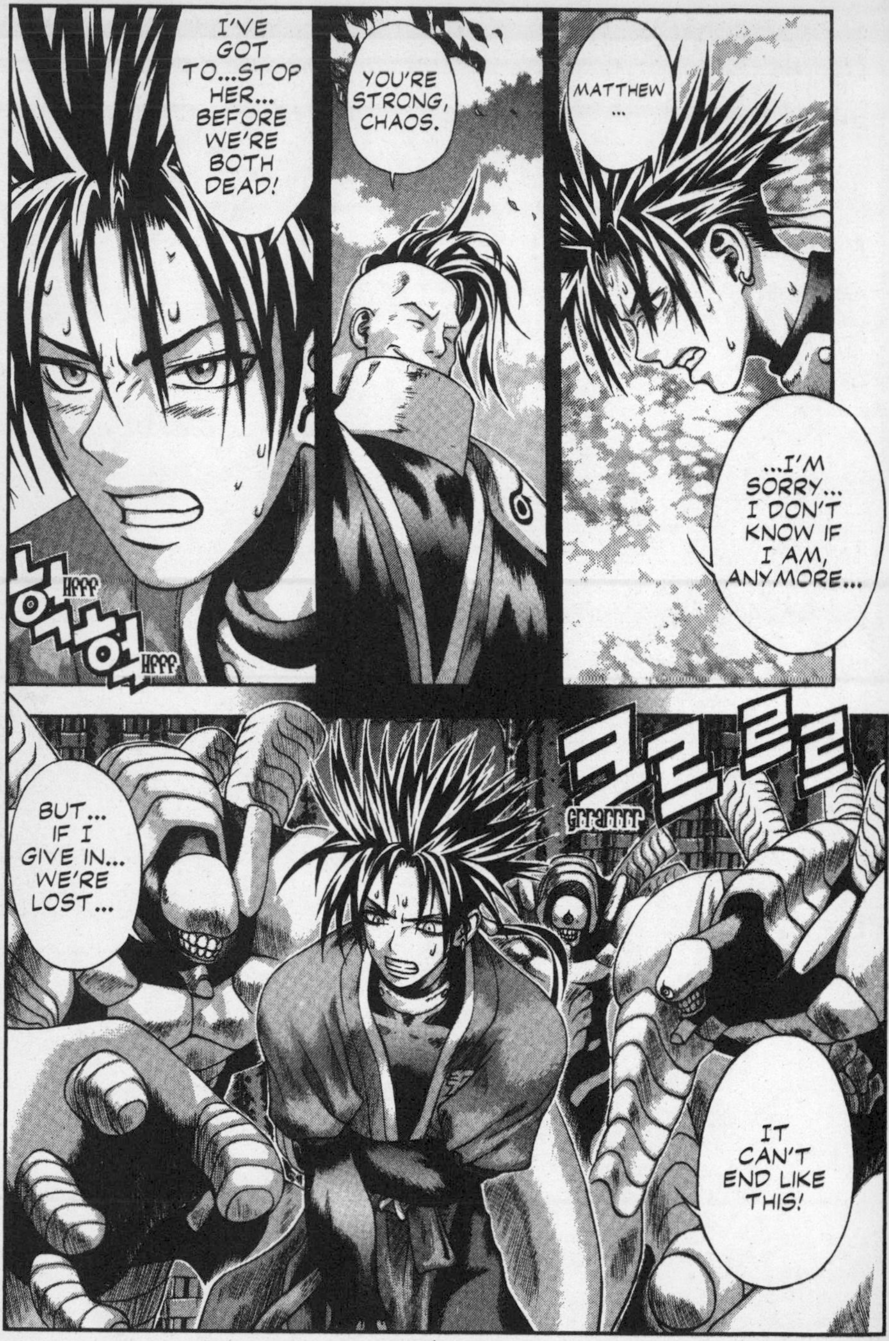
I'VE GOT TO...STOP HER... BEFORE WE'RE BOTH DEAD!
HFFF
HFFF
YOU'RE STRONG, CHAOS.
MATTHEW ...
...I'M SORRY... I DON'T KNOW IF I AM, ANYMORE...
BUT... IF I GIVE IN... WE'RE LOST...
IT CAN'T END LIKE THIS!

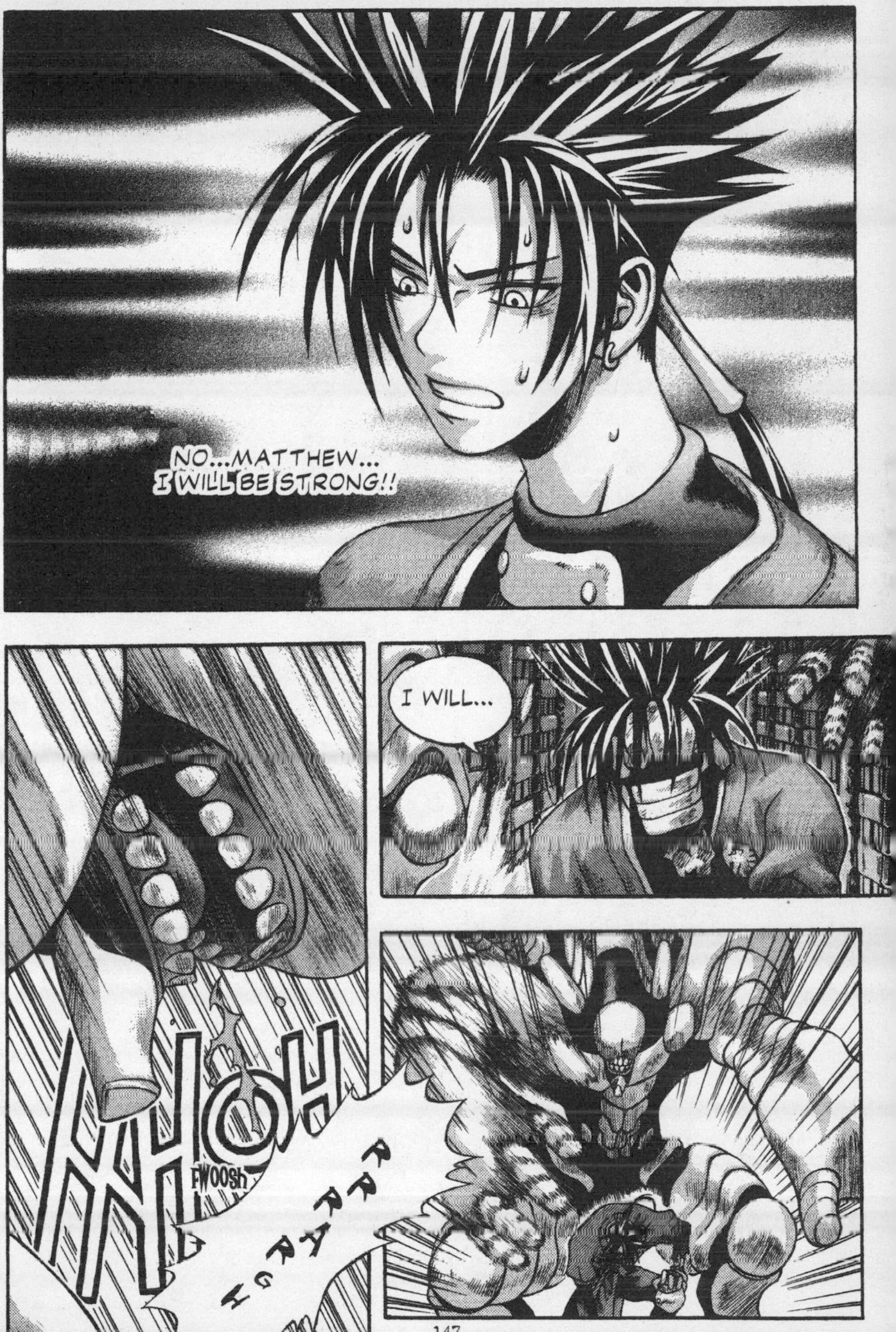
NO...MATTHEW...
I WILL BE STRONG!!
I WILL...
HHOH
FWOOSH
GRRRAA

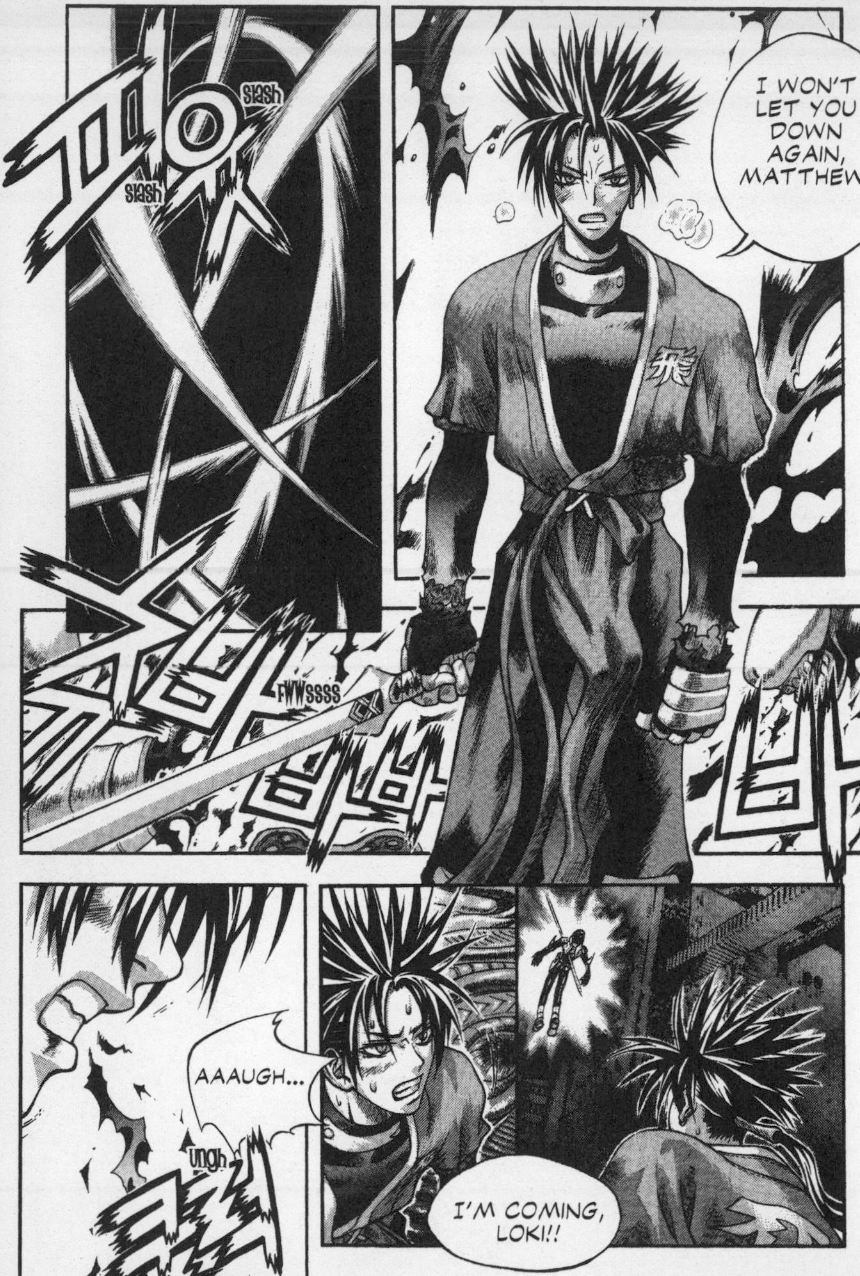
slash
slash
I WON'T LET YOU DOWN AGAIN, MATTHEW.
FWWSSSS
AAAUGH...
ungh
I'M COMING, LOKI!!

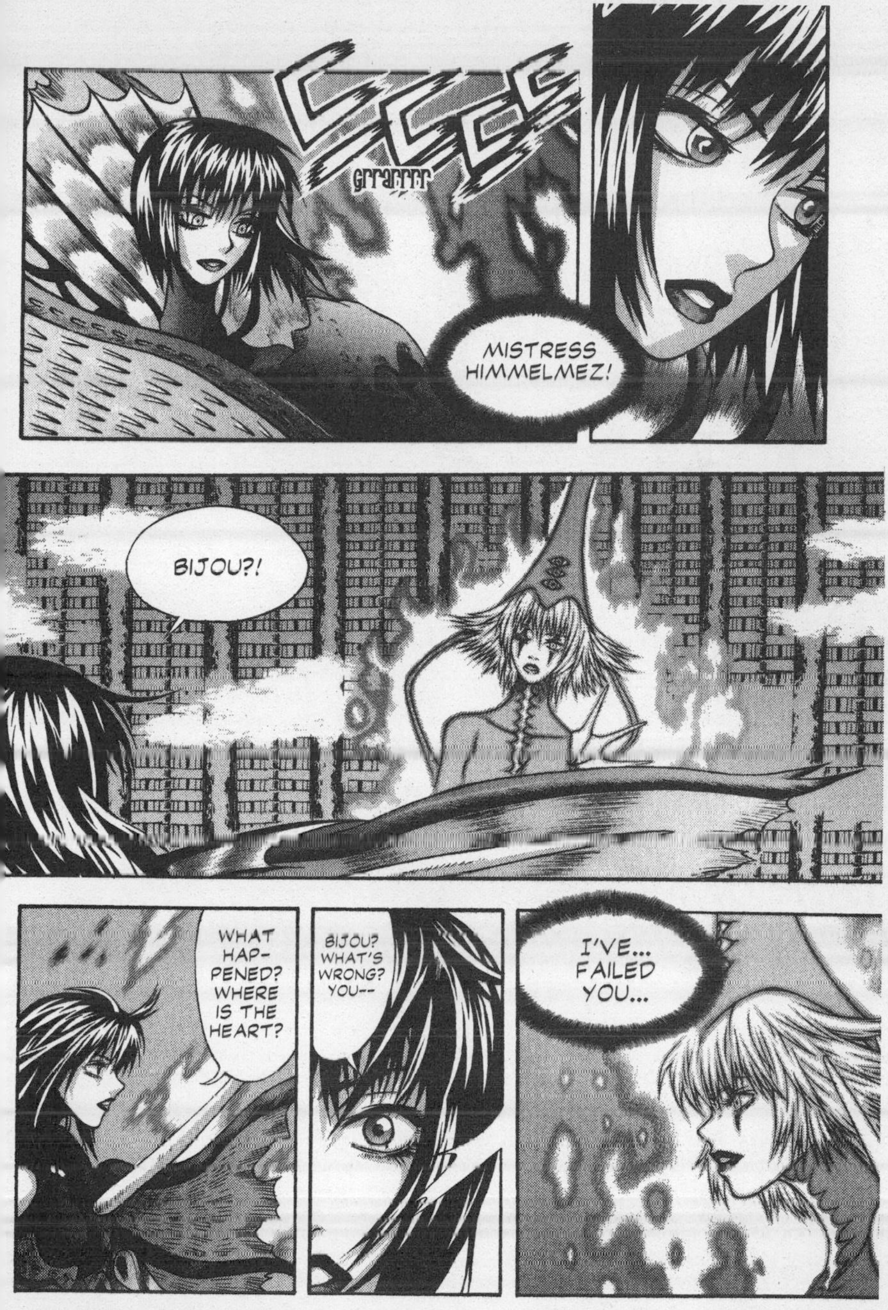
grrarrrr
MISTRESS HIMMELMEZ!
BIJOU?!
WHAT HAP-PENED? WHERE IS THE HEART?
BIJOU? WHAT'S WRONG? YOU--
I'VE... FAILED YOU...

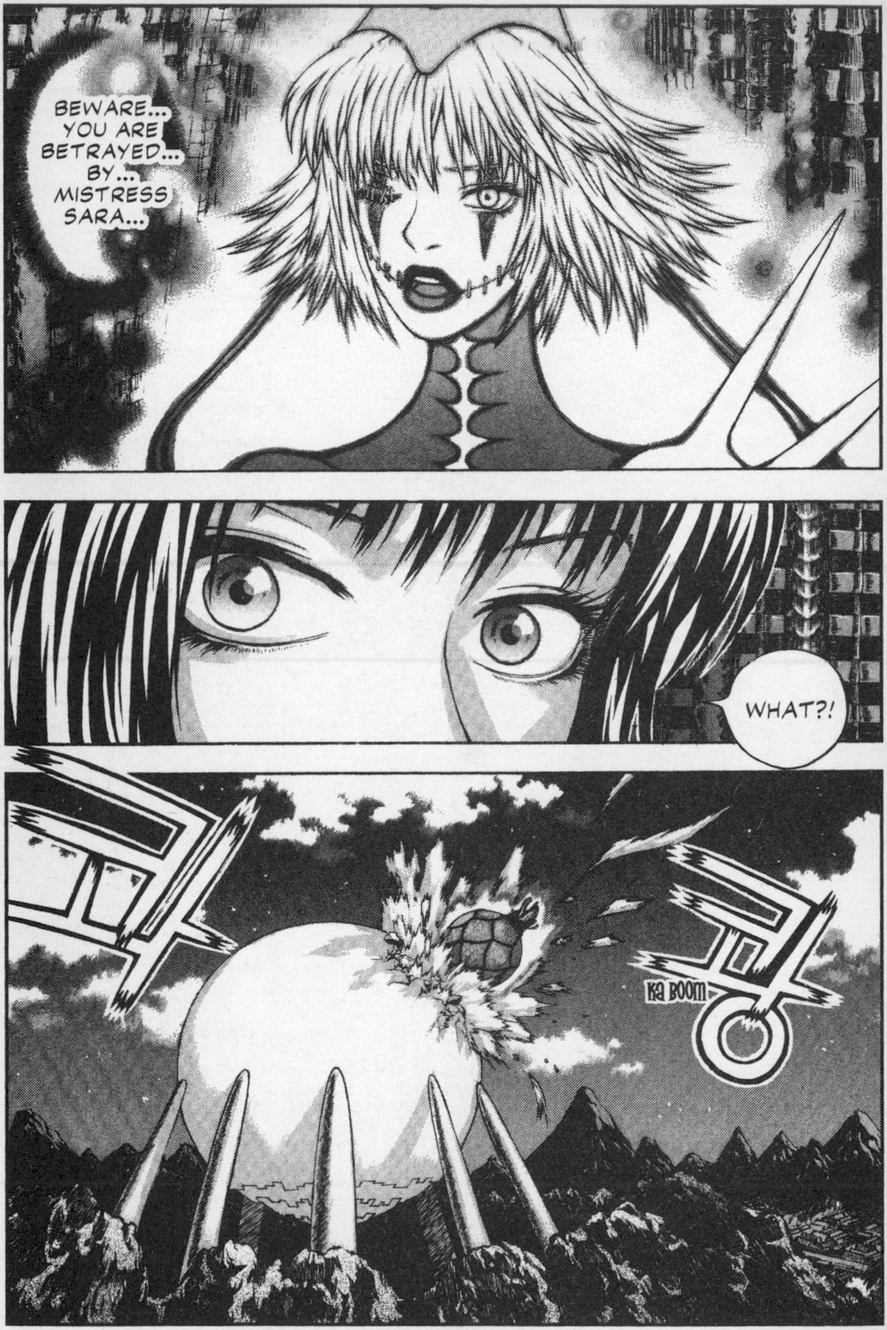
BEWARE... YOU ARE BETRAYED... BY... MISTRESS SARA...
WHAT?!
KA BOOM

RAGNAROK
라그나로크
IN TO THE ABYSS

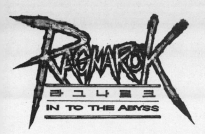

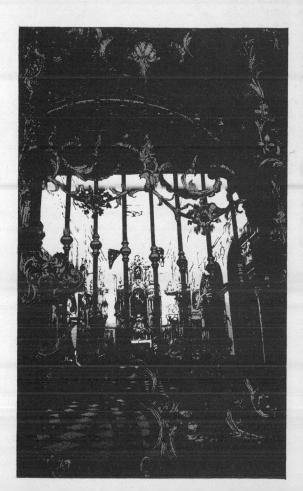

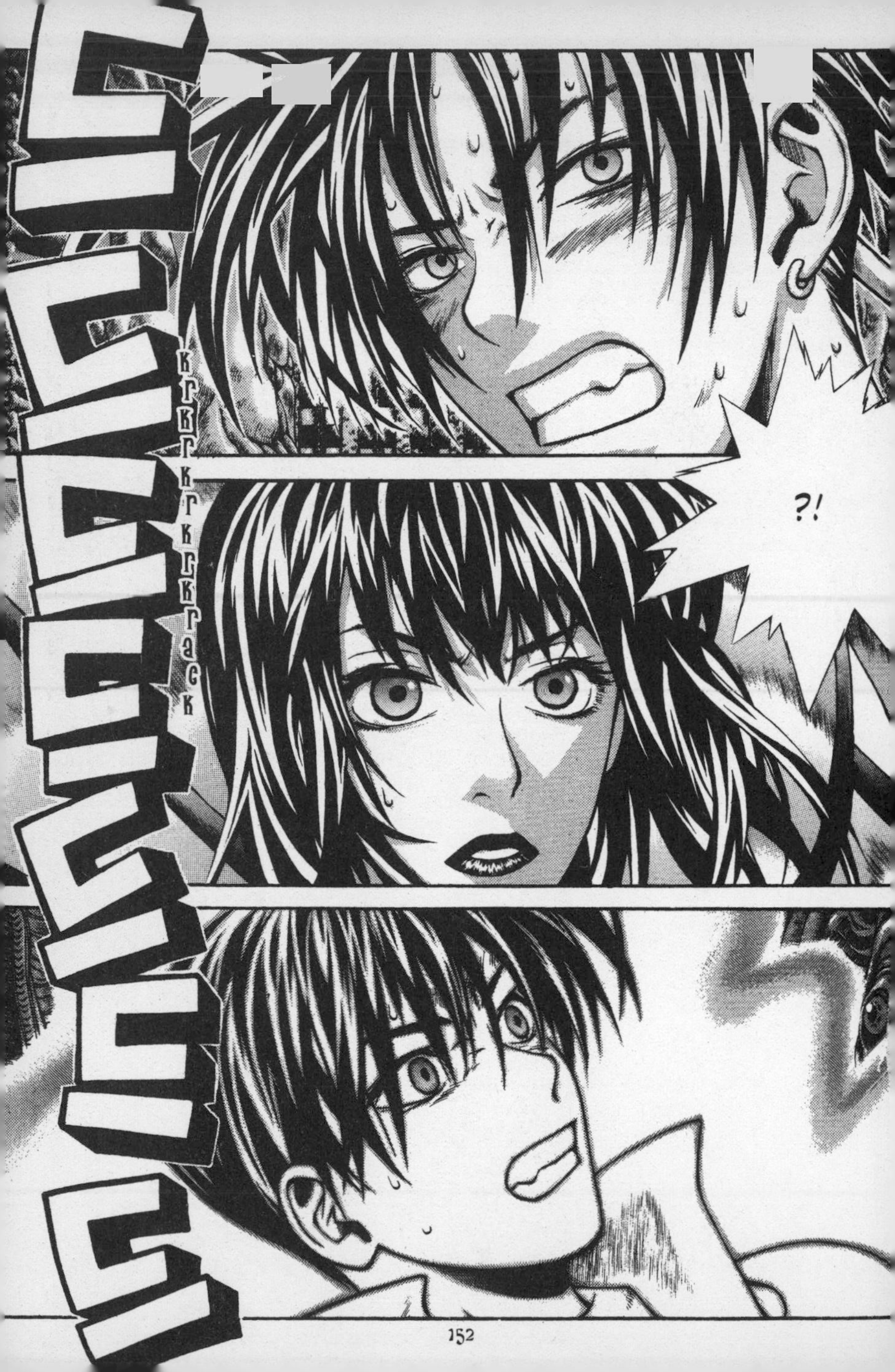
krkrkrkrkrack
?!

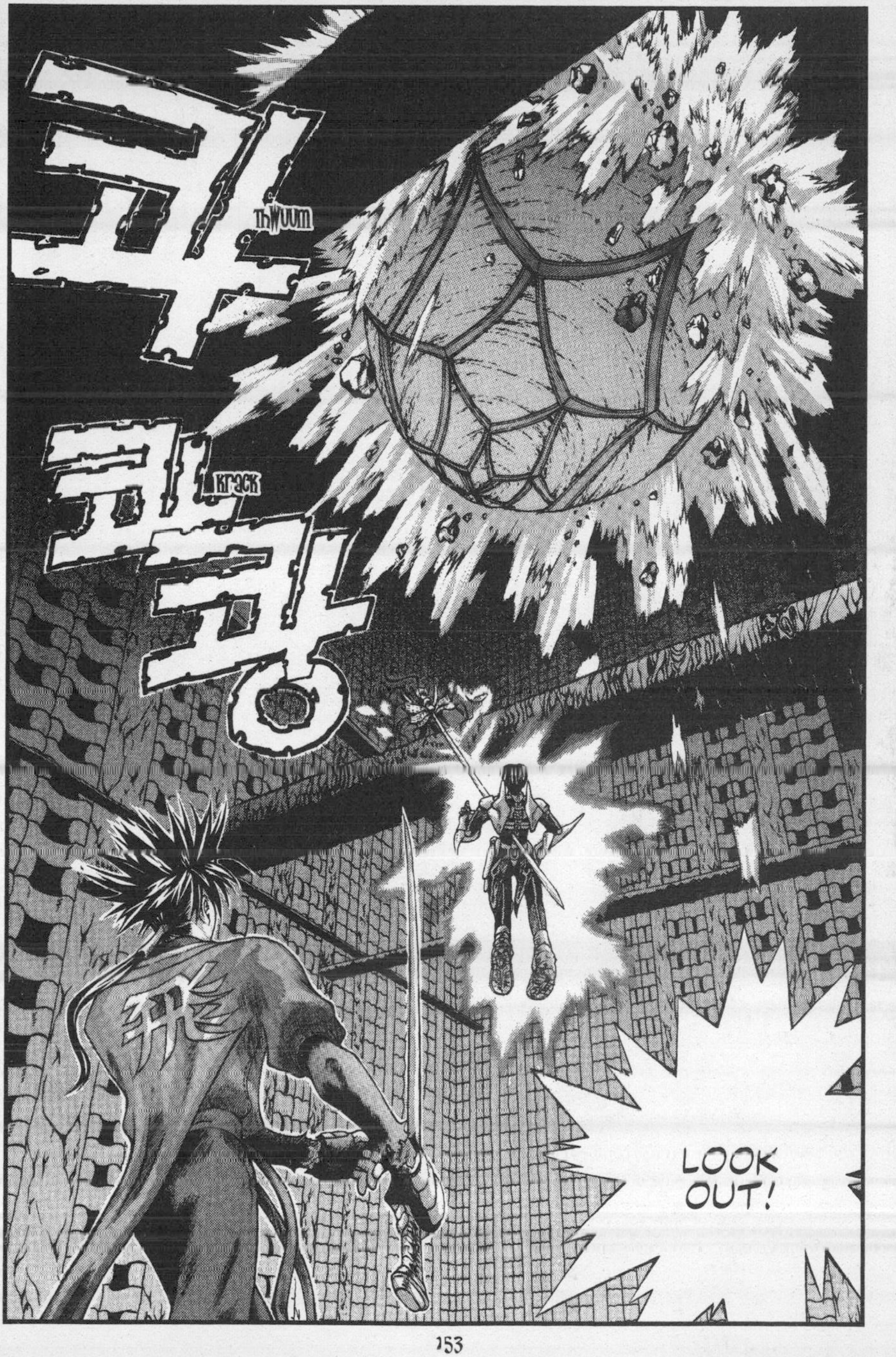

ThWUUM
KRACK
LOOK OUT!

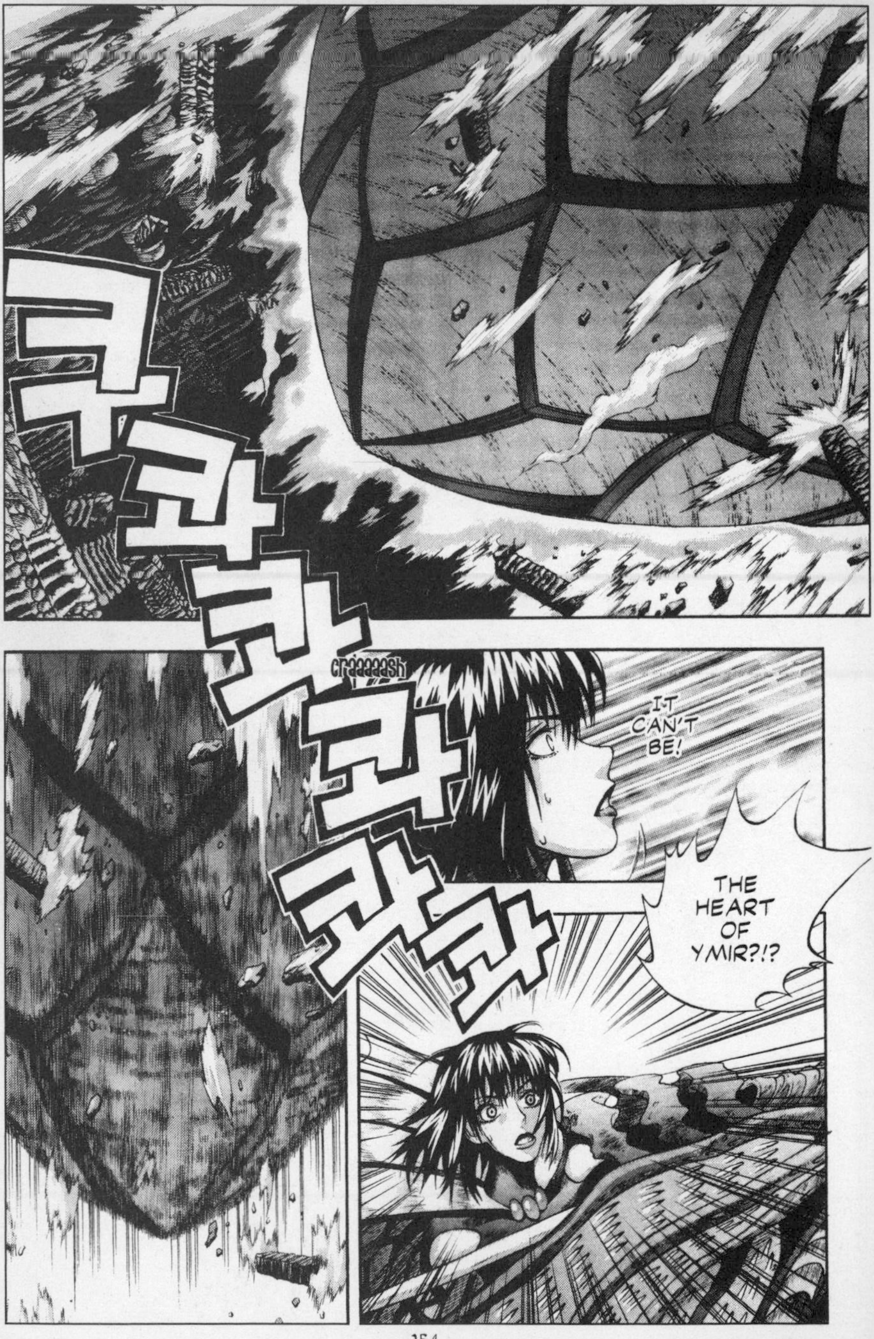
craaaaash
IT CAN'T BE!
THE HEART OF YMIR?!?

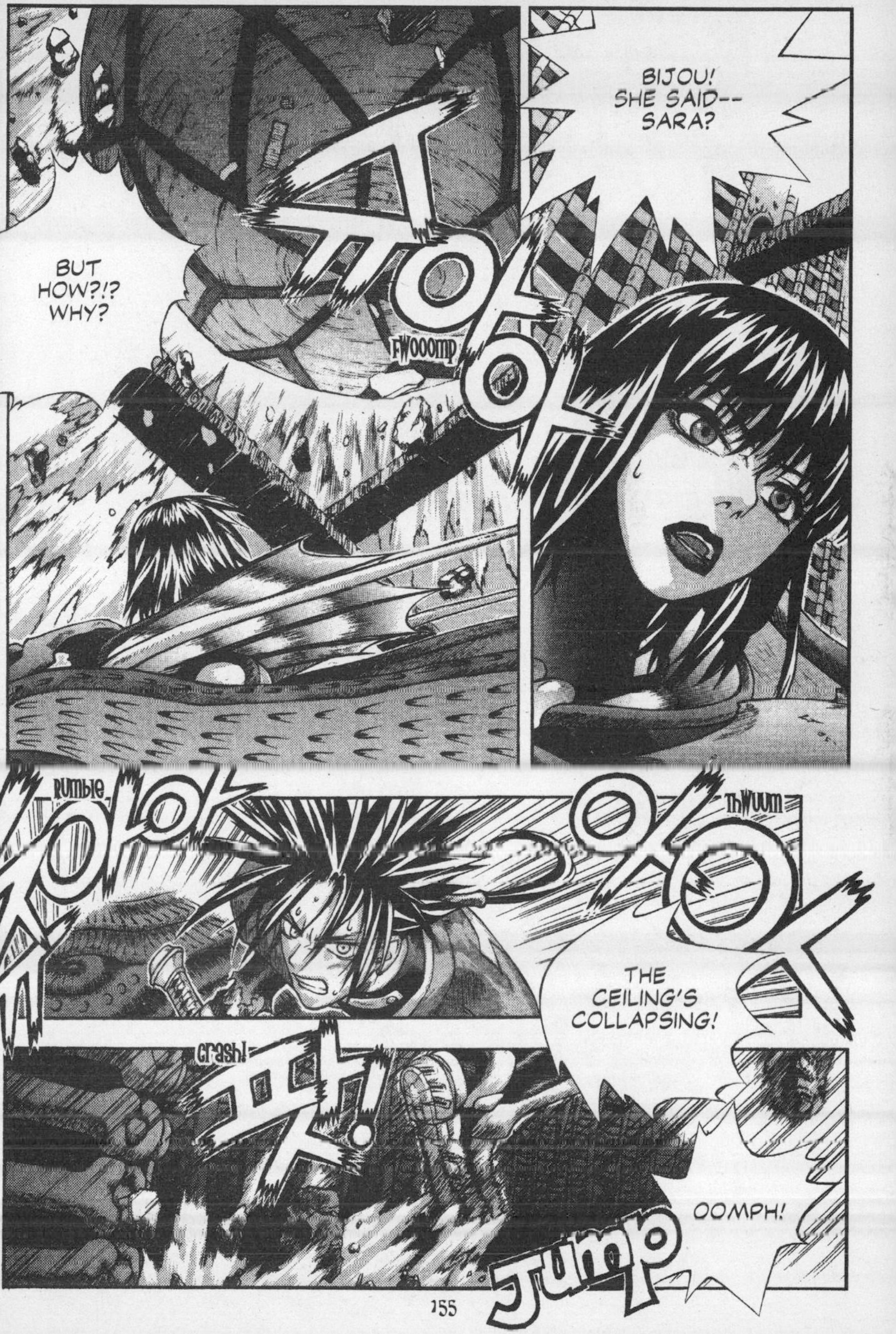
BUT HOW?!? WHY?
FWOOOMP
BIJOU! SHE SAID-- SARA?
Rumble
ThWuum
THE CEILING'S COLLAPSING!
Crash!
OOMPH!
Jump

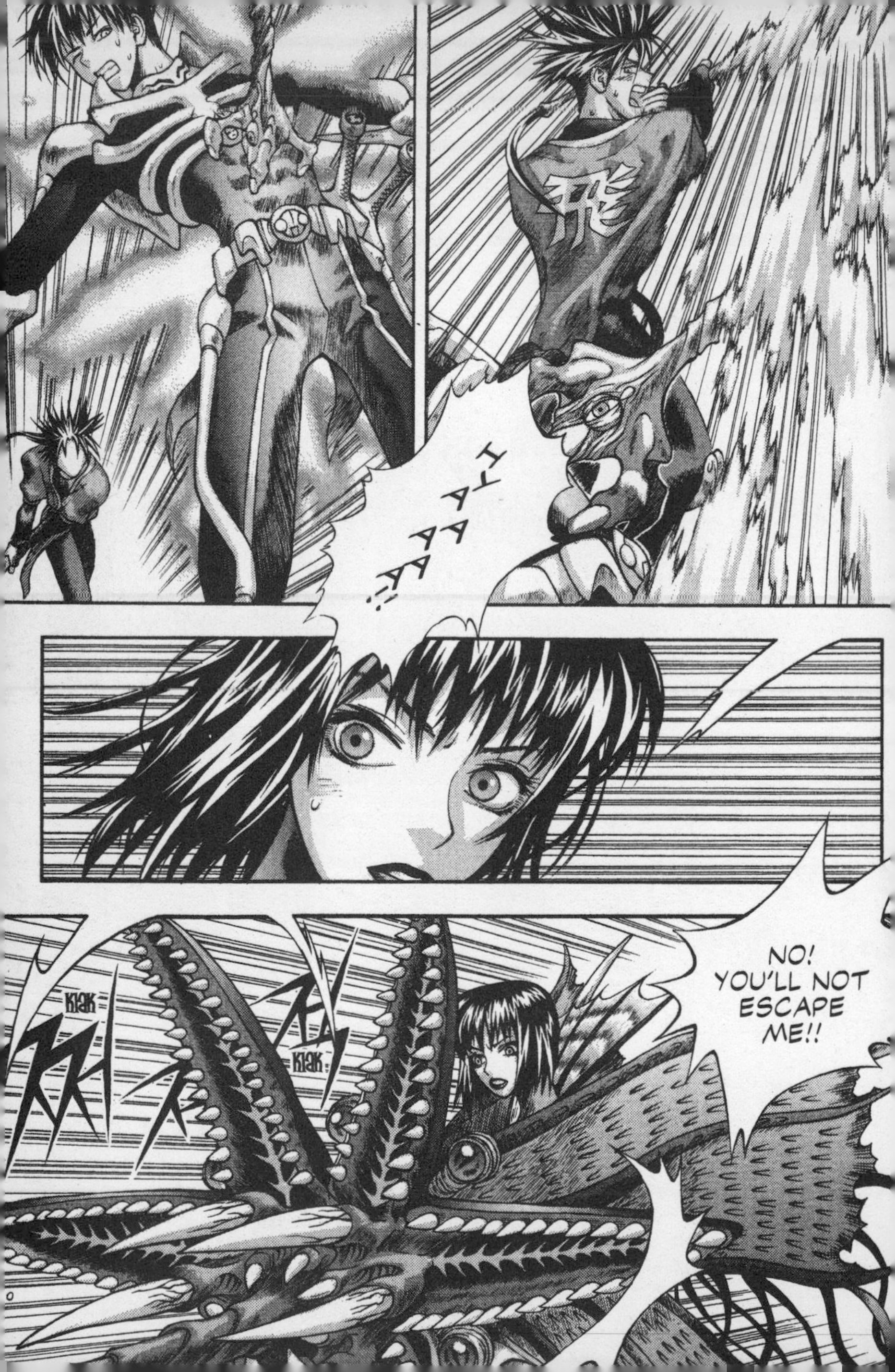
飛
HYAAAAA!!
KLAK
KLAK
NO! YOU'LL NOT ESCAPE ME!!

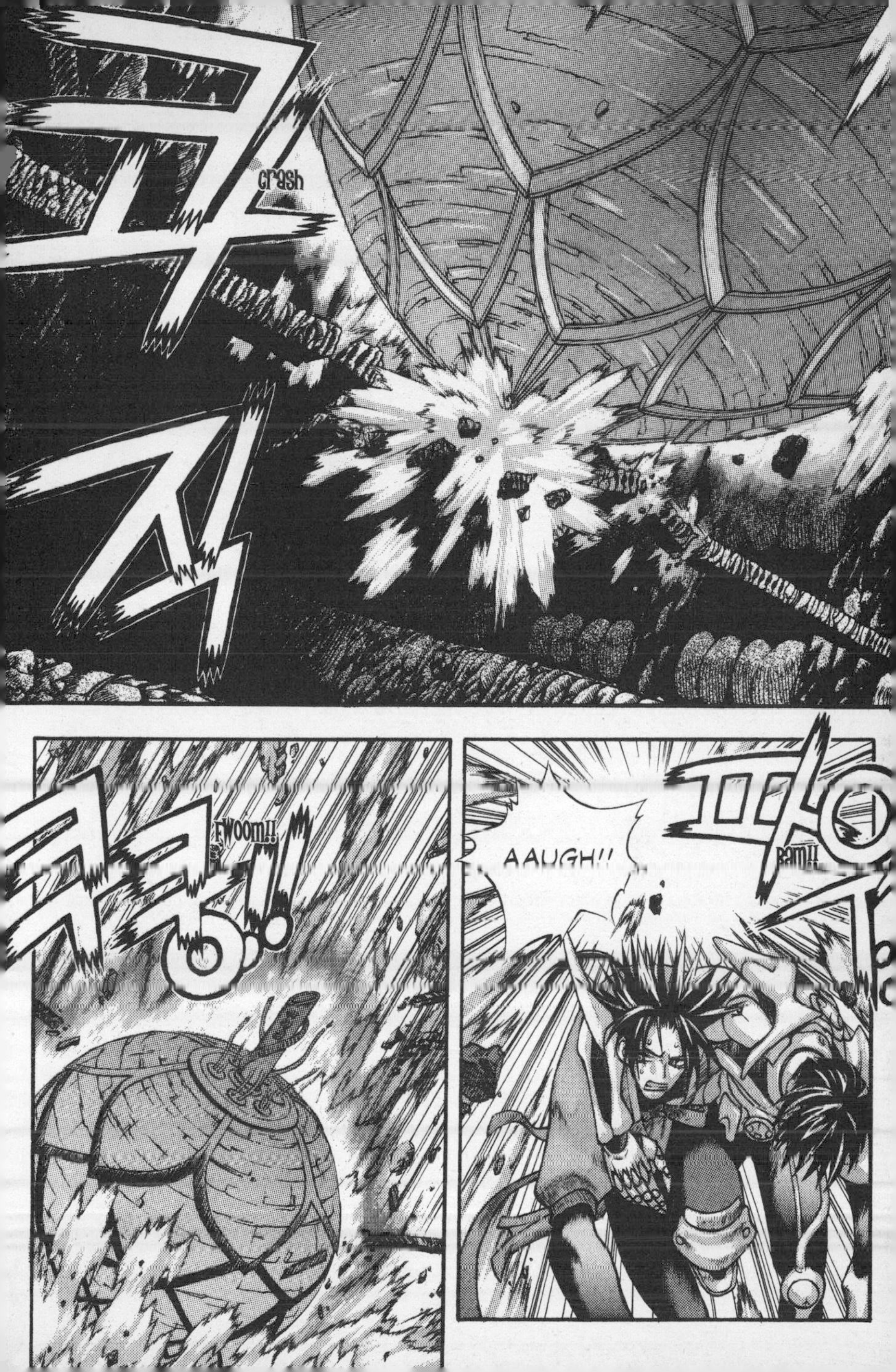

crash
FWOOM!!
AAUGH!!
BAM!!

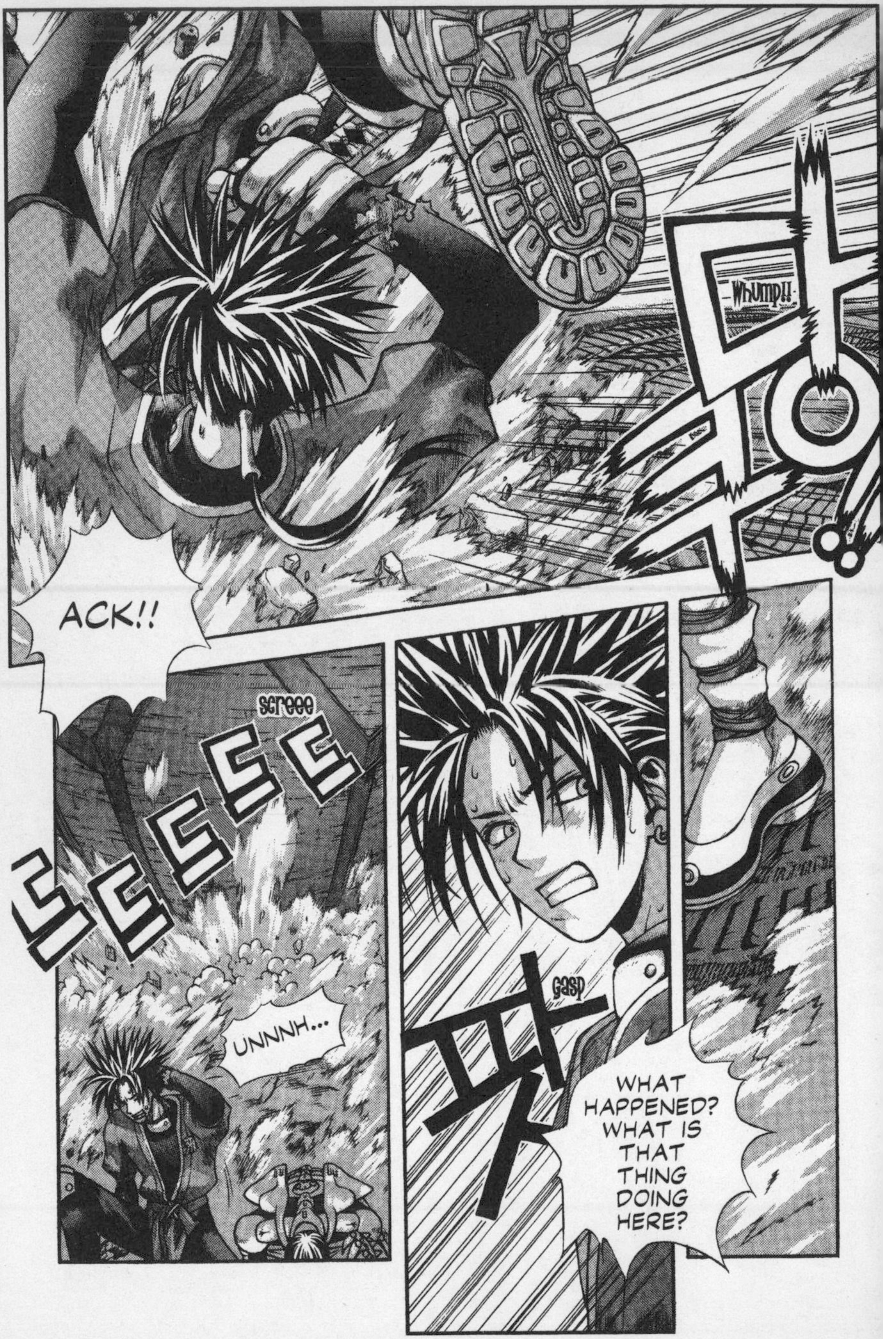
WHUMP!!
ACK!!
SCREEE
UNNNH...
GASP
WHAT HAPPENED? WHAT IS THAT THING DOING HERE?

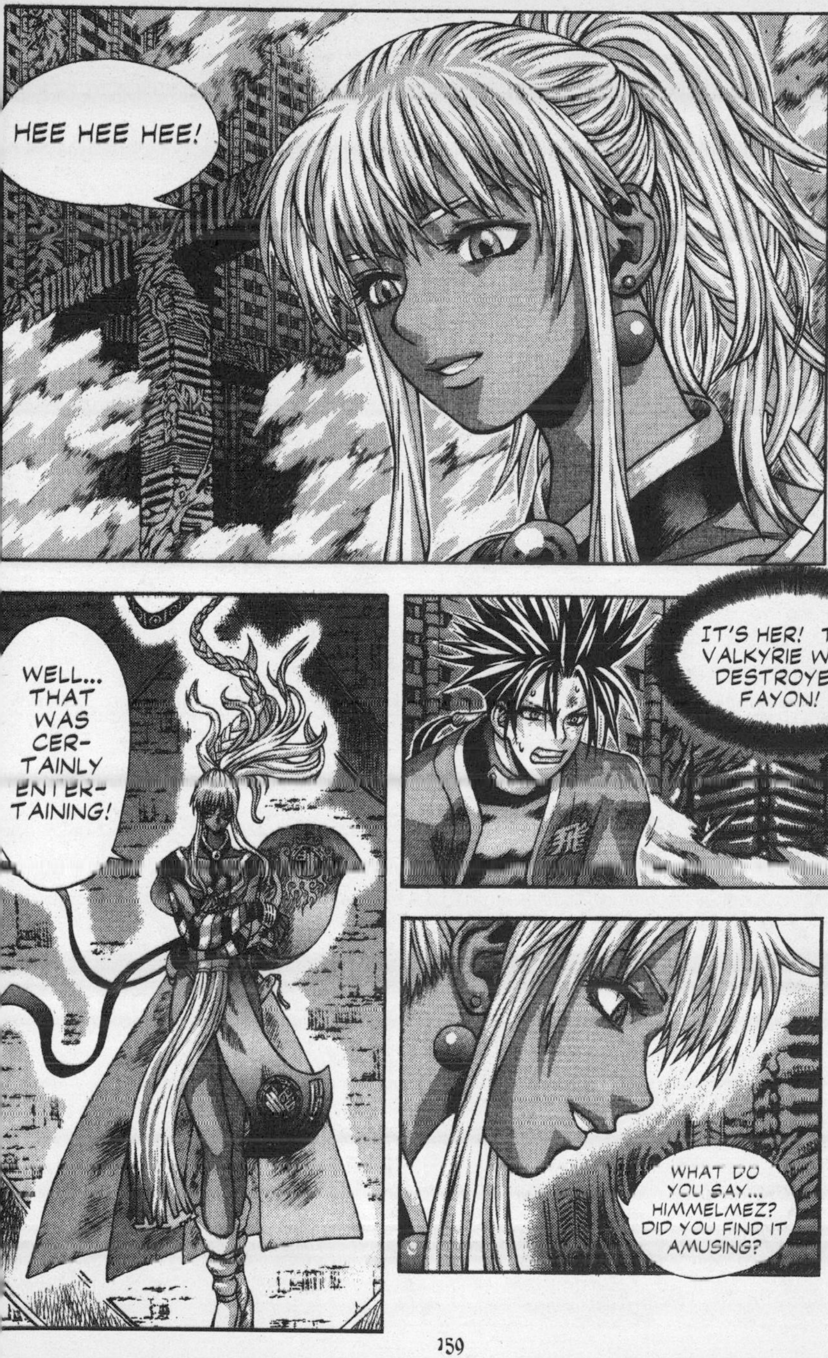
HEE HEE HEE!
WELL... THAT WAS CER-TAINLY ENTER-TAINING!
IT'S HER! THE VALKYRIE WHO DESTROYED FAYON!
WHAT DO YOU SAY... HIMMELMEZ? DID YOU FIND IT AMUSING?

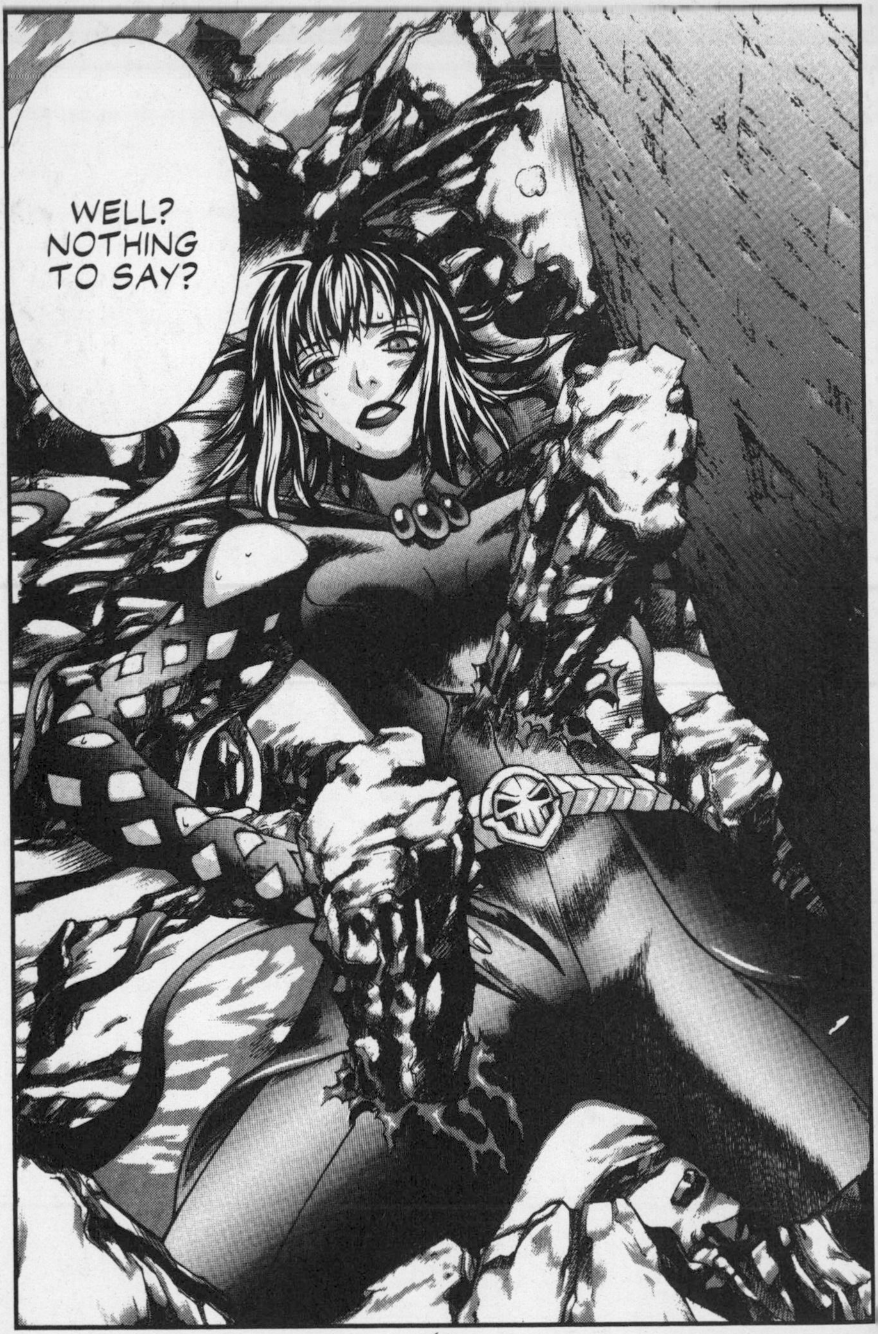
WELL? NOTHING TO SAY?

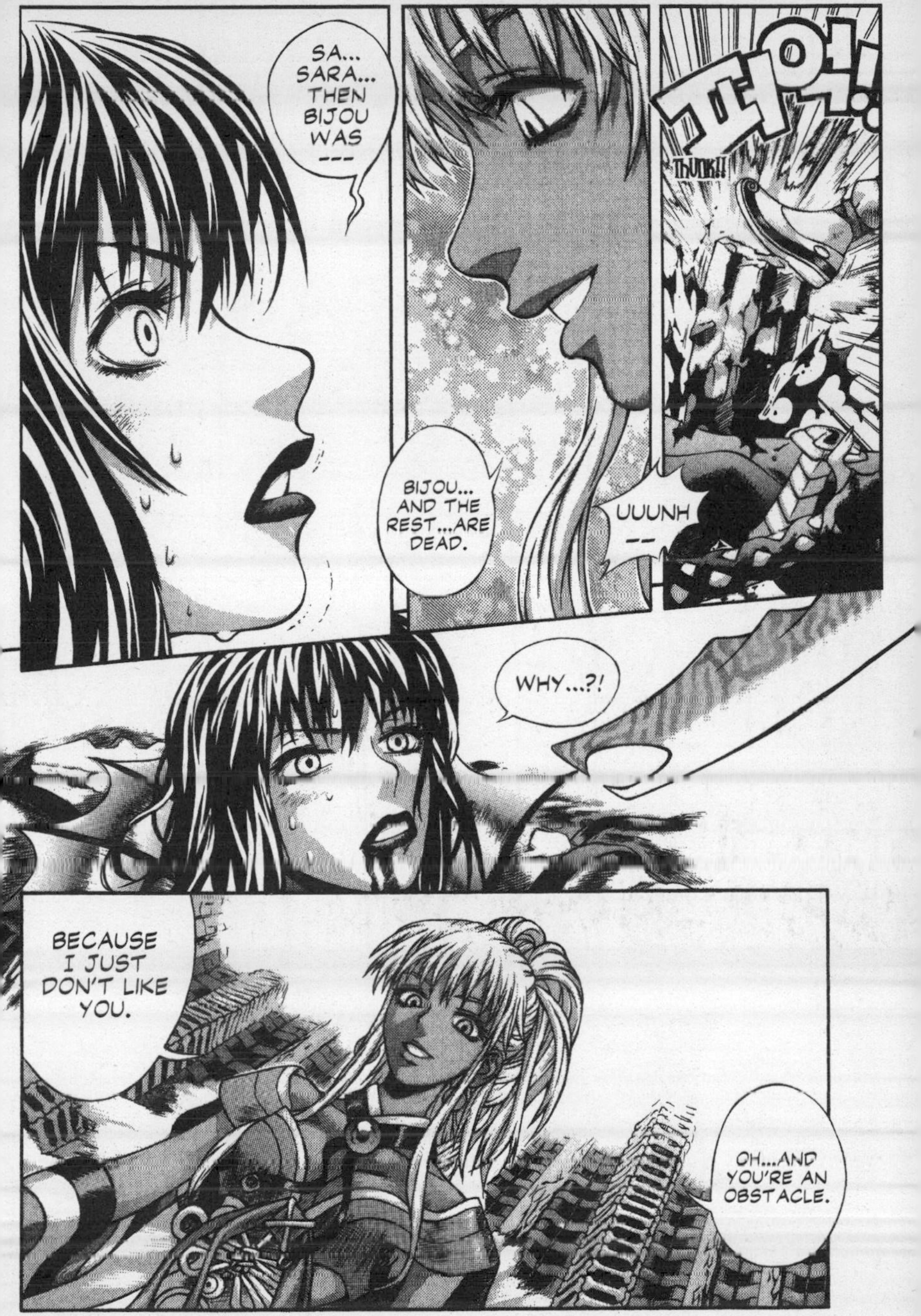
SA... SARA... THEN BIJOU WAS ---
BIJOU... AND THE REST...ARE DEAD.
ThUNK!!
UUUNH --
WHY...?!
BECAUSE I JUST DON'T LIKE YOU.
OH...AND YOU'RE AN OBSTACLE.

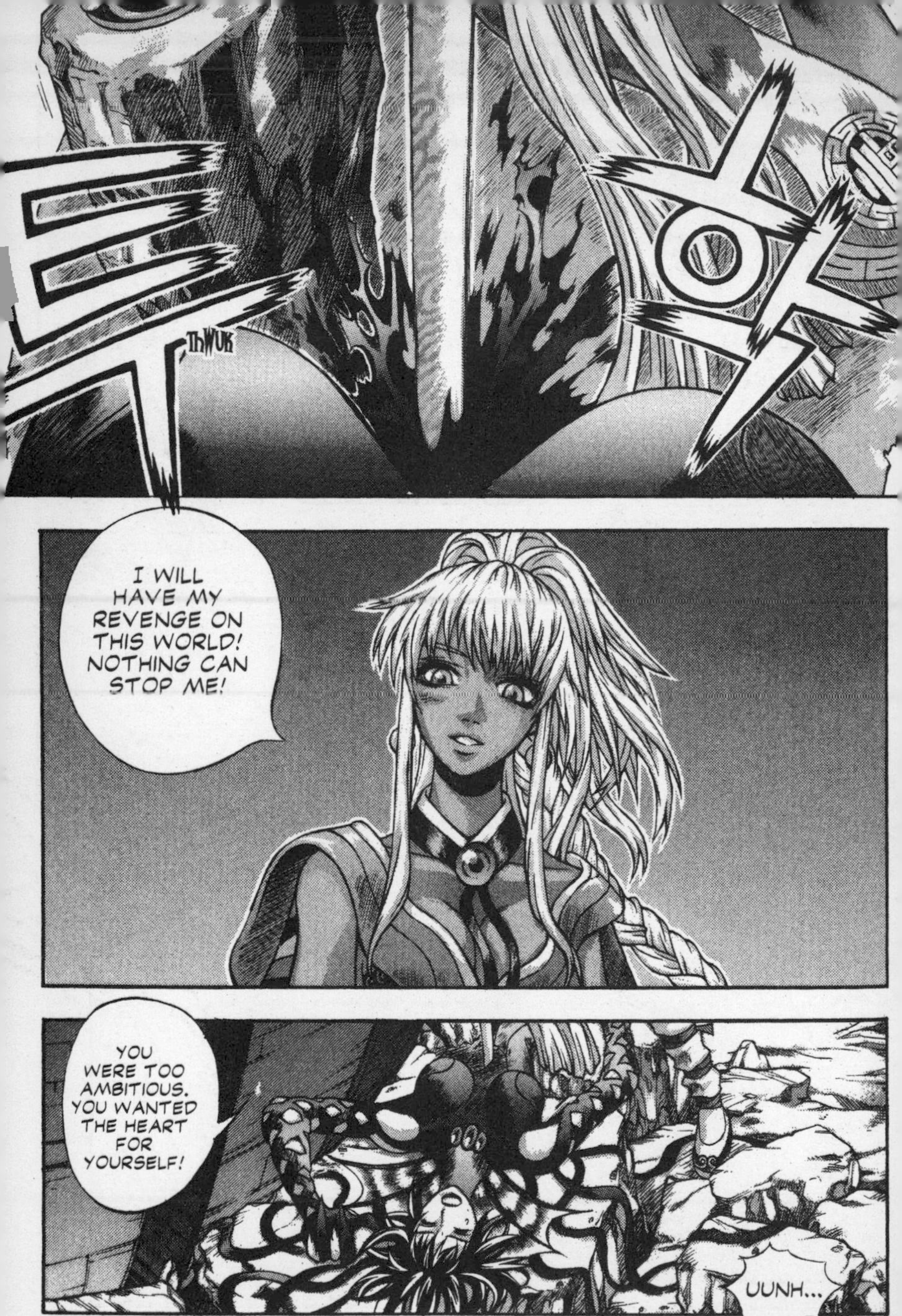
THWUK
I WILL HAVE MY REVENGE ON THIS WORLD! NOTHING CAN STOP ME!
YOU WERE TOO AMBITIOUS. YOU WANTED THE HEART FOR YOURSELF!
UUNH...

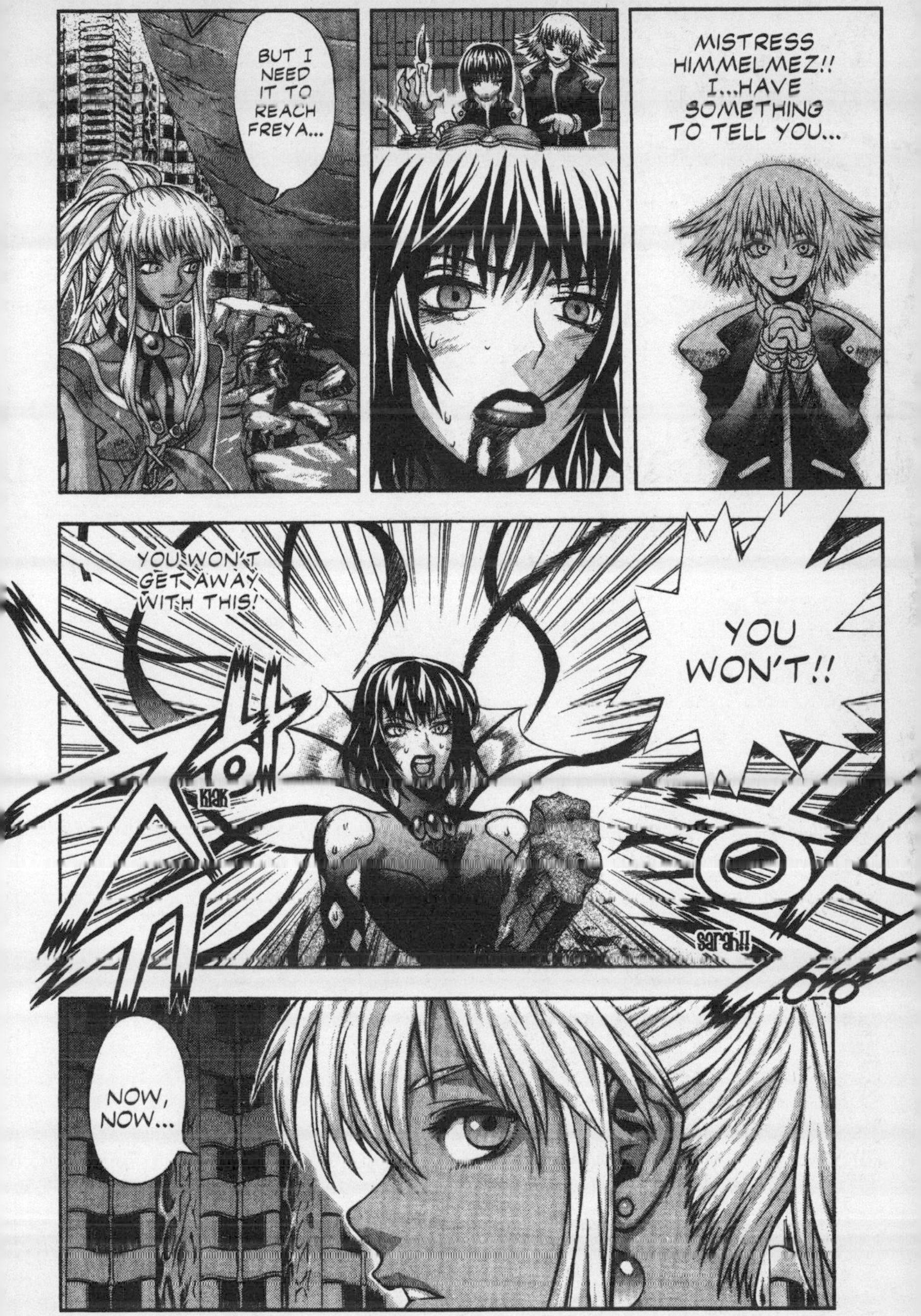
BUT I NEED IT TO REACH FREYA...
MISTRESS HIMMELMEZ!! I...HAVE SOMETHING TO TELL YOU...
YOU WON'T GET AWAY WITH THIS!
YOU WON'T!!
KIAK
sarah!!
NOW, NOW...

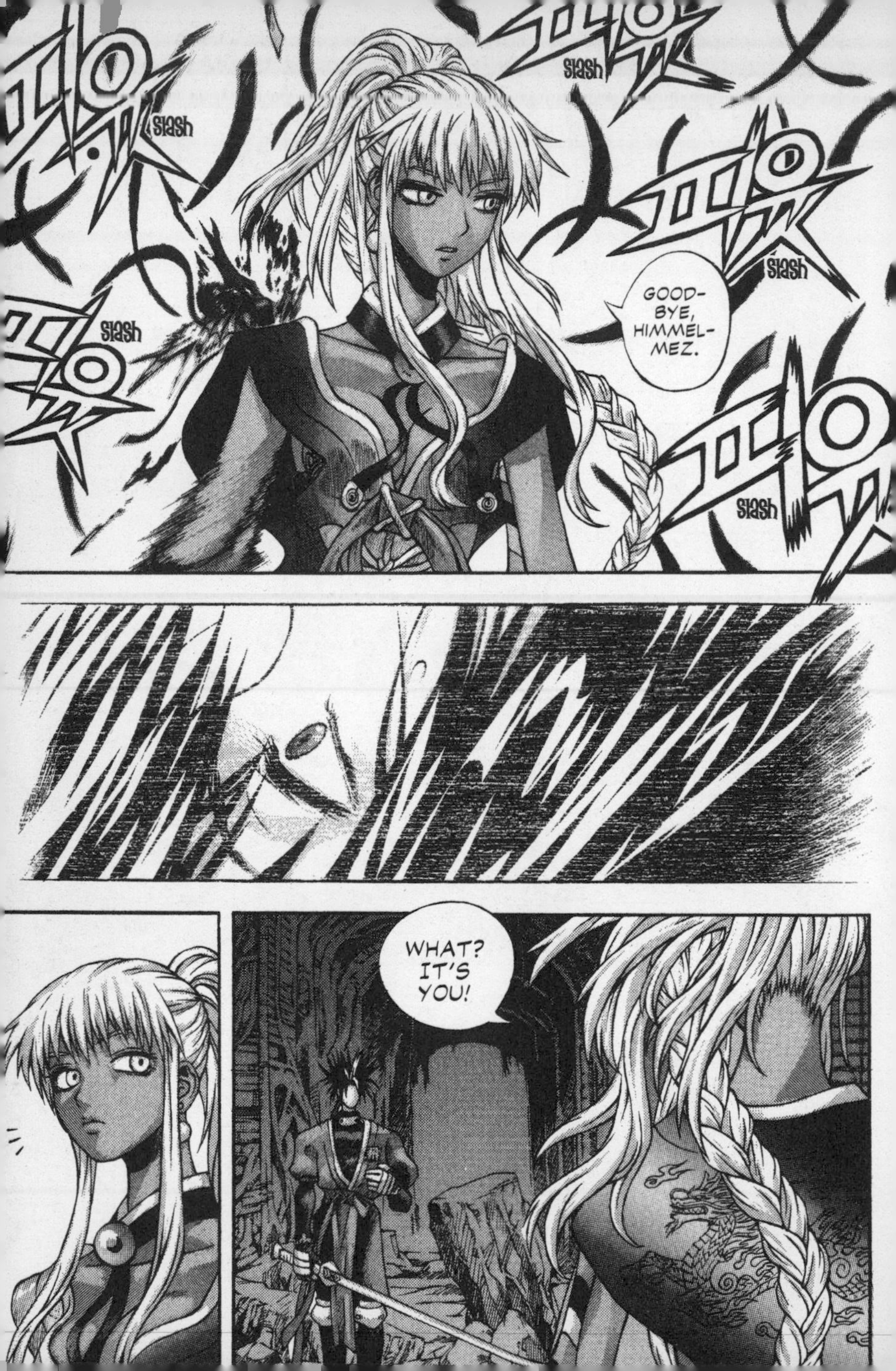
SLASH
SLASH
SLASH
SLASH
SLASH
GOOD-BYE, HIMMEL-MEZ.
WHAT? IT'S YOU!

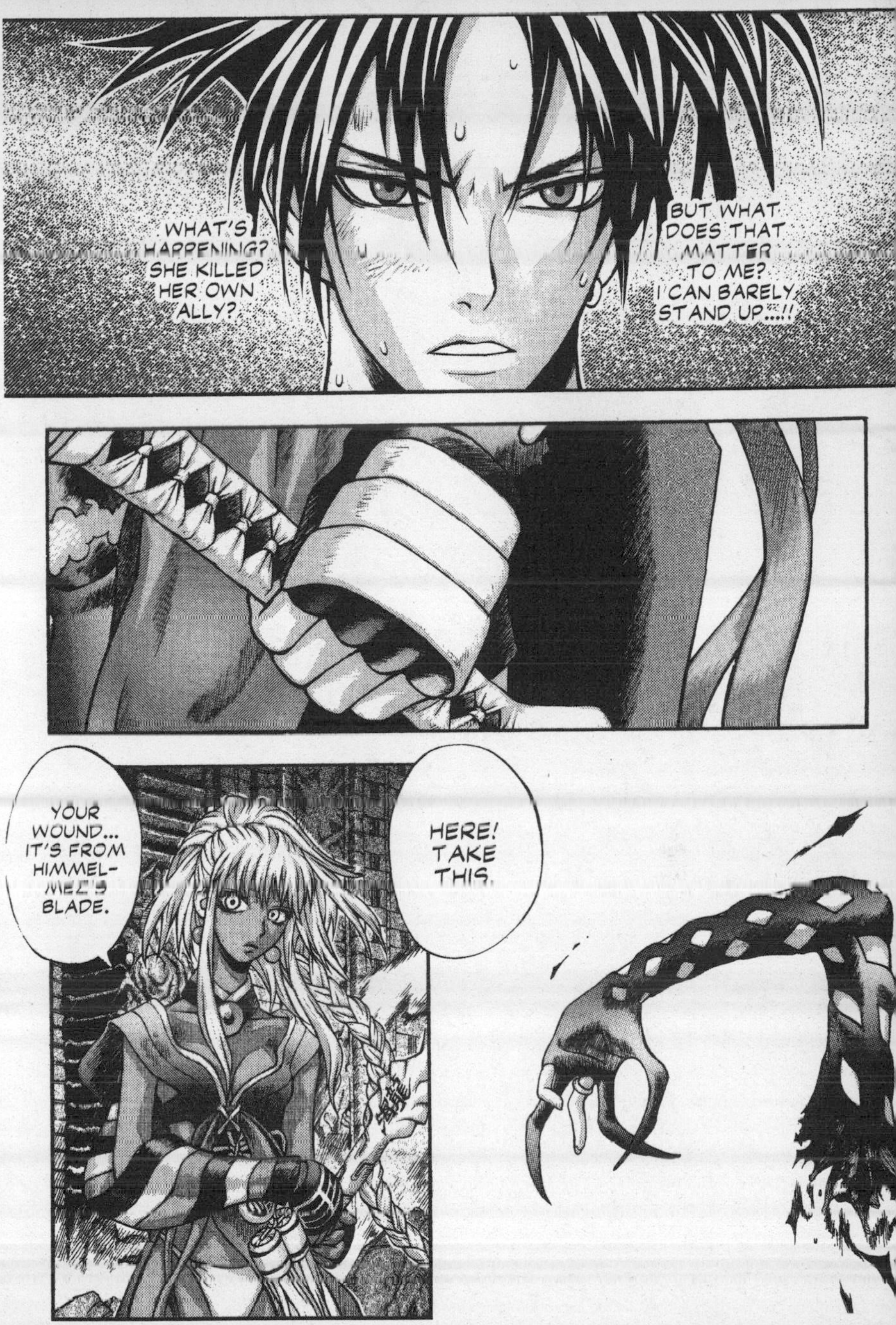
WHAT'S HAPPENING? SHE KILLED HER OWN ALLY?
BUT WHAT DOES THAT MATTER TO ME? I CAN BARELY STAND UP...!!
YOUR WOUND... IT'S FROM HIMMEL-MEL'S BLADE.
HERE! TAKE THIS.

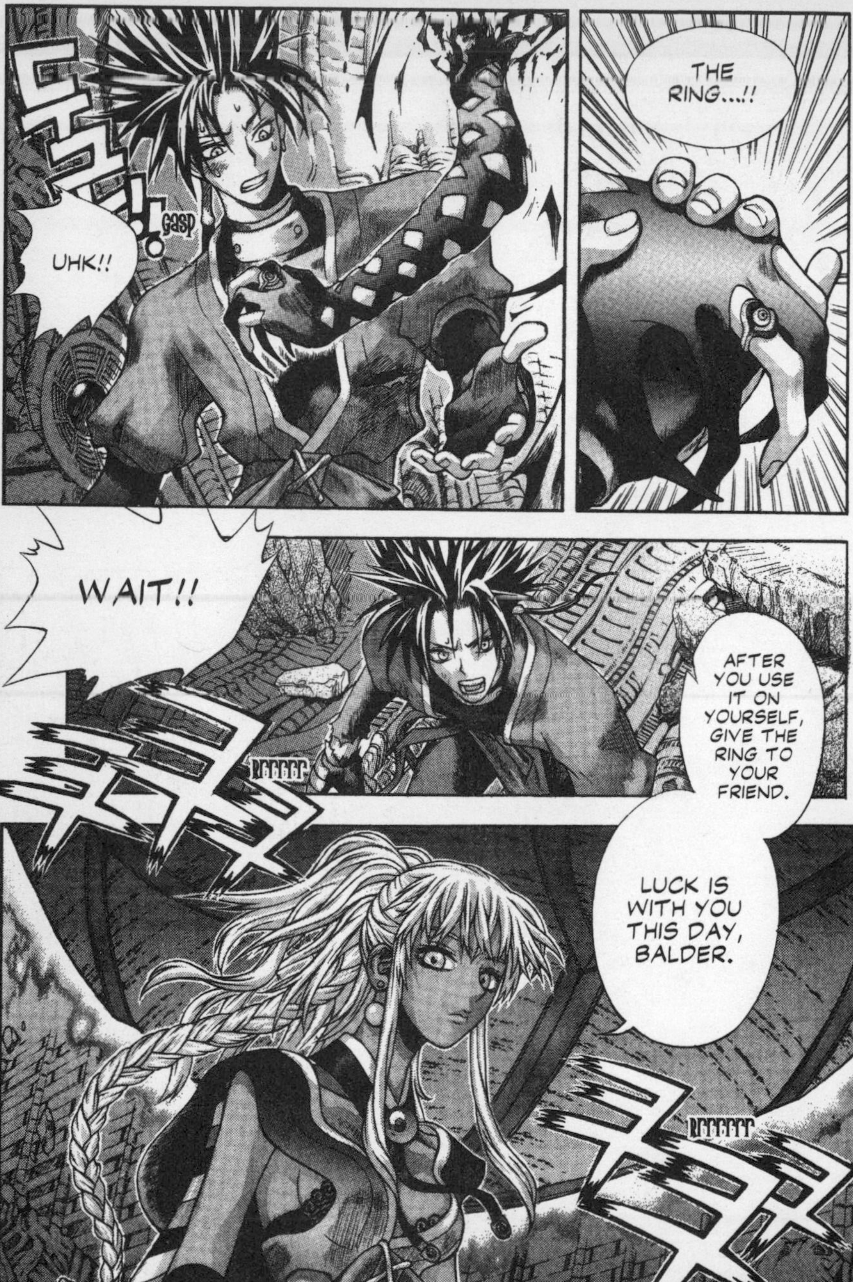
UHK!!
GASP
THE RING...!!
WAIT!!
RRRRRR
AFTER YOU USE IT ON YOURSELF, GIVE THE RING TO YOUR FRIEND.
LUCK IS WITH YOU THIS DAY, BALDER.
RRRRRRR

RAGNAROK
라그나로크
IN TO THE ABYSS

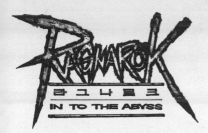

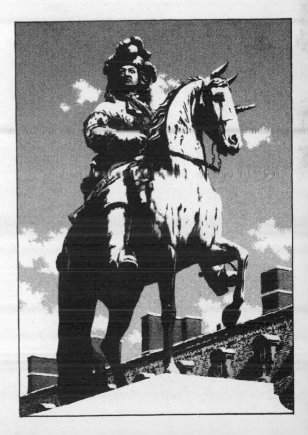

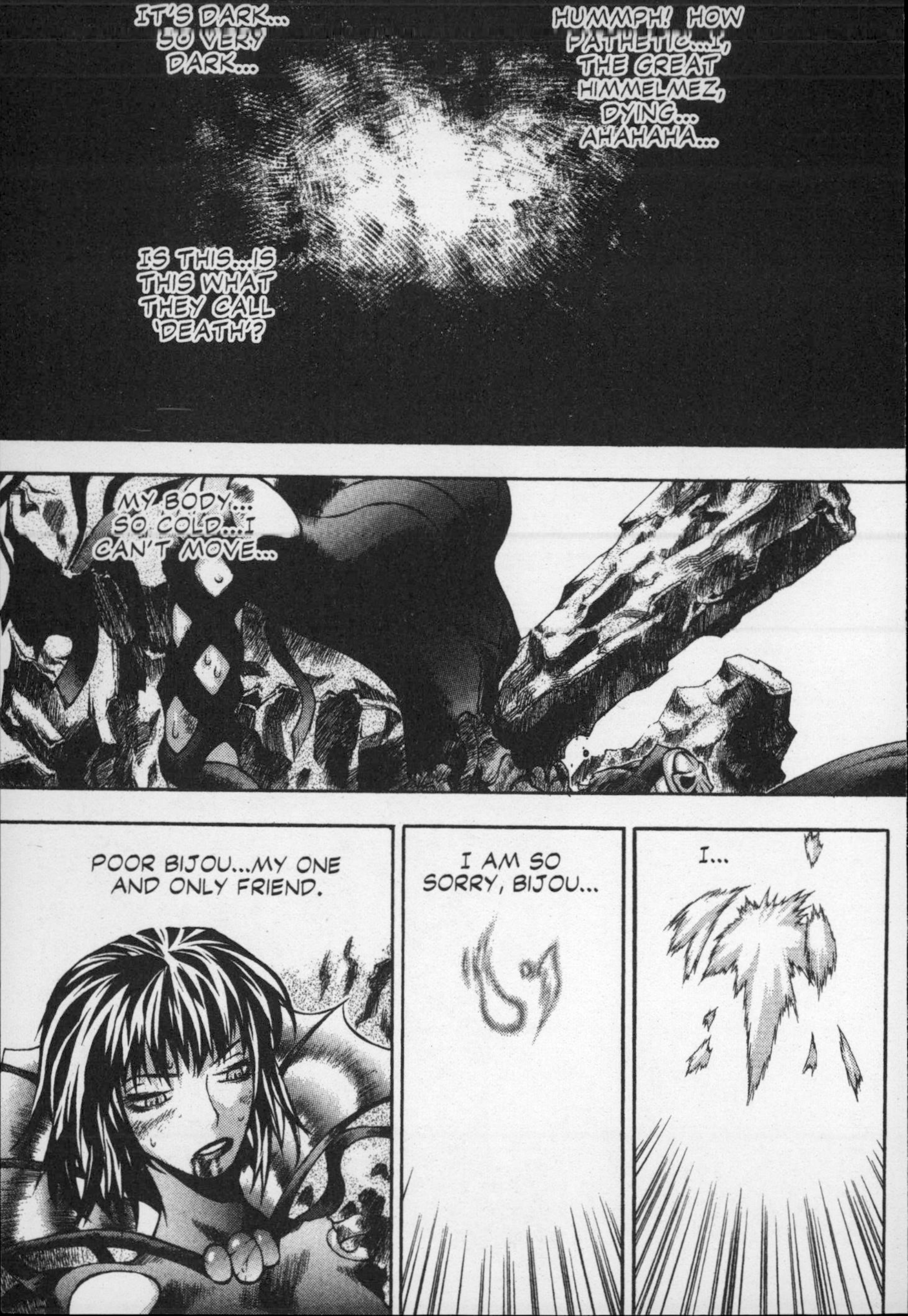
IT'S DARK... SO VERY DARK...
HUMMPH! HOW PATHETIC...I, THE GREAT HIMMELMEZ, DYING... AHAHAHA...
IS THIS...IS THIS WHAT THEY CALL 'DEATH'?
MY BODY... SO COLD...I CAN'T MOVE...
POOR BIJOU...MY ONE AND ONLY FRIEND.
I AM SO SORRY, BIJOU...
I...

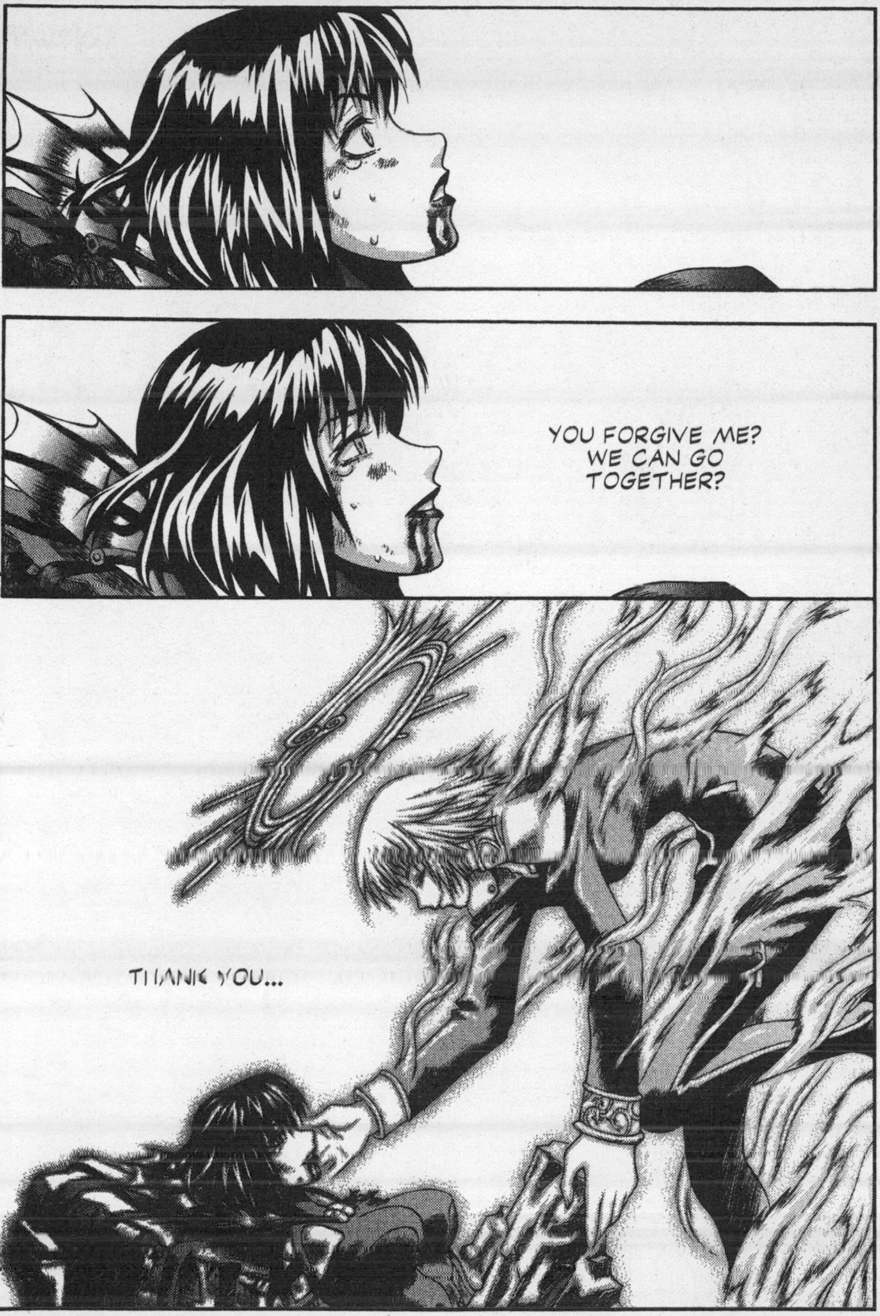
YOU FORGIVE ME? WE CAN GO TOGETHER?
THANK YOU...

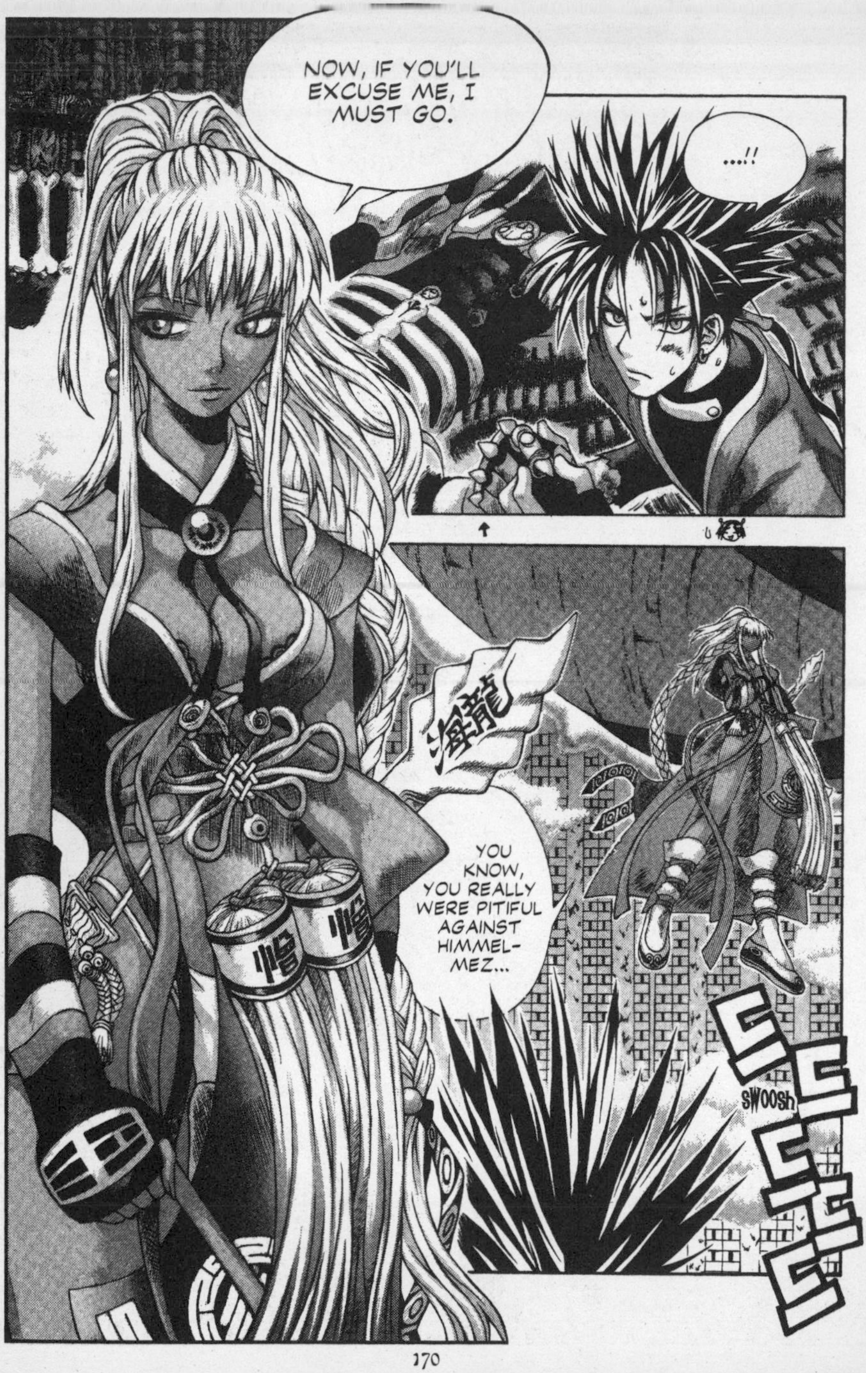
NOW, IF YOU'LL EXCUSE ME, I MUST GO.
...!!
YOU KNOW, YOU REALLY WERE PITIFUL AGAINST HIMMEL-MEZ...
SWOOSH

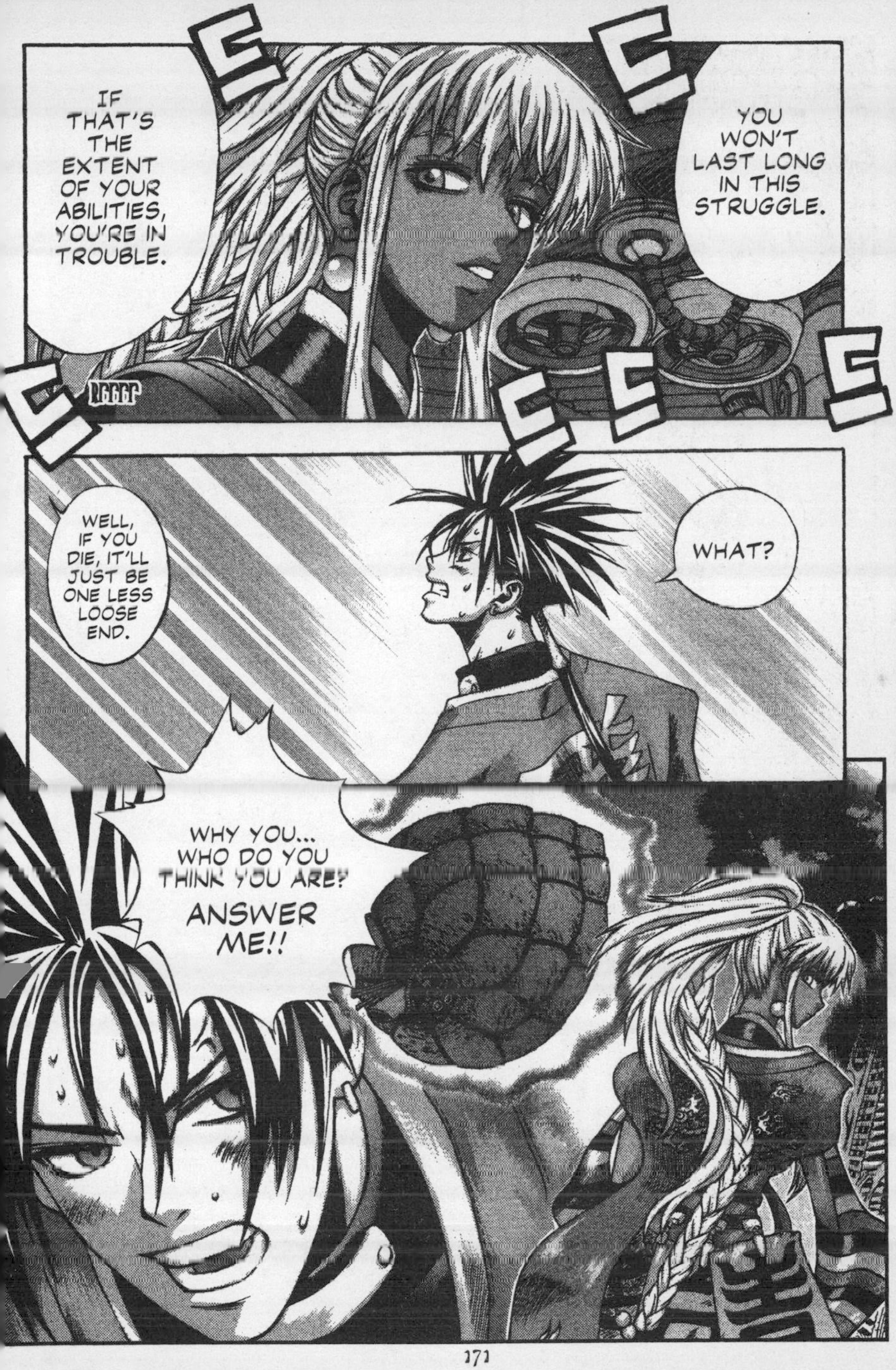
IF THAT'S THE EXTENT OF YOUR ABILITIES, YOU'RE IN TROUBLE.
YOU WON'T LAST LONG IN THIS STRUGGLE.
WELL, IF YOU DIE, IT'LL JUST BE ONE LESS LOOSE END.
WHAT?
WHY YOU... WHO DO YOU THINK YOU ARE?
ANSWER ME!!

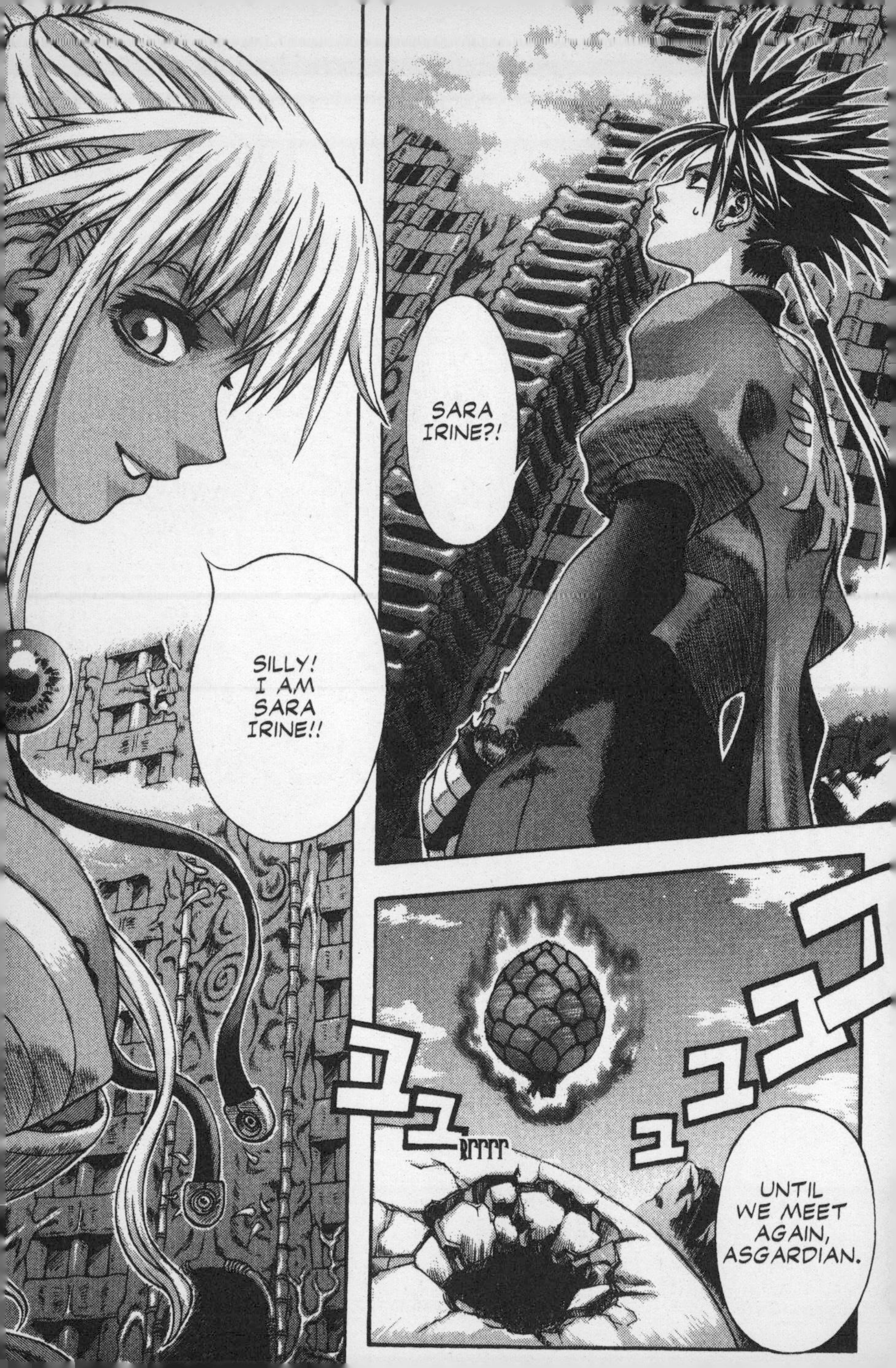
SILLY! I AM SARA IRINE!!
SARA IRINE?!
RRRRR
UNTIL WE MEET AGAIN, ASGARDIAN.

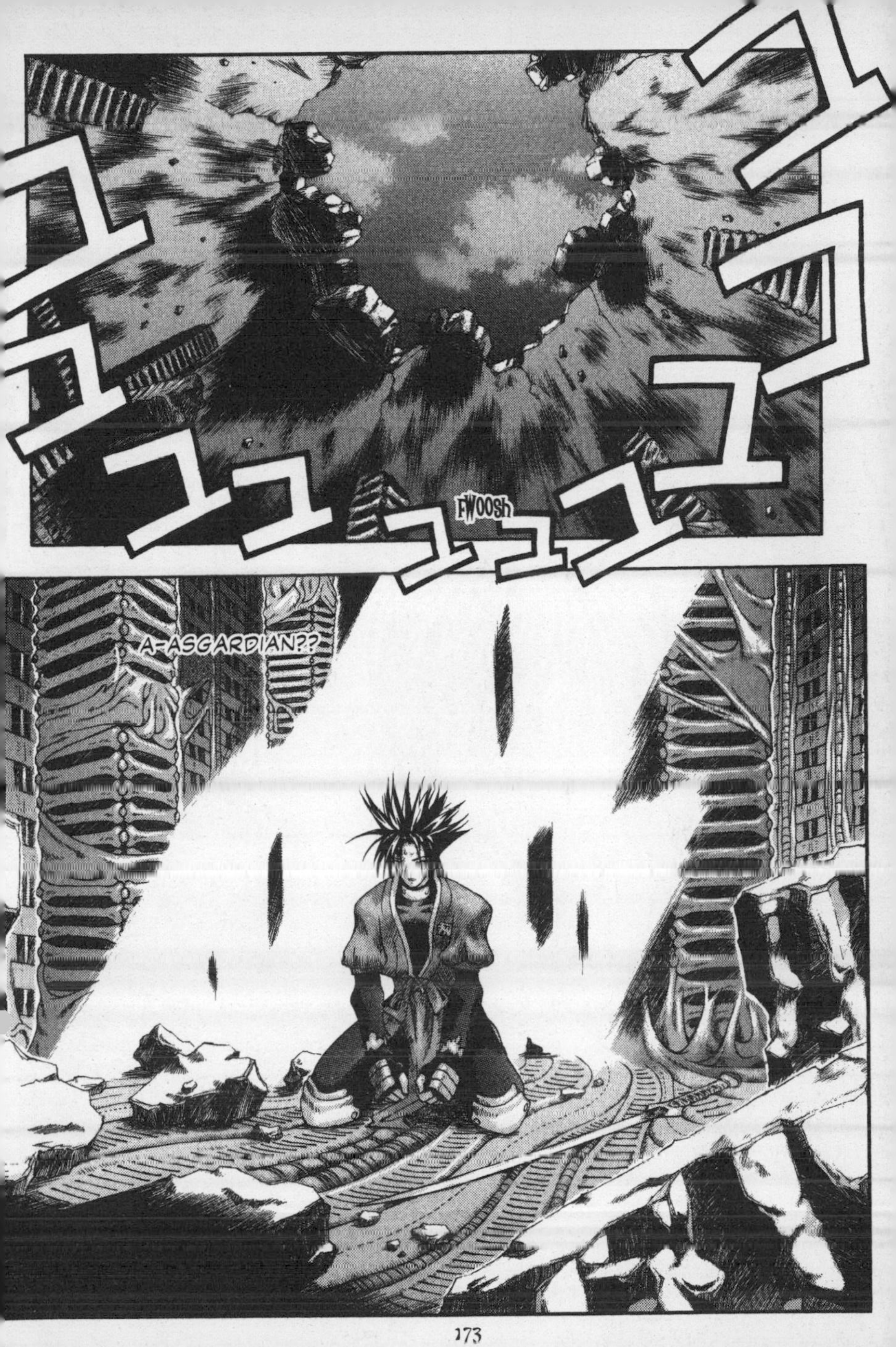
FWOOSH
A-ASGARDIAN??

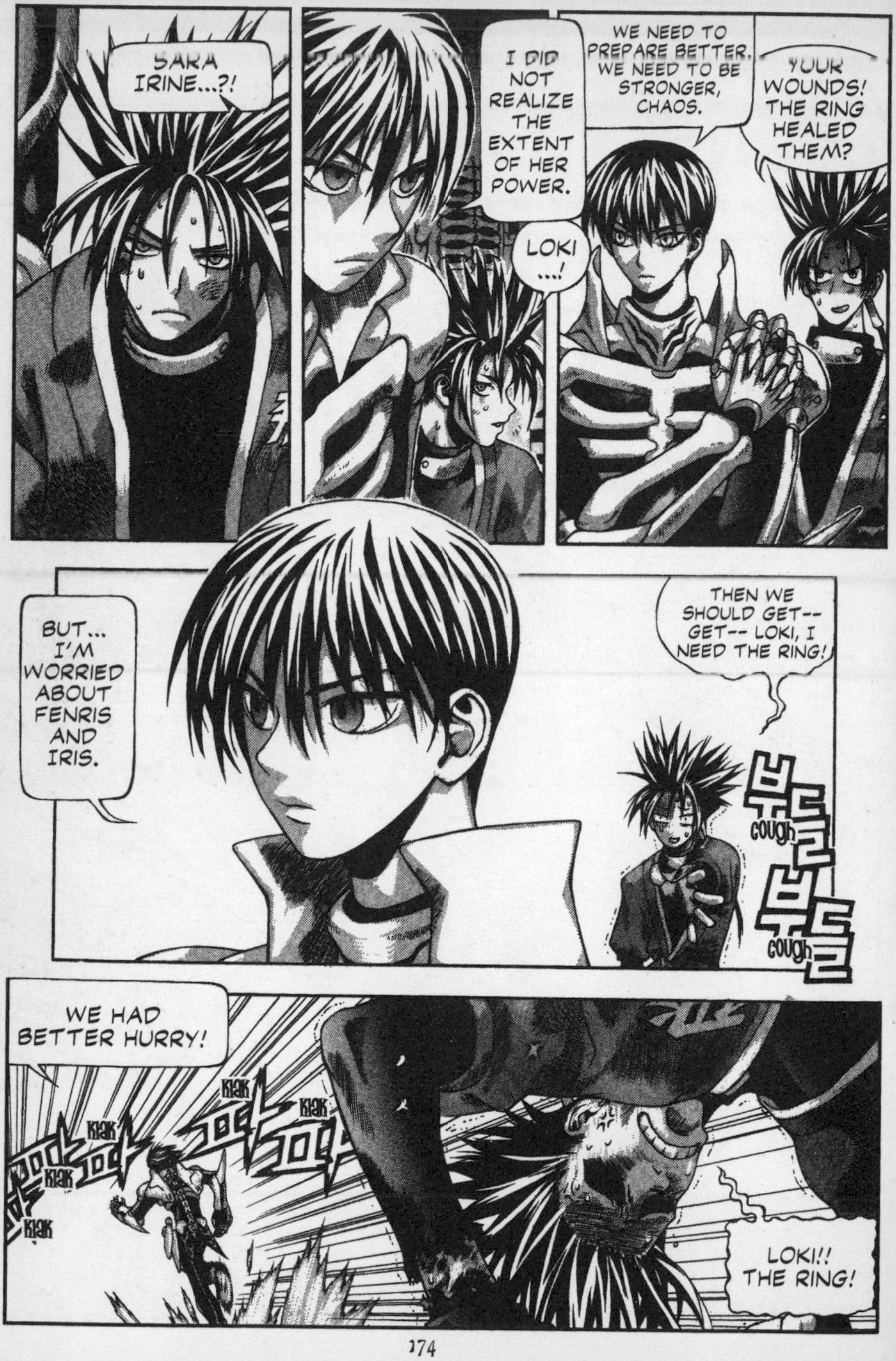
SARA IRINE...?!
I DID NOT REALIZE THE EXTENT OF HER POWER.
LOKI ....!
WE NEED TO PREPARE BETTER. WE NEED TO BE STRONGER, CHAOS.
YOUR WOUNDS! THE RING HEALED THEM?
BUT... I'M WORRIED ABOUT FENRIS AND IRIS.
THEN WE SHOULD GET-- GET-- LOKI, I NEED THE RING!
cough
cough
WE HAD BETTER HURRY!
klak
klak
klak
klak
klak
LOKI!! THE RING!

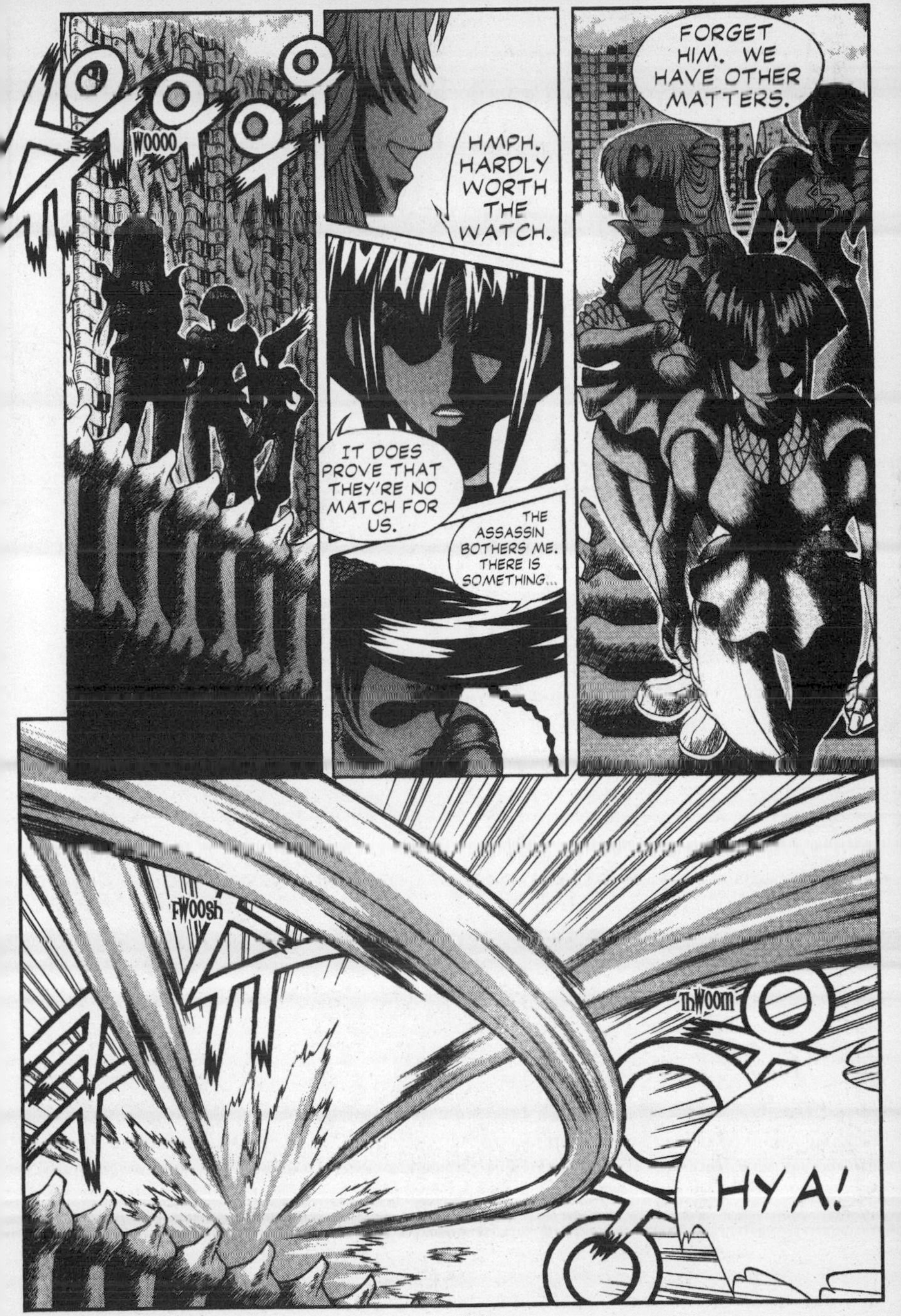
WOOOO
HMPH. HARDLY WORTH THE WATCH.
IT DOES PROVE THAT THEY'RE NO MATCH FOR US.
THE ASSASSIN BOTHERS ME. THERE IS SOMETHING...
FORGET HIM. WE HAVE OTHER MATTERS.
FWOOSH
ThWoom
HYA!

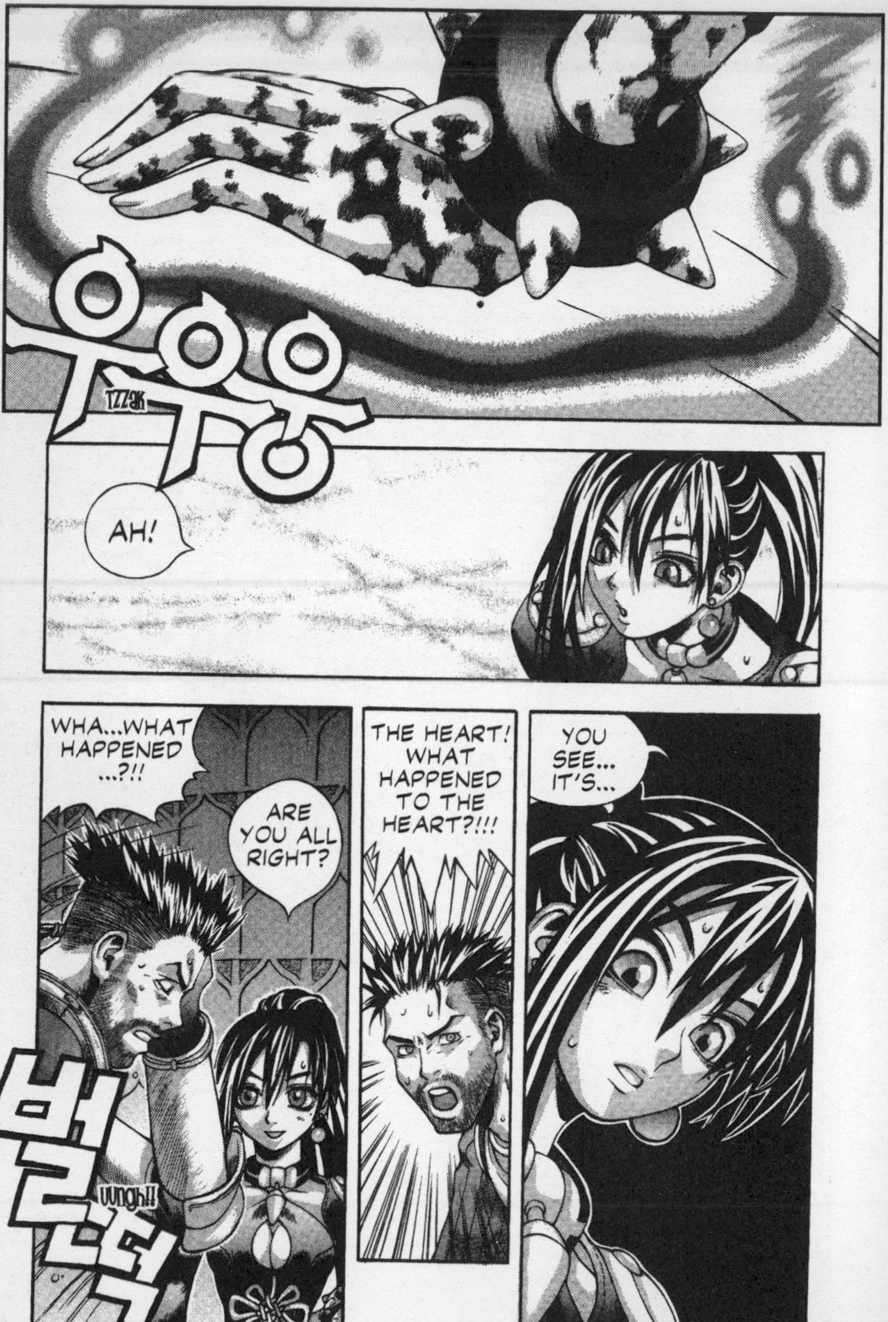
우우웅
TZZAK
AH!
WHA...WHAT HAPPENED ...?!!
ARE YOU ALL RIGHT?
벌떡
UUNGH!!
THE HEART! WHAT HAPPENED TO THE HEART?!!!
YOU SEE... IT'S...

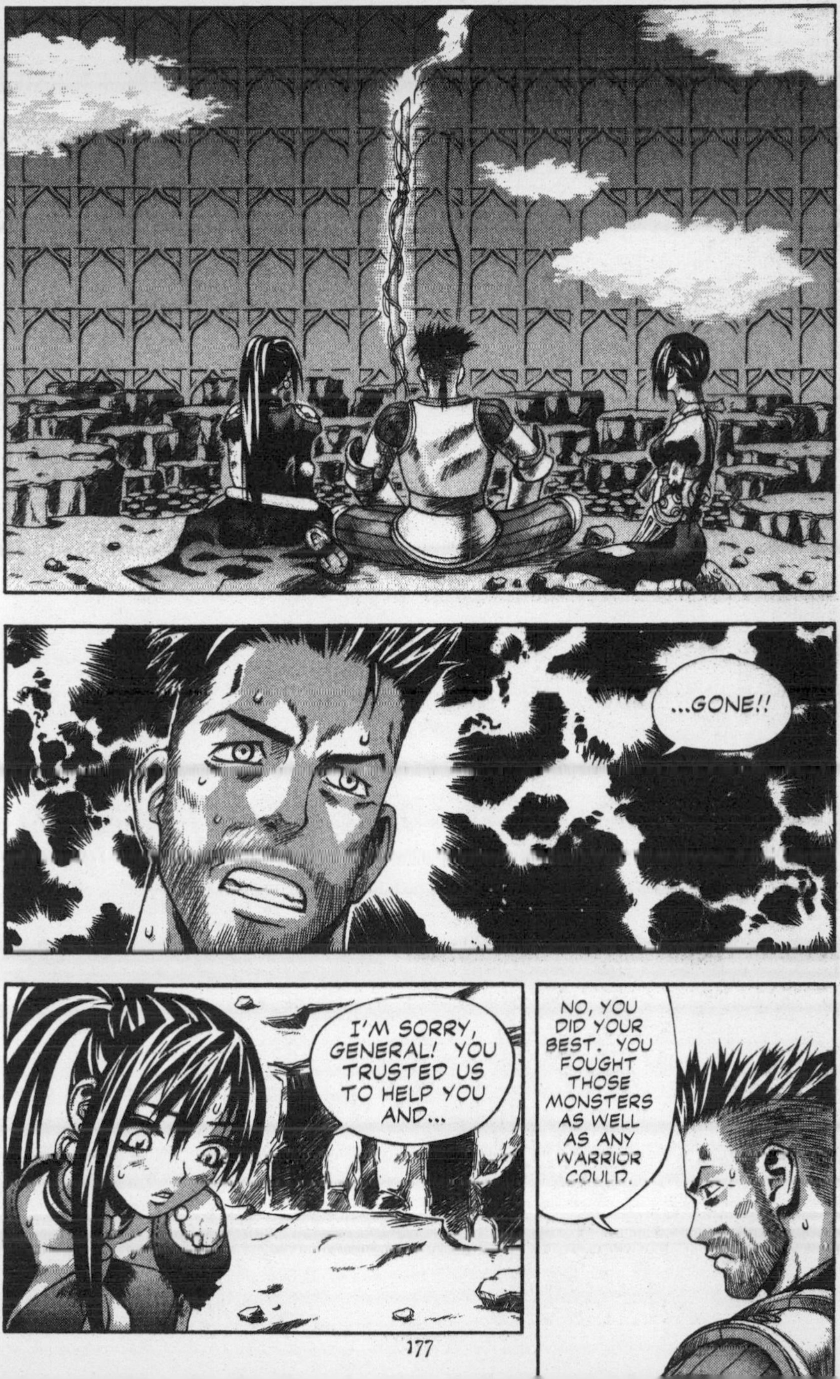
...GONE!!
I'M SORRY, GENERAL! YOU TRUSTED US TO HELP YOU AND...
NO, YOU DID YOUR BEST. YOU FOUGHT THOSE MONSTERS AS WELL AS ANY WARRIOR COULD.

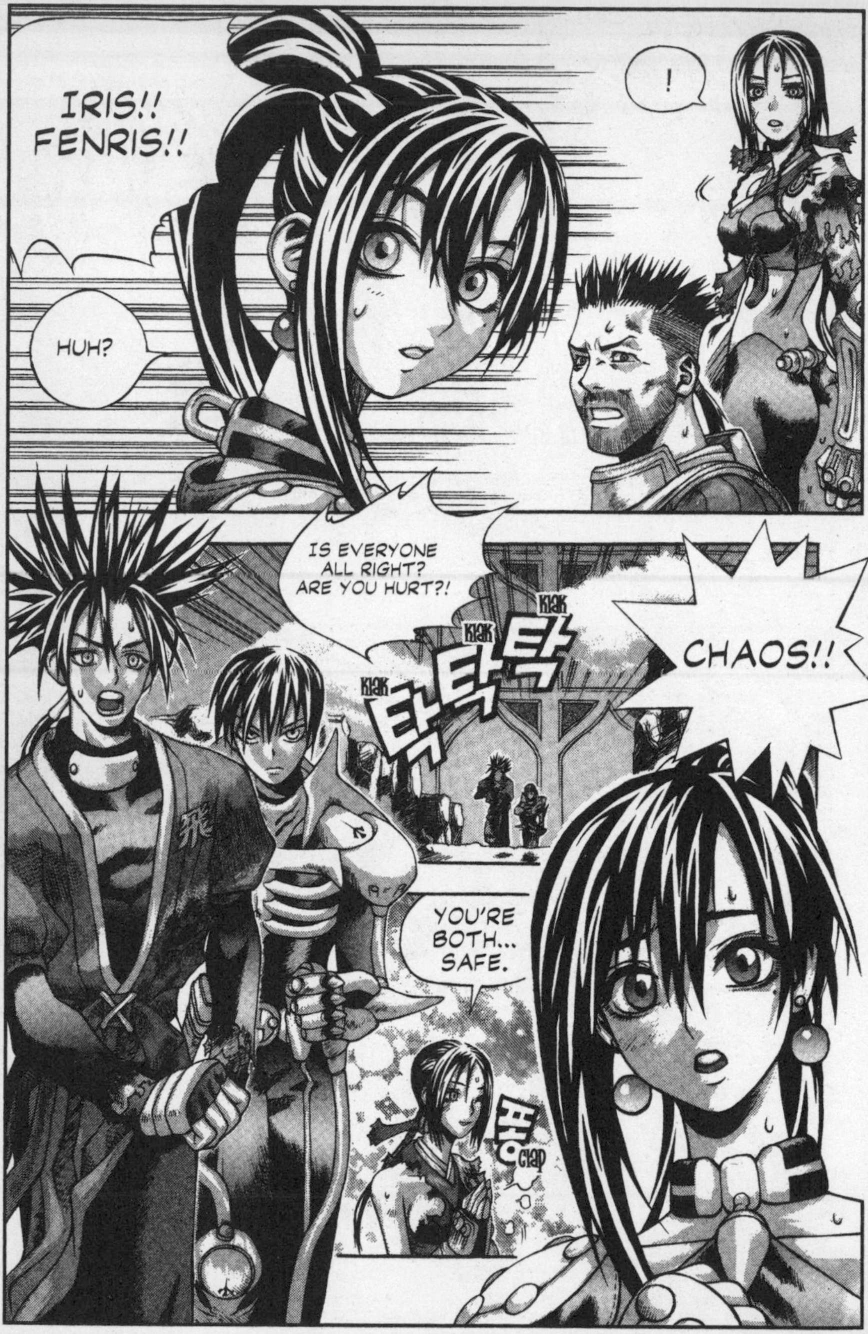
IRIS!! FENRIS!!
!
HUH?
IS EVERYONE ALL RIGHT? ARE YOU HURT?!
KLAK 탁
KLAK 탁
KLAK 탁
CHAOS!!
YOU'RE BOTH... SAFE.
clap

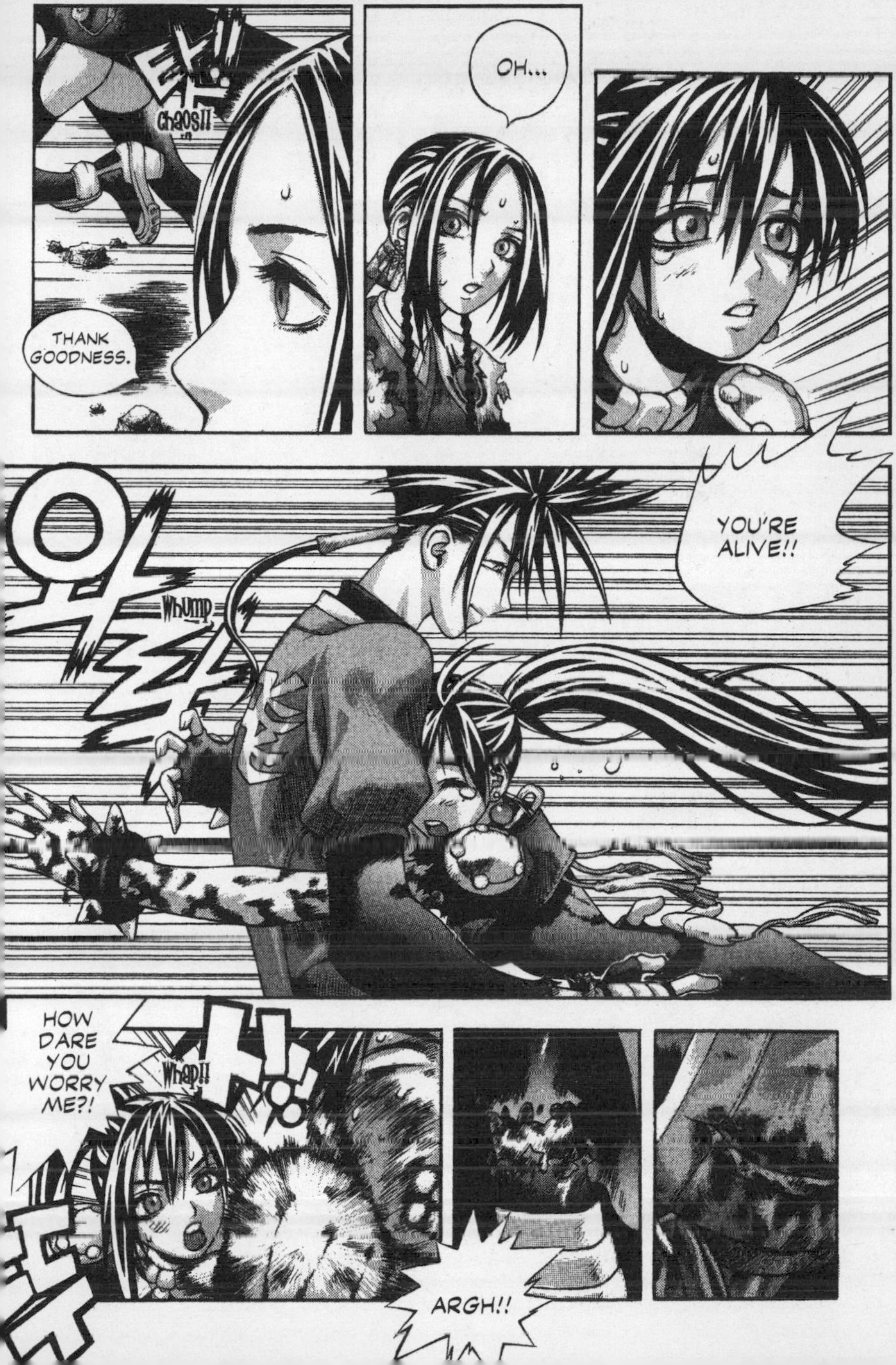

CHAOS!!
THANK GOODNESS.
OH...
YOU'RE ALIVE!!
WHUMP
HOW DARE YOU WORRY ME?!
WHAP!!
ARGH!!

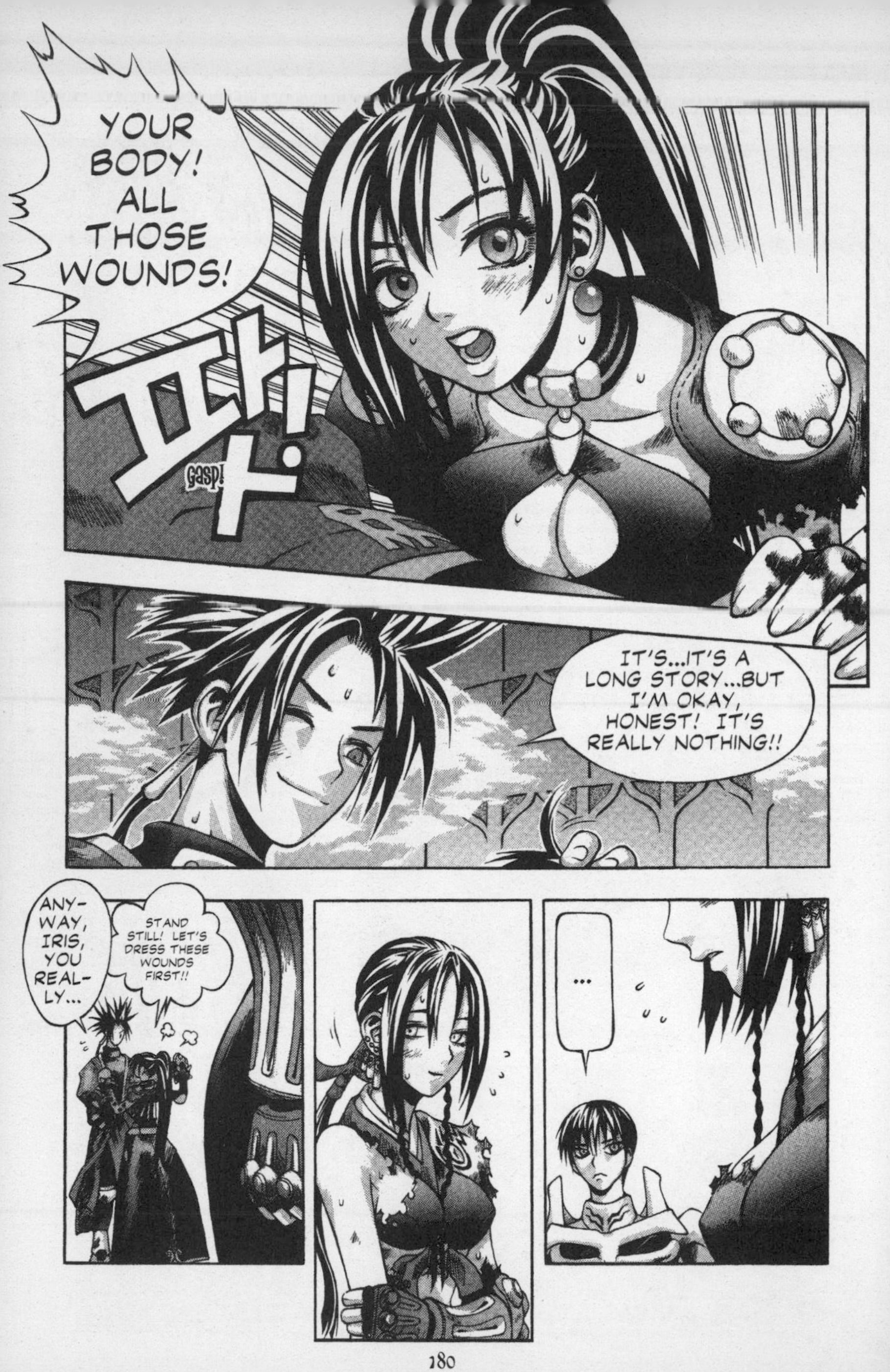
YOUR BODY! ALL THOSE WOUNDS!
GASP!
IT'S...IT'S A LONG STORY...BUT I'M OKAY, HONEST! IT'S REALLY NOTHING!!
ANY-WAY, IRIS, YOU REAL-LY...
STAND STILL! LET'S DRESS THESE WOUNDS FIRST!!
...

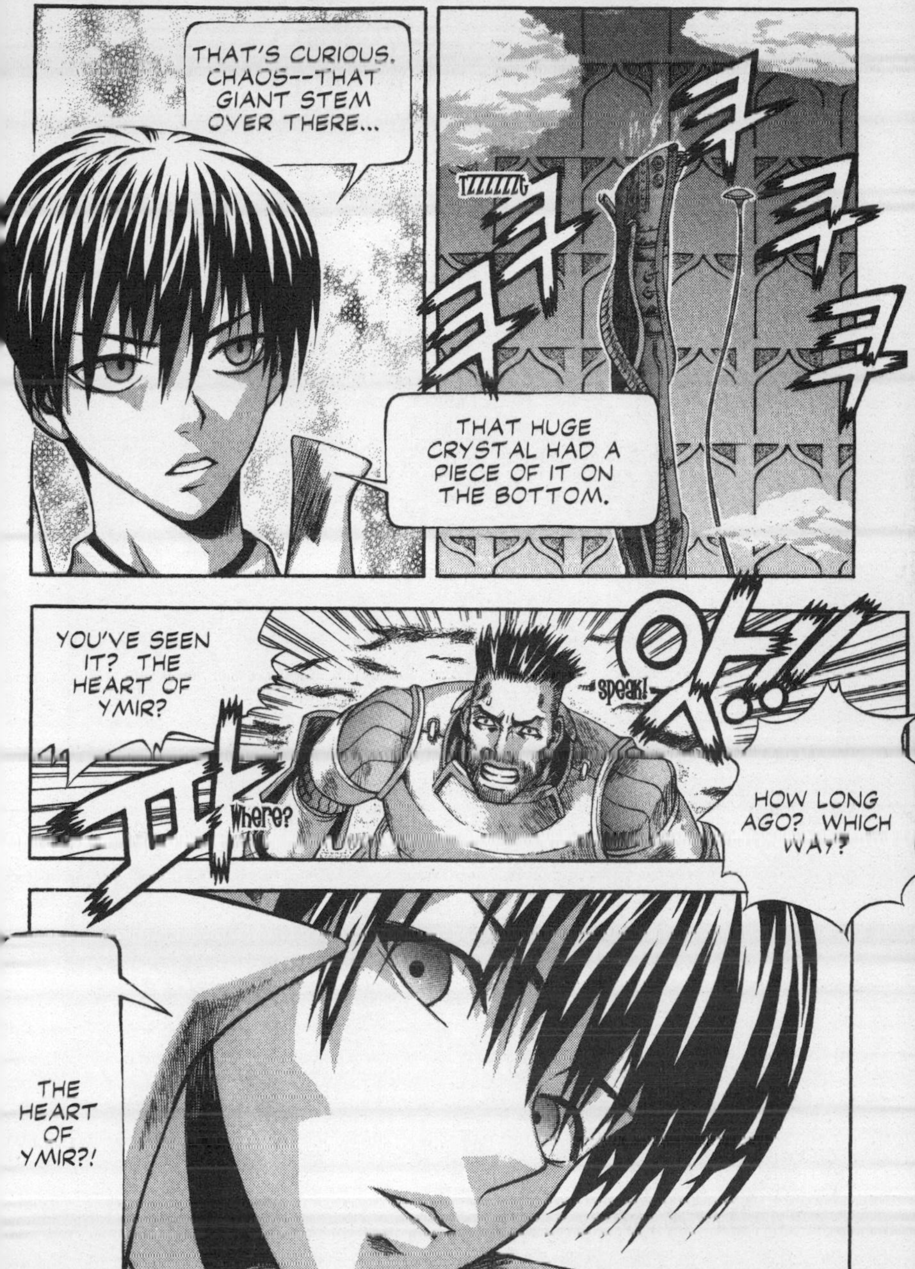
THAT'S CURIOUS. CHAOS--THAT GIANT STEM OVER THERE...
TZZZZZZG
THAT HUGE CRYSTAL HAD A PIECE OF IT ON THE BOTTOM.
YOU'VE SEEN IT? THE HEART OF YMIR?
speak!
Where?
HOW LONG AGO? WHICH WAY?
THE HEART OF YMIR?!

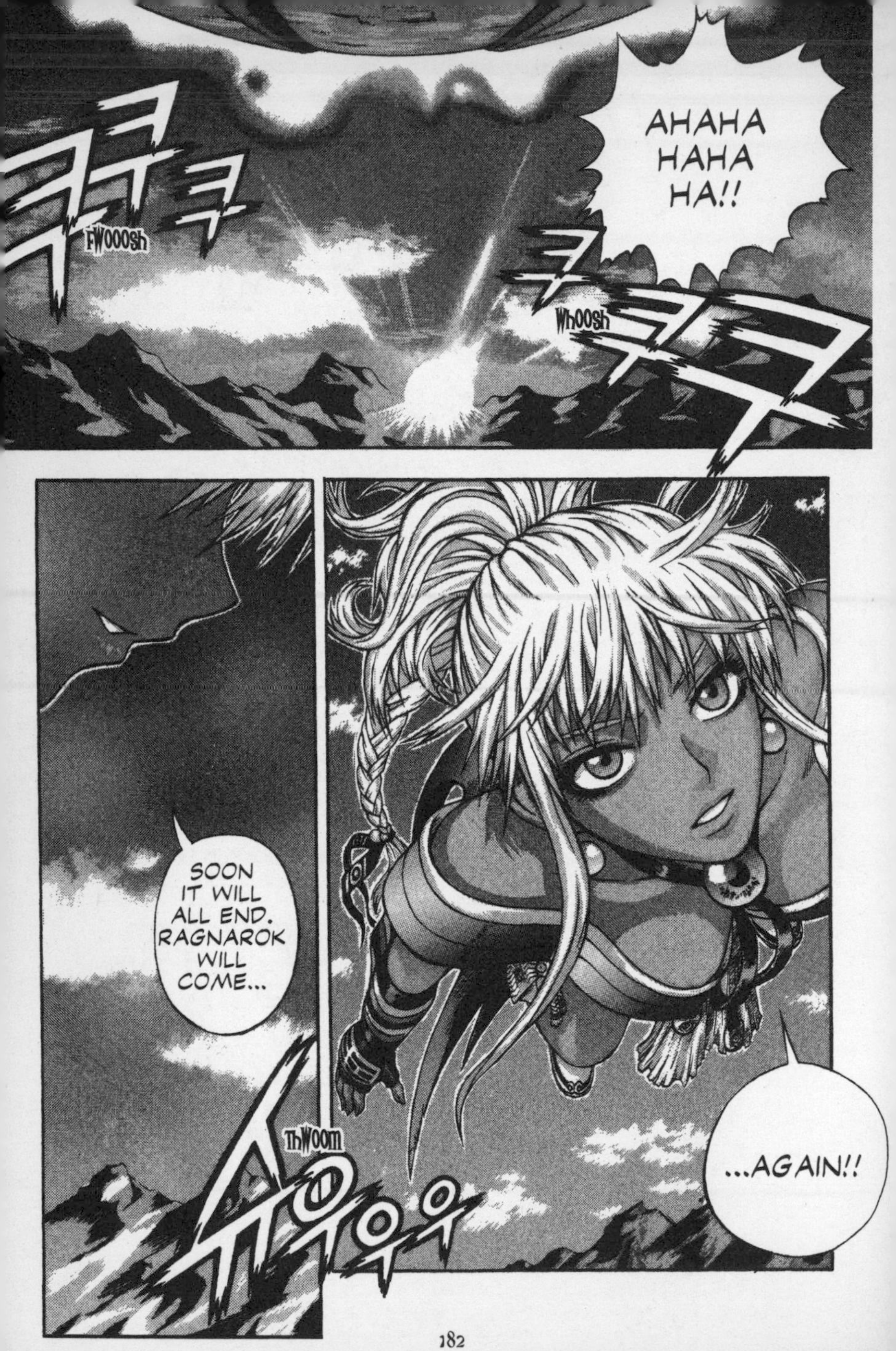
FWOOOSH
AHAHA HAHA HA!!
WHOOSH
SOON IT WILL ALL END. RAGNAROK WILL COME...
THWOOM
...AGAIN!!

TOKYOPOP®

RAGNARÖK

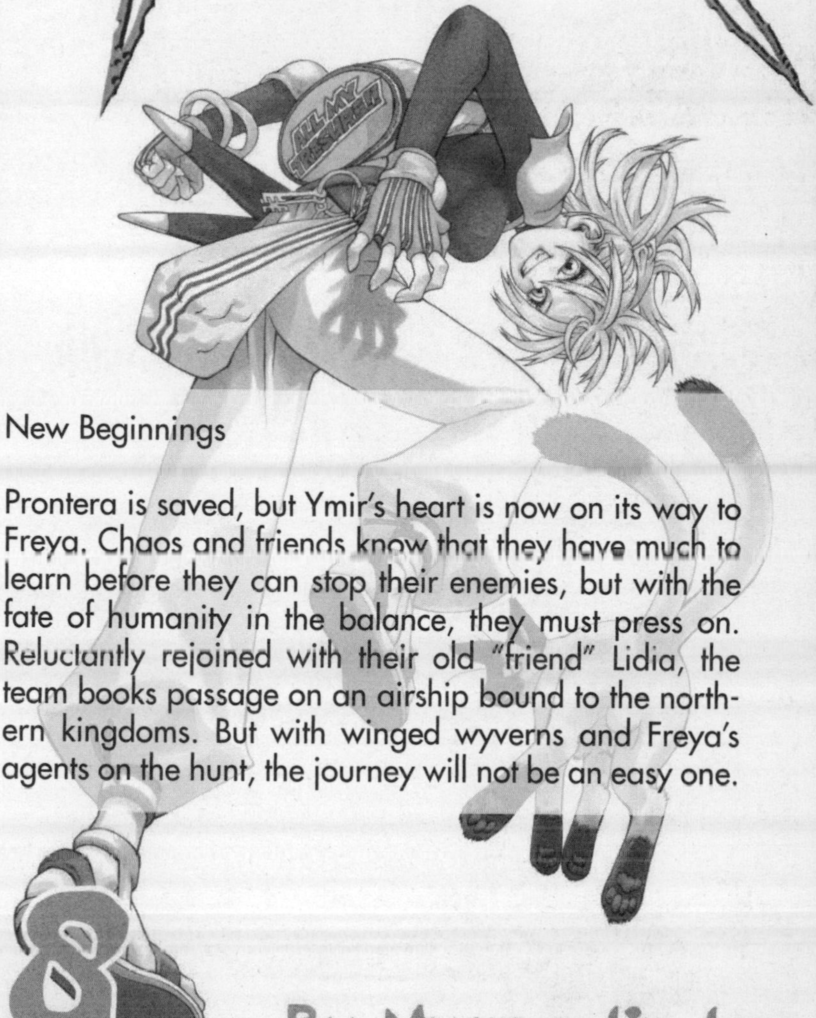

New Beginnings

Prontera is saved, but Ymir's heart is now on its way to Freya. Chaos and friends know that they have much to learn before they can stop their enemies, but with the fate of humanity in the balance, they must press on. Reluctantly rejoined with their old "friend" Lidia, the team books passage on an airship bound to the northern kingdoms. But with winged wyverns and Freya's agents on the hunt, the journey will not be an easy one.

8

By Myung-Jin Lee

RAGNAROK BONUS 4-PANEL STRIPS!

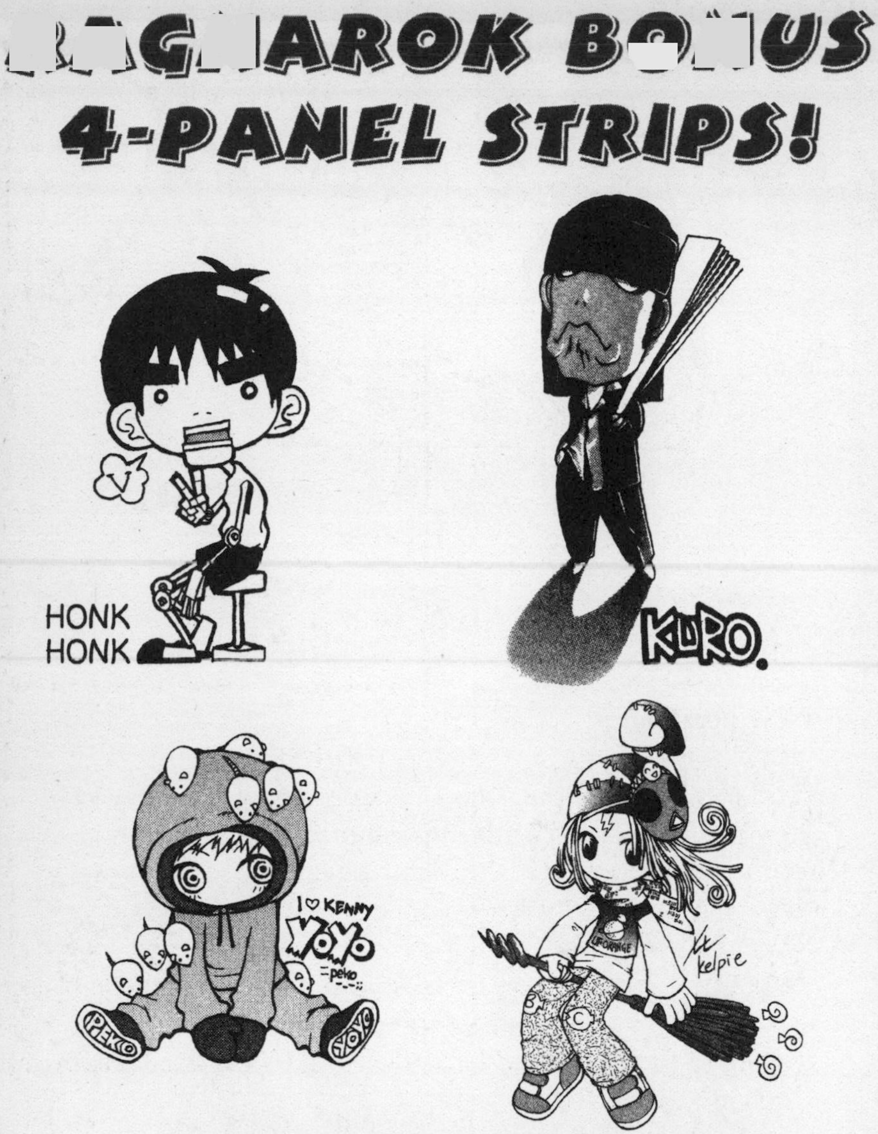
HONK HONK
KURO.
I ♥ KENNY
YOYO
=peko
PEKO
kelpie

Four Ragnarok assistants from our DIVE TO DREAM SEA studio came up with the following comic scenarios. Their dreams are to become famous manhwa creators of their own. Okay then, let's DIVE into the sea of dreams!!

Loki Unzipped

by Honk Honk

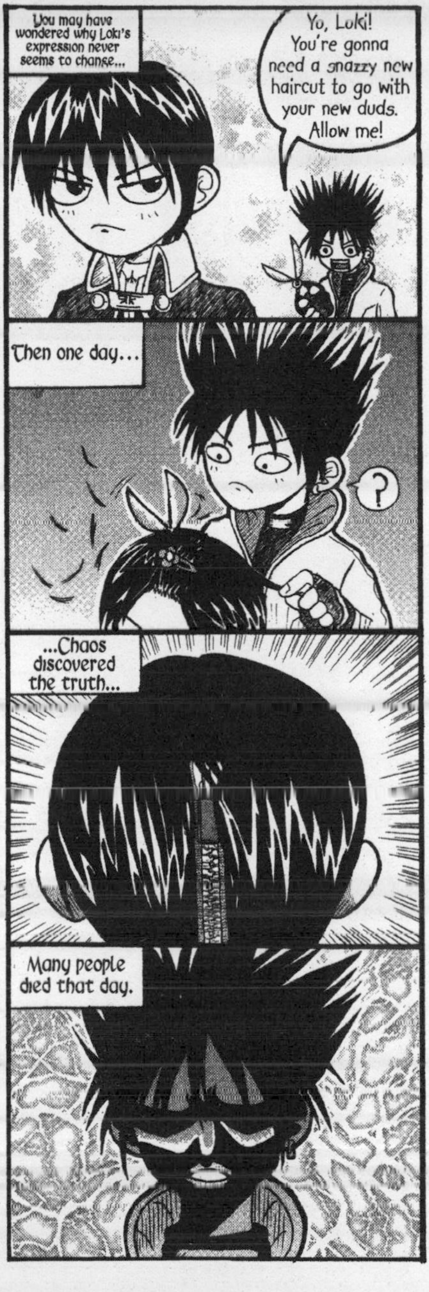
You may have wondered why Loki's expression never seems to change...
Yo, Loki! You're gonna need a snazzy new haircut to go with your new duds. Allow me!
Then one day...
?
...Chaos discovered the truth...
Many people died that day.

Miracle Cure

By Kuro

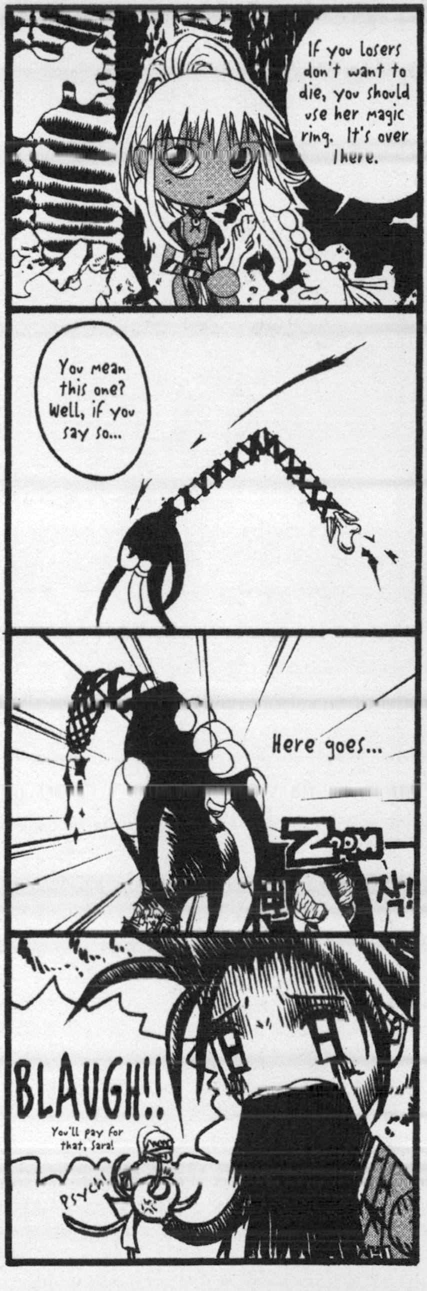
If you losers don't want to die, you should use her magic ring. It's over there.
You mean this one? Well, if you say so...
Here goes...
ZOOM
착!
BLAUGH!!
You'll pay for that, Sara!
Psych!

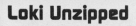

Ambrosia

by Peko

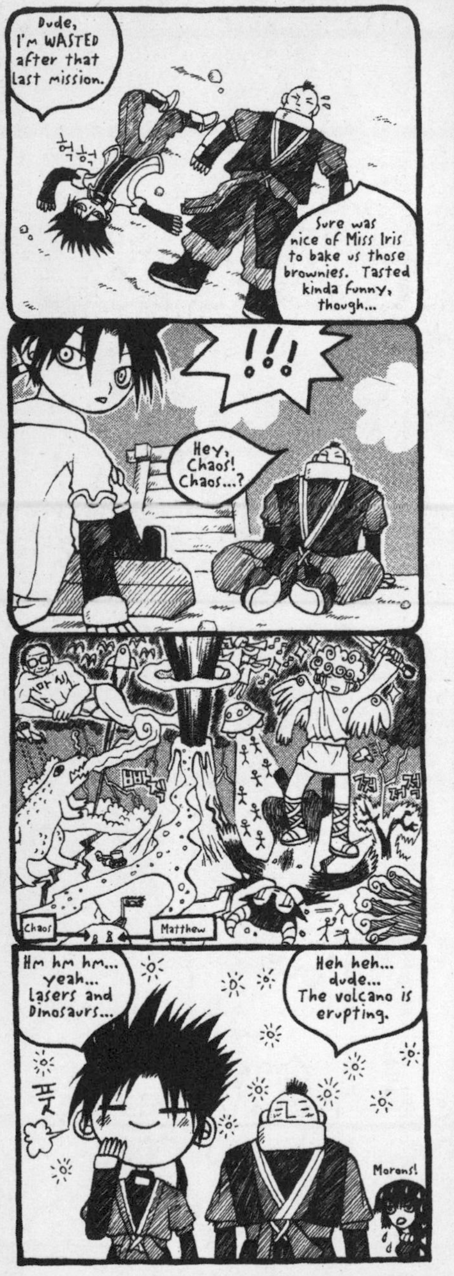
Dude, I'm WASTED after that last mission.
헉헉
Sure was nice of Miss Iris to bake us those brownies. Tasted kinda funny, though...
!!!
Hey, Chaos! Chaos...?
Chaos
Matthew
Hm hm hm... yeah... Lasers and Dinosaurs...
Heh heh... dude... The volcano is erupting.
Morons!

Idle Hands

by Kelpie

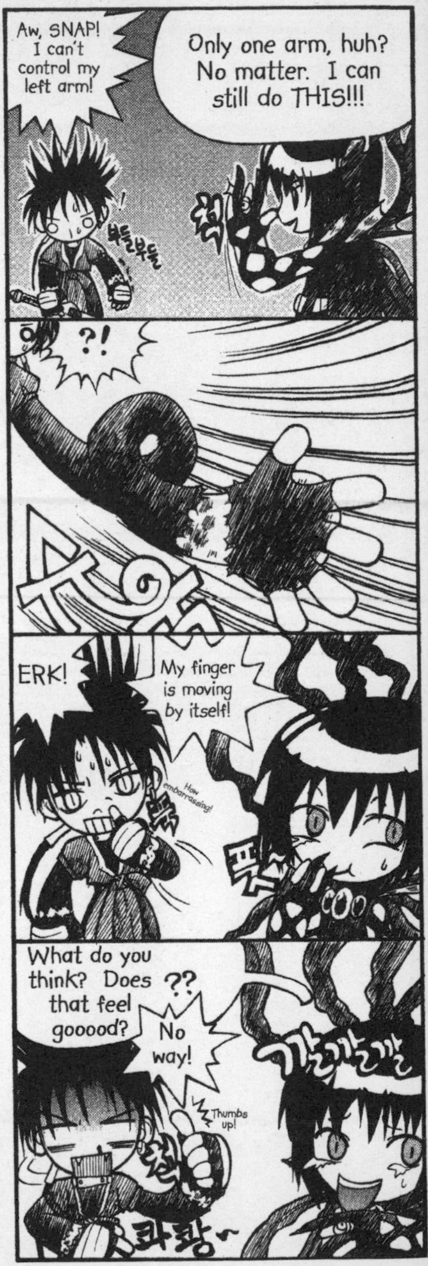
Aw, SNAP! I can't control my left arm!
Only one arm, huh? No matter. I can still do THIS!!!
부들부들
?!
ERK!
My finger is moving by itself!
How embarrassing!
What do you think? Does that feel gooood?
??
No way!
Thumbs up!

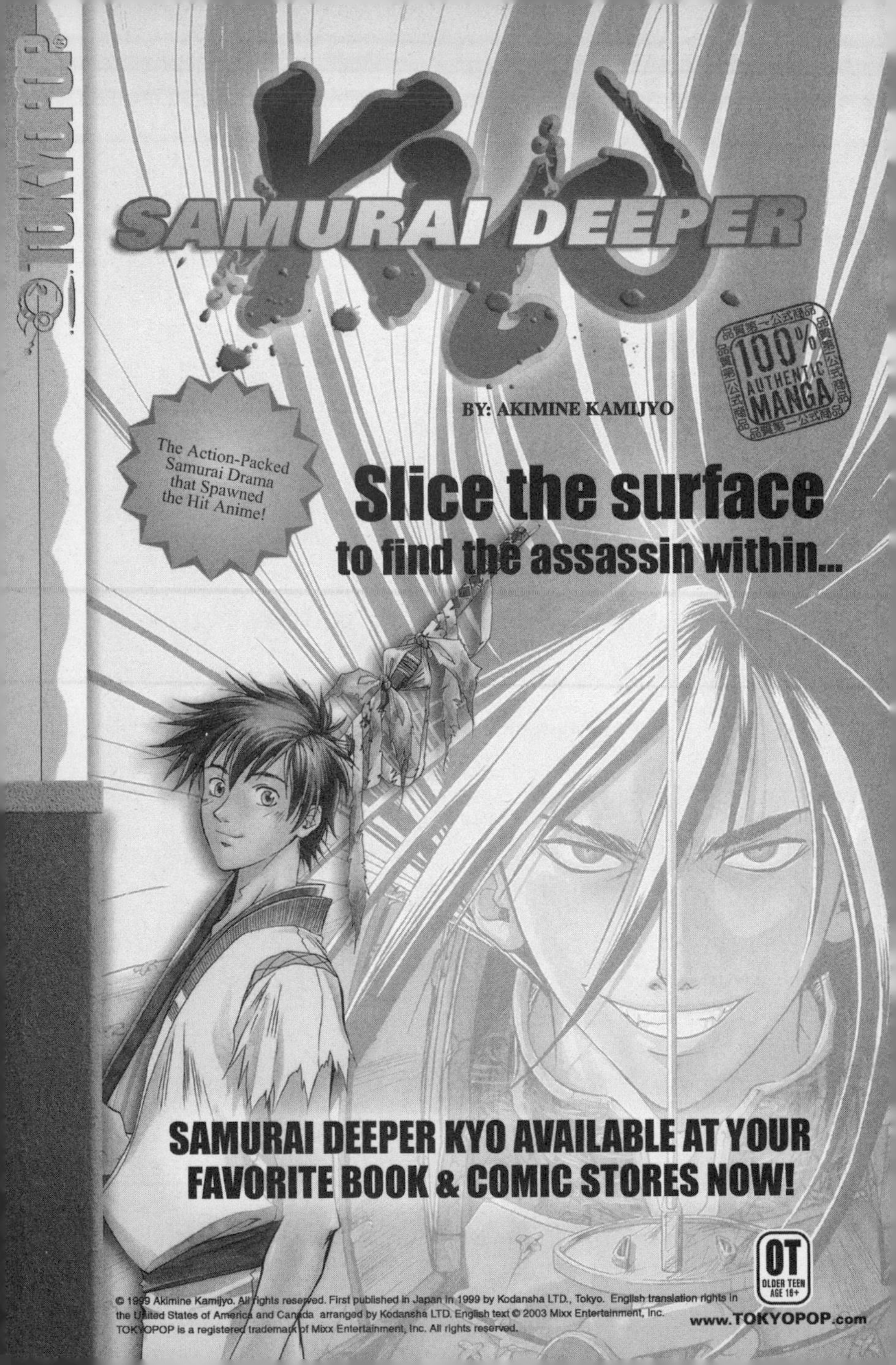

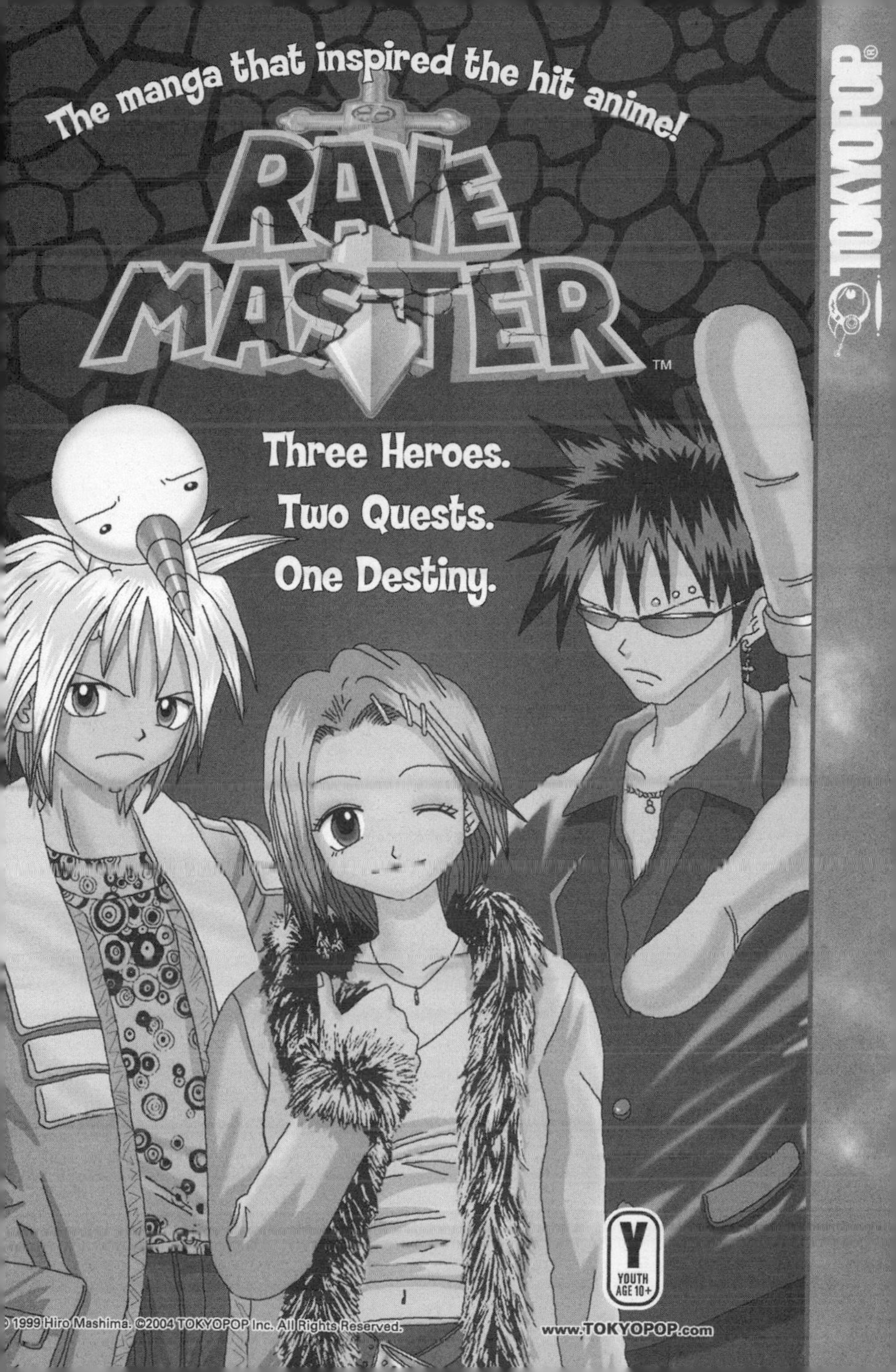
The manga that inspired the hit anime!
RAVE MASTER™
Three Heroes.
Two Quests.
One Destiny.
TOKYOPOP
Y
YOUTH AGE 10+
© 1999 Hiro Mashima. ©2004 TOKYOPOP Inc. All Rights Reserved.
www.TOKYOPOP.com

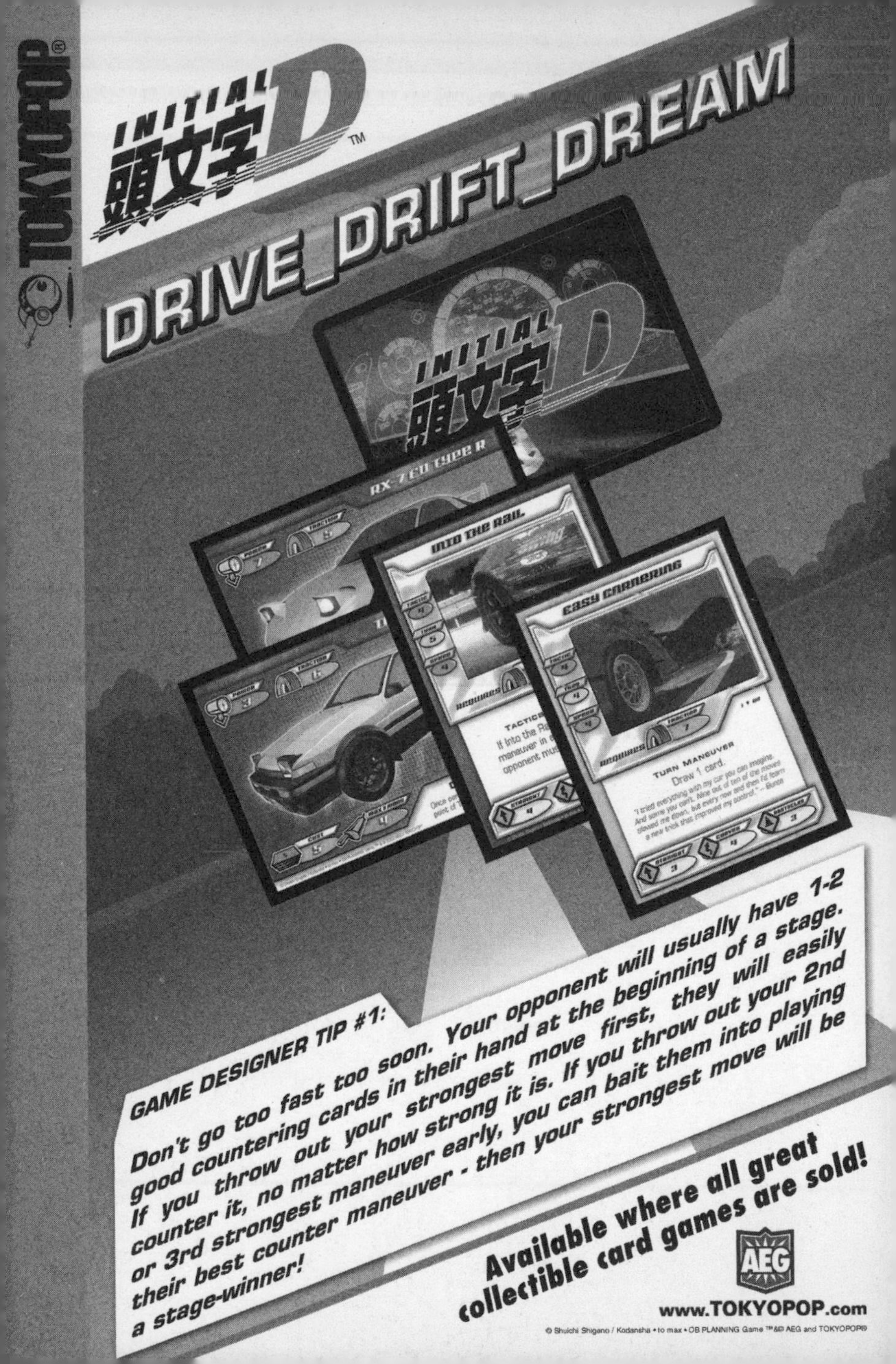

TOKYOPOP®
INITIAL D™
DRIVE_DRIFT_DREAM
INITIAL D
INTO THE RAIL
EASY CORNERING
TURN MANEUVER
Draw 1 card.
GAME DESIGNER TIP #1:
Don't go too fast too soon. Your opponent will usually have 1-2 good countering cards in their hand at the beginning of a stage. If you throw out your strongest move first, they will easily counter it, no matter how strong it is. If you throw out your 2nd or 3rd strongest maneuver early, you can bait them into playing their best counter maneuver - then your strongest move will be a stage-winner!
Available where all great collectible card games are sold!
AEG
www.TOKYOPOP.com
© Shuichi Shigeno / Kodansha • to max • OB PLANNING Game ™&© AEG and TOKYOPOP®

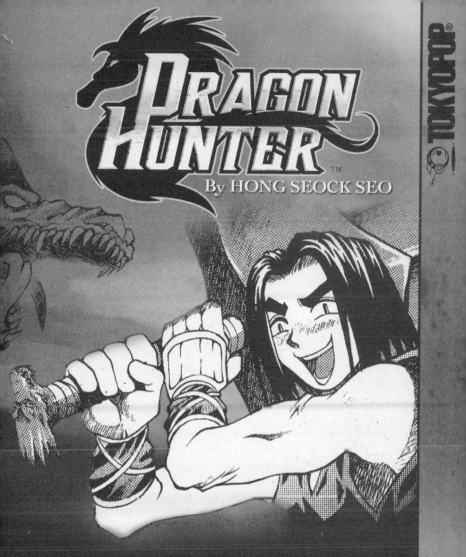

SLAYING DRAGONS IS HARD...
MAKING A LIVING
FROM IT IS BRUTAL!

www.TOKYOPOP.com

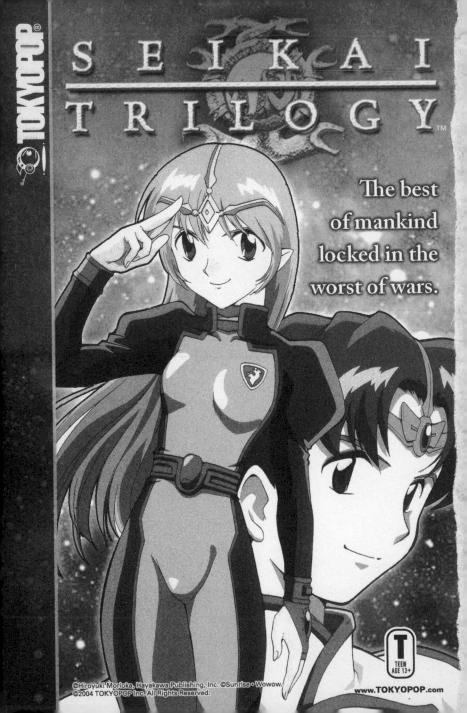

SEIKAI TRILOGY™

The best
of mankind
locked in the
worst of wars.